S0-BKU-064

Irreconcilable Differences?

DB
2228.7
.I77
2000

Irreconcilable Differences?

Explaining Czechoslovakia's Dissolution

Edited and translated by
Michael Kraus & Allison Stanger

Foreword by
Václav Havel

ROWMAN & LITTLEFIELD PUBLISHERS, INC.
Lanham • Boulder • New York • Oxford

CHABOT COLLEGE LIBRARY

ROWMAN & LITTLEFIELD PUBLISHERS, INC.

Published in the United States of America
by Rowman & Littlefield Publishers, Inc.
4720 Boston Way, Lanham, Maryland 20706
http://www.rowmanlittlefield.com

12 Hid's Copse Road
Cumnor Hill, Oxford OX2 9JJ, England

Copyright © 2000 by Rowman & Littlefield Publishers, Inc.

All rights reserved. No part of this publication may be reproduced,
stored in a retrieval system, or transmitted in any form or by any
means, electronic, mechanical, photocopying, recording, or otherwise,
without the prior permission of the publisher.

British Library Cataloguing in Publication Information Available

Library of Congress Cataloging-in-Publication Data

Irreconcilable differences? : explaining Czechoslovakia's dissolution
/ edited by Michael Kraus & Allison Stanger.
  p. cm.
Includes bibliographical references and index.
ISBN 0-8476-9020-2 (cloth : alk. paper).—ISBN 0-8476-9021-0
(pbk. : alk. paper)
 1. Czechoslovakia—Politics and government—1945–1992.
2. Czechoslovakia—Ethnic relations. I. Kraus, Michael, 1949–
II. Stanger, Allison.
DB2228.7.I77 1999
943.704'3—dc21   99-41680
                                                            CIP

Printed in the United States of America

♾ ™ The paper used in this publication meets the minimum requirements of
American National Standard for Information Sciences—Permanence of Paper
for Printed Library Materials, ANSI Z39.48–1992.

CHABOT COLLEGE LIBRARY

Contents

Předmluva

Jako občané jsme se vždycky ztotožňovali se státností československou. Československo jsme pociťovali jako svůj přirozený domov a sama myšlenka na jeho rozdělení byla tvrdým útokem na tuto naši identifikaci. Proto mnozí z nás vložili nemálo sil do pokusu přebudovat tehdejší formální federaci na federaci skutečnou a demokratickou, v níž by se všichni cítili dobře. Toto úsilí nevedlo k úspěchu. Historikové s odstupem času posoudí, zda bylo neúspěšné proto, že bylo nekoncepční, nedůsledné nebo v samých svých východiscích tak či onak vadné, anebo proto, že tváří v tvář slovenským tužbám úspěšné prostě být nemohlo. Ať tak či onak, po parlamentních volbách v roce 1992 bylo už zřejmé, že se náš dosavadní stát rozdělí. České politické reprezentaci patří uznání za to, že tak náročnou operaci, jakou je rozdělení státu, se jí podařilo—v trvalé a trpělivé součinnosti se slovenskou stranou—provést pokojným, právním a spořádaným způsobem. Zakládá to důvěryhodnost obou nástupnických států i perspektivu jejich dobrých vzájemných vztahů.

Rozdělení Československa bylo nepochybně pro mnohé z nás bolestivé. Přesto nebylo provázeno z české strany pocitem křivdy, bolestínstvím, výčitkami či dokonce odporem ke Slovensku a ke Slovákům. Pochopili jsme, že Slováci mají právo na samostatnost. I tato okolnost je nesmírně důležitá: kdyby náš rozchod byl provázen trpkostí, zatížilo by to nadlouho naše vztahy, což by se posléze obrátilo proti všem.

Václav Havel

Foreword

Václav Havel

As citizens, we have always identified with Czechoslovak statehood. We have felt that Czechoslovakia was our natural home, and the very idea of its division was a harsh assault on our sense of identity. That is why many among us expended considerable effort in the attempt to rebuild the existing formal federation into a genuine and democratic federation in which all would feel at home. This effort was unsuccessful. With the passage of time, historians will judge whether it was unsuccessful because it lacked a clear vision, because it was inconsistent or somehow flawed in its very points of departure, or because face to face with Slovak aspirations, it quite simply could not have been successful.

Whatever the answer, after the parliamentary elections of 1992, it was quite apparent that our existing state would have to be divided. Czech political representatives deserve recognition for carrying out this demanding operation—in persistent and patient cooperation with the Slovak side—in a peaceful, legal, and orderly manner. It lays the foundation for the credibility of both successor states and the prospect of good mutual relations.

Undoubtedly, the division of Czechoslovakia was painful for many of us. Despite that, it was not accompanied on the Czech side by a feeling of injury, by self-pity, by reproachfulness, or even by disgust for Slovakia and the Slovaks. We came to realize that the Slovaks had the right to independence. This fact, too, is immensely important: had our parting of ways been accompanied by bitterness, it would have burdened our relations for a long time. Eventually, this burden of bitterness would have turned against us.

Translated from Czech by Michael Kraus and Allison Stanger

Acknowledgments

This modest volume would never have seen the light of day without assistance and inspiration from a wide range of sources. An International Research & Exchanges Board (IREX) Special Projects grant provided the primary funding for the June 1996 Prague conference that led to this book. Our research in the Czech Republic and Slovakia during 1995–1996 was also generously funded by twin IREX individual advanced research grants and a joint grant from the National Council for Soviet and East European Research (contract 810-30). Along the way, Middlebury College has been exceptionally supportive of our quest to transform a set of conference papers in three languages into a coherent book. For this invaluable financial assistance and the vote of confidence it represented, we are very grateful.

We remain indebted to Jan Svejnar, Director of the Economics Institute (EI), and František Turnovec, Director of the Center for Economic Research and Graduate Education (CERGE), and the always accommodating staff of CERGE–EI for providing us with a stimulating intellectual environment, both during our sabbatical year in Prague and in subsequent summers, as well as the most gracious of conference facilities. The Institute of Political Studies at Charles University as well as its director, Rudolf Kučera, deserve acknowledgment for their support of our conference endeavors.

In addition to the individuals whose formidable contributions comprise this volume, we would like to thank the other conference participants, whose participation enriched the quality of our exchanges over that two-day period: Rudolf Battěk, Daniel Bútora, Martin Bútora, Zora Bútorová, Karen Henderson, Jozef Horal, Josef Kotrba, Kevin Krause, Oskar Krejčí, Jiří Musil, Soňa Szomolányi, Václav Žák, Ernest Valko, and Milan Žitný. Our thinking on ethnic conflict has also been energized by countless conversations with friends and colleagues too numerous to thank individually but too important not to mention here.

Our research and writing benefited enormously from the exceptional dedication and research assistance of Benjamin Block, David Cohen, Damjan de

xi

Krnjevic Miskovic, and Daniel Mucha in Middlebury and Marián Nič and Igor Slovak in Prague. Many thanks to Linda Booska for valuable and timely technological assistance and to George Bellerose for his keen editorial eye. Looking across the Atlantic, gratitude must also be expressed to Milena Zeithamlová for guiding us through the planning of a conference in Prague, to the entire Koucký family for their friendship and hospitality, to Naďa Charvátová for running the best restaurant in Prague, and to Ludvík and Jiřina Rybáček for their outstanding translation work.

Finally, we dedicate this book to Hannah Kraus. For a three-year-old in transition, she showed a remarkable reservoir of patience and understanding in coping with her parents' joint or individual disappearances caused by this project. She is not responsible for any errors contained in the pages that follow.

Major Parties and Coalitions

CZECH REPUBLIC

ČSSD—*Czechoslovak Social Democratic Party*

HSD-SMS—*Movement for Self-Administration Democracy–Society for Moravia and Silesia*

KDU-ČSL—*Christian and Democratic Union–Czechoslovak People's Party*

LBL—*Left Block*

LSU—*Liberal Social Union*

ODA—*Civic Democratic Alliance*

ODS-KDS—*Coalition of Civic Democratic Party and Christian Democratic Party*

OF—*Civic Forum*

OH—*Civic Movement*

SPR-RSČ—*Alliance for Republic–Czechoslovak Republican Party*

SLOVAK REPUBLIC

HZDS—*Movement for a Democratic Slovakia*

KDH—*Christian Democratic Movement*

MKDH-ESWS—*Coalition of Hungarian Parties*

SDL—*Party of Democratic Left*

SDSS—*Slovak Social Democratic Party*

SNS—*Slovak National Party*

VPN—*Public Against Violence*

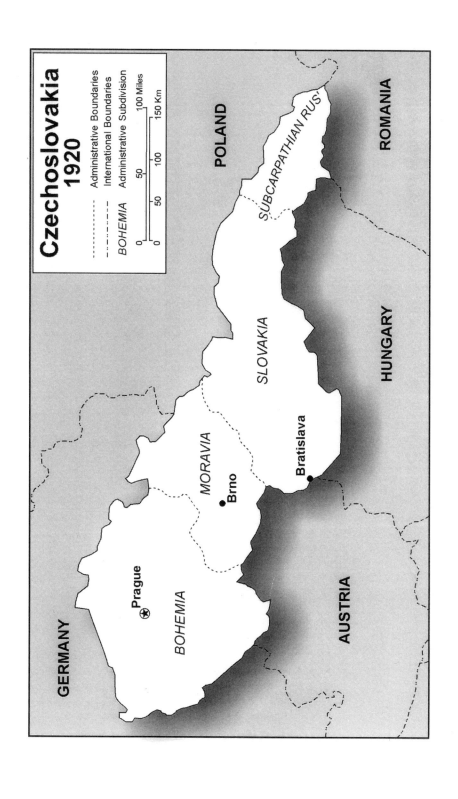

Czechoslovakia
1920

.... Administrative Boundaries
—·—·— International Boundaries
BOHEMIA Administrative Subdivision

0   50   100   150 Km
0   50   100 Miles

POLAND

SUBCARPATHIAN RUS'

ROMANIA

SLOVAKIA

HUNGARY

MORAVIA

Bratislava

Brno

BOHEMIA

Prague

GERMANY

AUSTRIA

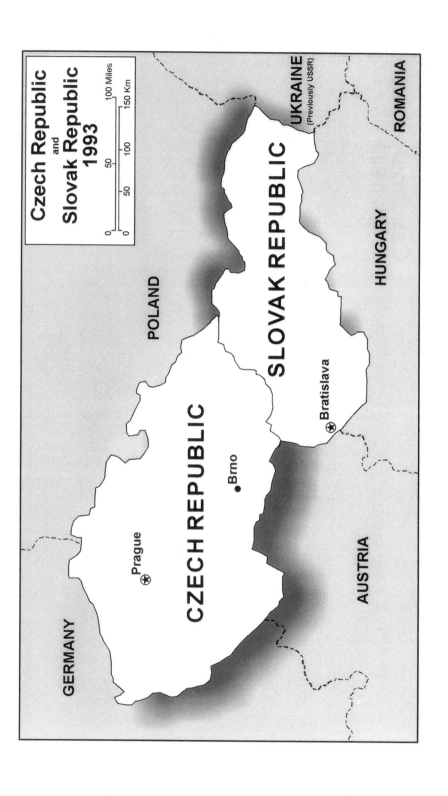

Czech Republic and Slovak Republic 1993

GERMANY
POLAND
CZECH REPUBLIC
Prague
Brno
SLOVAK REPUBLIC
Bratislava
AUSTRIA
HUNGARY
UKRAINE
(Previously USSR)
ROMANIA

0 50 100 Miles
0 50 100 150 Km

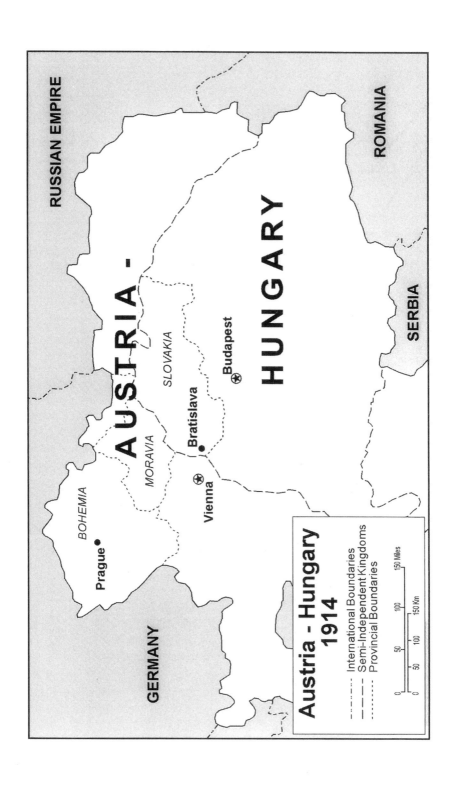

RUSSIAN EMPIRE

ROMANIA

SERBIA

GERMANY

AUSTRIA -

HUNGARY

BOHEMIA

MORAVIA

SLOVAKIA

Prague

Vienna

Bratislava

Budapest

Austria - Hungary
1914

- - - - International Boundaries
— — Semi-Independent Kingdoms
· · · · · Provincial Boundaries

0   50   100   150 Miles
0   50   100   150 Km

The Past as Prologue

Michael Kraus and Allison Stanger

Czechoslovakia's history faithfully reflects the trials and the tribulations of twentieth-century Europe in general and Central Europe in particular. Born in 1918 out of the wreckage of the Austro-Hungarian Empire, the new Czech and Slovak homeland enjoyed its most peaceful and prosperous years in the interwar period, when it was the only functioning liberal democracy in Central Europe. Following the Munich Agreement of September 1938, Czechoslovakia was partitioned into a Slovak state and the separate German-controlled Protectorate of Bohemia and Moravia. The Czechs and the Slovaks reunited after the war but soon succumbed to a communist takeover in February 1948, and, over the next decade, were integrated into the Soviet sphere of domination. During the quickly suppressed "Prague Spring" of 1968, Czechoslovakia attempted to emancipate itself from Soviet hegemony, but not until November 1989 did Prague's hard-line regime fall, in part collapsing of its own defective weight, in part overturned by the surging forces of the Velvet Revolution, led by Václav Havel. For the next three years, the Czechs and Slovaks tried to redefine their relationship within the common state. But, by the end of 1992, their differences turned politically insurmountable, and, on the last day of December 1992, Czechoslovakia ceased to exist, and two new republics, Czech and Slovak, were born.

Yet the history of the peoples of the area is not only much older and richer than this capsule history of modern Czechoslovak statehood but also reveals the deeper reasons a union was forged in 1918 and, more recently, was dissolved. The first phase of shared Czech and Slovak destiny dates back to the Great Moravian Empire, which in the ninth century also included parts of southern Poland and northern Hungary. By the end of the tenth century, that empire was divided between the Germans and the Hungarians, setting the neighboring Czechs and the Slovaks on two separate paths of political development for the next millennium.

1

The territory of Bohemia, Moravia, and Silesia, which comprises the Czech Republic today, existed in the framework of one state as early as the Middle Ages. The Kingdom of Bohemia's greatest glory occurred in the fourteenth century, when its ruler, Charles IV, was crowned Holy Roman Emperor, and Prague became the empire's capital and Europe's major political and cultural center. On several occasions, the lands of Bohemia became the epicenter of Europe's turmoil, as the Czechs rose in defiance of their more powerful neighbors. In 1415, Jan Hus, who had been a reformist preacher and the head of Prague University, was burned at the stake in Constance for heretical teachings. His followers, the Czech Hussites, rebelled in 1420 against the Roman Church and the Roman Empire; their actions established the legal foundations of Protestantism in Bohemia for the next 200 years. In 1618, the Protestant Bohemian estates rose again against the Habsburgs to reassert their religious and political rights, thereby unleashing the Thirty Years' War that pitted Protestant and Catholic forces against each other throughout Europe. The 1620 defeat of the Czech nobility brought on the downfall of the Bohemian kingdom, and, for the next three centuries, Protestant Prague was subjected to Catholic domination and Habsburg rule from Vienna.

Unlike the territory of the Czechs, which had retained its independence until 1620, the Slovak lands remained an integral part of the Hungarian kingdom from around the tenth century until 1918. In that sense, the Slovaks shared in Hungarian triumphs and defeats. For more than two hundred years, Bratislava, today's Slovak capital, served as the capital of Hungary; the kingdom's coronations were held there. By the second half of the nineteenth century, ethnically related Czechs and Slovaks increased their contacts and found a common denominator in their quests for self-determination.

Foreign domination and economic hardships spurred on major waves of emigration from East and Central Europe. Between 1870 and 1914, some 250,000 Czechs and 650,000 Slovaks emigrated to the United States and Canada alone. Among some 500,000 refugees who left Czechoslovakia after 1945, many, if not most, landed on American shores.

As was true of other countries in Central Europe, the Czech and Slovak diaspora played an important role in the political and cultural life of their homelands. During the period from 1914 to 1918, exiles such as future presidents Tomáš Masaryk and Edvard Beneš, working in tandem with loyalists at home, drew their support from the diaspora, lobbied for an independent state, organized liberation armies, and played a decisive role in impressing the Czech and Slovak case for independence upon Western allies, including President Woodrow Wilson. These efforts came to fruition in Pittsburgh on 30 May 1918, when the Czech and Slovak leaders in America agreed upon the creation of an independent Czecho–Slovak state. The Czechoslovak Declaration of Independence, issued by Masaryk in October of that year in Washington, D.C., was clearly inspired by its American counterpart.

The creation of the common state in 1918 was rooted, at least in part, in the perception that the two related Slavic nations would be in a better position together, rather than each on its own, to contend with the long-standing external threats to their existence. But given that the new state contained large German and Hungarian minorities, external concerns became linked to questions of internal stability. To compound the problem, two incompatible ideological propositions were built into the political system from the start. The first proclaimed that all individual Czechoslovak citizens enjoyed equal political and civil rights. The second insisted that the state had a "Czechoslovak" character, thus elevating Czechoslovak national culture to a higher plane, whereby some ethnic groups were accorded a more equal place than others. The constitution guaranteed equal rights for all citizens, irrespective of ethnic background, and various laws stipulated the right of all to educational opportunities and religious activities in one's native language. But, at the same time, the state retained a nationalist character whereby it excluded members of ethnic groups besides the Czechs and Slovaks from Czechoslovak nationality and did not recognize in principle the equality of these other groups and languages. While Masaryk's nationalist philosophy—embraced by Beneš as well—had a large following among the dominant nationalities (more among the Czechs than the Slovaks), it could not generate broad support for the Czechoslovak state among the substantial minorities that constituted a full third of the population.

As a "successor" state to the Habsburg Empire, Czechoslovakia inherited over two-thirds of the empire's industries, one-fifth of its former territory, and one-fourth of its population. More fortunate than most of the successor states carved out of the old empire, Czechoslovakia ranked among the top ten industrialized states of the world in terms of industrial endowment. Its newly acquired independence, however, had brought under one state umbrella regions characterized by very different levels of socioeconomic development. By and large, the industrial sector was concentrated in the western ex-Austrian (Czech) region. The ex-Hungarian provinces of Slovakia and Ruthenia (Carpathian Ukraine, which was annexed by Moscow in 1944), on the other hand, were predominantly agrarian.

The economic disparities among its provinces coincided with ethnic divisions. In 1921 (and for the next twenty-five years), the republic's territory was inhabited by seven million Czechs and over two million Slovaks; over three million (Sudeten) Germans, who enjoyed the highest standard of living; three-quarters of a million Hungarians, most of whom resided in Slovakia; and nearly half a million Ukrainians and Russians in Ruthenia, the easternmost province and economically the poorest stratum of Czechoslovak society between the wars. Overlapping in terms of its national identification (especially with the Czechs) but separate in religious terms was the 350,000-strong Jewish community (including some 100,000 in Ruthenia).

The potential for ethnic tensions was further enhanced by inequities of income and status. The Germans, over 90 percent of whom lived in the Czech lands, on the whole enjoyed a higher standard of living than the more numerous Czechs; similarly, the Hungarians were, on average, better off than the Slovaks who surrounded them. The generally secular, progressive, and rationalistic Czechs lived side by side with the more religious, conservative, and tradition-bound Slovaks. But divisions between the Czechs and the Slovaks, stemming in large part from the separate development under the centuries-old rule of Vienna and Budapest, respectively, were also in evidence.

Thus considerable economic, social, cultural, and ethnic heterogeneity characterized the years of the First Republic (1918–1938). Not surprisingly, such disparities, enhanced by the economic strains of the 1930s, translated into political conflicts. On one level, they fueled Slovak demands for the home rule and governmental and administrative autonomy promised in the Pittsburgh Agreement. On another, they provided the ammunition for the increasingly nationalist orientation of the Sudeten Germans' parties. Yet in hindsight, it is clear that even a federal system of rule could not have ameliorated the dramatic plunge in fortunes experienced by the formerly "ruling" German and Hungarian nationalities or prevented Hitler from using the German minority issue as a pretext for his war of aggression.

Although it is a historical fact that interwar Czechoslovakia treated its ethnic minorities with greater tolerance than any other country in East and Central Europe, including Germany, Prague's relationship with its Sudeten German minority would become an international issue. Seen in that light, the First Republic's twenty-year record of political stability and liberal democracy was a notable achievement in the history of democratic constitutional experiments, especially when contrasted with the political circumstances of the neighboring countries, which, one after another, in the 1920s and 1930s, succumbed to authoritarian rule, or worse.

This political record was complemented by the highly creative efforts of artists, writers, musicians, and scientists. Its Western political orientation rendered Czechoslovakia particularly receptive to cultural influences from England, Italy, Weimar Germany, and especially France. Cubism in architecture and design; modernism in painting, sculpture, and photography; surrealism in literature, poetry, and photography—all these cultural crosscurrents found expressions in interwar Czechoslovakia. The innovative contributions of Czech and Slovak artists, painters such as Oskar Kokoschka, František Kupka, and Alfons Mucha, writers and poets such as Karel Čapek and Jaroslav Seifert (the future Nobel Prize winner), and composers of the caliber of Leoš Janáček and Bohuslav Martinů, to mention only a few, have received their due recognition from Western publics for their universality and quality.

Moreover, an integral part of Czechoslovakia's cultural scene was the presence of German and Jewish intelligentsia represented by Franz Kafka, Max Brod, Rainer Maria Rilke, Karl Kraus, Franz Werfel, and Edmund Husserl. The hospitable climate of liberal democracy provided a new home to refugees from Bolshevik Russia, such as Roman Jakobson and Nikolai S. Trubetskoi, cofounders of the Prague Linguistic Circle, which laid the foundations for the school of Prague structuralism, or exiles from Nazi Germany such as Thomas Mann. Interwar Prague also hosted the young Ernst Mach and Albert Einstein, who taught physics there. No such list would be complete without noting that Bohemia and Moravia were the birth lands of Sigmund Freud, Ernst Mandel, and Gustav Mahler. In short, Czechoslovakia's First Republic enjoyed a rich period of sustained artistic and scientific growth, nourished by the presence of some of the luminaries of our age and stemming in large measure from the cultural and ethnic diversity that comprised its lands.

But the same ethnic mosaic also gave rise to forces that ultimately proved Czechoslovakia's undoing. As the Sudeten Germans gradually fell under the spell of Hitler's call for the unification of all Germans in one state, Prague came, by 1938, to occupy the central stage of another European crisis. In the September 1938 Munich Agreement between France, Great Britain, and Germany (to which Czechoslovakia was not a party), Prague was forced to cede to Hitler the border districts largely (but not exclusively) populated by Germans. The crisis culminated as Hitler occupied Prague in March 1939 and created the Protectorate of Bohemia and Moravia as part of the Greater German Reich. At the same time, he ordered the leading Slovak nationalists to establish their own "independent" state under German protection and encouraged Hungary's seizure of Ruthenia.

That bitter series of events and developments had a shattering impact upon the twenty-year-old democracy, bringing on an agonizing crisis of legitimacy, a reassessment of the institutions and practices of democracy, and a reappraisal of the country's international position. After all, the external blows were inflicted by enemies and allies alike, and democratic Czechoslovakia was in the final analysis a victim of Britain and France—Western democracies. For the next six years Czechoslovakia disappeared from the map of Europe. German occupation brought devastation, especially aimed at the intelligentsia, including some 360,000 victims who perished in concentration camps and prisons, about half of whom were of Jewish origin.

While the successive catastrophes of 1938 to 1945 weakened the forces of interwar democracy after the war, they also enhanced the postwar stock of the communists, who portrayed Stalin's Soviet Union as the only reliable ally against German revanchism. Hitler's acts of barbarism also put an end to the long history of Czech–German cohabitation in the historic lands of Bohemia and Moravia. Due to the fact that, from 1938 on, the vast majority of Sudeten Germans had rallied behind Berlin's cause, the Prague government won the approval of the Great Powers at the Potsdam Conference to expel these ethnic Germans from Czechoslovak territory into Germany. This policy was also fully exploited by the communists, who controlled the redistribution of the expellees' farms and property, which they conferred, if temporarily, upon their supporters. So with the advent of the Cold War in 1948, the doors were wide open for the communist seizure of power.

After 1948, Czechoslovakia's history is the story of the vicissitudes accompanying Soviet rule in East and Central Europe in general: from the Stalinist terror and purges, nationalization of property and collectivization of land in the 1950s, to the thaw and gradual relaxation of party control in the 1960s, which resulted in the 1968 Prague Spring. Motivated in part by Slovak perceptions of inequality vis-á-vis the more numerous Czechs and led by the Slovak communist reformer Alexander Dubček, the Communist Party's program—an early version of Gorbachev's *perestroika*—embarked on a search for "socialism with a human face." Snuffed out in August 1968 by the allied armies of the Warsaw Pact, the only lasting legacy of the Prague Spring was the establishment of the federal state that put the Czechs and the Slovaks on an equal footing and thereby removed, at least constitutionally, a long-standing Slovak grievance.

For the next two decades after 1968, Czechoslovakia was subject to a thorough program of counterreformation, or "normalization," as it was officially called. The restoration of totalitarian practices included a massive purge of party and nonparty nonconformists, the reestablishment of strict censorship in the mass media, and a renewed emphasis on ideology in the arts, literature, and scholarship. The goal was to eradicate democratic traditions and aspirations once and for all. In 1977 the normalization campaign led to the emergence of Charter 77, the dissident human rights movement headed by Václav Havel, which openly chronicled and protested the regime-organized indignities and human rights violations.

Persisting doggedly for the next twelve years in the face of severe police repression, the Chartists and other dissidents acted as the repository of national conscience and provided the leadership for the Velvet Revolution of 1989. In December of that year, Havel, a veteran of communist prisons, became the new president and the belatedly vindicated Dubček the head of the federal parliament. A few days later, on the occasion of the traditional New Year's day address to the country, Havel ended his speech by paraphrasing Comenius, the great Czech educator: "People, your government has returned to you!"

Over the next three years, the euphoria of 1989 gave way to the hard-hitting realities of coping with the legacies of fifty years of dictatorship. One such inheritance that proved much too weighty for the young democracy was the recasting of the deformed relationship between the Czechs and the Slovaks. While the communist era provided at best Band-Aids and at worst fresh wounds for the long-ailing Czech/Slovak marriage, Havel spared no effort in his search for a viable formula that might prolong the life of the Czech and Slovak Federal Republic. The June 1992 elections, however, propelled into Czech and Slovak leadership contrasting political elites with different outlooks and diametrically opposed political agendas; the result of their negotiations was the peaceful parting of ways. From a broader historical perspective, the 1993 creation of distinct Czech and Slovak states must be seen, in part, as a legacy of a millennium of separate development, the forces of which have carried the day, at least for now.

1

Contending Views of Czechoslovakia's Demise

Michael Kraus and Allison Stanger

If 1989 will go down in history as the annus mirabilis, marking the peaceful de-mise of communism in Eastern Europe, the 1990s will be remembered as "the springtime of ethnicity." In the wake of the collapse of the Cold War order, con-flicts and not only have tensions between ethnic groups brought about the disinte-gration of the multinational federations of the Soviet Union, Yugoslavia, and Czechoslovakia, but many of the new successor states also face the prospect of fur-ther territorial divisions. At the time of this writing, the Czech and Slovak republics are in their seventh year as independent states. The Czech Republic has received the honor of NATO membership, while Slovakia remains at the margins of inter-national life, despite the ouster of its authoritarian prime minister, Vladimír Mečiar, in November 1998 (after his electoral defeat in September of that year). The di-vergent paths that each took over the course of the past seven years only serve to confer an additional aura of inevitability upon Czechoslovakia's extinction.

As scholars, however, we need to be wary of declaring historical events in-evitable, particularly since the former Czechoslovakia, Yugoslavia, and Soviet Union each disintegrated in very different fashion. The most striking feature of Czechoslovakia's demise was the peaceful resolution of ethnic conflict. If Czechs and Slovaks were able to part ways in civil fashion, the question arises of why they were unable to work out their differences within the framework of a com-mon state. In this sense, the presumption of inevitability can potentially obscure more than it reveals. To advance our understanding of the sources of state cohe-sion, the key question should instead be: At what point in time did Czechoslova-kia's disintegration become inevitable, and what steps, if any, might political elites have taken to preempt the country's arrival at this point of no return?

Cataloging the most salient forces, the collapse of the Czechoslovak federation might be seen as the product of (1) the legacies of the communist and precom-

7

munist eras (the inevitability thesis), (2) the rational or erratic actions of post-communist political elites, (3) constitutional deadlock, (4) the absence of political parties as well as other associations and groupings that unite people across ethnic lines, (5) the role of the mass media, (6) regional economic disparities, and (7) demonstration effects (international factors fostering separatism). Obviously, these factors are often overlapping and interrelated, but approaching the question of Czechoslovakia's breakup from each vantage point yields valuable insights. Although they are largely applied to the Czecho–Slovak case in this volume, each of these categories of explanation might also be used to shed light on disintegration processes in other countries and contexts.

HISTORICAL LEGACIES

The first analytical framework emphasizes those factors that rendered national division a potent political force in the precommunist and communist phases of development. They include the ideological character and the institutional structure of the new state created in 1918; the bipolar imbalance of power pitting the less numerous Slovaks against the more numerous Czechs; the cultural and economic disparities between the two societies during 1918–1989; the nature of Leninist politics as a source of ethnonational identification; and the impact of external factors upon Prague's policies of centralism.[1] In short, the tortured history of Czech–Slovak relations is the obvious point of departure for examining Czechoslovakia's fate.

Carol Skalnik Leff's opening essay builds on the work of her successful 1987 book on the Czech–Slovak relationship, which remains one of the best available in the English language. Leff puts the events of the 1990s in their appropriate historical context, demonstrating that Czechoslovakia suffered from what Juan Linz and Alfred Stepan have termed a "stateness" problem since its very inception. Since Czechoslovakia was forged in an atmosphere of crisis largely generated beyond its immediate borders, the institutional solutions that were successively embraced during both the interwar republic and the communist era were products of that context. Consequently, Czechoslovakia's internal political stability or lack thereof was strongly influenced by external factors.

Leff's chapter also highlights the elements of continuity in Czech–Slovak relations before and after 1989. In three important areas—quarreling over the constitutional form of the common state, the relationships between Czech and Slovak elites, and the attempts to forge a Czechoslovak national identity—she finds that history repeated itself. Mutual suspicion and institutional failure were historical constants throughout Czechoslovakia's relatively short lifetime. Do these historical patterns suggest that Czechoslovakia's dissolution was inevitable? Leff answers in the negative, concluding that the Velvet Divorce was "a probabilistic outcome . . . the historical deck was stacked, not definitively, but still substantially, against" the survival of the common state.

In exploring the possibilities for Czech–Slovak compromise that existed in 1989–1992, Jan Rychlík's contribution complements that of Leff, assessing the weight of history through a different lens. The first part of his chapter provides a retrospective look at Czecho–Slovak relations and institutions in the post-normalization period. Rychlík points out that while the normalization reforms never succeeded in fulfilling Slovak expectations, they did create a strong managerial class in Bratislava where one had never previously existed, which turned out to be useful for the newly independent Slovakia after the dissolution of the common state. Rychlík then surveys the subsequent negotiations over Czechoslovakia's constitutional future, emphasizing the further divergence of Czech and Slovak perceptions as the conflict unfolded. In his view, the Czech side believed that "Slovak negotiators were bent on squaring a circle, aspiring to have a Slovak state while at the same time resisting the same. From the Slovak perspective, however, it seemed that the Czechs did not want to accept legitimate Slovak demands."

Despite these differences, a compromise agreement was forged at Milovy in February 1992, which was then passed on to the Czech and Slovak national councils for ratification. A ratification vote would never take place, as the Milovy accord was killed by the Presidium of the Slovak National Council, which could not obtain a majority in favor of bringing it to a vote. After the failure of the Milovy compromise, both sides agreed that further negotiation should be left to the victors of the June 1992 elections. As Rychlík concludes, the outcome of the June 1992 elections rendered further compromise impossible. The negotiations between the victorious parties focused on how the existing federation was to be undone, with the most significant point of disagreement taking place over the optimal tempo. If the common state had no future, Václav Klaus's Civic Democratic Party (ODS), triumphant in the Czech lands, wanted to move as quickly as possible toward independence; in contrast, Vladimír Mečiar's Movement for a Democratic Slovakia (HZDS) was interested in slowing things down in order to negotiate the most favorable separation agreement. Opposition parties tried to save the state but were ultimately unsuccessful, for any talk of a renewed political union was a "project without a future."

THE ROLE OF POLITICAL ELITES

The second potential explanation focuses exclusively on the role of postcommunist political elites in the development of ethnic conflict. Research on "constitutional nationalism" in the former Yugoslavia and on "the politics of national identity" identifies political elites as critical agents in the rise of postcommunist nationalist ideologies.[2] The political dynamic whereby the quest for national self-determination serves as a vehicle for enhancing the political power of certain leaders and elites was a factor in both the Czech and Slovak contexts. Individual leaders such as Vladimír Mečiar and Václav Klaus, whose parties and coalitions emerged dominant from the June 1992 elections in Slovakia and the Czech Republic, respectively, increased their personal power through the dismemberment of Czechoslovakia.[3] Repeated promises of a referendum on the country's fate were never fulfilled; the narrative chronology found in the appendix to this volume highlights the critical role of political elites in Czechoslovakia's demise.

Given that the supporters of Slovak independence never counted more than a third of those polled (and the champions of Czech independence were even fewer) during 1990 to 1992, the fact that Czech and Slovak voters gave the largest electoral support to leaders who swiftly negotiated the separation merits investigation. In an effort to probe this seeming paradox, Petr Kopecký's chapter interprets the peaceful breakup of Czechoslovakia through the consociational lens first developed by Arend Lijphart. Lijphart argued that democratic stability could be maintained in a segmented society if political rule was based on power sharing—i.e., the inclusion of representatives of each group in decision-making structures so as to facilitate compromise. Kopecký argues that the pre-1989 institutional structure, largely retained until the end of the common state some three years later, should be viewed as a consociational system that failed.

To demonstrate that the newly democratic Czechoslovakia's inherited institutions and practices were consociational, Kopecký begins by reviewing the main tenets of consociational theory. Having surveyed the relevant literature, he then accounts for the failure of consociational democracy in Czechoslovakia. Put simply, consociational institutions alone are never enough to sustain democratic stability; as Lijphart emphasizes, the requisite groundwork must be in place for consociational democracy to flourish. In postcommunist Czechoslovakia, where there was no strong tradition of elite accommodation and compromise, the volatile, uncertain, and competitive nature of postcommunist politics mitigated the otherwise stabilizing factors of consociational arrangements. Kopecký points out that six out of Lijphart's nine preconditions for consociational democracy did not pertain in democratizing Czechoslovakia. In this soil, not surprisingly, consociational democracy did not take root.

While consociational institutions alone cannot ensure democratic stability in a divided society, they can potentially play a positive role when the common state fails to hold. Kopecký maintains that the same consociational institutions that proved incapable of holding Czechoslovakia together eventually fostered its peaceful partition. As he puts it, "Indeed, the impressively legalistic manner in which the dissolution was carried out—the agreement to form a federal government to divide the state, followed by a number of agreements to divide the assets of the state, as well as an agreement for accomplishing the division in legal fashion—was possible, at least in part, precisely because of the integrative and inclusive nature of existing consociational procedures."

CONSTITUTIONAL DEADLOCK

According to the third analytical framework, the origins of the split can be traced to the institutions that the makers of the Velvet Revolution willingly inherited from the outgoing order. Instead of taking decisive and immediate action to institutionalize the revolution in the form of a new federal constitution, the dissident leadership in Czechoslovakia wound up accepting the legitimacy of the communist constitution as an interim document, one that would be amended to be suitable until a replacement could be negotiated.[4] In this, the symbolic and substantive value of a legal break with the communist era for the cause of democracy was perhaps squandered at a time when there was a high degree of cooperation between Czech and Slovak political leaders.

Where Kopecký asks why bona fide consociational institutions did not produce democratic stability, Allison Stanger seeks to explore why democratizing elites embraced communism's institutional legacy in the first place when they were not forced to do so and what the consequences of those early choices were for Czechoslovakia's subsequent political development. She argues that dissident views of the relative importance of constitutional transformation changed after they had assumed power. Embracing the communist constitution as a stopgap measure "had the unfortunate byproduct of underscoring and encouraging what divided rather than united citizens of the common state." With the benefit of hindsight, the decision to set a two-year deadline for the drafting and ratification of a new federal constitution appears to have been a flawed strategy. The task of reconstructing federalism should have been either tackled in the Velvet Revolution's immediate aftermath or pursued without timetables.

Taking a closer look at the inherited constitution, Stanger points out that federalism Czecho–Slovak style had two distinctive features. First, it featured the sweeping *zákaz majorizace* (minority veto), which banned majority voting for extraordinary as well as a broad range of ordinary legislation. Given the structure of the federal parliament, the minority veto gave extraordinary powers to the Slovak nationalist minority and fostered unfathomable gridlock. Second, the fact that the federation was comprised of only two members meant that negotiations on any agenda item were easily perceived by both parties to be a zero-sum game. In Stanger's view, Czechoslovakia's institutional forms, especially as a backdrop to the democratic transition, were a recipe for disaster, for they were never designed to function under democratic conditions. "If the potential for Czechoslovakia to survive communism's demise indeed existed," she concludes, "the negotiation and implementation of new constitutional first principles for a democratic life were a necessary condition for the common state's continued viability."

Given that elite behavior was a critical variable in both the end of Czechoslovakia and the peaceful transition to two new states, to what extent can we fault the actions and inactions of members of the Czech, Slovak, and federal governments and the leadership of the major political parties for generating the irreconcilable differences that led to the dissolution of the country? Peter Rutland has argued that "Czech politicians (such as Klaus) who pressed for a clean break were largely motivated by economic considerations," while their Slovak counterparts "were motivated more by questions of identity and pride than by worries about the economy."[5] It is difficult to evaluate Rutland's proposition, for studies relying upon survey research data point in different directions. For example, one concludes that "the creation of an independent Slovak republic was more an unintended outcome of the postcommunist panic and confusion exploited by ambitious politicians than the culmination of Slovak national emancipation."[6] Another study based on many of the same sources suggests a more tentative finding, explaining the "increase in the political salience of ethnicity" on the basis of both the role of elites and the "important differences in the objectives and perspectives of the two groups involved."[7]

In an effort to weigh the relative role of mass and elite sentiment in Czechoslovakia's demise, Sharon Wolchik builds on the findings of Kopecký and Stanger to shed light on some of the less commonly appreciated factors that contributed to the election of pro-autonomy Slovaks and the parallel election of Czechs uninterested in making concessions to Slovak aspirations. The second section of Wolchik's essay traces the development of Slovak nationalism and discusses the rapid post-1989 politicization of ethnicity—the rapidity of which was facilitated by Czechoslovakia's institutional structure. Wolchik concludes that "the interaction of institutional forms and political factors, with underlying ethnic cleavages and economic change" were responsible for Czechoslovakia's fate. Czechoslovakia's peculiar variant of federalism discouraged cross-national interaction, which contributed to the drifting apart of the two national groups twenty years later, when the rule of law was allowed to be restored, albeit on a less than stable institutional foundation. In the final section of her essay, Wolchik reflects on the tumultuous state-building process in Czechoslovakia's two successor states. In some sense, Wolchik warns, Czechoslovakia's developmental trajectory may point to the limits of federalism as a device for containing ethnic conflict.

POLITICAL PARTIES

The fourth explanatory framework highlights the critical role of the political parties and of substate institutions and organizations that emerged in the transition period. The revolutionary movement in Czechoslovakia, while united in its general objective to overthrow communist power, was organized from the start along republic or regional lines (e.g., Civic Forum in the Czech lands and the Public Against Violence in Slovakia). Political parties in Czechoslovakia were quick to form and equally quick to splinter; twenty-three political parties participated in the 1990 federal elections.[8] Among these, no party—with the important exception of the communists—transcended the regional/ethnic divide; no party, that is, had strong appeal in both the Czech and Slovak republics. Though several parties made a modest effort to overcome the national division in the 1992 elections, none succeeded in winning seats in the parliament.[9] Moreover, in the Czech lands, Moravia-based parties, and in Slovakia, Hungarian-based groupings further fragmented the sources of cohesion during the rapid repluralization of politics. Put another way, political parties in postcommunist Czechoslovakia did not successfully perform the integrative function that mass political parties typically provide, compromising the prospects for preserving state unity.[10]

Relatedly, both Czech and Slovak political leaders faced the challenge of fostering the growth of civil society in postcommunist Czechoslovakia. A robust civil society is an essential facet of democratic consolidation. The presence of interest groups and voluntary associations plays a key role here, inasmuch as they draw and empower citizens to participate in the political process. The weakness of such actors on the Czechoslovak political stage, especially those seeking to organize around the platform of the common state, can be singled out as a crucial factor in the demise of the federation.[11]

Through a rational choice analysis of the June 1992 federal elections, the outcome of which sealed the fate of the common state, František Turnovec assesses the role of the electoral system in Czechoslovakia's deepening political crisis. Czechoslovakia's last elections were conducted under proportional representation with a relatively high threshold (5 percent for singleton political parties, 7 percent for coalitions of two parties, and 10 percent for coalitions of greater than two parties). Using simulation techniques, he then varies the electoral rules and assesses the impact of these changes on political stability.

Turnovec finds that "proportional representation with thresholds led to a significant decrease in the number of parliamentary parties," yet its imposition did not succeed in eliminating extremist parties, largely due to the powerful effects of strategic voting (voting only for parties that have a chance of actually winning, rather than for one's top choice). The net effect of strategic voting was to increase the gap between what the electorate preferred in absolute terms and what it actually got representing it in parliament. "For the Czechs and Slovaks," he contends, "the choice of a high threshold may have enhanced 'governability' but also increased the relative power of the common state's enemies."

THE ROLE OF THE MASS MEDIA

Long before the country's dissolution, the Czechs and the Slovaks lived on separate islands of information. Slovak newspapers, for example, were virtually unobtainable in the Czech lands, thereby depriving any interested reader of Slovak perspectives on many issues dividing the leadership. Conversely, Slovak political leaders routinely complained about what they perceived to be biased coverage of Slovak issues emanating from the state-controlled Federal Czechoslovak Television, by far the most important source of news for most citizens. What role did the Czech and Slovak mass media—print, television, and radio—play in exacerbating or ameliorating the Czech/Slovak conflict? Contributions from Owen Johnson and Martin Vadas provide complementary answers to this question.

Throughout Czechoslovakia's existence, Johnson notes, the media were less likely to shape public opinion than they were to reinforce existing political attitudes. It follows that the media in and of themselves did not significantly increase the likelihood that the common state would break up; their influence was more subtle than that. In postcommunist states, the media's power did not rest in their ability to change people's minds but rather in their ability to reinforce the strength of the public's convictions. In post-1989 Czechoslovakia, the media did not so much tell people what to think as tell them what they should and should not be thinking about; in this way, they framed the agenda for the public. Although this meant different things in the Czech lands and in Slovakia, in both republics the media took their cue from political elites, who nurtured and manipulated the historical experiences of their respective nations for their own ends, just as they had in the first republic and under communism.

So did the media contribute to Czechoslovakia's demise? The media's lack of objectivity and balance reminds Johnson of the sort of "schizophrenic" journalism that was practiced in the United States in the nineteenth century. In both cases, the media wanted to be independent and professional while at the same time wanting to support particular political positions. With these conflicting aspirations, truly objective coverage was an unattainable goal. In serving as the political elite's megaphone in post-1989 Czechoslovakia, especially in Slovakia, the media inadvertently became a "transmission belt" for the voices of dissolution. Had a referendum actually been held, it would have been easier for the media to play "an informational and organizational role," in turn sparking genuine public debate on critical issues facing the besieged federation. For that to happen, however, journalists would have had to relinquish their long-standing leadership position, thereby bringing the public more directly into the political process. This they did not do, and as a result, the media were unable to play an independent role. Johnson concludes, therefore, that journalists "largely did not seek to serve the public" but rather the political elites—thus unintentionally and indirectly contributing to the breakup of Czechoslovakia.

While Johnson's chapter focuses on the print media, the contribution from Martin Vadas assesses the role of broadcast media, especially television, in the breakup of Czechoslovakia. Having served as Czechoslovak Television's last news director, Vadas provides unique insight into the challenges of reporting the news objectively as the drive for Slovak autonomy intensified. Vadas argues that the mass media "played an important, if subsidiary, role in the unraveling of the federation." At a time when Czechoslovakia was gearing up for its most important elections in June 1992, Czechoslovak Television, which might have served as a unifying force, was in its death throes.

For coverage of the run up to the June 1992 elections, both republics had at least three sources of television news: Czechoslovak Television, Czech Television, and Slovak Television. During his tenure as news director, Vadas assigned top priority to providing quality coverage from Slovakia, yet both organizational and personnel problems rendered this task quite difficult. After over forty years of communist rule, professional journalists were virtually nonexistent. The choice was often between an individual with experience and hence a tainted past or a person of character with no experience whatsoever. Since many television employees, both federal and national, were culpable for their service to the old regime, they were equally eager to assist the new regime. The result was a continuation of the unfortunate tradition of mass media servility to political power. The new political elites, acting out of self-interest, did not object to this subservient relationship.

After the official creation of an independent Slovak Television (ST) in 1991, federal television had to rely almost entirely on the work of ST for its Slovakia coverage. Since Slovak Television needed to justify its independent existence, it was unlikely to provide federal television with wholly objective coverage of the Czech–Slovak conflict; friction was built into this relationship from the start. In this context, Vadas admits that he was relieved that the matter of Czechoslovakia's future was never actually put to a referendum. He feared that the referendum campaign would only have further exacerbated existing tensions. As for the official position of Czechoslovak Television, Vadas tells us that it endeavored to present the full array of views on the referendum issue, while never advocating that one take place.

As Vadas's account amply illustrates, federal television faced extraordinarily difficult obstacles, which account "for the very superficial and inadequate way in which radio and television covered political events and developments during 1990–1991." Like Johnson, Vadas believes that "this coverage almost always failed to serve the public interest." Yet Vadas sees a silver lining in this lackluster tale. Unlike its Yugoslav counterpart, federal television in Czechoslovakia "contributed to a peaceful parting of the ways."

REGIONAL ECONOMIC DISPARITIES

With respect to the sixth working hypothesis, theories that focus on economic factors postulate that ethnic separatism is likely to emerge when one substate is discriminated against economically by the state.[12] Put another way, ethnic conflict is likely to develop as the product of growing regional economic disparities. At first glance, such explanations would seem to be of little relevance to the Czechoslovak case, since the Slovaks received a disproportionately larger share of state investment during the communist era. While the status of Czechs and Slovaks was markedly different at the beginning of the communist period, because of a higher level of capital investment per capita in Slovakia than in the Czech lands, the communist regime in Czechoslovakia had largely eliminated gaps in the living standards and levels of economic development by the end of the 1980s.[13] However, those funds were disproportionately devoted to the development of heavy industry, especially the weapons industry, for which markets largely dried up after the collapse of Soviet power.

The economic inequalities thesis also pertains to the differential impact of economic reforms enacted by the postcommunist government, which hit the Slovak economy harder than that of the Czech lands. Slovakia's experience with high rates of unemployment during 1991 and 1992 vis-á-vis the Czech lands (the ratio was about 3:1) was readily translated into the conviction that the Czech-dominated economic ministries of the federation failed to serve Slovak interests. Side by side with Slovak grievances, the Czech public grew increasingly weary of the proposition that Czech revenues should continue to pour into Slovakia, where they seemed to meet with little or no appreciation. By the fall of 1991, both Czech and Slovak government leaders engaged in mutual recriminations over who subsidized whom and issued their respective projections concerning the economy in the event of dissolution.[14] In this sense, actual or perceived regional economic differences played a role in fueling the forces of separation.

To assess the role of economic factors in Czechoslovakia's disintegration, Jan Svejnar compares the economic performance of the Czech and Slovak republics before and after the dissolution of the common state. Svejnar presents a time series analysis of key performance indicators in both the Czech and Slovak republics and by drawing comparisons with the economic performance of other postcommunist states, places those figures into a broader context. The chapter begins by surveying the relative economic performance of the two republics from 1918 to 1989. By 1989, Slovakia had for all practical purposes caught up to the Czech lands, so there were surprisingly similar initial economic conditions at the onset of the transition to a market economy. The chapter then evaluates seven economic indicators from the period 1989–1998 (the rate of inflation, unit labor cost, budgetary policies, income distribution, foreign trade rates, gross domestic product numbers, and unemployment). Contrary to the prevailing conventional wisdom, which emphasized Slovakia's relative economic failure in the immediate post-November 1989 years, Svejnar concludes that the recorded economic performance of the two republics was more similar than different in all examined areas, save that of the unemployment rate, especially when compared with the performance of other East–Central European economies. Though they went largely unrecognized at the time, these shared economic realities prevailed in both the predissolution 1989–92 period as well as in the postpartition 1993–98 epoch. While some of these similarities were not fully known to the decision makers at the time, Svejnar maintains that even had "full knowledge of the economic similarities between the two countries and the growth potential of Slovakia" been attainable, it probably would not have been enough to prevent the breakup. Politics and perceptions largely trumped economic realities. "The struggle," Svejnar concludes, "was elsewhere."

DEMONSTRATION EFFECTS

The demise of Czechoslovakia cannot be viewed in isolation from the larger international context. By demonstration effects, we simply mean the influence of international developments on domestic political developments.[15] The debate preceding the separation took place at a time when the successful negotiation of the Maastricht treaty had captured the imagination of European politicians. Concurrently, subnational units in Western Europe, such as the Scots, demanded greater autonomy within the larger European Union context. Drawing their own conclusions about what was possible, Slovak leaders repeatedly insisted that what they wanted was a "Czechoslovak Maastricht," which for them meant Slovak sovereignty, international recognition, and preservation of a loose union with the Czechs.

Another source of external influence working in the same direction stemmed from the successful quest for sovereignty and independence by some of the republics comprising the former Soviet Union and Yugoslavia, which received a stamp of Western approval in the form of international recognition. These developments, though they reflected forces and factors working at cross-purposes, provided grist for the mill of Slovak advocates of independence. Moreover, they fueled demands for a greater expression of the Slovak national interest in foreign affairs than that provided under the auspices of the federal ministry.

Like most studies of ethnic conflict, the majority of contributions to this volume focus on the domestic factors that spawned the demise of Czechoslovakia. Michael Kraus's chapter fills an important gap by emphasizing the critical role of the international context in determining whether states succeed or fail. History shows that regime change in Central and Eastern Europe in general and Czechoslovakia in particular was typically shaped by outside powers or by changes in the international environment. As Kraus's contribution highlights, disintegrative forces in Czechoslovakia were similarly a product of an international system in transition; "domestic conflict was ultimately inseparable from the international context." He makes this point by analyzing the influence of external factors from three distinctive perspectives: (1) the impact of a transformed international system on the shared Czech and Slovak sense of vulnerability; (2) the legacies of federalized totalitarianism, an import from Moscow, for Czechoslovak political development; and (3) the influence of integrative forces at work in the West on the manner in which Czech and Slovak individual actors perceived the realm of the possible for their own futures.

Kraus begins by reminding the reader that states form in response to "external dangers that unify people across class and ethnic boundaries." For Czechoslovakia, fear of German and Hungarian domination forged an uneasy alliance between the Czech and the Slovak peoples and continued to reinforce state cohesion in the First Republic. Hitler's rise destroyed this bond, which was replaced by Soviet imperialism. The end of the Cold War further diminished a long-standing shared sense of Czech and Slovak vulnerability. In 1989, the threat from Hungary and Germany seemed minimal, and the imploding Soviet Union's attention was focused inward. In these circumstances, a vital link between Czechs and Slovaks was severed.

The legacy of what Havel called "federalized totalitarianism," a constitutional import from the former Soviet Union, is another factor that played its part in Czechoslovakia's demise. It is important to note the extent to which Czech–Slovak agreements from the communist era were shaped by Moscow's self-interested designs. The asymmetrical constitutional model, whereby Slovaks had party and government institutions in a federal structure with no Czech counterparts, was very much tailored to Soviet specifications. The Soviet experience also shaped patterns of resource allocation in communist Czechoslovakia. In this way, the international balance of power was embedded in Czechoslovakia's political institutions.

What might be labeled the Maastricht phenomenon played a profound role in the divergence of Czech and Slovak attitudes after November 1989. Calls for a Czechoslovak Maastricht accompanied the birth and institutionalization of Slovak foreign policy as an entity distinct from the foreign policy of Czechoslovakia. By 1991, Czechoslovakia's foreign policy wore two faces: federal and Slovak. As Kraus puts it, "Clearly, Maastricht encouraged the illusion in the Slovak ranks that the hard choices between national sovereignty and supranational institutions were fast losing their salience."

THE VIEW FROM THE GROUND:
CZECH AND SLOVAK PERSPECTIVES

The fourth section of the book presents the views of prominent Czechs and Slovaks who were actually firsthand witnesses to and participants in the process of dissolution. Ján Čarnogurský, prime minister of the Slovak Republic at the time of the split, leads off by arguing that the reasons for the Czech–Slovak breakup have an interesting and paradoxical intellectual kinship with Francis Fukuyama's end-of-history hypothesis. In Čarnogurský's view, Europe's multinational states first had to dissolve for rationalism to triumph in Europe. The dominant Czech theme in the early 1990s, Čarnogurský tells us, was economic autonomy, with each republic living on the basis of its own means. In contrast, the predominant Slovak theme was the demand for equal treatment and autonomy both within the common state and on the international stage. These two animating aims became irreconcilable over time, making divorce the only feasible option. That is the reason why Čarnogurský insists that even had the common state held together, it still would have been very difficult, if not impossible, to put together a federal budget for 1993.

The Velvet Divorce was possible only because of the heightened rationalism that now characterizes the majority of European relations (the situation in the former Yugoslavia being a prominent exception). The relative stability in the relations of post-Cold War Europe had rid the Czechs and the Slovaks of their long-standing historical suspicion of their neighbors. The common state, Čarnoguský suggests, was never really more than a pragmatic solution and was therefore rendered obsolete by post-Cold War events. He describes the futile negotiation effort to save Czechoslovakia, in which he was an important participant; it lacked any sort of overarching idea or aspiration that might have united both parties to the conflict. The national mood in Slovakia was unprepared to accept a continuation of status quo constitutional arrangements. For all of these reasons, Čarnogurský's political party, the Christian Democratic Movement (KDH), believed that the Slovak "process of emancipation" was best accomplished "in the framework of European integration." In his view, the June 1992 elections, which resulted in the almost complete defeat of the former dissident parties, severed one of the last remaining bonds of solidarity between Czech and Slovak political elites. Čarnogurský concludes by suggesting that the subsequent deterioration in relations between the Czech and Slovak republics proves ex post facto that "we were peoples too different to comprise one state."

In a provocatively titled chapter, "The Division/Dissolution of Czechoslovakia: Old Sins and New Forms of Selfishness," Petr Pithart, the prime minister of the Czech Republic at the time of the split, provides an alternative perspective. While it might have been possible to preserve the common state, the costs of completing this agenda were far too high. Pithart was an opponent of partitioning Czechoslovakia until the bitter end, which was a politically suicidal stance to take at the time.[16] For Pithart, those who advocated that each republic go its own way took the easy way out. In so doing, they compromised liberal principles and in some sense still do so, since legitimacy had to be bestowed on the division after the fact. Not surprisingly, relations between the Czech and Slovak republics are today less than neighborly. The split established unfortunate incentives for continued ill will between the Czech and Slovak governments; contemporary flashpoints of conflict only appear to prove that it would have been impossible for Czech and Slovak political elites to cohabitate in democratic times.

Urging us to let the Slovaks speak for themselves, Pithart goes on to consider the principal causes of the dissolution on the Czech side. First, Czech chauvinism and Pragocentrism vis-á-vis Slovakia is a long-standing phenomenon, one that made it easy for Czechs to misgauge the seriousness of Slovak strivings for autonomy. Second, over forty years of "real socialism" destroyed any sense of civic community that had once existed. The absence of civic community made short-term material arguments for dividing Czechoslovakia only all the more appealing. Third, it is surprising how little Czechs actually knew about their Slovak sisters and brothers. "Czech haughtiness was sky-high—not only did they know nothing about the Slovaks, but they didn't even know that they knew nothing. As a result, the Slovaks were in a state of permanent alert." Finally, Czechs and Slovaks interpreted and recollected the forty years of communist rule in wholly different ways. The Slovaks, who, according to Pithart, were "initially less enamored of communism, experienced the normalization years favorably, while the Czechs lived through the same period as the most repulsive of times. After November 1989, the Czechs imagined that they were reawakening into freedom as right wingers, while the Slovaks were concurrently the most receptive to socialism." Obviously, this gave rise to "a host of misconceptions and misunderstandings."

From Pithart's perspective, therefore, the processes that ultimately culminated in Czechoslovakia's end had long been under way, even though many did not realize or refused to acknowledge that this was indeed the case. There was no "decisive moment in the process of division" but rather an "unending series of . . . misunderstandings, conflicts, and embarrassments." Pithart cites only one post-November 1989 error as fundamental, concurring with Stanger's assessment: the two-year deadline for drafting a new constitution was a mistake. He goes on to tell us that the two-year deadline was primarily a product of Havel's initial hesitation to assume the presidency. A two-year deadline for constitutional renovations meant that Havel would have to be president for a maximum of only two years, which was important to Civic Forum's leader, who, interestingly enough, could not at that time contemplate serving any longer. "In the final analysis," Pithart concludes, "the state fell apart, above all, because neither the Czechs nor the Slovaks showed at any time enough political will to create a common political nation."

Responding to the first two contributions in this section of the book, Daniel Kroupa criticizes Čarnogurský and Pithart for conflating sociological (deterministic) and subjective (free will) factors in their accounts. In Kroupa's view, sociological analysis is a legitimate approach, but it does not get one very far in explaining post-1989 events in the former Czechoslovakia, nor does the attempt to identify whether the Czech or the Slovak side is most to blame. As Kroupa puts it, "The differences between the Czechs and the Slovaks are far smaller than the proponents of the theory that Czechoslovakia broke up because of these differences would allow. Such disparities did not prevent the existence of a common state, and such differences are often far greater within each individual republic than between them."

Instead, Kroupa points a finger at a very small group of elite political figures and the choices they made as bearing much of the responsibility for the breakup. For those who would identify Slovak nationalism as the source of the common state's disintegration, Kroupa responds that the more important question is why nationalist forces acquired such great political influence, since survey research indicates that their platforms were initially embraced only by marginalized social groups. In Kroupa's view, nonnationalist political parties in Slovakia, such as the Public Against Violence, made a tactical error when they decided to co-opt the nationalist agenda—thereby legitimizing it—in an effort to court additional voters rather than continuing to take a firm stand against the nationalist orientation. Echoing a point emphasized by Pithart and Stanger in earlier chapters, Kroupa insists that "the main cause of the dissolution was the inherited constitutional framework, which narrowed considerably the range of options after the 1992 elections." Czechoslovakia's centrifugal forces "could not have brought on the dissolution of the state without the federal constitution's minority veto."

In contrast, the contribution from Miroslav Macek provides evidence for Pithart's assessment of the Czech contribution to the split. A flamboyant leader of the now-fragmented Civic Democratic Party (ODS), Macek was one of the earliest and most outspoken advocates of Czechoslovakia's dissolution.[17] Macek begins by laying out the two fundamental reasons why he subscribed to this view. First, the Czechs and Slovaks had had wholly different historical experiences, which accounts for the unbridgeable differences that developed following the November 1989 revolution. Second, Czechoslovakia's two-member federation was by nature institutionally dysfunctional and unstable. Without external or internal coercion, it was incapable of independent existence.

Macek proceeds to support his argument with five eyewitness anecdotes from 1989 through 1992. Macek's vignettes provide insight into previously undocumented incidents of Czech–Slovak friction as well as into some of the major political personalities of the time. They also demonstrate how the stance of key members of ODS accelerated the formal dissolution of Czechoslovakia.

Macek's fifth illustrative story is a firsthand account of the post-June 1992 election negotiations between ODS and HZDS on preserving the union. Macek recounts how he engaged the Slovak Republic's future president, Michal Kováč, in conversation just before the formal negotiation session began. In that corridor exchange, Macek claims that Kováč committed a negotiating blunder: he prematurely revealed that HZDS planned to resurrect the 1968 notion of an economic and defense union, a loose Czech–Slovak administrative arrangement that involved a common currency defended by two separate armies and treasuries. Macek coined the phrase for this arrangement as "Slovak independence with Czech insurance." Mečiar's negotiating style, however, where "yesterday's concession is presented as today's starting point," required that HZDS's extremist positions only be revealed gradually over time. Of course, Macek immediately informed Klaus (in Mečiar's presence) of HZDS intentions, and this new piece of information only confirmed the Czech side's preexistent opinions about Mečiar's lack of good faith. Mečiar turned ashen, Macek reports, at the realization that one of his deputies had revealed his ultimate goals.[18] In Macek's view, this critical incident sealed the fate of the common state: "The battle was over before it had begun. It was time to haggle and to sign a peace treaty." For Macek, that such an event could determine the outcome of this most serious of questions proves that the ties that had connected the Czech lands with Slovakia were uncommonly weak.

The chapter by Milan Zemko, historian and presently (1999) chief of staff of the president's office in the Slovak Republic, draws comparisons between the 1939 and 1989 demises of Czechoslovakia. In each instance, external factors played an important role, yet in 1939, totalitarianism was ascendant and in 1989, democracy. The latter international circumstances made independence an easier step for a small state to take. This changed environment was a necessary although not sufficient condition for the split. Zemko argues that the entire trajectory of the Czech–Slovak conflict after 1989 was very much a product of unacknowledged nationalism on both sides. That neither party recognized its own nationalist orientation generated the most difficult obstacle to overcome: a lack of empathy for the other. In this way, the revival of nationalist sentiments discouraged feelings of a shared future. Without some degree of empathy, no negotiation process can move forward.

Like many Slovaks, Zemko sees the March 1990 quarrel over what name the newly democratic country should wear—the so-called hyphen war—as symbolic of larger problems inherent in the Czech–Slovak relationship. In this dispute, Czechs displayed limited sensitivity to long-denied Slovak aspirations. Slovaks demonstrated an equally limited understanding of the significance for Czechs both of tradition and of their preferred hyphenated name, which reminded Czechs of the post-Munich republic.

In subsequent sections, Zemko provides the reader with an account of the ill-fated efforts to maintain unity. Zemko usually refrains from blaming one side more than the other, although he does criticize Czech hockey-style "power plays"—i.e., Czech attempts to preserve the common state by controlling both federal- and republic-level institutions—more than he does Slovak threats of unilateral action in such areas as foreign policy and economic development. While there were numerous searches for solutions to the federation's structural problems, no proposal was ever agreeable to the elites of both sides at the same time. Interestingly, Zemko touches on the failed Milovy accord, for which he cast the fateful "no" vote, yet he does not present it as a turning point. Zemko reports that he voted against the Milovy compromise simply because he felt it had no chance of ever being approved by the Slovak National Council. In general, throughout the constitutional discussions, Czechs were inclined to endorse the notion of a functioning federation, while Slovaks proposed a range of alternatives to federalism. The problem, in Zemko's view, was that the Slovak elite was highly divided on the question of optimal future constitutional arrangements, so any sort of forward momentum was difficult to generate. Despite these trends, as constitutional deliberations ground to a halt and the support for dissolution increased among the political elites of both nations, it did not for the public at large. In this way, peaceful partition became the "second-best solution," and hence one that the public in neither the Czech lands nor Slovakia openly protested.

A contribution from a former leader of the Public Against Violence rounds out the final section of the volume. Peter Zajac seeks to understand why Czechoslovakia dissolved in the absence of significant public pressure to do so. He notes that, paradoxically, "at precisely the time when a petition supporting the common state had secured more than a million signatures, the Czech and Slovak national councils were incapable of agreeing on practically anything." Surveying the competing explanations, Zajac points out that many of them are interrelated. This fact needs to be acknowledged if students of state disintegration hope to get to the heart of the matter.

In the course of elaborating on his thesis, Zajac provides many important details about the gridlock that surrounded the numerous constitutional negotiating sessions from 1989 to 1992. He concludes that one can view the dissolution of Czechoslovakia from two perspectives: "The first is a historical–teleological one, where the event is seen as a historical inevitability. The second argues that Czechoslovakia might have been preserved as a common state only if it had been capable of changing, to quote Tomáš Masaryk, 'the ideas that gave rise to it,' and for that, after 1989, there was neither opportunity nor time." Zajac faults the "arrogance of *nomenklatura* capitalism," a characteristic shared by all postcommunist elites, for eventually leading to the loss of public support for new and hence fragile democratic arrangements.

CZECHOSLOVAKIA'S DISSOLUTION
IN COMPARATIVE PERSPECTIVE

The concluding section has two components. In the first, Stanley Hoffmann provides a distinguished and incisive survey of the international context in which Czechoslovakia's peaceful partition took place. In inimitable style, Hoffmann begins by comparing the Cold War international system with that of the present to assess the key factors underlying the increased prevalence of ethnic conflict. Through numerous illuminating examples, he demonstrates not only that ethnic conflict has "multiple faces" but also that it has "multiple parents." Having established the importance and the consequences of the problem, Hoffmann then turns to an examination of potential solutions, from international intervention to prevention. Placing it in comparative perspective, he characterizes Czechoslovakia's Velvet Divorce as an unusual case of voluntary secession, where political elites decided the country's fate over the heads of the people. Hoffmann points out that most political philosophers insist on indisputable popular support if a secession effort is to be considered legitimate.

Looking to the future, Hoffmann ends with "three sets of exhortations." First, the tasks of prevention and settlement "cannot be left to often questionable, fragile, and selfish states"; the distinction between interstate and intrastate conflict is no longer viable and should cease to be treated as such. Second, the tension between the norm of state sovereignty and the principle of self-determination is best addressed through "strict limitations on both." International and regional organizations can combat the excesses of the former. As for the latter, despite the Czech and Slovak example, secession should always be a last resort and "endorsed by a qualified majority of the people who claim independence." Finally, efforts to reduce the significance of ethnicity in international relations, as represented by the European Union, must be encouraged. While this task may at times seem impossible, Hoffmann concludes by reminding us "that it is not necessary to hope in order to undertake, or to succeed in order to persevere."

In the second component of the concluding section, Michael Kraus and Allison Stanger reflect on the larger implications of this collaborative project. To accomplish this task, we begin by comparing the breakup of Yugoslavia, the Soviet Union, and Czechoslovakia to shed light on the question of why the Czechs and the Slovaks were able to part ways without violence. We then survey the general findings of this volume and end by reflecting on the lessons of the Czecho–Slovak case for other states torn by ethnic conflict.

NOTES

1. Carol Skalnik Leff's *National Conflict in Czechoslovakia: The Making and Remaking of a State, 1918–1987* (Princeton: Princeton University Press, 1988), identifies several similar "conflict-intensifying" factors as determinants of Czechoslovak national conflict. See esp. ch. 9.

2. See Robert Hayden, "Constitutional Nationalism in the Formerly Yugoslav Republics," *Slavic Review*, 51, no. 4, Winter 1992, pp. 654–673; Julie Mostov, "Democracy and the Politics of National Identity," paper presented at the 1992 Annual Meeting of the American Political Science Association, Chicago, Ill., September 1992.

3. Noting the different levels of economic development, Ellen Comisso writes: "Czechs may have needed the Slovak hinterland in 1918 but in 1992 it was Václav Klaus, not the Slovak nationalists, who forced the separation." See her "Prediction versus Diagnosis: Comments on a Ken Jowitt Retrospective" (review article), *Slavic Review*, 53, no. 1, Spring 1994, p. 191.

4. This is a decision that merits explanation, given that the dissidents around Václav Havel had worked on constitution drafting prior to November 1989 and had actually prepared a draft of a new federal constitution. Interview with Rudolf Battěk, Prague, July 1994.

5. Peter Rutland, "Thatcherism, Czech-style: Transition to Capitalism in the Czech Republic," *Telos*, no. 94, Winter 1993–94, p. 104.

6. Martin Bútora and Zora Bútorová, "Slovakia: The Identity Challenges of the Newly Born State," *Social Research*, 10, no. 2, Winter 1993, p. 720.

7. Sharon L. Wolchik, "The Politics of Ethnicity in Post-Communist Czechoslovakia," *East European Politics and Societies*, 8, no. 1, Winter 1994, p. 187.

8. On the role of political parties in national integration, see William N. Chambers, "Parties and Nation-Building," in Joseph LaPalombara and Myron Weiner, eds., *Political Parties and Political Development* (Princeton: Princeton University Press, 1966), pp. 98–104.

9. On this point, see David Olson, "Dissolution of the State: Political Parties and the 1992 Election in Czechoslovakia," *Communist and Post-Communist Studies*, 26, no. 3, September 1993, pp. 301–314; and Sharon Wolchik, "The Repluralization of Politics in Czechoslovakia," *Communist and Post-Communist Studies*, 26, no. 4, December 1993, pp. 412–431.

10. Otto Kirchheimer, "The Transformation of the Western European Party Systems," in LaPalombara and Weiner, eds., *Political Parties and Political Develoment,* pp. 188–189.

11. Martin Bútora and Zora Bútorová, "Slovakia: The Identity Challenges of the Newly Born State," *Social Research*, 10, no. 2, Winter 1993, p. 721.

12. For a list of social scientists who have ascribed great significance to economic forces in explaining nationalism, see Walter Connor, *Ethnonationalism: The Quest for Understanding* (Princeton: Princeton University Press, 1994), pp. 161–162, note 1.

13. For evidence, see Sharon L. Wolchik, *Czechoslovakia in Transition: Politics, Economics and Society* (London and New York: Pinter Publishers, 1991), pp. 186–195.

14. See, for example, the December 1991 report of the Slovak government on this subject, "Správa o ekonomických dosledkoch pripadného rozdelenia ČSFR na dve samostatné republiky," *Hospodárské noviny*, 12 December 1991, pp. 7–10.

15. The "demonstration effect" is Arend Lijphart's concept. See Arend Lijphart, "Political Theories and the Explanation of Ethnic Conflict in the Western World: Falsified Predictions and Plausible Postdictions," in Milton J. Esman, ed., *Ethnic Conflict in the Western World* (Ithaca: Cornell University Press, 1977), pp. 63–64.

16. His views initially cost him a position in the newborn Czech Republic's political leadership, although he has subsequently returned to political prominence, in no small part because he is seen as a man of principle.

17. Macek served as Klaus's campaign manager during the 1996 elections.

18. This story is consistent with the public animosity that existed between Kováč and Mečiar after Kováč had become president.

Part I

The Legacies of the Past

2

Inevitability, Probability, Possibility: The Legacies of the Czech–Slovak Relationship, 1918–1989, and the Disintegration of the State

Carol Skalnik Leff

INTRODUCTION

Juan Linz and Alfred Stepan define a "stateness" problem to exist "when a significant proportion of the population does not accept the boundaries of the state (whether constituted democratically or not) as a legitimate political unit to which they owe obedience."[1] The Linz-Stepan definition, however, may be somewhat too restrictive. In a multinational state, a stateness problem can exist not only in the presence of a defined secessionist impulse of disallegiance to the established territorial unit but also when a significant proportion of the population is merely *agnostic* about loyalty owed to the state. The crux of the matter is whether the relevant actors can agree on the proper institutional form for a multinational state, the proper safeguards for national identity. If there are pronounced ethnonational differences on this issue, the stateness question remains open even if there is no clear impulse to independence. In such circumstances, successive generations of politicians are confronted with challenges to the existing constitutional bargain—in the name of a federal or confederal arrangement, for example—to the pronounced detriment of political stability. Such a state is thus especially vulnerable to the vagaries of international politics to the extent that external threats amplify internal divisions.

Czechoslovakia clearly suffered from such a stateness problem from its inception in 1918. It was a state born abruptly in an atmosphere of crisis that precluded serious, sustained negotiations on the national character of the state,[2] and a state

29

that underwent a series of wrenching regime changes, each of which reopened the stateness question. Throughout, the central Czech–Slovak relationship, which was ambiguously defined at the outset, remained problematic, and its successive institutional expressions were never fully legitimized and accepted throughout the territory.

In the 1980s, I attempted to decipher the evolution of the Czech–Slovak relationship since 1918 and the long Czech–Slovak stateness quarrel in a book that analyzed how the issue persisted and redefined itself across generations from the germinal period of state formation to what we know were the final years of the communist regime. I also sought to anticipate its future course.[3] The conflict appeared from abroad to be both civilized and momentous. It was civilized because of the absence of violence, a minimalist definition that looks increasingly valuable when viewed through the prism of the Yugoslav tragedy. It was momentous because Czechoslovakia's multinational character so often proved to be the Achilles' heel of an otherwise rather prosperous and viable state. The book focused on two questions: why the conflict persisted, and why it was never satisfactorily resolved.

The following propositions compress the arguments of three hundred pages, organized around three central issues: the institutional expression of the Czech–Slovak relationship in electoral politics and governance, the patterning of elite relations, and the mutual perceptions and social engineering of national identity. In each case, the emphasis is on the parallels that emerged between the interwar republic and the communist regime in the management and mismanagement of the national question and the logic of the persistent failure to—as the Košice Program of 1945 too optimistically put it—"put an end to all former quarrels."[4] Once the framework is set, the analysis that follows revisits the conclusions I reached in that study in light of the subsequent collapse of the state.

CZECH–SLOVAK RELATIONS BEFORE 1989

Institutional Setting

Between 1918 and 1989, the institutional framework of Czechoslovak politics functioned to control and contain the national question rather than to resolve it. This was true of both the First Republic and its eventual communist successor.

Scholars and journalists alike widely hail the First Czechoslovak Republic of 1919–1938 as the sole functioning parliamentary democracy in interwar Central Europe. But it achieved this status—in a complex and threatening international environment and in an equally complex domestic multinational environment—at certain costs to the flexibility with which successive governments could respond to festering problems, particularly tensions generated by that very multinational complexity. The electoral process itself was quite open to the representation of a broad spectrum of views, generating an extraordinary array of parties stratified by class, religion, and ethnicity. But in part because of that openness and the proliferation of small parties, each with its own niche in a complex socioeconomic and multinational setting, the process of governance was all the more complicated: political management centered on multiparty government coalitions; the persistence of core parties that remained in power from election to election (in particular the Agrarians, who soon dominated every government); unofficial back-corridor mechanisms that regulated policy and government composition; repeated cabinet reshufflings; and caretaker governments. Later, after the war, there was a strong sense in many quarters that First Republic governance had been too much a closely held corporation of aging leaders, too rigid to respond effectively to questions of both survival and social justice. Politicians streamlined the tasks of governance by streamlining the agenda, especially when it came to national questions facing the republic. Parties that accepted the founding premises of the state, including the unitary logic of the 1920 constitution, were acceptable partners in government. Those that did not—who challenged in particular the need for a centralized state—were not generally eligible, notably the Hlinka Populists with their Slovak autonomist program. In short, the governing parties of the First Republic governed *around* the national question and consistently resisted proposals to subject the centralized institutional form of the state to serious reconsideration. As Kenneth Jowitt has observed, an "effective nation-building strategy depends on an elite's minimizing the number and character of its commitments, holding certain issues as resolved, and preventing their continuous espousal by counterelites."[5] This was the strategy of interwar governance.

Of course, the politicians of the First Republic did not try to finesse the national question merely because they were busy with an overloaded agenda. As a *multi*national state, and one in which two substantial German and Hungarian minorities were linked to potentially threatening neighboring states, Czechoslovakia was vulnerable to centrifugal pulls on its political stability and even its territorial integrity; most Czech politicians and a number of Slovaks therefore saw the unitary state as a national security safeguard and feared that the differentiation of Slovak institutions would provide impetus for a move down the slippery slope to further, possibly state-destroying, claims from disaffected minorities.[6] Even before the inception of the state, the Czech–Slovak alliance had been seen as a useful demographic counterweight to those very minorities.[7]

The result was that in the interwar republic, a broad spectrum of Slovak views found ready expression in electoral politics and assured parliamentary representation but not a decisive voice in governance—a formula under which grievances about the constitutional order could neither die nor be resolved. In the communist state, the institutional setting was of course rather different. The postwar institutional "asymmetry" of a Slovak Communist Party (KSS) and a Slovak National Council without equivalent organs in the Czech lands did create a potential Slovak bureaucratic power base. This framework provided Slovaks a different, but equally problematic, form of access. Although the ČSSR became ever more decentralized in formal institutional terms after the decision to federalize the state in 1968, the continued control of the Communist Party inhibited the full political logic of those changes, and the system remained markedly "Pragocentric." In the parlance of later times, this was not an "authentic" federalism, and it did not represent a permanent resolution of the stateness question any more than the unitary interwar state had.

Yet the Czechoslovak federation was not politically insignificant. In "ethnofederalism" of this sort, regional institutions could reinforce national cohesion and prospectively create regional political marketplaces, thus nurturing regional elites and segmenting the statewide leadership.[8] Until 1989, of course, a statewide KSČ glued these political subsystems together, as did the CPSU in the former Soviet Union. Once again, there was an institutional foothold to sustain national identity without the capacity for genuine Slovak autonomy.

Elite Relations

If the evolving institutional frame of Czech–Slovak relations was a containment chamber for the stateness problem rather than a means of resolving it, so too was the pattern of elite relations that evolved in tandem with it. In the area of elite interaction, Czech–Slovak conflict persisted because of a Czech misapprehension, a misapprehension that in addition provided the rationale for continued postponement of a reckoning on institutional redesign. This is because the conflict was regulated and contained in both the interwar and communist states by a distinctive pattern of elite relations. Historically, Czechoslovakia had neither a single integrated multinational leadership nor a segmented configuration of autonomous ethnically based elites. Instead, the norm was a triangular leadership pattern in which Czech politicians always had the cooperation of some Slovak allies—whose participation in governance formed the basis of a claim for the acknowledgment of legitimate Slovak interests. The "real" Slovak leaders were those who shared Czech premises and cooperated in governance. Vocal nationalists, the other leg of the triangle, were demagogues and populists capitalizing on the naiveté of the immature Slovak public.

In the First Republic, this triadic pattern was reflected in Slovak politics by a peculiar hybrid of regionally based parties and parties with a statewide base, a division that overlapped considerably with the division between government and nongovernment parties. The ethnically Slovak electorate consistently returned the autonomist Hlinka Populists as the single largest Slovak delegation to the National Assembly in Prague, but it also regularly returned substantial numbers of representatives of the statewide parties. Some highly respected scholars have read this bifurcation in the Slovak elite as evidence that the real problem was not Czech–Slovak discord but rather an internecine split within the Slovak leadership. Yet it was hardly a matter of indifference to Prague which of the Slovak elite groups had the upper hand. Only once during the interwar period did the central government experiment with the inclusion of the Hlinka party in power, and that experiment broke down in a welter of mutual accusations and a spectacular treason trial of one of the party's chief ideologues. A small core of Slovak leaders from statewide parties, on the other hand, were consistently represented in government. In fact, one could argue that Czechs governed interwar Slovakia primarily on a narrow base of only three Slovak lieutenants—Ivan Derer, Vavro Šrobár, and Milan Hodža—who were allotted three-fifths of the cabinet assignments and 94 percent of the substantive policy posts accorded to Slovak ministers in the interwar period.[9]

Under communism, while the triangulation of leadership was less clear-cut, the Czech Communists continued to find it necessary and politic to incorporate reliable Slovak allies into governance. The inclusion of a proportionate number of Slovaks in party presidia and government consistently accorded formalistic recognition of Slovak claims to representation. Although there was, of course, no electorally validated Czech or Slovak alternative, there was clear tension over who could credibly speak for the Slovaks and recurrent evidence that an alternative Slovak perspective existed. Not only did the leadership purges of the 1950s target a renegade corps of communist "bourgeois nationalists" charged with isolating themselves from the premises of the larger Czechoslovak state, but the act of excluding them provided a focus for those who challenged the logic of the communist solution to the national problem. In the 1960s, the rehabilitation of purged "bourgeois nationalists" became part of the larger Czech–Slovak debate, in which Prague lost partial control of the designation of appropriate Slovak leaders in Bratislava even prior to 1968.[10] The quarrel over who could credibly speak for Slovak interests persisted.

This triangular model of elite relations oversimplifies the very real trade-offs that Slovak allies of the center had to make in order to maintain a delicate balancing act between the expectations of Prague and the interests of Slovakia—for example, the compromises of the interwar Slovak Agrarians or the tightrope act of some later Slovak communist leaders, balancing between the interests of socialism and the interests of Slovak national identity. But the patterning of elite relations helps to explain why it was often difficult for Czechs to accept the argument that Slovak interests would be better served by greater decentralization, federalization, or even confederation. Czech politicians saw their own Slovak allies as the responsible and undemagogic leaders—the true voice of Slovak self-interest, had the entire Slovak public only been mature enough to see it that way.[11] The Czech public and leadership could thus argue that Slovaks had an established and enduring voice in governance, while Slovak proponents of greater institutional autonomy could respond that this voice did not give full expression to Slovak interests. Thus the triadic structure of elite relation was a coping mechanism but also a perceptual obstacle to managing the question of state organization. Interwar and communist governments could and did govern without fully addressing this constitutional question, but at the price of postponing any stable resolution.

The Failure of Social Engineering to Generate Agreement

The third and final core issue considered in *National Conflict in Czechoslovakia* was the evolving complex of attitudes and mutual perceptions that surrounded the long quarrel over the stateness question in Czechoslovakia. Here, two points are critical. The first was that successive regimes dealt with the Slovak question with long-term strategies that, it was vainly hoped, would liquidate national tensions without necessitating a grand constitutional revision. This approach in itself was productive of tension. Second, the record of successive crises and disappointments in dealing with the national question imposed its own cumulative burden on resolution of the issue and produced characteristic patterns of conflicting perceptions that remained recognizable over time and were reinforced by repetition.

To understand the actual impact of those long-term strategies designed to liquidate national tensions, it is important to recognize that the proper form of the Czech–Slovak relationship did not remain contentious for reasons of force majeure; Czechs, who heavily outnumbered Slovaks, did not rely cynically on the imposition of a centralized and repressive Pragocentric regime. To the contrary, successive leaderships consistently acted on a series of assumptions—flawed assumptions, to be sure—about the character of the stateness problem and the means by which it could be resolved. In a manner that foreshadowed a now widely criticized Western scholarship on modernization, the architects of policy on the national issue in Czechoslovakia acted as social scientists (some of them *were* indeed social scientists) who supposed Slovak nationalism to be a "childhood disease" that would succumb to the medicinal treatment of political, cultural, and economic development.[12] Politicians saw the development gap between Czech lands and Slovakia as the root of conflict and sought a remedy in the narrowing of that gap. In the First Republic, the governing powers of the state regarded the national fabric as malleable and engaged in sustained social engineering to try to generate a "Czechoslovak" consciousness consonant with the aspiration encapsulated in the unhyphenated name of the state. It is striking how often cultural remedies were proposed for the bridging of Czech–Slovak differences—particularly notable was the expectation that the educational advances in Slovakia would produce a generation more receptive to the acceptance of a common Czechoslovak identity.[13] This assumption had clearly been shown to be false by the 1930s: the first generation of Slovak students educated in the First Republic proved if anything more radical in its national self-assertion than had previous generations.

The postwar Marxist analysis of the problem accented a perceived flaw in the calculations of earlier leaders, without abandoning the logic of modernization and development as a force for national cooperation. In this case, however, the emphasis was on the promotion of economic development within the framework of the socialist state, an approach that communists charged the interwar leadership with neglecting. Indeed, scholars do not seriously question the sustained commitment of economic resources to Slovakia after 1948.[14] The gap in economic development did narrow during the subsequent decades, although the investment priorities embedded in the strategy of equalization were hardly optimal for Slovakia's development any more than the Soviet model was for the Czech Republic. What is clear, however, is that the modernization strategy in its economic form proved no more viable in resolving national tensions than did the variant form it took in the First Republic. Over decades of experimentation, Czechoslovakia provided a laboratory test for a proposition now widely accepted: greater literacy and social and economic development do *not* quash nationalist assertiveness, nor do they promote an integrated identity for multiethnic states. To the contrary, such an evolution may feed national assertion by providing resources for pursuit of the cause. By 1968, Marxist theorists were rejecting the simplistic thesis that economics was a cure for inconvenient identity politics and began to accept the need for a federal solution, but the full logic of that acknowledgment was stunted by the postinvasion normalization period.

This prolonged experimentation with modernization strategy as a liquidator of national tensions is not merely significant for its flawed assumptions. It is also a clue to an important parallel dynamic. Paradoxically, the fact that successive political leaderships saw themselves as offering a solution to the Slovak question and assistance to the Slovaks in itself contributed to further deadlock and misunderstanding, because it reinforced the perceptual blinders that generated a sense of mutual grievance. Anyone who looks at the twentieth-century experiment in Czechoslovak statehood as a whole will be struck by the recurrence of certain perennial arguments. On the one hand, responsible political actors on the Czech side (and their Slovak allies) were indignant that Slovaks did not appreciate Czech sacrifices and subsidies. The theme of alleged Slovak ingratitude runs through the history of the common state. Slovaks, in turn, were frequently exasperated that the Czechs persisted in seeing national self-assertion as a provincial manifestation of backwardness that would disappear with cultural and economic uplift. This continued perceptual mismatch gave both contestants a clear conscience about their own rectitude and erected further barriers to understanding.

This analysis suggests that a combination of factors—Czech numerical dominance, institutional control from the center, undue optimism that social engineering would pacify Slovak aspirations, the pressure of international influences—blocked substantial reconsideration of the constitutional order in the course of normal politics. As a consequence, Slovak national self-assertion reappeared on the agenda in times of crisis and systemic change, as any broader regime crisis triggered the reconsideration of the Czech–Slovak bargain as well.[15] Such episodes include the founding of the state in 1918 amidst the chaos and uncertainty of the end of World War I (and the acceptance of a unitary constitutional settlement in the aftermath of Bela Kun's incursion into Slovakia thereafter); the reconfiguration of the state following Munich, in which the Slovaks first gained autonomy and later a German-circumscribed independence; the reconstruction of the state following World War II; and its federalization in the wake of the Soviet invasion in 1968. Notice that it was not the Slovak question itself that had generated these earlier crises; only in 1968 could one clearly see Slovak self-assertion as directly fueling regime crisis. Rather, these historical moments were broadly dependent on the international context of the state—the chronic fate of small nations embedded in a larger framework of power politics. Nonetheless, such critical junctures provided an opening for reformulation of the Slovak question, and that question in turn complicated the response to crisis. The common denominator of these crisis periods was the Czech perception that Slovaks had capitalized on the international pressures and uncertainties to extract concessions in conditions that precluded a sustained and mutually beneficial period of negotiation:

> The unfortunate circumstance that Slovak demands climaxed in periods of greatest crisis and uncertainty is no accident. Only in such periods does the previous logic of evolutionary assimilation break down; only in such periods does the fulfillment of Slovak demands become sufficiently critical as to induce decisive action. The unhappy consequence is that Slovak nationalism then appears as the blackmailer of the state's survival.[16]

The circumstances under which the Slovak question could effectively be raised, then, created a negative historical learning curve, an accumulation of mythologies about the insensitivities of the Czechs and the treachery of the Slovaks in salvaging national gains from crises such as Munich or the Soviet invasion of 1968. This cumulative record of past misunderstanding framed each subsequent crisis, undercutting tolerance and trust, as each new opening resurrected the historical disputes of previous periods.[17]

In predictable fashion, the Czech–Slovak debate rehearsed a litany of increasingly well-worn themes: the question of who subsidized whom, the depiction of Slovak nationalism as a childhood disease, the charges of insufficient Slovak commitment to democratic as opposed to nationalist values, the countercharges of inadequate economic development policy for Slovakia, all amplified with recriminations about previous behavior.

In this respect, the historical context for the interpretation of the present was always highly problematic. Some might virtuously argue that revisiting the past is a means of avoiding its repetition, and in fact that argument did surface after 1989. However, the prior experience of such politicized historicism offered fair warning that the net impact was likely to be inflammatory.

The primary legacies bequeathed to the postcommunist period therefore were multifaceted. In the first place, of course, there was the unfinished business of finding a mutually acceptable constitutional format for the expression of Czech–Slovak commonality and difference—the legacy of repeated inconclusive struggles over that issue. Institutionally, the argument would begin again in the framework of the most recent attempt at resolution and rectification—the federalized state of 1968 as it evolved over the next two decades. But there was also the baggage of sustained mutual incomprehension: about the validity of Slovak claims, about the sincerity and utility of Czech responses, about the import of past strategies to resolve the conflict.

The democratic but centralized interwar republic had provided a framework for the expression of Slovak grievances without providing the mechanism for their resolution, and the formally federalized communist regime after 1969 was merely a simulacrum of "authentic federalism." The convergence of federalized structure and democratization after 1989 created a power equation that could either have generated a Czech–Slovak consensus or stalemate. Although the latter outcome—deadlock and dissolution—was not inevitable, the interwar state and the communist regime, as well as the troubled interregnum surrounding World War II, bequeathed a legacy difficult to surmount: a long history of mutual misunderstanding and past failures to construct a durable institutional framework for Czech–Slovak relations. This legacy manifested itself institutionally in a stunted communist federalism that, once energized by democratization, accorded both Czechs and Slovaks veto power over any constitutional settlement. The legacy of elite interaction was one of elite segmentation. Above all, the historical record of joint statehood bequeathed a well-rehearsed language of dispute—a patterned argument that reemerged in historically recognizable form in the newly opened media and political forums after 1989 to poison the debate.

CZECH–SLOVAK RELATIONS AFTER 1989

Clearly, there was a distinct patterning to the Czech–Slovak relationship between 1918 and 1989. The question is whether this patterning persisted, in what ways and with what consequences, after the collapse of communist power. In the period after 1989, some elements of this historical pattern did indeed resurface. Once again, the Slovak question reemerged on the political agenda in a period of regime collapse and reconstruction in a parallel climate of international instability and change. Once again, the Slovak position in the state was not central to the initial opening for change; the challenge to communist rule in November 1989 would have occurred regardless of the level of Slovak satisfaction or dissatisfaction with the existing formulation of Czech–Slovak relations. What had changed after 1989 was not the character and logic of the Czech–Slovak dispute over the appropriate relationship, but the *context* of that dispute—the political arena in which it was conducted. Democratization in general, and regionally based competitive elections and the free press in particular, provided a forum for the activation of the latent quarrels of the normalization period, energized partially constrained federal institutions at the republic level, and thus created a new institutional setting in which to address the enduring conflict.

It at first appeared that the past record of failure would provide an additional prod to a thorough reordering of the troubled relationship, an incentive in the search for the authentic federalism that had been announced as the objective in 1989. To reword a Slovak campaign slogan of 1990—it was a "chance for Czechoslovakia." Democratization might have validated any consensual solution reached by Czech and Slovak leaders. And there was a further reason for optimism. Although negotiations after 1989 did follow the historical pattern of reconsideration of the stateness question during periods of regime collapse and change, the international context after 1989 was far more conducive than it had been in previous periods to the provision of breathing space for systemic and exhaustive negotiations. The external threat level was uncharacteristically low compared to earlier reorientation periods and thus did not mandate rapid and unbalanced negotiations in a crisis atmosphere. The postcommunist period may have been the first historical opportunity to settle the national question on a timetable dictated by the long-term needs of the affected parties rather than by the pressure of crisis and international threat. In contrast with some earlier periods, there was time to negotiate and reach consensus. This point should not be overemphasized, however; the time to reach consensus was not unlimited. Ultimately, deadlock on the appropriate constitutional form of the postcommunist state did exact clear costs, both domestic and international. Despite the absence of external threats to state survival, constitutional postponement impeded the scope and pace of domestic economic and political transformation, holding the agenda of general transformation hostage to the stalemate over Czech–Slovak relations. Moreover, the unprecedentedly benign international environment eventually became an inducement either to complete the bargaining process or to abort it; protracted and unseemly controversy over the proper form of the state jeopardized the aspiration to join Europe.

Other indicators were still more ominous. The triadic leadership structure in earlier periods—and in particular the ability of Czechs and a core of Slovak allies to govern—had been central both to the short-term stability of the system and to the state's longer-term problems; it served as a partial legitimation for the Czech–Slovak relationship as it existed under earlier regimes and as a reason not to revisit the larger question of the allocation of state power. The breakdown of an effective triadic pattern would be in itself a signal of systemic crisis. Such a breakdown was both theoretically and empirically predictable after 1989.[18] One empirical indicator that pointed toward the emergence of two increasingly discrete political subsystems was the secular trend that appeared in the life histories of Czech and Slovak elites. An analysis of the elite biographies included in *Kdo je Kdo* during the communist period suggested that Czechs and Slovaks, instead of growing together over the course of the joint state, were rather moving apart. The younger the Slovak notable, the more likely he or she was to be educated and to work in Slovakia. The Slovak elites most likely to circulate across republic lines were in the older-age cohort. This finding suggests that Czechoslovakia was an increasingly segmented country without an overarching sense of common identity.[19]

A further empirical basis for the prediction of elite bipolarity was the experience of the short-lived Second Republic of 1945–1948. The most striking political feature of that interregnum period was the segmentation of the Czech and Slovak electoral politics into two separate party subsystems—a reflection both of heightened Slovak national awareness following the wartime experience of statehood and of the existence for the first time of a significant Slovak institutional base. These signals in turn suggest the logic of a theoretical prediction: a democratized Czechoslovakia in which the substate republican governments had real voice would be a Czechoslovakia in which parties and leaderships would segment along republic lines, as in fact they did after 1989. Where the Communist Party, even with its separate Slovak organization, had bridged the national divide and enforced a common agenda in the prior regime, the subsequent competitive elections established the predicted new pattern: two almost completely segmented party systems in the Czech Republic and Slovakia.[20]

Federation plus democratization, in other words, was a formula that reconfigured the power equation and undercut the political incentives for the continuance of the triadic pattern of previous periods. Earlier Slovak politicians received clear political payoffs for cooperation with Czech counterparts: power centered in Prague and so therefore did access to the most important political forums. In retrospect, it is likely that at least since 1945, the triangulation of the elite structure was essentially the artifact of central control. Indeed, even in the First Republic, the Slovak political forces who worked harmoniously with Czech politicians were continually cross-pressured by the effort to maintain credibility both with their electorates and with their Czech colleagues. Democratized federalism after 1989, even an unreconstructed federalism, recontoured the incentive structure previously imposed by the concentration of power at the center and recontoured as well the gateways of the Slovak politician's access to power. As Vladimír Goati noted in his analysis of the breakup of Yugoslavia, opening the political system led less to pluralization than to segmentation of the national publics,[21] a segmentation that lent still greater weight to the republican governments, since it legitimated them with two distinct electoral bases and autonomy of political action from the center.

Just as significantly, it afforded the federal government no cross-national statewide constituency of its own with which to lay claim to the exclusive license to define the new rules of the game. In this context, politicians who tried to speak for the larger interests of Czechoslovakia as a whole faced an intractable task. In Bratislava, federal government officials of either nationality were tarred with the brush of Pragocentrism and castigated as spokesmen for a federal bureaucratic interest in maintaining power at the center. Slovak politicians ready to show flexibility on the form of statehood could be, and were, electorally outbid and ritually denounced as "anti-Slovak." Even Czech politicians who urged greater understanding of Slovak interests and perceptions were vulnerable to charges of neglecting purely Czech interests.[22] The clearest expression of the changed environment was the shift in the locus of decision making from the Federal Assembly to ad hoc summits comprised of republic leaders, a summitry in which federal government negotiators were increasingly marginalized and eventually, after the 1992 elections, excluded. What is especially important here was the disappearance of the prior overarching statewide party systems, whether communist or democratically competitive, a framework in which a jointly designed constitutional structure might have had a fighting chance for ratification.

In effect, the disappearance of the triadic leadership structure that had regulated past Czech–Slovak relations was symptomatic of two legacies. The first was the legacy of successive previous adjustments to the constitutional structure of the state, culminating in the decision for federalization in 1968, which created an institutional base from which Slovak politicians could effectively pursue alternative visions of constitutional design. The second was the legacy of evolving Slovak resources to sustain nationally self-conscious elite development. In turn, the more pronounced bipolarization of elite politics after 1989 fed back into the invigorated federal structures, giving serious meaning to the formal veto power possessed by each republic. The impact of this consociational institutional setting will be addressed by others in this volume, but its existence was a product of past attempts to regulate the national question.

In this changed setting, itself the reworking of historical materials, the impact of the cumulative record of past grievances merits careful attention. There were many who wished to learn from that record how to overcome past misperceptions and set the course of discussion on a more productive plane; this concern generated periodic admonishments from politicians and journalists not to revisit the contentious and unproductive terrain of the past with the same perceptual blinders. Pleaded one Czech journalist, "We must stop thinking [of the Slovaks] as immature children, who are deluded and don't know what they want."[23] Václav Havel warned that indifference to national identity questions could make Czechs appear arrogant, condescending, and paternalistic in their dealings with Slovaks.[24]

Despite such warnings, the historical pattern of mutual grievance and suspicion reemerged in familiar outlines after 1989, covering well-trodden ground and rehearsing established themes of earlier conflicts in a nightmarish historical pageant. Old quarrels were refought: the missionary Czechs of the First Republic and their exodus in 1939,[25] the checkered record of the Slovak state in World War II, the fate of Josef Tiso. Czech fears of the escalation of Slovak demands in 1990 were couched in terms of historical analogy—the failure of the 1938 Žilina Accords that belatedly provided Slovak autonomy to satisfy nationalist aspirations and the subsequent splintering of the state in 1939.[26] The KSS warned of a "return to the year 1939" in its draft action program of December 1989.[27] The invocation of a problematic past was virtually a cottage industry in postcommunist discourse, and the examples could be multiplied indefinitely.

It is worthwhile to sketch some of the most prominent themes in the postcommunist Czech–Slovak debate, precisely because they will not strike an observer of the postcommunist dispute as at all novel. These themes include:

1. *The linkage of Slovak national assertion with antidemocratic tendencies.* In earlier periods, critics saw the autonomist drive of the interwar period as culminating in the "clerico-fascism" of the wartime Slovak state. The debate over the federalization of the state in 1968 was attended by reformist concern that the federal question might detract from and supplant the process of opening up the system: hence the slogan, "democratization first, then federation." In short, Czechs feared a Slovak focus on identity politics that was indifferent to democratic logic and found Slovaks too immature and nationally obsessed for democratic governance. When the solidity of Slovak commitment to democratization was questioned in the 1990s, therefore, the past provided a context and the present extended an old argument.[28]

2. *Problem of "Czechoslovakism" as a negation of Slovak identity.* Contrapuntally to the first theme, there was enduring Slovak resentment that the Czechs saw the national question as a primitive or trivial concern. Historically, Slovak critics frequently perceived Czechoslovakia as a Pragocentric *Czech* state masquerading in the guise of an inclusive Czechoslovakism or neo-Czechoslovakism. While in the interwar period it was possible, though not always popular, for Slovak politicians to declare a Czechoslovak orientation and survive, Czechoslovakism was roundly rejected as a state ideology by all major political forces after World War II.[29] The concept lingered as a whipping boy for communist ideologists and as a term of opprobrium to delegitimize attitudes destructive to Slovak identity. Vladimír Mečiar himself was charged with "Czechoslovak leanings" during his first tenure as prime minister by Marian Andel of the Slovak National Party.[30] Nonetheless, Slovak commentators frequently invoked the persistence of interwar "Czechoslovak" attitudes and "Beneš stereotypes."[31]

3. *The suffusion of the agenda of economic policy with unresolved national tensions.* Problems that might, in a homogeneous society, assume a technical character or be amenable to negotiation in class terms tend to be refracted in a multinational society through the prism of national identity and interests. Here, the reference point for economic policy readily becomes its impact on national communities. Hence, the weakening of the interwar Slovak economy when exposed to competition from the industrial Czech lands after 1918 was interpreted in almost colonial terms, and the missionary Czechs sent to Slovakia were reviled as superfluous and incompetent bureaucrats feeding on Slovak weakness and displacing Slovakia's own work force. In the communist period, reform programs that might interrupt the allocation of investment to less developed Slovakia provoked resistance there, while Czechs tended to see Slovaks as resistant to reform

and unenthusiastic about economic revitalization. Thus, the pattern of Slovak ambivalence about the postcommunist economic transformation created tensions with Prague that echoed yet another long-standing argument and created additional grounds for Prague to insist on a centrally coordinated constitutional order—a "functional" federation—and Bratislava to argue for more local control over substantive policy.

It can be very difficult to determine who is "right" in such circumstances, but it is also beside the point in many respects to attempt to find that elusive truth. No economic policy is ethnically neutral, and the economic truth is less important than the political truth that each national grouping interprets economic outcomes through a different perceptual lens. Thus Czechs could understand their economic relationship with Slovakia as one of beneficent subsidy that encountered only ingratitude, while the Slovaks just as readily understood that relationship as exploitative.[32]

Among the clearest persistent historical disputes was the question of cui bono—Czechs and Slovaks harbored mutually discordant elite and popular perceptions of who benefited from the existing state structure—a question that speaks to the heart of the rationale for commitment to the common state. Czechs consistently believed that they were carrying a long-term burden of assistance to Slovak development. To cite some representative examples of this perspective, Karel Kramář addressed the Slovaks heatedly in the 1920s that "if it were possible to experiment with the constitutional order without fear of the future, I would give you full freedom so that you could know how we subsidize you . . . in a half year you would beg on your knees for us to take you back," while generations later, during the Prague Spring, Vilém Prečan conveyed his sense that "in the Czech public and not only in conservative political circles, the widespread conception obtains that Slovakia is something on which a great amount is spent for some kind of poorly understood state interest, into which investment is squeezed and crammed, and from which as a whole only an incomprehensible national sentiment is expected."[33]

This central historical conflict over the benefits of the experiment in joint statehood of course resurfaced after 1989. The previous pattern of discordant perception emerged vividly in public opinion surveys. In an Association for Independent Social Analysis (AISA) poll of May 1992, nearly 70 percent of those questioned in Slovakia thought that the current system favored the Czechs—only 16 percent of Czech respondents agreed.[34] Indeed, from the outset, postcommunist Czech and Slovak opinion surveys showed that each national group tended to view the existing situation inherited from the communist era as one in which the *other* nation had been the primary beneficiary, a confirmation of more impressionistic evidence in the 1980s. Such attitudes had not bred a climate of ready understanding of the other nation's grievances and concerns in the past, and they continued to haunt the debate in the 1990s.[35] The almost eerie familiarity of the arguments of the 1990s lends additional credence to the conclusion drawn in the 1980s: "With regard to the Slovak question, the past has not been reinterpreted; it has merely been recycled, with all the old grievances laid bare."[36] The discourse of earlier Czech–Slovak conflict—its structure and logic—continued in the postcommunist period.

On this basis, one could reasonably argue that, although the consociational veto power embedded in the inherited communist federal structure and the release of the structure of elite politics from the constraints of centralized authority were important components in the creation of the deadlock that destroyed Czechoslovakia, neither of these factors in themselves need to have been determinant in the face of a clear will to preserve the state. It may well be that the climate in which the negotiations took place—a climate shaped by the freeing of the press and the relaunching of political competition but also heavily burdened with the resurrection of past grievance—was the single most important contributor to the stalemated search for a new constitutional order. This climate was especially relevant in creating an atmosphere in which mutual intentions were routinely and skeptically scrutinized. Many Slovak politicians believed, or for political reasons professed to believe, for example, that the Czech "functional" or "rational" federalism was a mask for continued Slovak subordination in a cosmetically decentralized constitutional framework. In turn, Czechs often interpreted the Slovak confederal posture as a mask for Slovak secessionist designs, as a tactical maneuver calculated to produce deadlock and to justify independence. As one Czech journalist described it:

> For Slovakia, it would not be desirable to separate by Slovakia's own decision. Everyone realizes that the world would not accept it kindly. This is why a sort of "secret strategy" has been established in Slovakia. . . . First of all, it is necessary to continuously increase demands, even demands that are nonsensical, whose goal is to disgust the other side. . . . When the Czech side does not comply with a nonsensical demand, this serves as further proof of Prague's unwillingness to negotiate and colonial behavior.[37]

An overt commitment to the state thus becomes a disguise for a covert secessionist agenda. Klaus pointedly raised the question of whether Slovak leaders intended to "break up the federation" with their economic demands.[38] The frequency with which both sides charged the other with failing to bargain in good faith is a signpost to the core failure of the negotiations; it is difficult to account for this atmosphere of distrust entirely in terms of current politics, the frailties of individual leaders, or institutional impediments. Lying behind that contemporary reality was the fact that a completely fresh start, unencumbered by past conflict, was impossible in the context of a democratized politics in which old quarrels could be revisited and resurrected daily. In the face of protracted stalemate and disagreement, historical tensions undermined the bargaining process by intensifying the perception that current incompatible positions—themselves a response to historical experience—were symptomatic of long-term irreconcilable differences. Successful negotiations require a modicum of trust, and the historical learning experience tended to undermine trust, coloring mutual perceptions and inviting repeated and invidious interpretations of the deeper historical meanings of contemporary negotiations. None of this context benefited the search for compromise, unduly burdening politics with history.

All this being said, past legacies were not entirely negative and subversive of the process of seeking agreement. To encapsulate some complex arguments in summary form, one could argue that the absence of violence in the historical record reduced the sense of threat to either party from the continued common state.[39] The historical failure was political failure rather than the Yugoslav memory of bloody mutual slaughter. Czechs and Slovaks, as the polls repeatedly showed, did not hate and fear each other. In fact, an Institut pro výzkum veřejného mínění (IVVM) survey conducted just before the critical elections of June 1992 showed 64 percent of Czech Republic respondents and 72 percent of those in Slovakia defining mutual relations as very good or rather good[40]—a startlingly positive response for a couple on the verge of divorce! A lack of intensity and commitment killed Czechoslovakia, but this relative apathy might also have given latitude to the leaderships of the two republics to strike a bargain. It is true that the continuing plurality support among the Czech and Slovak publics for joint statehood was somewhat misleading, since the Czech and Slovak publics were as divided over the preferred form of the state as were their leaders.[41] However, it would not be unreasonable to argue that the climate of public opinion was such that the majority of citizens would have accepted a constitutional bargain that both leaderships were willing to sanction—in short, that the ambiguities of popular opinion offered considerable scope for a settlement.

CONCLUSION

Was the breakup of Czechoslovakia therefore historically inevitable? Politics is human, and it is not about certainties and inevitabilities. It is about probabilities and possibilities. The draft treaty that might have preserved the state failed to be approved by the presidium of the Slovak National Council by a single vote in February 1992. Time might have improved the chances for state survival by alleviating some of the broader tensions surrounding the constitutional negotiations: in particular, the divergence in economic priorities attendant on Slovakia's greater postcommunist disruption. On the other hand, time was not available because of the energizing of the inherited federal structure by democratization and the mounting costs exacted on all societal change by the constitutional deadlock.

Ultimately, the judgment of inevitability on the Czech–Slovak divorce depends in significant measure on one's reading of the slipperiest of questions, the question of motivation and intention. If one accepts the proposition that Slovak desiderata for a common state were deliberately formulated and successively amplified in order to block any settlement and to diffuse the responsibility for a disguised secession, then of course the dissolution of the state would have the inevitability of a political design that comported well with the veto or deadlock machinery of the existing communist federation, in which pseudonegotiations—after a seemly interval—could give way to the acceptance of the disintegration of the state. If, however, one takes the position that the dissolution of the state was an unintended consequence of a genuine bargaining failure,[42] the question of inevitability remains. The disintegration of the state was not simply a leadership failure, if by that we mean that all that was needed was a different set of leaders to produce a mutually consensual settlement. The outcome was not merely bad luck; the possibility of deadlock was foreshadowed in the long history of previous conflict and conditioned by that history.

The key historical legacies that contributed to state disintegration were twofold. The first was a history of mutual suspicion and discord on the constitutional form of the state, poisoned by variant historical readings of the meaning of the past that bled into the bargaining environment. Ultimately, neither Czech nor Slovak leaders were convinced of the good faith of the other, nor did they find a sufficiently compelling reason to stay together in the face of competing priorities. In Prague just after the first elections, in July 1990, one heard an ominous tone to the Czech perception of the problem, the pervasive attitude that a settlement was desirable but that *this time* no one would let the Slovaks act the martyr on the stateness issue—if agreement was elusive, it was time to let them go. After seventy years, Czech patience with the perpetual conflict was clearly wearing thin, and it is striking that throughout that period, Czech publics and leaderships had never found a value of their own in decentralization and national self-assertion, a perspective that would have given both sides a common starting point for a durable bargain. The evidence seems to indicate that Czechoslovakia was a state that everyone wanted, but no one wanted enough.

The second important legacy, somewhat ironically, was the problematic impact of previous efforts to resolve that long-standing conflict. A federal institutional framework that was in itself a flawed product of the most recent previous attempt to resolve the Czech–Slovak quarrel created the formal conditions under which deadlock was possible. The efforts to create a stronger cultural and economic base for Slovakia over the years also created the conditions for an increasingly separate and self-sustaining Slovak elite. The fact that either party could veto a constitutional settlement and block decision was particularly important to the logic of the breakup. Deadlock—the absence of mutual agreement, the effect of deciding nothing—would under normal circumstances have provided for the continuation of the existing order or given the Czech majority a decisive say in constitutional revision. In the special circumstances, however, only affirmative action would have preserved Czechoslovakia: doing nothing and deciding nothing was the death sentence of the common state. Weighing all these considerations, in choosing from the menu of inevitability, probability, and possibility, perhaps the fairest conclusion is that the disintegration of the state was a probablistic outcome—one that might have been avoided but only with greater luck and skill. The historical deck was stacked, not definitively but still substantially, against state survival.

NOTES

1. Juan J. Linz and Alfred Stepan, *Problems of Democratic Transition and Consolidation: Southern Europe, South America, and Post-Communist Europe* (Baltimore, MD: The Johns Hopkins University Press, 1996), p. 123.

2. Nothing could better capture the ambiguous spirit of statehood attained than the fact that the two component parts of the new state, the Czech lands and Slovakia, declared their adherence to it during the collapse of Habsburg rule in late October 1918, each unbeknownst to the other.

3. Carol Skalnik Leff, *National Conflict in Czechoslovakia: The Making and Remaking of a State* (Princeton, NJ: Princeton University Press, 1988).

4. Cited, with considerable irony, in "Máme, čo sme chceli? Historické i súčasné peripetie koexistencie," *Národná obroda*, 17 July 1992.

5. Kenneth Jowitt, *Revolutionary Breakthroughs and National Development: The Case of Romania, 1944-1965* (Berkeley: University of California Press, 1971), p. 11.

6. In 1932, Foreign Minister Beneš argued that greater autonomy for Slovakia would "mean for this state the slogan Slovakia to the Slovaks, German regions to the Germans, Magyar regions to the Magyars." Beneš quoted in František Janáček, "Poznámky k hodnocení Čechoslovakismu v odboji," *Československá revoluce 1944–1948*, ed. Jaroslav César and Zdeněk Snítil (Prague: Academia, 1979), p. 79.

7. Even after 1989, Czech and Slovak journalists occasionally taunted each other with the prospect that independence would mean that the next generations would be speaking German or Hungarian (or, for Slovakia, occasionally Russian).

8. Philip G. Roeder would later so designate Soviet federalism in "Soviet Federalism and Ethnic Mobilization," *World Politics*, January 1991, pp. 196–232.

9. Leff, *National Conflict,* p. 192.

10. Most notable was the grudging reluctance with which KSČ First Secretary Novotný accepted the replacement as KSS First Secretary of Karol Bacílek by Alexander Dubček in 1963.

11. As Susan Mikula and Carol Leff ("Ethnic Fragmentation of Post-Communist Party Systems," paper presented at a conference, American Political Science Association, Chicago, August 1995) recently argued, the Slovak Agrarians found themselves increasingly cross-pressured by the pull of the language of national identity on the one hand and the language of Czechoslovakism and of Agrarianism on the other, and unable to chart an independent course that would give adequate expression to the national sentiments of the younger generation of Slovak leaders in particular. See also Vladimír Zuberec, "Republikanská strana zemědělského a malorolnického ludu," in *Politické strany na Slovensku, 1860–1989* (Bratislava: ARCHA, 1992).

12. This argument is elaborated in Leff, *National Conflict*, and Leff, "Czech and Slovak Nationalism in the Twentieth Century," in Peter F. Sugar, ed., *Eastern European Nationalism in the Twentieth Century* (Washington, D.C.: American University Press, 1995), pp. 103–162.

13. Particularly famous is Masaryk's often cited assertion that only cultural level separated the two nations and that following the founding of Slovak schools, "in one generation there will be no difference between the two branches of our national family." T. G. Masaryk, interview with *Petit Parisien*, reprinted in T. G. Masaryk, *Spisy*, vol. 2 (Prague, 1934), p. 78.

14. See, for example, the evidence in Sharon Wolchik's important baseline study, *Czechoslovakia in Transition: Politics, Economics and Society* (London: Pinter, 1991), pp. 186–91.

15. Resistance to renegotiating a constitutional bargain on the national question during periods of normalcy is not, of course, unique to Czechoslovakia. Donald Horowitz has argued that periods of regime change generally offer a window of opportunity to revisit the constitutional ordering of ethnonational relations, and the Czechoslovak case illustrates this generalization very convincingly. Horowitz, *Ethnic Groups in Conflict* (Berkeley, CA: University of California Press, 1985), p. 10.

16. Leff, *National Conflict*, p. 177.

17. Indeed, L'ubomir Lipták remarked in the debate leading up to the federalization of the state in the 1960s that in the revisiting of the Slovak question, "not one argument has surfaced that a historian would not recognize from the polemics of the pre-Munich republic." See Karel Bartošek, "Diskusia—k československým vzt'ahom," *Historický časopis* 15:4, 1967.

18. See especially Mikula and Leff, "Ethnic Fragmentation."

19. Leff, *National Conflict*, p. 287. The watershed in this pattern appeared to be the expansion of Slovak educational facilities, since Slovaks educated at home tended to work there. Economic and cultural development therefore gave Slovaks the resources to sustain their own elite. Czech elite circulation had in any case always been largely on Czech territory. Moreover, it became clear after the dissolution of the state that those Slovaks who left Slovakia for careers in the Czech lands were effectively no longer oriented to Slovak republic politics: the overwhelming majority of Slovaks resident in the Czech Republic in 1992 opted for Czech citizenship.

20. See, for example, František Turnovec, "The Political Background of Economic Transformation in the Czech Republic," *Discussion Paper No. 25*, November 1993, Center for Economic Research and Graduate Education, Charles University.

21. Vladimír Goati, "The Challenge of Post-Communism," in Jim Seroka and Vukašin Pavlović, eds., *The Tragedy of Yugoslavia: The Failure of Democratic Transformation* (Armonk, NY: M. E. Sharpe, 1992), p. 6.

22. For example, Czech Prime Minister Pithart's expressed willingness in November 1991 to start talks on "a type of coexistence that would be looser than the present state, towards something I call a semi-detached house" triggered a failed effort—"an indirect motion of no-confidence in the prime minister"—to condemn Pithart's "policy of concessions" toward the Slovaks as an impediment to constitutional resolution. Klaus also attacked Pithart's formulation as "unstable and unviable." See *Rudé právo*, 15 November 1991, pp. 1–2; and Prague, ČSTK, 11 November 1991, in FBIS-EEU-91–220, 14 November 1991, p. 12; and Prague, ČSTK, 9 November 1991, in FBIS-EEU-91–218, 12 November 1991, p. 13.

23. Vladislav Krásný, "Přestaňme již strašit Slováky!" *Český deník*, 29 June 1992.

24. "C Václavom Havlom o jedenástej večer," *Verejnost'*, 19 May 1990, p. 2.

25. See, for example, "Kto koho vyháňal?" *Slovenský národ*, 9 October 1991.

26. See, for example, "Češi o Slovácích," *Tvorba*, 12 December 1990, p. 3. Czech hostility to the Žilina agreement is quite palpable: "Slovakia attained autonomy in 1938 as a consequence of the Munich disaster. . . . If a justified demand is carried through in the shadow of injustice and violence, its justification is automatically in doubt." Jan Petr, "Česko–slovensko není samozřejmosti: Triasedmdesát let oproti tisíci leté odlišnosti," *Respekt*, 27 October 1991, p. 4.

27. Bratislava *Pravda*, 19 December 1989, p. 3.

28. The issue of democratization touched a chord even with those who expressed sympathy with Slovak national aspirations. See, for example, Boris Zala, "Česká zodpovednosť za československé vyrovnanie," *Literárný týždenník*, 29 February 1992.

29. The wartime Slovak state, however controversial in other respects, had been a landmark for consolidating national consciousness and permanently destroyed the legitimacy of a Czech–Slovak relationship based on an assimilative Czechoslovak ideal.

30. Interview, *Zemědělské noviny*, 11 May 1990.

31. "Slovensko na svuj obraz," *Národná obroda*, 13 April 1992; and Igor Cibulka, *Národná obroda*, 4 December 1990.

32. Leff, *National Conflict*, pp. 278–82.

33. Cited in Karol Sidor, *Slovenská politika na pôde pražského snemu (1918-1938)*, vol. 1 (Bratislava: Andreja, 1943), p. 274; "Je čas mluvit o Slovensku," *Reportér*, 20–27 March 1968, p. 7.

34. "AISA ke vztahům Čechů a Slováků: Komplex nedospělého," *Lidové noviny*, 15 May 1992.

35. See, for example, Josef Kotrba and Karel Kříž, "Cui bono? The Common State in Economic Perspective," *East European Reporter* 5:5, September/October 1992, pp. 3–6.

36. Leff, *National Conflict*, p. 163.

37. Pavel Černocký, *Občanský deník*, 30 August 1991, p. 3.

38. Cited in *Mladá fronta dnes*, 10 April 1991, p. 2.

39. Of course, the relatively benign character of the Czech–Slovak dispute also contributed to a peaceful dissolution.

40. Cited in *Hospodářské noviny*, 5 June 1992.

41. See Carol Skalnik Leff, *The Czech and Slovak Republics* (Boulder, CO: Westview Press, 1997); Carol Skalnik Leff, "Could This Marriage Have Been Saved? The Czechoslovak Divorce," *Current History* 95:599, March 1996, pp. 129–139; and Sharon Wolchik, "The Politics of Ethnicity in Post-Communist Czechoslovakia," *East European Politics and Societies* 8:1, Winter 1994, pp. 167–186.

42. A reading of the endgame of 1992, for which considerations of focus and space prohibit elaboration, is that Mečiar and the HZDS came to the table after the elections, not with an agenda of "stealth secession," but rather with the intention of driving a hard bargain—a conclusion based in part on the vehemence with which the Slovak prime minister cried foul when faced with Klaus's unwillingness to negotiate, claiming that Klaus and his party had "decreed the disintegration of the state after forty minutes of discussion." (Vladimír Mečiar, interview with *Le Monde*, 7 July 1992, in FBIS-EEU-92–131, 8 July 1992, p. 12.); and on the Slovak efforts to improvise a continued Czech–Slovak relationship in autumn 1992.

3

The Possibilities for Czech–Slovak Compromise, 1989–1992

Jan Rychlík

BACKGROUND, 1968–1989

In 1968, Czech–Slovak relations were formally refounded on the basis of a federation.[1] The constitutional law number 143/1968 of 27 October 1968 established on the territory of the former unitary Czechoslovak Socialist Republic (ČSSR) two new states: the Czech Socialist Republic (ČSR) and the Slovak Socialist Republic (SSR), each with its own parliament (the Czech and the Slovak national councils) and its own government, effective 1 January 1969. According to the preamble of the law, the ČSR and the SSR were, in theory, two completely sovereign states who voluntarily delegated part of their sovereignty to federal organs, the Federal Assembly and the federal government. The latter could make decisions only in a narrowly delimited realm.

The Federal Assembly had two chambers, the Chamber of the People and the Chamber of the Nations. The Chamber of the People was elected on the basis of proportional representation throughout the country, so that the Czech Republic had a larger number of deputies. The Chamber of the Nations had equal representation whereby each republic elected seventy-five deputies. Passage of laws required majority approval from both chambers, while the passage of constitutional laws required a three-fifths majority in both chambers. The peculiarity of the new constitutional system was the so-called minority veto (*zákaz majorizace*), which made it impossible for the majority Czech deputies to override the votes of their Slovak counterparts. Some ordinary legislation, especially concerning issues of economic significance, required for passage a majority of deputies in the Chamber of the People and a majority of both Czech and Slovak deputies (voting separately) in the Chamber of the Nations. Further, constitutional amendments and the election of the president required a three-fifths majority of deputies in the

Chamber of the People and a majority of both Czech and Slovak deputies (again voting separately) in the Chamber of the Nations. This consensus principle in fact embodied a strong confederative element and signaled the potential for constitutional crisis.

For the majority of Slovaks, the establishment of the federation in 1968 seemed to be a sufficient guarantee for further national development. Most Slovaks truly believed that the federation would make possible both Slovak statehood and a common Czech–Slovak state. Therefore, the Slovaks did not raise the question of an independent Slovak state in 1968. To the extent that such an issue arose at all, it was presented by the Czech side, where some radical fringe opinions held that Slovakia was a needless burden for the Czechs and it would be best to get rid of it.[2] Most Czechs, however, were prepared to accept the federation and regarded it as a necessary concession to the Slovaks, hoping that it would secure long-term, if not permanent, stability for Czechoslovakia.

In actuality, the 1969–1989 federal framework had minimal significance. For starters, a series of laws beginning in December 1970 greatly limited the prerogatives of the republic organs in favor of the federation.[3] The passage of the constitutional law on federation took place only after the August 1968 Soviet occupation of Czechoslovakia and the launch of the so-called normalization, i.e., the gradual undoing of the democratic reforms from spring 1968 and the restoration of the communist dictatorship. The parliaments—federal, Czech, and Slovak—had no significance, nor did the elections in which voters were given the "choice" of only one candidate. Just like the parliaments, the governments—federal and republican—were mere transmission belts for the Communist Party of Czechoslovakia.[4]

For all these reasons, the federation had, in its own way, a strange impact on Czech–Slovak relations. The Czechs saw the federation only as an endless procession of Slovak officials at the federal ministries and as a transfer of resources from the federal budget to Slovakia. From 1969 to 1987, the first secretary of the Communist Party was a Slovak, Gustav Husák, who was also president of the republic from 1975 to 1989.[5] The éminence grise of the communist leadership was the Ukrainian Vasil Bil'ak, who was mistakenly regarded as a Slovak in the Czech lands. Consequently, a widespread feeling arose in the Czech lands that the state was run by Slovak communist normalizers, who were shifting resources from the federal budget to benefit Slovakia. In effect, they believed that the Czech lands were subsidizing Slovakia.

The Slovaks no less than the Czechs were also dissatisfied with the federation, because it did not fulfill their expectations. The Slovaks wanted Slovak matters to be decided in Bratislava and not in Prague. They also expected that the federation would give Slovakia increased visibility on the world stage. Neither of these aims was realized. The outside world continued to view Czechoslovakia as a Czech state, so that the adjectives Czechoslovak and Czech were frequently interchangeable in foreign languages. Husák and Bil'ak were just as unpopular in

Slovakia as they were in the Czech lands. In general, the Slovaks regarded the federal ministers, deputies, and bureaucrats in Prague as turncoats and traitors who were not defending Slovak interests. A significant segment of the Slovak population continued to feel that they lived in Czech bondage and that Slovakia was being economically exploited by the Czechs.

For Slovakia, arguably, the normalized federation had some positive effects. A strong Slovak managerial class was born, where Slovakia previously had had none. The federation meant the creation of a Slovak government and Slovak ministries in Bratislava, which, even though for the time being they only functioned as a branch office of Prague federal offices, could begin to work quite independently at any time.

The fall of the communist regime in November 1989 reopened the question of Czech–Slovak relations, a problem with which Czechoslovakia had wrestled since its very inception in 1918. In November 1989, two different organizations were founded: the Public Against Violence in Slovakia and Civic Forum in the Czech lands. The attempts to found Civic Forum in those Slovak areas where the citizenry traditionally felt strongly pro-Czechoslovak (especially in Eastern Slovakia) were quickly liquidated by the Public Against Violence (VPN), and Civic Forum, in agreement with the Public Against Violence, later proceeded to abolish those chapters of Civic Forum in Slovakia that had already formed. It became evident, right at the outset of 1990, that no political force on the Slovak scene could ignore the question of Czech–Slovak relations. Czech political parties, especially those that had been active before the communist takeover in 1948,[6] attempted to make inroads in Slovakia, but they encountered a total lack of voter interest because they were unable to offer any new ideas on Czech–Slovak relations. Conversely, the Slovak Democratic Party, the largest anticommunist Slovak political party during 1945–1948, could not gain influence in the Czech lands, as its emphasis on Slovak issues did not interest the Czech voter.[7]

After November 1989, Slovakia's proper status was a plank in the platform of every political party in Slovakia; the differences among them turning only on the degree of Slovak autonomy they favored. In this regard, the Public Against Violence and the Democratic Party were moderate parties, which supported the modification of the existing Czechoslovak federation, while the Christian Democratic Party (KDH) was more radical in its proposals. At the extreme, the Slovak National Party (SNS) of Vit'azoslav Móric and Jozef Prokeš demanded only a very loose Czech–Slovak connection. In both the KDH and SNS, there were many proponents of an independent Slovak state, but in the first half of 1990, even the SNS had not yet formally introduced this demand. While Czech and Slovak communists gradually parted ways, and an independent Slovak communist party was born (KSS, later the Party of the Democratic Left, SDL); the latter's embrace of the Slovak national program positioned the Slovak communists nicely in the new political scene.[8]

1990: FROM THE HYPHEN WAR TOWARD POWER SHARING

The first open Czech–Slovak conflict took place in connection with the Federal Assembly's deliberations on the country's new name. Given the political and socioeconomic changes that had occurred since November 1989, in early 1990, President Václav Havel proposed that the officially used title—the Czechoslovak Socialist Republic—be amended to the Czechoslovak Republic, which had been in use prior to 1960. A similar proposal had been made at the end of December 1989. It had been rejected because the communists still held a majority in the Federal Assembly and in both national parliaments at the time. Constitutional law 14/1990, passed 23 January 1990, however, removed this obstacle. All the legislative assemblies underwent reconstruction: a portion of deputies lost their mandates and were replaced by new representatives, mostly from the ranks of Civic Forum and the Public Against Violence. That is why Havel assumed that his proposal would be accepted without any problems. It was not the case.

The Slovak National Council fundamentally opposed the proposed name change (to the Czechoslovak Republic), demanding instead that the new state be called the Federation of Czecho-Slovakia. In this fashion, the world would be put on notice that Czechoslovakia was not comprised of one state but instead consisted of two. This proposal was supported by a clear majority of the Slovak public, but it was rejected in the Czech lands. For the Czechs, the name Czecho-Slovakia evoked bitter memories of the post-Munich (or the Second) Republic, when it was officially used during the German occupation. On 29 March 1990, after long discussions, the Federal Assembly approved constitutional law 81/1990 and established the official name as the Czechoslovak Federal Republic. Demonstrations against the new name immediately erupted in Slovakia, and for the first time, slogans demanding an independent Slovakia appeared. VPN had accepted the new name during the Federal Assembly deliberations, so Slovak critics now charged the party with the betrayal of Slovak national interests. Czech deputies in the Federal Assembly backed down in the end. On 20 April 1990, another constitutional law (101/1990) proclaimed the official name to be the Czech and Slovak Federative Republic (ČSFR). The unofficial name, Czechoslovakia, and the adjective, Czechoslovak, would thereafter be written in Czech as one word but in Slovak with a hyphen (e.g., Czecho-Slovakia).

The so-called hyphen war indicated that subsequent discussions were not going to be easy and that the Slovak side would propose a maximal loosening of the federation. While VPN participated in the negotiations that produced the interim federal government, and the first premier, Marián Čalfa was a Slovak, Slovaks did not trust the federal organs of government. Even the pro-Czechoslovak VPN insisted that the issues concerning the new framework of Czech–Slovak relations were beyond the purview of the federal government and that they should be negotiated on a bilateral, republic-level basis. The first such unofficial talks took place on 11 April 1990 between the Czech premier, Petr Pithart, and the Slovak premier, Milan Čič. Čič outlined for Pithart the principles of the future Czech–Slovak relationship. These, in turn, were based on key principles that had been developed by VPN. The program was also based on the principles of 1968, anticipating two essentially independent republics, which would delegate some of their competencies to common federal organs. Formal negotiations were to begin after the June 1990 elections.[9]

The Czechoslovak Federal Republic's first free elections took place on 8 and 9 June 1990. The elections were based on the principle of proportional representation, but parties that did not receive at least 5 percent of the vote, and in the elections to the Slovak parliament, 3 percent, received no seats in parliament. In Slovakia, VPN won with 29.3 percent, followed by KDH's 19.2 percent, SNS's 13.9 percent, KSS-SDL's 13.3 percent, and the Hungarian coalition with 8.7 percent. The Democratic Party and the Green Ecological Party also made it into the Slovak National Council. In the Czech Republic, Civic Forum was victorious, as well as ČSL, the Communist Party, and the Movement for Self-Governing Democracy—the Society for Moravia and Silesia (HSD-SMS), which propounded a three-way federation of Bohemia, Moravia, and Slovakia, also took seats in parliament. The new federal government was comprised essentially of a coalition between VPN and Civic Forum with the support of the Czech and Slovak center-right parties (the coalition of ČSL-KDS and KDH), and it was headed again by Marián Čalfa. The Czech government was again headed by Petr Pithart, but the Slovak government's leadership changed: Milan Čič was replaced by the former Slovak minister of the interior, Vladimír Mečiar. Negotiations between the Czech and Slovak governments were not affected by this and continued. In addition, there were also negotiations between the chair of the Slovak National Council, František Mikloško (VPN), and his counterpart in the Czech lands, Dagmar Burešová (OF), and their colleagues.

Official negotiations between the Czech and Slovak governments took place on 8 and 9 August 1990 in Trenčianské Teplice. They continued on 10 and 11 September in Piešt'any, 27 September in Kroměříž, and 28 October in Slavkov, where President Havel also participated. On 5 November 1990, the Czech–Slovak relationship was the subject of negotiations between the prime ministers of all three governments. Four days later, in Luhačovice, premiers Pithart and Mečiar met again.

Taken together, the negotiations showed that an agreement was impossible, because both sides approached them from very different philosophical points of view. The Czechs wanted to preserve Czechoslovakia, and took its continued existence for granted. They understood the federation as a shift in competencies. Their criterion for any shift was the functionality of the federal state. This meant that certain prerogatives—foreign policy, defense, finance—had to be retained by the federation without interference from the republics.

In contrast, the Slovak side's approach assumed the existence of two states, which then were to delegate powers to common organs. The question of functionality was secondary and subordinated to the principle that Czech and Slovak governing elites had the prerogative either to maintain the state or to divide it. Because fundamental agreement proved impossible, the representatives of the governing parties, along with President Havel and representatives of all three governments, issued a declaration on 28 October 1990, which emphasized their will to maintain the ČSFR.[10] The Czech and Slovak sides also simultaneously agreed that the division of powers would be rearranged and a definitive solution would subsequently be worked out. The final shaping of the division of powers took place in the presence of President Havel and all three premiers at the Prague Castle on 12 November 1990. The proposal was then evaluated by the national councils and passed on to the Federal Assembly.

In the version of the power-sharing law presented to the Federal Assembly, the Czech National Council and the Czech government proposed several changes (to the 12 November 1990 proposal). In this context, an expanded presidium of the Slovak government, headed by Mečiar, suddenly came to Prague on 6 December 1990. Mečiar presented Pithart with an ultimatum: if the power-sharing law was not adopted in its original form, i.e., if the Czech National Council or the Federal Assembly amended the draft version of the law, the Slovak National Council would declare the supremacy of Slovak laws over the laws of the federation. This would mean de facto paralysis and dissolution of the Czecho–Slovak federal republic. The Slovak side also further emphasized that the Federal Assembly had no business interfering in Czech–Slovak negotiations. The Czech government and Czech National Council submitted to this demand. The government parties, especially Civic Forum, instructed their deputies to vote for their original version of the power-sharing law, which was adopted on 12 December 1990 as constitutional amendment 556/1990.[11]

The new power-sharing law significantly reduced the power of the central (federal) organs. In contrast to the 1968 constitutional amendment that created the federation, this law eliminated the exclusive prerogative of the federation in foreign policy and defense, which opened up the future possibility of separate international treaties and even the creation of republic-level armed forces. The power-sharing law, however, did not remove the crux of the problem and therefore represented only a temporary compromise. While the Czechs viewed the amendment as their maximum concession, for the Slovaks, it was only the first step toward their final goal—the attainment of a loose Czech–Slovak commonwealth, in which Slovakia could reap the benefits of its own statehood while retaining all the advantages of a common state.

SQUARING THE CIRCLE

In 1991, the changing political landscape in the Czech and Slovak republics transformed the negotiating atmosphere. On 24 February 1991, Civic Forum splintered into Václav Klaus's right of center Civic Democratic Party (ODS)[12] and Jiří Dienstbier's Center–Left Civic Movement (OH). Immediately after the elections of June 1990, the Slovak National Party declared full Slovak independence as its ultimate goal. Simultaneously, several smaller parties and movements emerged, which openly evoked the traditions of the totalitarian Slovak state (1939–1945) and of the interwar fascist Slovak People's Party. On 3 March 1991, the conflict between Vladimír Mečiar and VPN's leadership—above all with Fedor Gál, the representative of its liberal wing—caused an acute crisis to erupt within the VPN. Under the auspices of VPN, Mečiar founded his own platform, "For a Democratic Slovakia," and before long, he separated completely from VPN, creating an independent Movement for a Democratic Slovakia (HZDS).

On 23 April 1991, the presidium of the Slovak National Council recalled Mečiar from his position as prime minister of the Slovak government, as well as all his supporters, who refused to respect the decisions of the VPN leadership. As a result, the government was reconstructed, with Ján Čarnogurský, the chairman of KDH, becoming the new prime minister. Čarnogurský was a proponent of Slovak independence, but for the time being, he did not regard it as the republic's most pressing issue. In his view, Slovakia would become independent only after Czechoslovakia had joined the then European Community. In contrast to the representatives of VPN, who favored an enduring state bond with the Czechs, Čarnogurský viewed Czechoslovakia as a temporary formation, and he made no secret of this. When negotiating with Petr Pithart, a former fellow dissident, Čarnogurský demanded that the foundation of Czech and Slovak cohabitation should rest on a legally binding treaty between the two republics, whose acceptance should precede the adoption of any new constitution.

During 1991, Czech–Slovak negotiations continued. At first, Dagmar Burešová, the chair of the Czech National Council, rejected the Čarnogurský notion of a treaty between the two republics. Eventually, the Czech side accepted it as a political initiative. In contrast, the Slovak side demanded that the treaty should have a binding character, which meant, in effect, that it should assume the form of an international treaty, creating an association of two states. Such a solution was unacceptable to the Czech side, because it presupposed the transitory nature of the Czecho–Slovak state or commonwealth. The Czech side rightly feared that Slovakia would take advantage of the existence of any common state so defined so as to fortify its own position and then declare its independence anyway. In May and June 1991, negotiations continued in a series of meetings: 12 May 1991 in Lány, at the end of May in Budmerice, and 19 June 1991 in Kroměříž, all without results. After the November negotiations at Hrádeček with President Havel, the Czech side had the impression that Slovak negotiators were bent on squaring a circle, aspiring to have a Slovak state while at the same time resisting the same. From the Slovak perspective, however, it seemed that the Czechs did not want to accept legitimate Slovak demands.

A turning point in the balance of political power came when Mečiar's HZDS adopted an antifederation stance, i.e., its support for the notion of Slovak *svrchovanost*. The notion of Slovak *svrchovanost*, propounded in the spring of 1991 by the Slovak National Party and other nationalists, demanded the immediate transfer of all competencies to Slovak organs, and only thereafter would an agreement with the Czech Republic be possible. Mečiar, who had been a federalist up until that point, engaged in demagoguery by announcing that *svrchovanost* meant neither state sovereignty nor the destruction of Czechoslovakia. HZDS explicitly demanded international recognition of Slovakia, while claiming (and the Slovak public had largely come to believe this claim) that even this demand was compatible with the continued existence of the common state.

Another contributing factor to the changing balance of political power was the gradual fragmentation within KDH. A nationalistically oriented KDH splinter group, headed by Ján Klepáč, demanded a confederation, even though the Czech side repeatedly declared that such a temporary formation did not interest them and would be unacceptable. On 4 November 1991, HZDS, SNS, and the Klepáč nationalist faction submitted a proposal which they had already made public on 12 September 1991,[13] for the declaration of Slovak sovereignty to the Slovak National Council.[14] To be sure, Slovak public support for this project was by no means clear. In reaction to the proclamation for a sovereign Slovakia, another petition was immediately born: for a common state, which received roughly equal support.[15] Such conflicting responses demonstrate the deep divisions that existed in Slovak society.

In this situation, Čarnogurský was forced to seek a compromise with the Czechs. In the fall of 1991, it seemed that a compromise between Pithart and Čarnogurský, i.e., between Civic Movement on the one hand, and KDH and VPN on the other, would be possible. The Pithart government was willing to accept a *smlouva* (treaty) between the Czech and the Slovak republics, even though the matter was complicated by the formal legal conflict (in reality, groundless) over whether the republics could even enter into such a smlouva while the federation still existed. The smlouva was supposed to precede the federal constitution, which would then be bound by it. In October 1991, the Pithart cabinet was willing to agree that the federal ministries would be reduced to a minimum number in the areas of foreign policy, defense, and finance (or a ministry with broader responsibilities for the economy). On 3 November 1991, the top representatives of all three governments and parliaments gathered informally at the private villa of President Václav Havel in Hrádeček near Trutnov. With the exception of the deputy chair of the Czech National Council, Jan Kalvoda (Civic Democratic Alliance), an agreement was reached among all those present on a binding Czech–Slovak smlouva, even though the legal procedure for the incorporation of the smlouva into the national and federal constitutions remained undefined.[16] This solution would have turned Czechoslovakia into a dualistic state formation on the model of the 1867 Compromise between Austria and Hungary.

The desire to reach a compromise was also evident at a conference at Oxford University in December 1991. At the invitation of the university, fifteen politicians and various experts from the Czech Republic, led by Petr Pithart, met with fifteen politicians and experts from Slovakia, led by Jan Čarnogurský. But the question of how to make the smlouva binding and preclude future constitutions from abolishing or amending it was not answered.[17]

A compromise, however, was eventually reached even on that issue. On 10 January 1992, representatives of the Czech and Slovak national councils agreed in Prague that the smlouva would be signed by the Czech and Slovak republics, represented by their respective national councils. On 23 January 1992, a commission representing both national councils was created in Bratislava and charged with the responsibility of preparing the smlouva language.[18]

During 3–8 February 1992, in Milovy near Žd'ár nad Sázavou, there was a final round of negotiations between expert commissions of the Czech and Slovak national councils and the governments of both republics as well as the federation. The result was a draft smlouva between the two republic parliaments. On the one hand, KDH gave up its original demand that the smlouva be signed by the republics (which would render it an international treaty between two independent states). On the other hand, the smlouva language stipulated the framework of the future federal constitution, and, in this respect, accommodated Slovak demands. The agreement was to be ratified by both national councils, which represented a concession from the Czech side.[19]

On 12 February 1992, the presidium of the Slovak National Council considered the draft. Ten members voted for the proposal, and ten voted against. Therefore, the proposal was defeated and could not be submitted to the Slovak National Council as a whole. On 5 March 1992, the presidium of the Czech National Council declared that further negotiation with the Slovak side would be pointless. Furthermore, on 7 March, the treaty draft from Milovy caused the definitive fragmentation of the KDH. The Klepáč wing formally separated and created the Slovak Christian Democratic Movement (SKDH). As a result, the government coalition, comprised of KDH-VPN-DS-MOS, became a minority government. On 11 March, the chairs of the Czech and Slovak national councils, Dagmar Burešová and František Mikloško, agreed that further negotiation should be left to the victors of the next elections.[20]

KLAUS AND MEČIAR: PARTING IS SUCH SWEET SORROW

New elections to the Federal Assembly and both national councils took place on 5–6 June 1992. In the Czech Republic, Václav Klaus's ODS (in coalition with the tiny Christian Democratic Party (KDS), won. The ODS-KDS coalition had entered the election campaign with a program of completing the economic reform and completing the transition to a democratic and capitalist society. On the matter of constitutional framework, it had adopted the slogan, "Either a functioning federation or the division of Czechoslovakia into two states," while clearly preferring the former to the latter.[21] In Slovakia, Vladimír Mečiar's HZDS won with a program of social compromises that endorsed various populist demands. As far as the constitutional framework was concerned, it was a vague platform, which combined (in reality) mutually exclusive demands for sovereignty, international recognition for Slovakia, and the maintenance of a common state with the Czechs.[22] Mečiar succeeded in persuading a substantial part of the wider Slovak public that demand for international recognition was fully compatible with the continued existence of Czechoslovakia. At the same time, he claimed that he had five variants of constitutional arrangements (including confederation, which, in reality, is not a common state) for Czech–Slovak relations, whose ultimate fate was to be decided by a referendum. The HZDS leadership chose to ignore objections that any of these variants would require the agreement of the Czech side, which had made it clear that it would insist on dividing the state if Slovaks rejected the federation.[23] In this fashion, HZDS won a substantial number of votes from supporters of the common state, especially voters with less education.[24] The supporters of an independent Slovakia gave most of their votes to the Slovak National Party.

The results of the elections to the Federal Assembly were the key to the fate of Czechoslovakia. Civic Movement, which had been the mainstay of Czech politics until then, was defeated in the elections, failing to win seats in either the Federal Assembly or the Czech National Council. The results in Slovakia were even more catastrophic for the pro-Czechoslovakia, right-of-center forces. VPN, renamed as the Civic Democratic Union (ODU-VPN), campaigned independently, while the Democratic Party (DS) joined Klaus's ODS, in a campaign coalition. Other pro-Czechoslovakia forces forged a last minute electoral formation called Democrats 1992 (D-92), while the Hungarian Civic Party joined the opposition Hungarian parties to create an electoral bloc. In addition, ODU-VPN and KDH, expecting an election victory, raised the threshold for entering the Slovak National Council from the existing 3 percent to 5 percent. The result was that neither ODU-VPN nor DS-ODS and D-92 gained seats in either the Federal Assembly or the Slovak National Council. KDH, after the departure of the Klepáč wing (which also failed to make it into parliament), was weakened. ODS-KDS obtained 33.9 percent of the vote and forty-eight seats in the Chamber of the People, and 33.4 percent and thirty-seven seats in the Chamber of the Nations. The necessary majority in the Chamber of the People was seventy-six deputies, in the Czech part of the Chamber of the Nations, thirty-eight deputies. This meant that ODS-KDS was just one vote short of a majority in the Czech part of the Chamber of the Nations.

As a result, ODS-KDS was forced to look for allies, not only on the Czech but also on the Slovak political scene. Since another potential ally, the rightist Civic Democratic Alliance, had entered the Czech National Council but not the Federal Assembly, only the centrist Catholic Christian Democratic Union–Czechoslovak People's Party (KDU-ČSL) was a candidate for this role on the Czech political scene. It won seven seats in the Chamber of the People and six in the Chamber of the Nations, and the ODS-KDS was preparing to create a coalition with it in the Czech government. In Slovakia, Čarnogurský's KDH was another potential ally, but it won only six seats in the Chamber of the People and eight seats in the Chamber of the Nations. Therefore, the ODS-KDS-KDU-ČSL-KDH combination could not garner a majority in the Chamber of the People.

The situation in the Chamber of the Nations was even more tragic, because ODS-KDS needed allies in the Slovak part of the chamber to pass any law where the minority veto applied, such as the government program, votes of confidence, and the election of the president. Apart from HZDS, however, there were no parties on the Slovak side that could be effective legislative partners. A conglomeration of smaller Slovak parties, which had emerged in the Federal Assembly after the elections, could not be relied upon, for they spanned incompatible ideologies and could never have agreed on a common program. [25]

As early as Sunday, 6 June 1992, Václav Havel had asked Václav Klaus to begin negotiations to form a new federal government and designated him as its next prime minister. Even though Klaus represented the largest party in parliament, Havel's move was most unfortunate. It violated an unwritten tradition that when the president of the country was a Czech, the federal prime minister had to be a Slovak. Yet even in the event that Vladimír Mečiar had become the new federal prime minister, the underlying political situation could not have been altered. The minority veto meant that HZDS could not have created a new cabinet without the support of ODS-KDS. As it soon turned out, however, Mečiar had not even considered entering the federal cabinet and instead intended to become the premier of the Slovak Republic. In the Slovak National Council, HZDS had a majority, and for the passage of constitutional amendments, it could rely on the support of the Slovak National Party and, if needed, the Party of the Democratic Left (SDL).

The first postelection negotiations between ODS and HZDS took place in Brno on 8 June 1992. Both parties assumed that these negotiations would be difficult but not impossible. ODS presumed that Mečiar's absurd demand for Slovak international recognition, which was fundamentally incompatible with Czechoslovakia's continued existence (if only because Slovakia and Czechoslovakia could not simultaneously be subjects of international law), was only a campaign trick by HZDS, seeking to win over SNS voters. ODS was willing to accept a substantial devolution of the federal government's powers, as long as it would not endanger the economic reforms. HZDS was willing to offer several key ministries as well as to make some concessions. The latter included, for example, recycling the demand of the Klepáč wing that Slovak soldiers wear separate insignias on their uniforms, that they might serve in separate units, or the proposals by the Slovak National Party for the creation of Slovak self-defense units, as well as the request that only the Slovak part of the national anthem be played in Slovakia.

Along parallel lines, HZDS approached the negotiations convinced that the ODS claim that the only alternative to federation was a complete division of the state was only a campaign slogan. The HZDS leadership believed that ODS would accept a union or a confederation in the end. The Czech and Slovak republics would then each be independent subjects of international law, each having its own representatives in international bodies. For the purposes of defense, coordination of foreign policy, and economic affairs, they would create joint organs with equal representation of both sides. Each republic would have its own treasury, but both states would share a common currency.[26] The HZDS leadership was incapable of grasping that such an arrangement not only would be dysfunctional but also that for the Czech side it would bring about only problems, nothing positive. For where the weaker and smaller unit has the same powers as the stronger and larger unit, what is involved is not equality but rather a minority veto over the decisions of the majority. History from 1938, 1945, and 1968 was repeating itself: the Slovak side assumed that its proposals were mutually advantageous, but in reality, they were advantageous only for Slovakia.

According to the testimony of one of the meetings' participants, Miroslav Macek, the negotiations began with a private meeting between Klaus and Mečiar.[27] According to Macek, Mečiar was attempting, as usual, to use vague formulations to blur the irreconcilable conflict over international recognition. While the Klaus–Mečiar conversations were taking place, Macek spoke with Michal Kováč, who described a Slovak proposal for an economic and defense union, apparently without previous consultation with Mečiar. Macek, who subsequently dubbed this proposal a "Slovak state with Czech insurance,"[28] immediately realized that this project could not and must not be accepted by the Czech side, because it signified an evolutionary approach to Slovak state building, funded by Czech taxpayers. That is why after Klaus and Mečiar had joined the larger meeting, Macek declared that the matter had become quite clear; the only solution was the dissolution of Czechoslovakia.[29]

Even after the Brno talks, Klaus apparently had not given up all hope that Mečiar would back away from some of his demands and that the dissolution of the state could be averted. That is why that subject was on the agenda at subsequent meetings in Prague on 11 and 17 June 1992. At these negotiations, ODS put pressure on HZDS to give a clear response: either a functioning federation or two separate states. After six hours of futile negotiations, during which HZDS again blurred the distinction between the two alternatives, relying on such contradictory formulations as "a common state in the form of a confederation" or "defense and economic union," Klaus's patience had run out. He asked the HZDS leaders whether they wanted to build a Slovak state with Czech money and whether or not the Slovaks were a proud nation. Mečiar replied that each republic would be responsible for its own finances. With this response, Mečiar sought to return to the question of confederation, but the Czech side interpreted his declaration as yet another step toward Slovak independence. In the end, they agreed on the composition of a reduced federal cabinet, which, in addition to the prime minister, would have only ten ministers. Apart from the premiership, which went to ODS, there was equal representation in the cabinet for each party, but HZDS demanded the ministry of foreign affairs and the ministry of defense.[30]

Václav Klaus apparently had changed his mind as early as 17 June 1992, but ODS made its position clear only after the fourth round of negotiations with HZDS, which took place in Bratislava on 19 June 1992. The negotiations lasted a full twelve hours and confirmed that the only thing on which the parties could agree was the division of the country. Following the negotiations, both parties issued a declaration, which stated in part: "ODS does not regard a confederation, in which both republics are subjects of international law (which was the HZDS proposal) as a common state, but instead as a union of two separate states. Rather than confederation, ODS prefers two completely independent states, i.e., a constitutional dissolution of the federation." On 24 June 1992, a new Slovak government, headed by Vladimír Mečiar, was formed. On 2 July, Václav Havel appointed the last federal cabinet of Jan Stráský. On the same day, a Czech government comprised of the coalition ODS-KDS-ČSL-ODA was formed under the leadership of Václav Klaus.

Both the Czech and the Slovak opposition protested the political agreement to divide Czechoslovakia. SDL rejected the notion of a confederation and instead proposed a "cooperating federation." KDH regarded independence as premature. On the Czech side, the Social Democrats (ČSSD), the Moravian and Liberal-Social Union (LSU), the Czech communists, and the extreme right Republicans (the Association for the Republic–Republican Party of Czechoslovakia, or SPR-RSČ) also opposed the agreement. The opposition demanded that the dissolution of the state be decided by a referendum. The opposition parties met with the chair of the Federal Assembly, Michal Kováč (HZDS), and welcomed the notion of Czecho–Slovak union. Jiří Horák, the chair of ČSSD, created a special commission of experts,[31] which was expected to develop this project, in agreement with the other opposition parties and HZDS. The proposal was inspired by the notion of dualism along the lines of the 1867 Austro-Hungarian Compromise model. While HZDS was sympathetic to this idea, not even ČSSD was able to solve the problem of international recognition for Slovakia. Lawyers considered the possibility that Slovakia could eventually receive special representation in the United Nations, much like Belarus and Ukraine had in addition to the USSR. There was also talk of Slovakia creating its own representation abroad, short of full diplomatic status. But when it turned out that HZDS demanded full diplomatic representation, the commission resigned and the project remained unfinished.

Both the opposition and the government repeatedly considered the question of a referendum. Surveys of public opinion showed that when asked, "Are you for a common state?" most voters in both the Czech and the Slovak republics responded positively. To rule out erroneous conclusions stemming from conceptual confusion promoted by HZDS, the opposition (ČSSD) maintained that the question should be worded to make it clear that in a common state, Slovakia would *not* have international recognition. But the problem of the referendum had several layers: even if it had affirmed popular support for the maintenance of the common state, the opposing political forces would have remained in power, making a compromise impossible. At the same time, surveys of voters' preferences indicated that new elections would not have brought about any change. Irrespective of the outcome of the referendum and thanks to a political system with a powerful minority veto, the stage was clearly set for government paralysis and the gradual dissolution of the state. *Legal* means could not overcome the *political* stalemate. Only the use of force could do that, i.e., the dissolution of the parliaments and the establishment of a Prague-based military dictatorship. Such a move would have created precisely the situation that the Slovak nationalists needed to sustain their claim that Slovakia was ruled by the Czechs. No one on the Czech side, however, actually considered this option. From 1990 on, there was consensus among Czech elites that if Slovakia should wish to become independent, no one was going to stand in its way.

With the end of Havel's presidential term and new presidential elections in the Federal Assembly, the unfolding dissolution became apparent. Havel's term ended on 5 July 1992.[32] HZDS not only refused to support the candidacy of Václav Havel for another term, but it also declined to propose and back its own alternative candidate. Given the minority veto and without the votes of HZDS and SNS, Havel could not be reelected. Such an attempt failed on 3 July 1992. On 17 July 1992, the Slovak National Council, with the support of HZDS, SNS, and surprisingly, SDL, passed the declaration of Slovak sovereignty, which declared Slovakia to be the state of the Slovak people. The declaration passed over the dissenting votes of KDH and the Hungarian parties. On the same day, Václav Havel resigned from his office; no new president was chosen for the remainder of Czechoslovakia's existence.

Following the promulgation of the declaration of sovereignty and during negotiations in Bratislava on 22–23 July 1992, HZDS attempted to stop further disintegration of the state, because it wanted to take advantage of the existing federation to prepare for an independent Slovakia. The Czech side, however, had lost its interest in Slovakia.[33] It was afraid that slowing the dissolution process at this point in time would only create economic chaos and financial losses, which the Czech taxpayers would have to bear. Therefore, the Czech side insisted on a speedy and complete division. Klaus presented Mečiar with a draft law on the end of federation, which the Federal Assembly was to approve by 20 September. The draft assumed four formal possibilities: (1) declaration by the Federal Assembly; (2) agreement of the national councils; (3) a referendum; and (4) a unilateral departure from the federation by one of the republics. Instead of a union, Klaus proposed a series of bilateral agreements. The final agreement was reached in Brno on 26 August, where a timetable was established, and the date was set for Czechoslovakia's expiration on 31 December 1992, the end of the budget year. On 1 September 1992, the Slovak Republic adopted a new constitution, which had been conceived to function as a constitution for an independent state. It did not reckon with the existence of Czechoslovakia and did not take it into account, except that the validity of some articles was to go into effect as of 1 January 1993. Nevertheless, as it turned out, the division of Czechoslovakia was not an easy matter. On 11 September, the opposition forced a special session of the Federal Assembly, which again demanded that a referendum be held. The federal government refused this demand, arguing that if the referendum were to endorse the continued maintenance of the common state—which surveys of public opinion indicated was virtually certain—it would be in no position to act on such a result, for the disintegration of the state had already gone too far. On 1 October 1992, the Federal Assembly had voted on the constitutional amendment concerning the end of the federation. The opposition defeated the proposal. Miloš Zeman, then deputy chair of ČSSD, took advantage of the situation and proposed a constitutional commission that would be charged with the transformation of the federation into a Czecho–Slovak union. The proposal, which enjoyed the support of the opposition as well as many of the HZDS deputies, was actually approved. ČSSD's proposal presupposed the existence of two states with common organs for foreign policy, defense, and finance. Decisions were to be made on the basis of parity, and the question of international recognition was left open.

The vote in favor of such a commission was a great victory for the opposition and HZDS. Nevertheless, ODS had already decided to divide the state at any price, and if no other way was open, it would proceed without the help of HZDS. The Czech governing coalition refused to send any representatives to the new commission. Instead, on 6 October 1992, the ODS and HZDS delegations met in Jihlava. Klaus insisted that HZDS explicitly reject union and confederation and commit itself to the division of Czechoslovakia into fully independent states. In the end, Mečiar agreed. As a result, the union project was shelved.

The next stage of Czecho–Slovak development took place under the banner of deconstruction. A 13 November 1992 constitutional amendment divided federal real estate property in a ratio of 2:1. A new law on the devolution of powers from 8 October transferred further responsibilities from the federation to the republics. On 18 November 1992, the Federal Assembly met to vote on a new version of the constitutional amendment concerning the end of the federation. The various modes of how the federation might end were no longer at issue. The new amendment was merely a modification of the existing law on the federation, which simply added a paragraph stipulating that the federation would end on 31 December 1992.

By the time the assembly voted on this law, Czechoslovakia had already been de facto partitioned. The law, however, was passed only in the Chamber of the People, and another vote had to be held a week later on 25 November. By lobbying the opposition deputies, the government coalition in the end persuaded some right-wing Republicans and some Czech and Slovak Social Democrats and succeeded in obtaining the needed votes. By a narrow majority and only on the second attempt, the constitutional amendment finally passed. On 31 December 1992, the Czech and Slovak Federal Republic officially expired.

CONCLUSIONS

Obviously, the question arises whether this end was inevitable or whether a Czecho–Slovak compromise was possible. As the foregoing narrative makes clear, until the June 1992 elections, such a compromise was possible, for the Slovak side had not placed the issue of full international recognition on the agenda. A compromise, however, would have required that the Czech side accept the Slovak demand for a treaty arrangement. The Czech side made a critical error in clinging excessively to legalistic formulas. In actuality, the issue as to whether republics could or could not enter into treaties was subsidiary. It was an academic discussion without any practical significance. Entering into agreements, inasmuch as it would have assisted in the creation of functioning common organs, could have preserved Czechoslovakia, at least for a time.

After the 1992 elections, however, there was no possibility of maintaining the common state; the only alternative was a union or a confederation, neither of which would satisfy the definition of a common state. Prospects for a union, which appeared quite viable at the time, do not seem so sanguine from today's (1997) perspective. The perils of a union became evident, for example, in the conflict between Hungary and Slovakia over the Gabčíkovo Dam, which showed that when decisions are based on parity, stalemate results.[34] Such problems would have undoubtedly, sooner or later, led to the dissolution of any union as well. Given the divergence of developments in the Czech lands and in Slovakia after the third Mečiar government of 1994, it is clear today that a Czecho–Slovak union would have brought little good for the Czech Republic. It was a project without a future. That is why there was no possibility for compromise after the June 1992 elections.

Translated from Czech by Michael Kraus and Allison Stanger

NOTES

1. For key documents concerning the establishment of the federation in 1968, see Jozef Žatkuliak, *Federalizacia československeho štátu 1968-1970: Vznik česko-slovenskej federácie roku 1968* (Prague-Brno: Ústav pro soudobé dějiny AV ČR, 1996). See also Žatkuliak's "Realizacia ústavného zákona o československej federácii od októbra 1968," *Historický časopis*, vol. 40, no. 3 (1992), pp. 356–369.

2. Viliam Plevza, *Československá štátnost a slovenská otázka v politike KSČ* (Bratislava: Práca, 1971), pp. 326–327.

3. Sbírka zákonů (Sb.), Constitutional laws no. 125/1970 Sb., no. 126/1970 Sb., 133/1970 Sb., 134/1970 Sb. For the origins of these changes, see Jozef Žatkuliak, "Deformácia ústavného zákona o československej federácii po októbri 1968, *Historický časopis,* vol. 40, no. 4 (1992), pp. 473–485.

4. Real power in the state was vested in the eleven-member presidium of the Central Committee of the Communist Party of Czechoslovakia (KSČ), where the decisive

word belonged to the party's first secretary. The Communist Party itself was not federalized. While there was a Communist Party of Slovakia (KSS), it was not independent but represented the territorial organization of the KSČ in Slovakia, to whom it was fully subordinated.

5. The circumstances of Husák's 1987 departure from his position as first secretary of the KSČ are described in the memoirs of his successor, Miloš Jakeš, *Dva roky generálním tajemníkem* (Prague: Regulus, 1996), pp. 67–73.

6. These were especially the Czechoslovak Socialist Party (ČSS) and Czechoslovak Social Democratic Party (ČSSD). While the former founded its own branch in Slovakia, the latter created a separate Slovak organization (SDSS).

7. Similarly oriented parties in the Czech Republic and Slovakia even went as far as to conclude special agreements committing them not to launch activities in the other republic. For example, the Catholic Czechoslovak People's Party (ČSL) as well as the Christian Democratic Party (KDS) entered into such agreements with Ján Čarnogurský's Christian Democratic Movement (KDH).

8. To make this account complete, we need to note that in Slovakia an attempt was made to launch a statewide Czechoslovak party, the Movement for Czechoslovak Understanding, in February-March 1990. The movement was founded on 22 February 1990 by a former Slovak dissident and signatory of Charter 77, Vladimír Čech, but it never acquired a large following.

9. Based on conversations with Petr Pithart.

10. Jan Měchýř, *Slovensko v Československu: Slovensko-české vztahy, 1918-1991: Dokumenty, názory, komentáře* (Prague: Práce, 1991), doc. XVII, p. 114.

11. Karel Pacner, *Osudové okamžiky Československa* (Prague: Themis, 1997), pp. 609–611.

12. Previously, two other parties had split from Civic Forum, the Christian Democratic Party (KDS) and the Civic Democratic Alliance (ODA).

13. Měchýř, *Slovenskov Československu,* p. 111.

14. Měchýř, *Slovenskov Československu,* p. 115.

15. Měchýř, *Slovenskov Československu,* p. 112.

16. The transcript of the recording of the negotiations at Hrádeček was published under the title of *Poločas rozpadu,* as a supplement to *Slovenské listy,* vol. 2, nos. 2–6 (1994).

17. For the views of the Oxford discussions' participants, see *Výber,* no. 3, 1992, and no. 4, 1992. Also, see the interview with Petr Pithart in *Mladá fronta dnes* (MFD), no. 296, 1991.

18. Pacner, *Osudové okamžiky Československa,* pp. 630–631.

19. The smlouva text was published in most Slovak dailies in February 1992.

20. Dušan Škvarna et al., *Lexikón slovenských dejín* (Bratislava: Slovenské pedagogickénakl. 1997), pp. 173–174. Pacner, *Osudové okamziky Československa,* p. 631.

21. *Cesta k prosperitě: Programové prohlášení ODS* (Prague, 1991), p. 5.

22. *Tézy volebného programu HZDS* (Bratislava, 1992), p. 18.

23. Marián Leško, *Mečiar a mečiarismus* (Bratislava, 1996), p. 76.

24. Rüdiger Kipke and Karel Vodička, eds., *Rozloučení s Československem* (Prague: Český spisovatel, 1993), p. 88.

25. For results of the elections, see Kipke and Vodička, *Rozloučení s Československem,* p. 87. See also *Volby 92* (Prague: Federalní statistický úřad, 1992).

26. A draft of the Slovak proposal is in my personal archive. See also Jan Rychlík, "Bol možný česko-slovenský kompromis?" *Literárny týždenník,* no. 18 (1993), p. 13.

27. Eds. note. For further details, see Macek's chapter in this volume.
28. *Mladá fronta dnes* (22 September 1992), p. 7.
29. See Macek's chapter in this book.
30. Pacner, *Osudové okamžiky Československa,* p. 634 and ff.
31. These and the following observations are based on my personal notes concerning the deliberations of the ČSSD commission, of which I was a member.
32. According to the constitution, a new president was to be elected within three months of the expiration of his predecessor's term, i.e., no later than 5 October 1992. Before the election of the new president, the current holder of the post was to stay in office. The constitution was silent as to how to proceed in the event that no new president could be elected.
33. When Czechoslovakia was born in 1918, the Czechs needed Slovakia for strategic reasons, to obtain an escape corridor to the East from German encirclement; the Slovak population fortified the Czechs against the German minority. But with the expulsion of the Germans after 1945, and especially with the fall of communism in Eastern Europe, the situation changed considerably. In the eyes of contemporary Czech policymakers, not only are corridors to the East unnecessary, they are unwelcome.
34. After the Hungarian abrogation of the agreement on the Gabčíkovo Dam, the Slovak side decided in 1990 to bridge the Danube on Slovak territory and to proceed with the construction unilaterally. In turn, the Hungarian government protested and presented its conflict with Czechoslovakia to the International Court of Justice in the Hague. The latter ordered Czechoslovakia to refrain from proceeding any further with the construction until the court had completed its deliberations. On 26 October 1992, the Czechoslovak government considered the matter. Slovak ministers voted against the court-mandated work stoppage, and Slovak government bodies ignored the commitment of the Czechoslovak government to cease work on the project. This incident demonstrated that the Czechoslovak government could no longer undertake international commitments in good faith, for it was impossible to implement the federal government's decisions in Slovakia.

Part II

Institutional Challenges and Constitutional Controversies

4

From "Velvet Revolution" to "Velvet Split": Consociational Institutions and the Disintegration of Czechoslovakia

Petr Kopecký

INTRODUCTION

This chapter aims to contribute to explanations of the peaceful breakup of Czechoslovakia through a consociational interpretation.[1] The focus is on the role of institutions, and the conditions in which they operated. The consociational theory, developed by Arend Lijphart, holds that stable democracy is possible in a segmented society if that democracy is based on power sharing. Ethnically, religiously, and linguistically divided societies need peaceful coexistence among their contending groups; this requires the inclusion of their representatives in decision-making structures in order to facilitate conciliation and compromise. That Czechoslovakia was a segmented society, consisting of two large and distinct linguistic groups from the beginning of its existence in 1918, hardly needs clarification.[2] However, it is less well acknowledged that the largely inherited institutional structure in postcommunist Czechoslovakia—in place until the split in 1992 and the result of historical compromises made between the Czechs and Slovaks—was also a prominent example of a consociational system. What we need to understand, then, is why consociationalism failed in Czechoslovakia: in other words, why a consociational system of institutions did not provide for a stable and functioning consociational democracy.

In essence, it will be argued that consociational structures alone could not provide for the preservation of unity between the Czechs and Slovaks in one state because of the unfavorable context: the volatile, uncertain, and competitive character of postcommunist politics. However, and somewhat paradoxically, it will also be argued that the same consociational institutions that proved incapable of hold-

Petr Kopecký

ing Czechoslovakia together facilitated its peaceful partition. Consociational theory is of particular relevance for this discussion in at least two important respects. First, it draws attention to the composition and behavior of political elites representing the segments of a divided society, an aspect that will be identified as critical in the turmoil leading to the split of Czechoslovakia. Second, consociational theory tries to predict the probability that power sharing will be maintained (and introduced) in a segmented society by looking at certain background conditions. An examination of the functioning of institutions and political elites in postcommunist Czechoslovakia will show that while these conditions were largely unfavorable to preserving a common state, some of them left a legacy that facilitated the partition of the country.

Consociational Theory

Consociational theory was originally formulated to explain the achievement and maintenance of stable democratic systems in deeply divided smaller European countries—the Netherlands, Belgium, Austria, and Switzerland. For Lijphart, they represented a deviant case, since conventional wisdom associated political stability with homogeneous political culture and its autonomous political parties and interests groups, and political instability with the fragmented cultures and mutual dependence of parties and interest groups of continental European countries. Based on empirical observations of the four small countries, which were characterized on the one hand by subcultural segmentation and, on the other hand, by political, social, and economic stability, Lijphart maintained that stable democracy is possible in such deeply divided societies if their type of democracy is based on power sharing. Lijphart's definition of power sharing has four characteristics: (1) government by a grand coalition of political leaders of all significant political segments; (2) (mutual) minority veto; (3) proportionality as the principal standard of political representation, civil service appointment, and allocation of public funds; and (4) a high degree of autonomy for each segment to run its own internal affairs.[3]

Each of these four devices can take on a variety of forms. Government by grand coalition can be an inclusive cabinet coalition of ethnic or religious parties, as was the case in Austria after the Second World War.[4] Other possibilities include the formation of inclusive grand coalition councils and advisory boards enjoying tremendous influence, as used to be the case in the Netherlands,[5] or simply the representation of relevant groups in the cabinet and presidency in a predetermined ratio, such as in Belgium.[6] Minority veto can be a purely informal understanding that minority groups can effectively block proposals that affect their autonomy, but it can also be constitutionally entrenched, especially in a country where the minority faces a solid majority. As will be shown later, Czechoslovakia had such a device. Proportionality is most clearly exhibited in the adoption of a proportional representation (PR) electoral system. But as Lijphart showed, power sharing can also coexist with the plurality electoral system, if the minorities are geographically concentrated (India) or if a right of exclusive nomination is given to minority groups in a number of electoral districts (Malaysia).[7] Finally, cultural autonomy is most clearly instituted in federal systems, such as cantonal Switzerland, where state and linguistic boundaries largely coincide.[8] In nonfederal states, where ethnic, religious, or linguistic groups are not regionally based, cultural autonomy can be secured by granting minorities the right of, and providing public assistance for, establishing their own schools and cultural and religious institutions.

In addition to these formal and informal institutional devices, consociational theory places extra emphasis on the constructive role of political leadership in a divided society. The leaders must make a commitment to maintaining democratic practices as well as have "a basic willingness to engage in cooperative efforts with the leaders of other segments in a spirit of moderation and compromise."[9] Thus, if willing and if possessing a sufficient capacity, political elites can stabilize the system through an overarching accommodative pattern of behavior. To engage in such a pattern of behavior, political elites need to be sure that they enjoy stable support and legitimacy within their respective political subcultures. It is obviously possible to imagine that incorporated elites are accommodative toward each other *despite* possible dissent on the mass level, but especially in the long-term, the erosion of subcultural cohesion usually leads toward the erosion of consociational democracy.[10]

Therefore, while consociational theory can explain stability in a particular segmented society by referring to an observable accommodative pattern of elite behavior, it is less powerful in predicting whether political elites will engage in such behavior, even if all four consociational devices mentioned above are adopted. In other words, there remains a question of which comes first: institutions or elite behavior? Can consociational democracy be produced by means of a constitutionally mandated set of institutions that, in turn, will enhance or even induce a certain pattern of elite behavior? Can a power-sharing system be introduced and maintained if moderate leaders face opposition from secessionist-minded leaders, undermining their ability to speak on behalf of their segment? Consociational theory does not give a clear answer to these questions, but it suggests a set of nine factors that help explain why elites in some systems, at particular times, decide to engage in accommodative behavior and why they introduce and maintain a power-sharing system.

In a later elaboration of consociational theory, Lijphart formulated these nine background conditions as follows:[11] (1) a long-standing tradition of elite accommodation; (2) the existence of overarching loyalties to the system, which reduce the strength of particularistic tendencies; (3) only moderate socioeconomic differences between segments of society; (4) the nonexistence of a united majority segment, which would be tempted to revert to majoritarian methods; (5) segments of equal size, so that there is a balance of power between them; (6) the presence of external threats to the country, which promote internal unity; (7) geographically concentrated groups, so that a territorially based federation could be established; (8) a small number of segments, so that negotiations between them are less complicated; and (9) a small total population within the country, so that leaders can know each other personally. It should be stressed that these are neither sufficient in and of themselves nor are they all necessary if a consociational democracy is to function. Rather, they are factors that enhance or hinder it.

However, and crucially, consociational theory holds that power sharing is a necessary condition for managing conflicts in divided societies, even though it does not guarantee that a stable democracy will be constituted and maintained. It holds that the alternative to power sharing is either assimilation (which is problematic in the short term) or partition (which is often violent). Empirically as well as normatively, consociational democracy has become a widely practiced and influential form of conflict management, applicable as much to federal societies, with hostile segments that are geographically separated, as to nonfederal states, with geographically intermingled groups. The section that follows will argue that the structure of Czechoslovak institutions reflected a persistent attempt to accommodate the national conflict between the Czech and Slovaks with a number of institutional devices. Indeed, it will demonstrate that, from 1989 until the 1992 split, Czechoslovakia could be classified as a textbook example of a consociational system of institutions.[12]

THE STRUCTURE OF STATE INSTITUTIONS IN THE FORMER CZECHOSLOVAKIA

The structure of democratic institutions and, in particular, the extent of decentralization, autonomy, or federalism for Slovakia had been the subject of serious political disputes among successive political elites ever since the establishment of Czechoslovakia in 1918. During the First Republic (1918–1939), political consolidation of the whole system was secured because of a remarkably divided Slovak intelligentsia. The fear of an eventual relapse into Hungarian domination, as well as a skepticism among many Slovak representatives regarding their incapacity to manage a truly independent state, led them to accept the unitary structure of the new Czechoslovakia, embodied in the 1920 constitution.[13]

At the end of World War II, during which the Czech lands were occupied by Nazi Germany and Slovakia enjoyed independent status, both regions were again reunited into a common state. In 1948, the Communist Party organized its coup and took over power in the whole of Czechoslovakia. The result was a new constitution (in 1960), which proclaimed a unitary, socialist state and subjected the Czech and Slovak regions to totalitarian doctrines for nearly thirty years. The political legacy of the war period in Slovakia, however, was the political elite's recognition of Slovak nationhood. In institutional terms, this meant the creation of an asymmetrical political structure. This structure was, in fact, provided for by the 1948 constitution (written before the communist coup), and was largely accepted by the communist regime. An ultimately sovereign federal government ran affairs for the entire country, and the Slovak National Council ran affairs within the Slovak Republic. Moreover, this asymmetry in institutional structure was paralleled during the whole communist period in the party structure, where both the nationwide Czechoslovak Communist Party and the Slovak Communist Party coexisted.

In 1968, during the Prague Spring movement led by Alexander Dubček, the pressures to further reconstitute Slovak autonomy came to a head as part of a general campaign for democratization. The Slovak political elite in particular considered further progress in federalization as an integral, if not crucial, part of a broader package of political reforms. The result was again a new constitution, providing for a symmetrical federal state. This federal system, only marginally amended, was used as a basic institutional structure after the fall of the communist regime in 1989, and it was this system that constituted the Czechoslovak power-sharing mechanism.[14] Jon Elster argues that the 1968 constitution may be "a unique example of a text that came into life only after death—after the abolition of the regime whose affairs it was supposed to regulate."[15]

It is important to emphasize at this point that the Czechoslovak consociational system was as much the legacy of a long-lasting attempt to find acceptable solutions for Czech–Slovak disputes as it was the more recent legacy of highly contingent decisions made during the Round Table talks between opposition forces and the communist regime in autumn 1989. Given that writing a new constitution was the primary objective assigned to the first freely elected Federal Assembly, and given that the old constitution was hardly considered to be a perfect solution, consociationalism in postcommunist Czechoslovakia was instituted more by accident than by a conscious and deliberative decision.[16]

What were the principle features of the system? The 1968 law on the federation provided the most prominent consociational device. It established Czechoslovakia, like Belgium, as a federal state. However, unlike Belgium, which consists of three constituent parts, Czechoslovakia was established as a federal state comprised of only two separate republics.[17] The territorially based federation was the institutional embodiment of the geographical concentration of both nations. The state and linguistic boundaries coincided. Both the Czech and Slovak republics had their own separate legislative assemblies, the Czech and Slovak national councils, and both republics had their own national governments. At the federal level, there was the Federal Assembly and the federal government.

The Federal Assembly consisted of two chambers: the Chamber of the People, elected by the entire population of Czechoslovakia on a proportional basis; and the Chamber of the Nations, with seventy-five Members of Parliament (MPs) elected in the Czech Republic and seventy-five MPs elected in the Slovak Republic. Each of the two republics acquired a relatively high degree of autonomy to run its own affairs within a given jurisdiction. Education and cultural affairs were exclusive republic domains from 1968 onward, with the 1990 constitutional act on the "new competencies" for the two republics extending the areas of autonomous jurisdiction even further.

The principle of proportionality further complemented the federal arrangements. Proportionality was, first of all, embodied in an electoral law that employed a PR list system. There were twelve large multimember districts, eight in the Czech Republic and four in Slovakia. The threshold requirement to gain a seat in the Federal Assembly was 5 percent of the vote in *either* republic. As indicated above, the Chamber of the People was elected by the entire population, having approximately two-thirds of the MPs from the Czech lands (101) and one-third from Slovakia (49). The Chamber of the Nations had seventy-five MPs from each region, thereby overrepresenting the smaller of the two republics. More or less similar districts and electoral formulae were used for the elections to the national councils.

Top civil servant positions were also allocated on an informally proportional basis (if not always strictly), both during the communist regime as well as in the postcommunist period. But this kind of "bias toward proportionality" was most clearly exhibited in the alternation of nationality between the office of prime minister and the president. If the prime minister was of Slovak nationality, the president was to be a Czech and vice versa. The parity principle in representation applied also to the appointments to the supreme court and the attorney general and the governorship of the central bank.[18] Both state television and radio broadcasted a bilingual federal program and two national programs.

A strong minority veto was built into the voting procedures of the Federal Assembly by requiring a double majority within the Chamber of the Nations: each of the two republic sections of the Chamber of the Nations voted on all issues separately; to pass a bill, a majority had to be obtained in both sections of the Chamber of the Nations as well as in the Chamber of the People. Such a structure already granted a veto power to one of the two national representations in the Federal Assembly on all issues. Most important, however, all constitutional amendments, constitutional laws, and votes of no confidence required a qualified majority in each of the two voting sections of the Chamber of the Nations, leaving a small number of either Czech or Slovak deputies (thirty-one) an effective veto power within the Federal Assembly.[19]

Government by grand coalition took on two specific forms in Czechoslovakia. The most visible was the formation of a broad coalition cabinet. During the 1989 revolutionary changes, two mass political movements—Civic Forum (OF) in the Czech lands and Public Against Violence (VPN) in Slovakia—emerged simultaneously. These two movements tried to appeal to society at large, encompassing basically all sections of society. From December 1989 until June 1991 the representatives of both movements managed the interim federal government and held a majority of seats in the federal parliament. The landslide victory of both movements in the first free elections of June 1990 made possible the formation of a grand coalition of the OF and the VPN, together with the Slovak Christian Democrats. This coalition controlled 98 seats in the 150-member Chamber of the People, and 102 seats in the 150-member Chamber of the Nations. The parties losing out on power sharing were both the Slovak and Moravian nationalists, the Hungarian minority party, and the Communist Party.

The federal government was not, therefore, a perfect inclusive coalition of all parties, but arguably, it was a coalition government that secured the representation of both national groups, effectively excluding extremist forces, particularly the Slovak nationalists and the Communist Party. In fact, the fierce resistance to the communists and the fear of their strength was initially the main force that held the ideologically heterogeneous movements together. Later, in 1991, internal differentiations within both mass movements appeared, causing their disintegration and creating a simpler majority government of the successor parties. This notwithstanding, the informal rule stipulating that federal cabinets should be composed of ministers of both national groups stayed in place, but the cabinet was less inclusive in terms of representation *within* the groups than it had been previously at its inception.

Furthermore, the most visible element of government by grand coalition, the federal coalition cabinet, was complemented by a number of ad hoc Round Table talks, commissions, and councils, which brought together the representatives of both Czechs and Slovaks. This was especially the case with negotiations on the future institutional arrangement of the country, where both the national councils and the republics were represented. The talks also often included representatives of the federal institutions, President Havel, and later the leaders of the emerging political parties. These "para-constitutional," largely informal practices served one purpose: to bring together top representatives of both national groups and top representatives of all institutions to find a consensus on the future shape of the state, which would, in turn, guide the work on the drafts of the new Czechoslovak constitution. Instead of a new constitution, however, the breakup of the country followed the protracted disputes between Czech and Slovak elites, which were conducted within this consociational system of institutions.

WHAT HAPPENED? ELITES, PARTIES, AND THE ESCALATION OF THE CONFLICT

The first obvious answer is that the institutions, despite being consociational, were ill equipped for the conflict with which they had to deal.[20] Such arguments rightly point to the difficulties stemming from the practice of consociational arrangements in Czechoslovakia: supermajority voting requirements and the consequent frequent use of the minority veto by the Slovak deputies as well as the strong incentives to appeal to regional preferences that existed as a result of electoral law. However, these arguments do not examine the institutional alternatives for ameliorating the escalating conflict. It is true that Czechoslovak consociational devices put a significant burden on the decision-making capacity of the system. But with more majoritarian features, the conflict might have been even worse. Consociational institutions, or rather the outcome they produced, frustrated mainly the majority segment—the Czechs.[21] If the Czechs had been satisfied, that would very likely have meant that the Slovaks would have been dissatisfied and frustrated for the same reason, namely, the failure of institutions to fully meet their demands. Given this, it is very unlikely that a new constitution could have escaped or elided a Czech–Slovak dispute that had always necessitated compromises in the past. And one wonders how much different it would have been from the 1968 constitution.

The ingredient most needed for the success of Czechoslovak federalism was consensual and cooperative behavior on the part of political elites. However, while consensual behavior was needed to make consociational devices work, the conditions under which the postcommunist political elites in Czechoslovakia operated unfortunately provided every incentive not to compromise. Accordingly, the capacity of the leaders from both republics to reach any meaningful and lasting consensual agreement on the majority of issues involving the form of the state was strikingly low in all three years of the postcommunist federation. In fact, given the substantial number of ordinary Czech and Slovak citizens reluctant to accept the breakup of the country,[22] one could argue that political elites in the former Czechoslovakia were less tolerant and less accommodating than their electorates. At least three circumstances seem to be important in this respect.

The first relates to *the volatile pattern of elite–mass linkages* and its consequences. A characteristic feature of emerging Eastern European democracies in general has been the high level of voter volatility.[23] Compared to the earlier instances of democratization in Europe, very few potential voters entered the postcommunist period of democratization with preexisting party and social loyalties. The existence of such an open electoral market, it has been argued, is likely to encourage competitive behavior among the political elite, and hence potentially destabilize the conduct of democratic politics, since there is something substantial for which to compete.[24] As Barbara Geddes states: "In contemporary Eastern Europe, almost all votes are up for grabs . . . [which] not only increases the stakes and unpredictability of early electoral contests, it also contributes to the unpredictability and apparent opportunism of party behavior."[25] If the electoral market is by and large closed, as was the case in the four countries from which Lijphart developed his theory of consociational democracy, the stability of the electorate could discourage the competitive behavior of the political elite and hence contribute to issue stability within parties over time.

Among those in the former Czechoslovakia with existing loyalties were voters of the (former) Communist parties, parties representing ethnic minorities (in Slovakia), and the Christian-oriented parties, namely, KDU-ČSL in the Czech Republic. The rest—the overwhelming majority—was an available electorate with only one pervasive collective identity—national identity. When a relevant issue without other conflict dimensions (religion, class, etc.) presented itself, ethnicity offered fertile grounds for political exploitation, with potentially disintegrative effects.[26] Especially in the Slovak part of the former Czechoslovakia, ethnicity was a very rich source for these political entrepreneurs to mine—and many soon started digging. Before long, there could neither be a Slovak political party without a highly pronounced program of Czecho–Slovak coexistence nor a Slovak parliamentarian denying his or her national background.

Similarly, the institutional setup itself was open to political exploitation, thus further heightening the competition between political elites. In the absence of class and religious appeals, institutional squabbling is often an attractive way for an elite to achieve a distinctive political profile.[27] Moreover, and perhaps most important, the very process of constitutional reconstruction, starting basically from scratch, meant that the players in the game played for very high stakes. The institutional choices they made often predetermined what opportunities actors would enjoy in the future. Fierce competition among the elite was therefore to be expected, as they did compete not only for the available voters but also for favorable rules of the game under the emerging institutional system.

In this environment, almost the entire Slovak political spectrum began a perpetual shifting of positions on the national issue, paving the way for the conflicts with the Czech political elite, who often reacted in only an ad hoc manner to the new demands from the Slovak side.[28] The critical impulse, which forced the major Slovak political parties to relocate on national positions, was the split of the Public Against Violence (VPN) in 1991 and the subsequent emergence of Mečiar's Movement for a Democratic Slovakia. The popular success of his nationalist message, which evolved over time,[29] made the panorama of Slovak political parties dramatically different from that which had existed before the 1990 elections, when consensus on maintaining the federation prevailed. The Slovak Christian Democrats, led by Ján Čarnogurský, constructed the (in)famous vision of an independent Slovakia within the European Community—a move that shocked not only the Czech political elite but also the (few) remaining pro-federalists within the then VPN-dominated Slovak government. The Party of the Democratic Left (the ex-Communists), another major Slovak party, broke with its Czech counterpart partly because of the support it had expressed toward the more radical national standpoint of Mečiar in his negotiations within VPN and with Prague.

Simply put, given the historical salience of the ethnonational issue and the fact that the issue essentially involved bargaining on institutions, it should come as no surprise that the division along national lines between Czech and Slovak party leaders, and between Slovak party leaders themselves, gradually assumed a strongly divisive character. Within Slovakia, the mobilization of the population based on new interpretations of Czecho–Slovak relations and issue (re)formation led to all-too-frequent impasses on already existing agreements. Most of the Czech political parties, while competing among themselves on other issues,[30] gradually started to see the coexistence of the two "ethnona-tions" and the ever shifting positions of Slovak representatives as obstacles to the efficient decision-making capacity of democratic institutions, as well as a brake on rapid progress in economic transformation. In the course of three years, from a rather symbolic discussion about the name of the state (Czechoslovakia or Czecho-Slovakia?), and in spite of the "settlement" on the new competencies of both the federation and the republics (the November 1990 agreement), the de-bate had produced a climate of almost total political immobility as well as ad-versity and distrust between the politicians.

Second, the nonconsensual behavior of the politicians can also be explained in terms of *the lack of an elite tradition of accommodation.* Although there was long-term sympathy and appeal between the two nations, and although the nego-tiations around the birth of the common state of Czechs and Slovaks were carried out by representatives (mostly returning from exile) of both nations, the seventy-four years of Czechoslovakia's existence did not provide enough time to build a strong tradition of inter-elite cooperation and ties. Moreover, after forty years of communism, inter-elite exchange beyond the confines of the party had been vir-tually eliminated. Viewed in this light, the hostilities and uncertainties among the emerging Czech and Slovak political class are more understandable.

The only extraparty elite cooperation prior to the post-1989 period of democra-tization was the common clandestine activity of a group of dissidents. Yet, this was an activity directed primarily against one common enemy—the communist system, involving only a negligible number of intellectuals, mostly of Czech origin. Gor-don Wightman and Soňa Szomolányi write: "The [Slovak] dissident movement was much less public and limited to small groups of nonconformist individuals . . . who remained relatively isolated from each other and from Czech, Polish and Hungar-ian dissidents."[31] To this should be added that the former communist elite, which could be said to have had a tradition of inter-elite exchange within both the struc-ture of the Communist Party and the communist-dominated state and bureaucratic apparatus, was by and large out of the political process after the events of 1989.

The implication for the postcommunist period was that the new Slovak elites concentrated on their role in the Slovak National Council and government in Bratislava, while the Czech elites were based in Prague, balancing between fed-eral and Czech Republic institutions.[32] A good illustration of this division was the parties' strategies for candidate nomination before the elections. Prior to the 1992 elections, the Slovak parties nominated their top candidates by and large for the Slovak National Council, whereas the Czech parties targeted the Federal Assem-bly. Certainly there were Slovak politicians operating in Prague (so called profed-eral Slovaks) who had previously been in contact with the Czechs, but real diffi-culty arose when the members of the new Slovak elite, such as Vladimír Mečiar, had to bargain on the federal level.

The lack of long-standing mutual exchange was combined with the young political elite's obvious lack of experience in hard negotiations. The fact that the rules of the game were disputed, or not yet internalized into a set of commonly agreed-upon conventions and norms of behavior, meant only that the elite were poorly prepared for managing the critical situation that they had to face. Given the heavy decision-making load, stemming from the simultaneity of political and economic transition, there was little room for any piecemeal process of learning and getting accustomed to each other.

The third aspect relates to *the impact of socioeconomic variables*. The socioeconomic differences between the Czech lands and Slovakia were too large to sustain a common state. When the two areas were united into Czechoslovakia, the Czech lands were an economically advanced region. Its firmly based industrial structure almost single-handedly supplied the Austrian-Hungarian Empire with high-quality products. Slovakia, on the other hand, was traditionally an agricultural society with a very low level of industrial development and urbanization. Because of the lack of any plan to restructure the Slovak economy in the First Republic, the major differences in economic structures persisted in the communist era.

The implementation of the communist economy had one major aim: to decrease the macrostructural differences between the two regions. The result of the economic policies on the industrialization of Slovakia was that the Czech and Slovak societies became very similar in macroeconomic terms. However, the application of the unifying Soviet model, driven by strategic and military reasons, bore all the hallmarks of the distortions of a centrally planned economy from its very foundation. The communists grafted heavy industries (in particular armament) onto the largely rural-based Slovak economy. By creating large locations dependent on the functioning of one colossal enterprise, they gave birth to an almost immobile economic structure with relatively outdated production. Moreover, such an industrial structure produced a kind of dependence where one part of the country (Slovak) served as the basis of subcontractual production finalized and serviced in the other part (Czech).

With the end of redistributive economic measures through the state budget and without the subsidies to inefficient enterprises, which accounted for the optimistic picture concerning the "same" level of development in the two regions, large parts of these industries virtually collapsed in postcommunist Czechoslovakia. These key disadvantages in the structure of the Slovak economy are the main reasons behind the steeper decline in production and higher rate of unemployment in Slovakia compared to the Czech lands after the revolution. Given the industrial structure, some parts of Slovakia were, and still are, hopelessly bedeviled by social and economic problems, which provide a gloomy prospect for decisive improvement in the foreseeable future.

One result of these increasing socioeconomic differences between the two regions in the postcommunist period was the reinforcement of national identities. The emerging market/redistributive issue did not cut across the Czech and Slovak political space but tended to divide it even more than did the state arrangement alone. Not only were the Slovaks and their representatives dissatisfied with the form of the state, but they also felt that the share of material resources was unequal. The Czechs were blamed by Slovaks for holding the disposable resources in the Czech lands, whereas the Slovak region was seen in the Czech lands as a bottomless pit for dumping hard-earned national wealth. The material inequality between the two nations provided an additional competitive impetus and made eventual agreements between the two republics more difficult to achieve. Consequentially, economic inequality provided extra ground for national mobilization in Slovakia.

It appears from this inventory, then, that at least the last two factors above—the lack of a tradition of elite accommodation and the large socioeconomic differences among the Czechs and Slovaks—undermine two of nine background conditions considered by Lijphart to be favorable to the maintenance of consociational democracy. Moreover, it can be argued that at least four of the remaining seven did not fare any better by 1992:

1. It seemed that many Czech and Slovak political leaders did not show the kind of overarching loyalty to the federation that would weaken the growing strength of particularistic tendencies. A national sentiment called "Czechoslovakism" was appealing perhaps to the Czechs. In Slovakia it always symbolized an attempt at assimilation, Czech chauvinism, or an empty term derived from the optimism of some of the post-World War I Czech and Slovak intellectuals and politicians. As a result, for many Czech and Slovak postcommunist leaders, especially the new elite, the debate was more about whether Czechoslovakia should be one country at all, rather than about what would be the best way to run it.

2. In terms of population, the Czechs formed a solid two-thirds majority compared to one-third for the Slovaks. The jockeying on a more majoritarian decision-making procedure favoring the Czechs was present ever since the existence of the common state and even more so during the turmoil of the transition from authoritarian rule. As argued above, the Czechs were dissatisfied with the institutional structure, and it was largely the Czech elite that was focused on introducing a more majoritarian (in their perception more efficient) structure of institutions.

3. There were no external dangers in the post-1989 period that could have united the two nations. Such dangers disappeared with the fall of the Austrion–Hungarian Empire, and even the danger of German occupation in 1938 did not compel the two nations to joint resistance, despite the fact that they were at that time living in a common state. In the postcommunist circumstances, a threat from the Soviet Union was no longer urgent and the Western international community supported democratic changes as well as, in the end, the partition of the country.

4. Although the total population of the country was relatively small (15 million), and hence the leaders could know each other very well, we saw that as a distinct legacy of the communist regime, the postcommunist elite was not particularly characterized by long-standing mutual exchange.

In the end, therefore, only three out of Lijphart's nine conditions could be said to favor the maintenance of the Czechoslovak federal system: (1) the population disparity (imbalance of power) between the two groups was sufficiently responded to by a deliberate overrepresentation of Slovaks on the federal level; (2) the groups were geographically concentrated, so that a territorially based federation could be established, and (3) the negotiations did not involve an excessive number of groups. Given the other conditions in postcommunist Czechoslovakia, these three favorable aspects could hardly have resulted in the maintenance of the consociational system. The irresistible impression one gets from the three years that culminated in partition is that consociational devices, under such difficult conditions, turned out to be dysfunctional and exacerbated the Czech–Slovak dispute.

However, power-sharing mechanisms are not simply important (if not always successful) means for solving problems in an internally segmented country. On the contrary, and somewhat ironically, they can also function as a final remedy to irreconcilable differences by facilitating the peaceful division of the country. This is exactly what happened in the former Czechoslovakia. The three favorable factors mentioned above—the overrepresentation of Slovaks, the limited number of negotiators (particularly after the 1992 elections), and the geographical separation of Czechs and Slovaks—combined to play a positive role in the peaceful character of the Czechoslovak separation.

First (as shown in the previous section), the need to redress the permanent imbalance between Czechs and Slovaks resulted in the creation of a power-sharing system, one that overrepresented Slovaks on the federal level, establishing a system that relied on a dual balance of power. Neither Klaus and Mečiar alone, nor both of them together, possessed a majority and a mandate that would have allowed them to carry on with a partition unilaterally. They had to build a larger consensus with other parties, on whose support they had to rely to push through the vote on dissolution. Focusing on institutions, David Olson raises the point that while such an elaborated structure of federal institutions was used to encourage regional separation, it nevertheless helped to accomplish a negotiated settlement.[33] Indeed, the impressively legalistic manner in which the dissolution was carried out—the agreement to form a federal government to divide the state, followed by a number of agreements to divide the assets of the state, as well as an agreement on coordinated steps for accomplishing the division in legal fashion—was possible, at least in part, precisely because of the integrative and inclusive nature of existing consociational procedures.

Second, the great advantage of the process of partition in Czechoslovakia was the small number of negotiating parties involved. This proved advantageous on two levels. During the negotiations between Klaus and Mečiar after the 1992 elections, there were only two leaders and their political parties behind the closed doors. The discussions were therefore not overburdened by a wide variety of conflicting demands and interests. Furthermore, and in close relation to the favorable conditions mentioned above, the decision to disintegrate was going to affect only the two ethnic groups that were parties to the negotiations; therefore, there was no concern with eventual consequences of the agreements for third parties. This differs, for example, from the republics of the former Yugoslavia and those of the former Soviet Union, since in those two federal states, the leaders of the center were extremely concerned with the eventual snowball effect on other federal units, should they grant sovereignty to one of those entities demanding it. In contrast, the concerns of the Czech and Slovak leaders about the eventual effects of the split on the regionalist claims made by the Moravian groups in the Czech Republic and autonomist demands of the Hungarian minority in the Slovak Republic were negligible.

The final perhaps most crucial point is that the geographical concentration of Czechs and Slovaks and their neat separation from each other rendered partition quite easy. This autonomy was reinforced and cultivated by the existing consociational devices. Unlike, for example, in Bosnia and Herzegovina, Croatia, or even the Baltic republics, where ethnic segmental groups have been geographically intermingled, the split of Czechoslovakia involved by and large only the division of common material assets. The relatively few Czech citizens living in Slovakia and Slovaks living in the Czech lands were given a choice of the citizenship in one of the two new republics, thereby decreasing the potential insecurity of living in a new nation-state. Thus, while the separation of the Czechs and Slovaks might have provided for territorially based federal autonomy, it also made complete partition a viable alternative.

CONCLUSION

Crucial for the failure of the Czechoslovak power-sharing system was that it had to function under a set of extremely unfavorable conditions. Six out of nine of the background conditions identified by Lijphart as favoring the stability of any consociational democracy did not pertain to the former Czechoslovakia. There was no strong tradition of elite accommodation and compromise; hardly any overarching loyalties to the federal system; no single external threat forcing the Czechs and Slovaks to unity; the Czechs possessed a stable two-thirds majority creating the predominant group; the alternative elites were not well-known and accustomed to each other; the socioeconomic differences between the two regions were large and rapidly widening. Furthermore, in the absence of other relevant collective identities, which could have helped to close the electoral market, elite mobilization of the masses along national lines, especially in Slovakia, provided fertile and easy ground for political exploitation. The form of mobilization also inhibited the creation of new political institutions for a common state.

Given these circumstances, it is perhaps not surprising that the federation broke down. Its political elites did not have incentives to compromise but rather to perpetuate the conflict. Instead of a coalescent pattern of elite behavior, a competitive pattern became dominant. In turn, the issue of coexistence between the two nations in a common state swiftly evolved from a symbolic debate about the name of the state into an impasse over the form the state should take. Consistent with consociational theory, these combined factors seem to provide a better explanation than simply blaming an immobile and complicated institutional structure for the failure of power sharing in Czechoslovakia. The power-sharing mechanism would have provided an acceptable institutional framework for ameliorating the disputes between the Czechs and Slovaks if it had been accompanied by and fostered accommodative elite behavior.

However, and crucially, the case of the failed Czechoslovak federation strongly suggests that without a minimal prior level of consensus on the maintenance of the system, the institutions alone will not preserve it. Consociational institutions, if they are to secure a stable democracy in a segmented society, should be an embodiment of the existing will of the elite to compromise and to arrive at an acceptable solution. If the institutions are enforced or, as in the case of the Czechoslovak federation, inherited, they are more likely to frustrate the actors and exacerbate the conflict by providing opportunities for what one might term the misconduct of politics. Ironically, it was the same consociational inheritance, disliked and criticized as it was, that rendered the partition of Czechoslovakia peaceful.

NOTES

1. This is a revised version of a paper first presented at the COVICO and IPSA/SOG conference on Ethnonational Cleavages and Viable Constitutionalism, University of Hawaii, Honolulu, 5–8 January 1995. I would like to thank Tim Bale, Koen Koch, Kevin Krause, Arend Lijphart, Cas Mudde, Fred W. Riggs, and the editors of this volume for helpful comments on earlier drafts.

2. For a historical overview, see Victor S. Mamatey and Radomír Luža (eds.), *A History of the Czechoslovak Republic 1918–1948* (Princeton: Princeton University Press, 1973). For the postcommunist period see Zora Bútorová, "Premyslené 'ano' zániku ČSFR?" *Sociologický Časopis*, 29(1), 1993: 88–103; Vladimír Krivý , "Slovenská a česká definícia situace," *Sociologický Časopis*, 29(1), 1993; Petr Machonin, " Česko-Slovenské vztahy ve světle dat sociologického výzkumu," in Fedor Gál et al. (eds.), *Dnešní Krize Česko-Slovenských Vztahů* (Praha: Slon, 1992) 73–87; and Darina Malová, "Effect of Cultural Factors on the Promotion of the Relations of the Czech and Slovaks," in Dušan Kováč (ed.), *History and Politics,* (Bratislava: Czecho–Slovak Committee of the European Cultural Foundation, 1993) 129–134.

3. See Arend Lijphart, *Democracy in Plural Societies: A Comparative Exploration* (New Haven: Yale University Press, 1977).

4. See Kurt R. Luther and Wolfgang C. Müller (eds.), *Politics in Austria: Still the Case of Consociationalism?* (London: Frank Cass, 1992).

5. See Hans Daalder and Galen A. Irwin (eds.), *Politics in the Netherlands: How Much Change?* (London: Frank Cass, 1989).

6. See Lijphart, *Democracy in Plural Societies.*

7. See Arend Lijphart, "The Puzzle of Indian Democracy: A Consociational Interpretation," *American Political Science Review*, 90(2), 1996:258–268.

8. See Wolf Linder, *Swiss Democracy: Possible Solutions to Conflict in Multicultural Societies* (New York: St. Martin's Press, 1994).

9. Lijphart, *Democracy in Plural Societies,* 53. In this respect, consociationalism complements many general theories on ethnonational conflicts, which argue that the existence and behavior of a mobilizing elite, interpreting given grievances and social tensions and formulating them into political issues are of decisive importance. For a fuller discussion see Alexis Heraclides, *The Self-Determination of Minorities in International Politics* (Exeter: Frank Cass, 1991).

10. The erosion of a consociational democracy does not necessarily mean that it failed. On the contrary, a fundamental transformation of political values, urbanization, secularization, and deideologization, which undermine subcultural cohesion and in turn lead to the transformation of the whole (consociational) political system into a more pluralist and majoritarian system, can be seen as the very success of consociational democracy. The system simply becomes redundant after it helps to accommodate the conflict for which it was instituted.

11. See Arend Lijphart, *Power Sharing in South Africa* (Berkeley: Institute of International Studies, 1985), and also Lijphart, "The Puzzle of Indian Democracy," pp. 258–268.

12. For a similar classification, see Arend Lijphart, "Democratization and Constitutional Choices in Czecho–Slovakia, Hungary and Poland 1989–1991," *Journal of Theoretical Politics*, 4(2), 1992:207–223; and Karen Henderson, "Czechoslovakia: The Failure of Consensus Politics," *Regional and Federal Studies*, 5(2), 1993:111–133.

13. For a fuller discussion on the extent of Slovak autonomy in the First Republic, see Eva Broklová, "Češi a Slováci 1918–1938," *Sociologický Časopis*, 29(1), 1993:25–42; and Joseph Rothschild, *East Central Europe between the Two World Wars* (Seattle: University of Washington Press, 1992). For an overview of institutional developments until the 1980s, see Carol Skalnik Leff, *National Conflict in Czechoslovakia: The Making and Remaking of a State, 1918–1987* (Princeton: Princeton University Press, 1988).

14. One could argue, therefore, that Czechoslovakia was an example of a consociational system of institutions already before 1989, but I take it that to speak of a consociational system in a meaningful way is also to speak of a democracy.

15. See Jon Elster, "Transition, Constitution-Making and Separation of Czechoslovakia," *European Journal of Sociology*, 36, 1995:109.

16. For a fuller discussion on the reasons that led to the adoption of the 1968 constitution, see the chapter by Allison Stanger in this volume and Zdeněk Jičínský, *Československý parlament v polistopadovém vývoji* (Praha: NADAS-AFGH, 1993).

17. It is worth noting that with Belgium in mind, there were public discussions to reform the Czechoslovak federation by including Moravia (one of the historical regions) as a third member in order to curb the inherent instability involved in bargaining between only two subjects. However, as Elster ("Transition," 109) correctly asserts, because Moravia and Slovakia had hardly any interests in common, the smaller republics would have aligned so as to reconstitute the Czech–Slovak divide.

18. See Jana Reschová, "Parliaments and Constitutional Change: The Czechoslovak Experience," in Attila Ágh (ed.), *The Emergence of East Central European Parliaments: The First Steps* (Budapest: Hungarian Centre of Democracy Studies Foundation, 1994); and Elster, "Transition."

19. See David M. Olson, "The New Parliaments of New Democracies: The Experience of the Federal Assembly of the Czech and Slovak Federal Republic," in *The Emergence of East Central European Parliaments: The First Steps*, ed. Attila Ágh (Budapest: Hungarian Centre of Democracy Studies Foundation, 1994).

20. For such critical arguments, see Katherina Mathernova, "Czecho?Slovakia: Constitutional Disappointments," in A.E.D. Howard (ed.), *Constitution Making in Eastern Europe* (Washington: Woodrow Wilson Center Press, 1993); and David M. Olson, "Dissolution of the State: Political Parties and the 1992 Election in Czechoslovakia," *Communist and Post-Communist Studies*, 26(3), 1993:301–314.

21. Note that most of the constitutional proposals came from the Czech side. For example, majoritarian devices were included in several constitutional proposals of President Václav Havel, which were rejected by the Federal Assembly in January 1992. The proposals included the presidential right to call referenda, to dissolve parliament in the case of stalemate, to rule by decree prior to new elections, and also his proposals to change the existing PR electoral system.

22. For a review of popular preferences concerning the dissolution of the federation, see Jens Bastian, "From the Separation of Names: Czecho-Slovakia to the Velvet Divorce in 1992," paper presented at the ECPR Joint Sessions, Oslo, 27 March–3 April 1996.

23. See Peter Mair, "What is Different about Post-Communist Party Systems," *Stein Rokkan Memorial Lecture*, University of Bergen, 10 November 1995; and Richard Rose, "Mobilizing Demobilized Voters," *Party Politics*, 1(4), 1995:549–563.

24. See Peter Mair, "Electoral Markets and Stable States," in Michael Moran and Maurice Wright (eds.), *The Market and the State* (London: MacMillan, 1991).

25. The quote is from Barbara Geddes, "A Comparative Perspective on the Leninist Legacy in Eastern Europe," *Comparative Political Studies*, 28(2), 1995:252.

26. In a very stimulating essay, Frye pinpoints a number of reasons why class and religion, as opposed to ethnicity, could not easily become sources of popular mobilization in the Soviet Union, Czechoslovakia, and Yugoslavia. See Timothy M. Frye, "Ethnicity, Sovereignty and Transitions from Non-Democratic Rule," *Journal of International Affairs*, 45(2), 1992:599–623.

27. See Jan Zielonka, "New Institutions in the Old East Block," *Journal of Democracy*, 5(2), 1994:87–104.

28. Note that the only Slovak party with a relatively stable platform was the Slovak National Party, which consistently advocated full national independence, but even this party before the 1990 elections favored a confederal model.

29. Note that when Vladimír Mečiar, nominated by the Public Against Violence movement, became the prime minister of the Slovak government at the end of 1990, he favored a federal Czechoslovakia. Half a year later, he instead emphasized national principles and the importance of Slovakia's individuality. In 1991, when he was dismissed from the government and formed his Movement for a Democratic Slovakia, he largely abandoned the principle of federation. In 1992, Mečiar's party won the elections with a program to declare Slovakia's own sovereignty and full international subjectivity (while remaining within the Czechoslovak federation), thus substituting the previous federalist conviction with a drift toward some sort of confederation.

30. The most salient issues in the Czech lands were the character of the economic reforms and the communist/anticommunist debate on who was responsible for the last forty years and how to settle accounts with the past. Thus, while political discourse in the Czech

Republic provided a relatively simple left–right duality—something that has continued to shape the party system in the Czech Republic even after the split—the main dividing line in Slovakia was between nationalists and federalists, a divide that also continues, albeit in a different form, to shape the party system in the independent Slovak Republic.

31. The quote is from Gordon Wightman and Soňa Szomolányi, "Parties and Society in Slovakia," *Party Politics*, 1(4), 1995:615.

32. See Henderson, "Czechoslovakia: The Failure of Consensus Polities," 111–133.

33. See David M. Olson, "The Sundered State: Federalism and Parliament in Czechoslovakia," in Thomas Remington (ed.), *Parliaments in Transition* (Boulder, Colo.: Westview Press, 1994).

5

The Impact of Institutional Factors on the Breakup of the Czechoslovak Federation

Sharon Wolchik

The peaceful breakup of the Czechoslovak federation has been the subject of a good deal of analysis by scholars. Politicians and other activists who were involved in political life in the Czech lands and Slovakia between 1989 and 1993 have also shared their perspectives on this issue. As their analyses indicate, the breakup of the Czechoslovak federation reflected the influence of a variety of historical, economic, political, social, and psychological factors in the Czech lands and Slovakia. It also was influenced by the actions of outside actors.

The relative importance given to historical, economic, social, and political factors in accounting for the breakup of the common state differs in these treatments. One of the most evident areas of disagreement in the literature on the breakup centers on the issue of its inevitability, given the way in which Czechs and Slovaks came to be part of a common state at the beginning of this century and given the development of Slovak nationalism. Analysts also disagree on the weight they give to economic compared to political factors and to the responsibility of leaders and citizens.[1]

In earlier discussions, I have examined at some length the role of these and other factors, including the legacy of the precommunist and earlier periods, the different impact of the communist era in the Czech lands and Slovakia, and the impact of the particular conditions of political life in Czechoslovakia during the early years of the transition from communist rule. The purpose of this chapter is not to retrace this ground. Rather, it is to examine some of the less commonly appreciated factors that contributed to two important aspects of the breakup: first, the election of political leaders in Slovakia who came to support Slovak independence and the willingness of Czech leaders to agree to the breakup of the state. Second, after a brief look at the ways in which the Czechoslovak case compares to other examples of state breakup, I examine the development of Slovak nationalism and the institutional structure of the federation. As my discussion illustrates, the institutional structure that existed in Czechoslovakia was one of the primary factors that led to the rapid politicization of ethnicity in the wake of the collapse of communism in 1989. The institutional structure of the federation, as well as economic and social differences between the two regions, also conditioned the decision of Czech leaders to allow Slovakia to break away peacefully. My discussion also considers the implications of the way in which the common state broke up for state building in the new Czech and Slovak republics.

DEFINITION OF THE PROBLEM:
SECESSION, FRAGMENTATION, OR SOMETHING ELSE?

Efforts to understand the demise of all three federative communist states (Czechoslovakia, Yugoslavia, and the USSR) have been guided by a variety of theoretical perspectives. Mark Beissinger, for example, has argued that the breakup of the USSR involved both decolonization and secession, resulting from the failure of the Soviet state.[2] Michael Hechter, by way of contrast, has argued that the creation of independent states in the communist world has occurred largely as a result of fragmentation of host states rather than true secession.[3]

The dissolution of Czechoslovakia does not fit very well into any of these categories. Few would argue, for example, that the Czechs' relationship to Slovakia should properly be seen as imperial. Similarly, there is little evidence of the high degree of popular mobilization in support of the breakup of the state that viewing the end of the federation as the outcome of a process of secession would seem to require.[4] Although nationalist parties were active in Slovakia between 1989 and 1993, relatively few people in Slovakia supported the breakup of the state prior to its occurrence.

It is also difficult to portray the demise of the federation as a reflection of a process of state breakdown. As in other formerly communist states, the Czechoslovak state after 1989 faced a multitude of serious challenges and demanding tasks.[5] These challenges were compounded by the impact of economic reform on the population, as well as by the social and psychological impact of both communist rule and the transition from communism.[6] However, although it eventually proved impossible to resolve the political conflict between Czechs and Slovaks within the framework of the state, state organizations and officials continued to function relatively smoothly in Czechoslovakia up to the end of the state itself. The political system was influenced by the unusual circumstances of the transition, to be sure, but there was nothing like the decline in public authority and functioning of state structures that characterized the last years of the USSR. Nor, in contrast to the situation in Yugoslavia on the eve of its dissolution, were there significant groups that openly defied the authority of federal institutions.

In addition to the fact that it occurred peacefully, then, the breakup of Czechoslovakia also differs from that of other formerly communist states in the nature of the process that brought it about. Although many features of this process are similar to those that existed in other cases, there are also important differences that help to explain the ways in which the outcome in Czechoslovakia differed from that which occurred elsewhere.

One of the most important of these was the extent to which decisions about the future of the state were successfully confined to the elite level. Another was the nature of the conflict between the main ethnic groups in the state. In regard to the first issue, it is clear that ethnic cleavages had become very salient politically. As the section to follow will argue in greater detail, this salience was related to the ability of political elites to mobilize citizens around ethnic aims in the postcommunist period. As in other contexts, elite articulations of ethnic aims were also conditioned by mass responses. Although most Slovaks as well as Czechs continued to oppose the breakup of the state even as Václav Klaus and Vladimír Mečiar negotiated its end, significant portions of the Slovak electorate voted for political leaders who were advocates either of Slovak independence or of a radically revised position for Slovakia within the common state. However, the level of mass mobilization around separatist aims did not reach the level it did in the Baltic states prior to the breakup of the Soviet Union, nor did people in Slovakia or the Czech lands support armed intervention either to protect their independence or to recover territory and ensure the rights of fellow ethnic group members, as in Yugoslavia.[7]

Part of the explanation for these differences lies in the nature of the problem that brought about the end of the federal state in the three cases. As in the Soviet Union and Yugoslavia, the breakup of Czechoslovakia was intimately related to the country's ethnic composition. A multiethnic state that incorporated sizeable Hungarian and Roma communities as well as smaller Ruthenian/Ukrainian, Polish, and German minorities, Czechoslovakia's primary ethnic conflict was between Czechs and Slovaks. Political leaders thus faced a simpler task than that of dealing with the demands and perspectives of several important dissatisfied ethnic groups as in Yugoslavia and the Soviet Union.

As numerous analyses of the breakup of the federation have noted, there were important differences in the historical experiences, social structures, political traditions, and levels of economic development of Czechs and Slovaks.[8] Due in large part to the fact that the two regions were part of different larger states for nearly a thousand years prior to their unification in 1918, these differences were evident in the political traditions and opportunities for the development of a national movement in the two regions, as well as in their social structures and levels of economic development. Despite the efforts of the interwar elite to industrialize Slovakia and create a unified political culture, the experiences of the two regions continued to be very different in the period between the two world wars.

Slovak resentment over what was perceived to be Czech domination, together with the stagnation of living standards and the growing gap in development levels between the Czech lands and Slovakia, provided fuel for Slovak nationalist political leaders.[9] Many Slovaks saw the creation in 1939 of a pseudoindependent Slovak state that in reality had little real freedom to achieve national goals. When the two groups were brought back together in a common state, the legacy of this state remained a contentious issue.[10]

The forty-one years of communist rule saw a reduction of certain differences between the two regions. In contrast to the experiences of Yugoslavia and interwar Czechoslovakia, the development gap between Slovakia and the Czech lands decreased significantly under communism.[11] However, the legacy of communism, while decreasing certain differences between the two regions, exacerbated others. Even the decline in economic differences had consequences that proved problematic in the postcommunist period, because the fact that most of Slovakia's industrialization took place under communism meant that the economic reforms enacted after 1989 led to much greater hardship in Slovakia.[12] Similarly, both Czechs and Slovaks suffered from the inability to articulate grievances and openly discuss problems that prevailed in Czechoslovakia under communist rule due to the party's control of political life and the media. However, in Slovakia, with the exception of a brief period of reform in the mid- to late 1960s, these restrictions prevented the open articulation of dissatisfaction arising from ethnic as well as other issues.[13]

As I have argued in greater detail elsewhere, these differences in the impact of the communist period in Slovakia and the Czech lands were reflected in turn in the differing views of Czechs and Slovaks on issues related to economic reform, the role and form of the state, and the role of citizens in the postcommunist period.[14] Nonetheless, although Czechs and Slovaks differed in important ways, these differences were not as great as those that separated the various nationalities of the USSR or Yugoslavia.

Both the smaller number of groups involved and the relatively smaller differences that divided the two groups proved to be important to the way the common state ended. In the first instance, it was simply easier for Czech and Slovak leaders to agree on a strategy to end their common state than it was for leaders in Yugoslavia or the USSR. The relatively smaller differences that divided the two groups, together with the fact that neither national group had committed large-scale atrocities against the other, also contributed to the ability of political elites to contain conflict over ethnic issues to the elite level.

SLOVAK NATIONALISM: FRUIT OF A DELAYED NATIONAL MOVEMENT?

The ability of Slovak leaders to make ethnic issues politically salient is one of the fundamental points that must be examined in order to understand the breakup of the Czechoslovak federation. Both institutional and political factors and economic factors influenced this process. Prior to the creation of the Czechoslovak Republic in 1918, conditions for the development of a Slovak national movement were very poor. Part of Hungary for nearly one thousand years, Slovakia developed a culture and identity in connection with and in juxtaposition to Magyar culture and institutions. Particularly in the second half of the nineteenth century, Slovaks were subjected to intense pressure to give up their ethnic identity and assimilate with the dominant Magyar nationality. It was very difficult for Slovak children to be educated in Slovak schools or for Slovak intellectuals to publish in Slovak. In contrast to the situation in the Czech lands, where Austrian authorities' demands for autonomy gradually increased the role of local-level organizations and allowed Czech national organizations to grow, and where Czech deputies played an active role in the parliament in Vienna, Hungarian authorities made it very difficult for Slovak national organizations and movements to develop. Electoral restrictions also prevented most Slovaks from participating in public life.

For these reasons, the efforts of Slovak intellectuals to raise national awareness in the seventeenth and eighteenth centuries and to develop a national organization in the nineteenth and early twentieth centuries did not succeed in creating a national mass movement of Slovaks.[15] The nature of Slovak society also hindered efforts to create a national movement. Overwhelmingly agrarian, Slovaks were poorly educated. Levels of illiteracy were fairly high into the early part of the twentieth century. Dispersed in villages and smaller towns, most Slovaks were also difficult to mobilize politically.[16]

With the demise of the Austro-Hungarian Empire and the creation of the interwar Czechoslovak Republic, Slovak leaders were able, for the first time, to openly articulate national aims and organize the population politically to promote these aims. Although the Czechoslovak state was a unitary state, its democratic nature allowed the formulation of ethnically based political parties across the political spectrum. Associational life also flourished in Slovakia during this period.[17]

As the interwar period progressed, extreme nationalist political parties came to dominate political life in Slovakia as in the Sudetenland. In both cases, though for different reasons, political leaders succeeded in articulating popular grievances against the dominant Czech majority and mobilizing the electorate around ethnic issues.

Given the low levels of urbanization and literacy of Slovak society, the Catholic clergy became important political as well as spiritual leaders. Although Protestants had been important in the earlier efforts to develop Slovak national consciousness, in the interwar period, it was primarily the political parties affiliated with the Catholic Church that gained popular support.

Efforts to industrialize Slovakia during the interwar period failed, in part as a result of the Great Depression. The impact of the depression, which also created substantial hardship in the Czech lands, was particularly severe in Slovakia and led to large-scale emigration. The Czechoslovak economy recovered somewhat in the mid-1930s, but at the end of the interwar period, Slovakia's level of development was still far lower than that of the Czech lands.[18]

However, economic trends masked other changes that occurred during this period. These were especially noticeable in the area of education, where there was a substantial decrease in illiteracy, particularly among Slovaks, and the creation of a national intelligentsia. The expansion of educational opportunities and the end of restrictions on the press also allowed Slovak intellectuals to reach a much broader audience than in the period prior to 1918. The impact of these educational changes, together with the fact that Slovakia also became more urbanized during the interwar period, was to create resources that Slovak elites could use in the political realm. However, given the fact that most Slovaks still resided in rural areas, the form of nationalism that developed was not a middle-class nationalism centered in the cities but rather a peasant nationalism whose main centers of support were in rural areas of central and western Slovakia.[19]

The failure of efforts to industrialize Slovakia and the great hardship that existed in the country fueled support for extreme nationalist movements. The fact that the state bureaucracy was staffed largely by Czechs also reinforced the perception that it was Czechs rather than Slovaks who benefited from the new state and that Slovaks had merely exchanged the domination of Hungarians for that of Czechs.

As the interwar period progressed, relations between Czechs and Slovaks deteriorated. Demands for autonomy came to replace those of earlier moderate Slovak leaders for cooperation with the Czechs. These demands were expressed most stridently by the Slovak People's Party, led by Father Andrej Hlinka and later by Josef Tiso. Influenced by developments in Germany and the extremist views of Slovak nationalists such as Vojtech Tuka, the activities of this party paved the way for the establishment of a pseudoindependent Slovak state in 1939 under Hitler's tutelage. Reestablished in November 1918, the Christian Slovak People's Party gained the support of groups dissatisfied with the Czechoslovak state. These included many of the Catholic clergy who had originally supported the creation of Czechoslovakia. Faced with the threat to traditional, conservative values by the liberal ideas of the more secular Czechs, including those who came to Slovakia to staff the local administration and educational institutions after 1918, and frustrated by the anticlerical stance of the Czechoslovak state, many Catholic priests supported the party and brought their parishioners with them. Renamed the Hlinka Slovak People's Party in 1925, the party also drew support from Magyarized Slovaks whose newly discovered Slovak patriotism took the form of a virulent hatred of Czechs and the Czechoslovak state.[20] The party's defense of traditional Catholic values came to be reflected in increasingly virulent anti-Semitism.

The party's popularity grew as economic conditions deteriorated in Slovakia. Thus, the party gained 17.6 percent of the vote in Slovakia in the 1920 elections, compared to 45.2 percent for the Social Democratic Party. In 1923, the party obtained its highest share of the popular vote, 34 percent, and became the strongest political party in Slovakia. Known popularly as the "Ludaks" from the Slovak name of the party, Hlinka's party gained 28.2 percent of the vote in 1929 and 30.1 percent in 1935.[21] In the early years, the leaders of the People's Party professed their loyalty to the Czechoslovak state, even as they called for autonomy within it. By the late 1930s, more extremist elements with well-established contacts with fascist groups in Germany and Italy came to dominate the party.[22]

These groups moved quickly to take advantage of the situation created by the Munich ultimatum of 1938. At a 6 October meeting in Žilina, the Hlinka party forced the acceptance of the so-called Žilina agreement, calling for Slovak autonomy. In November 1938, the parliament in Prague passed a bill granting Slovakia autonomy. The so-called Second Republic of Czecho-Slovakia established at this time granted substantial power to Slovak governmental organs. These powers were formally increased in March 1939, when a separate Slovak state was created.

The creation of a separate Slovak state in March 1939 is one of the most controversial issues in Slovak history. Apologists and critics alike note the choice Slovak leaders faced between declaring their independence and being invaded. Both groups also note that, for many Slovaks, the creation of an independent Slovak state represented the fulfillment of their national aspirations, despite the way in which it was created and the limitations on the actions of its leaders. Finally, most analysts agree that the experience of having their own state, however circumscribed its powers and whatever the conditions under which it was formed, contributed to state building in Slovakia. Perhaps most important it created expectations concerning autonomy or parity for Slovakia that were disappointed by the re-creation of a unitary Czechoslovak state in 1945 and the gradual erosion of the power of Slovak national organs in the post-World War II period as the Stalinist system was consolidated in Czechoslovakia.[23]

The impact of modernization in Slovakia in the interwar period, then, allowed Slovak leaders to achieve what they had been unable to develop previously, a mass political movement.[24] However, although this movement succeeded in putting ethnic issues onto the agenda, it was not sufficient by itself to achieve the goal of Slovak independence. Rather, that step occurred as the result of intervention by an outside power: in this case, Nazi Germany.

The reunification of the Czech lands and Slovakia after the liberation of the country in May 1945 raised new questions about Slovakia's status in the common state. The Košice government program, which was the basis of the re-created state, included guarantees of Slovak autonomy and envisioned a sizeable decision-making role for Slovak national organs. However, these provisions were soon ignored, as Czechoslovakia experienced the consolidation of a Stalinist system and the impact of the purges and show trials in the late 1940s and 1950s. A disproportionate number of Slovak communist party leaders were victims of the purges; many were charged with bourgeois nationalism. The imposition of strict censorship, the institution of a one-party regime in which the Communist Party controlled political life, and a coercive system made it very difficult once again for Slovak elites to articulate their perspectives or work to change the unitary mechanism of the state.

It was only in the context of the reform era of the 1960s that Slovak leaders were able to once again mobilize the population around ethnic issues. Slovak efforts to gain a better position in the state were major factors that contributed to the reform movement that culminated in the Prague Spring. This process, which occurred first on the elite level among party-affiliated intellectuals and party leaders, spread in 1968 to ordinary citizens. Slovak national organizations (such as the *Matica Slovenska*, which had been outlawed) were revived, and Slovak leaders succeeded in bringing about a reform in the structure of the state. Slovak calls for the adoption of a federal system reflected the general intellectual ferment of the mid- to late 1960s in Czechoslovakia. They also reflected continued Slovak frustration at the inequalities in levels of development and living standards that existed in Czechoslovakia, despite disproportionate investment in Slovakia during the communist period and the substantial decrease in the gap between the two regions.

The ability of Slovak leaders to get ethnic issues onto the political agenda in the 1960s reflected the impact of the more successful development that occurred in Slovakia during the communist era. With the rise in educational levels and greater urbanization, as well as dramatic changes in the structure of occupations and concentration of the population in industry rather than agriculture, Slovak leaders had greater resources than those they had possessed in the interwar period to press national aims in the political arena.

The success of Slovak leaders in translating Slovak resentment, national aspirations, and desires for better treatment into political claims was also influenced by the changed political climate, which both allowed new demands to be articulated and limited the nature of those demands. In contrast to the situation in the interwar period, when there were many voices that called for independence rather than merely autonomy for Slovakia, Slovak leaders in the 1960s did not attempt to create support for an independent state. Rather, given the impact of the Soviet Union and Soviet control in fixing borders in the region, they concentrated on bettering Slovakia's position within the framework of federal institutions.

Their success in achieving a change in the framework of the state in part reflected the impact of mass mobilization. Once censorship was effectively stopped, Slovak citizens, as well as those in the Czech lands, became involved in the reform process. Public opinion polls conducted at the time indicate that Slovaks' support of the effort to create "socialism with a human face" rested more on national issues than on the effort to create a more democratic political system.[25] However, because the effort to change the political system in such a way as to give ordinary citizens a greater role in politics was still largely at the discussion stage in 1968, and the move to a true multiparty system in which there could be an organized opposition was explicitly rejected by the reformist Communist Party leadership in Czechoslovakia, the actual role of ordinary citizens in the process by which the federation was adopted was in fact minimal.

Federalization was one of the few elements of the reform project that survived the forcible end of the reform era. The powers of the two republic governments were subsequently reduced, particularly in the economic area. However, they did retain somewhat greater control over areas such as education, social policy, and culture than had been the case previously. Federalization was also important symbolically as a recognition of the validity of Slovak claims for parity in the common state. Because many Slovak party leaders were more involved in national issues than in efforts to democratize political life, the purge of reformists in the party and other areas of life was not as drastic in Slovakia as in the Czech lands. Many Slovak officials were brought to Prague to replace the reformists who had lost their posts and to fill newly created federal positions.

However, despite the change in the nature of the state and Slovak dominance of many of the top positions in the conservative party leadership that oversaw the reversal of the reforms that came to be known as "normalization," many Slovaks continued to be dissatisfied with their status in the joint state. The reimposition of tight political control after 1968 prevented this dissatisfaction from being openly articulated for almost twenty years.

With the slight loosening of the system that accompanied Mikhail Gorbachev's rise to power in the Soviet Union, Slovak intellectuals once again began articulating Slovak grievances. For the most part, this process took place within the framework of elite conferences and small circulation journals. But it also involved, in the late 1980s, the revival of the Slovak cultural organization, *Matica Slovenska*.

When the communist system fell, Slovakia's leaders once again gained a free hand to organize along ethnic lines. The Communist Party of Slovakia was soon joined by a variety of newly created or re-created political parties. Given Slovakia's history—the organization of most political parties on ethnic lines during the precommunist period, and the official division of the country into two republics for the preceding twenty years—it is not surprising that almost all of the newly created or revitalized political organizations formed within rather than across ethnic lines.[26]

The growth of support for the Slovak National Party and Vladimír Mečiar's Movement for Democratic Slovakia, the two main political groups that advocated national interests in Slovakia between 1989 and 1993, reflected the availability of nationalism as an organizing device as well as the political repercussions of the economic, social, and psychological costs of the transition to a market economy in Slovakia and the impact of certain institutional and political factors. One of the more interesting investigations of the sources of support for such parties has recently demonstrated that, although economic hardship (including levels of unemployment three times higher than those in the Czech lands prior to the split) clearly contributed to Slovaks' dissatisfaction with the federation, economic factors are not in fact the best predictor of support for nationalist parties in Slovakia. Support for the Slovak National Party and the Movement for Democratic Slovakia has been highest not in those districts of Slovakia with the highest unemployment rates but rather in those in which support for the Slovak People's Party in the interwar period was highest.[27]

It is tempting, then, to see the dissolution of the Czechoslovak federation as the culmination of a process of national development that had its roots in the early part of this century and, through the impact of successful economic development and changes in the political climate, succeeded in the late twentieth century in attaining its goal. The problem with this interpretation, of course, lies in the fact that, although significant proportions of the population in Slovakia supported parties that advocated Slovak national interests or independence, the end of the state came about not as the result of the actions of Slovak citizens but as the result of elite negotiation.[28] As Miroslav Kusy has written, "In spite of all the nationalistic excesses which appeared in Slovakia after the 1989 revolution . . . Slovakia did not suffer too severely from overexcited nationalistic passions: there were no wounded or dead, no looted shops, and there was no burning of state buildings. Hence, the Slovak nation as a whole remained relatively indifferent towards this movement; nationalism did not become a mass, nationwide movement."[29] Nonetheless, in the post-1989 political climate, leaders such as Mečiar, who eventually negotiated the end of the state with Václav Klaus, derived part of their support from groups who voted for them because they articulated Slovak grievances more effectively than other politicians. Although it was elite actions rather than mass mobilization that ended the common state, mass support of those political leaders as reflected in electoral results allowed them to take such actions.

THE POLITICIZATION OF ETHNICITY:
THE ROLE OF POLITICAL INSTITUTIONS

The role of institutional factors has generally been neglected in discussions of the process that led to the end of the Czechoslovak federation. Allison Stanger's and Petr Kopecký's chapters in this volume examine the impact of these factors. From my perspective, institutional factors were important in three main ways. First, the organization of political power in a federal system for the last twenty years of communist rule provided a structure that reinforced the development of Slovak nationalism. The institutional framework of the state also contributed to the inability of Czech and Slovak leaders to agree on a division of power between the republic and federal governments. Finally, it also affected the decision of Czech leaders to, in effect, allow Slovakia to go its own way, thus affecting the peaceful nature of the split.

In contrast to the situation in the Soviet Union and to Yugoslavia in its early communist period, there was never a serious effort in post-World War II Czechoslovakia to create a supranational Czechoslovak identity. The state that was re-created after the end of World War II was a unitary state. Although it included government bodies in Slovakia, such as the Slovak National Council, that had a good deal of autonomy at the outset, this autonomy was taken away in the course of the Stalinist purges and show trials of the late 1940s and early 1950s. The fact that the leadership reneged on promises made in 1945 to respect Slovakia's autonomy along with the fact that Slovak Communist Party leaders were disproportionately hit by the purges and trials were among the factors that led to support for national aims among party leaders in Slovakia in the mid-1960s and to the adoption of a federal system in the late 1960s. However, even during the period when Slovak national institutions came under strongest attack, there was little effort to create a supranational identity. Rather, Slovaks as well as Czechs were admonished to develop a form of patriotism compatible with socialist internationalism and friendship with the Soviet Union. In effect, both Czech and Slovak nationalism were discouraged.

The particular nature of the federal system that erupted during the communist period in Czechoslovakia was important from a number of perspectives. The powers of the republic-level governments were reduced, particularly in the economic sphere, in the early 1970s. Although the republic governments retained a certain degree of autonomy in the areas of education and culture that was reflected in divergences in the two areas, the federal government was clearly the locus of power. At the same time, however, the retention of the form of the federal structure meant that political life continued to be organized along republic lines in the eyes of the population.

This fact proved to have very important consequences for political life in the postcommunist period. When communist rule was overthrown, political leaders in Slovakia and in the Czech Republic began to breathe life into the existing governmental bodies at the republic level rather than creating new institutions. The repluralization of the country's political and associational life also took place within the framework of the existing federal structure. Thus, although there were several attempts to create political parties and other organizations that cut across republic lines, on the whole, these were not successful. As in the interwar period, Czechoslovakia's newly emerging multiparty system organized voters into groups divided along ethnic as well as other lines.

Most of the multitude of new voluntary associations, professional organizations, and charitable groups also operated only or primarily in one republic. In Slovakia, most interest groups and voluntary organizations were further divided into Slovak and Hungarian ethnic groups. Coupled with the fact that, as in all postcommunist societies, the legacy of central organization of political and associational life meant that many citizens were reluctant to join voluntary organizations of any kind, this separation meant that there were relatively few institutional mechanisms that linked Czechs and Slovaks across the institutional, republic divide.

Intellectuals and professionals clearly had a considerable amount of contact across regional boundaries. Intermarriage and tourism also brought significant numbers of Czechs and Slovaks into contact with each other. Public opinion surveys carried out in Slovakia in 1991 found, for example, that 31 percent of Slovaks had relatives and 57 percent had friends in the Czech lands.[30]

However, there were few institutional mechanisms that facilitated contact between Czechs and Slovaks on a regular basis or in a way that could influence political developments. Coupled with an electoral system organized along republic lines, the lack of such mechanisms meant that it was very easy for political leaders to mobilize voters along ethnic lines and around ethnic grievances. It was also impossible for those in Slovakia who opposed the breakup of the federation to cooperate politically (in the sense of creating an electoral bloc with any chance of seating deputies in parliament) with forces in the Czech Republic who also opposed the breakup.

Given the limited powers of the republic governments, the federal government was also important in other ways. The perceived defects in the federation from the Slovak perspective became one of the main issues of contention between Czech and Slovak leaders. Slovak dissatisfaction with what many perceived to be Slovakia's disadvantaged position within the existing federation also fueled popular support for nationalist movements and politicians in Slovakia after 1989.[31] The inability of Czech and Slovak leaders to agree on a new division of power between the federal and republic governments in turn proved to be an unresolvable stumbling block to the adoption of a new constitution. Originally scheduled to go into effect in October 1991, the new constitution was never adopted.[32]

As a result of this inability of Czech and Slovak elites to agree, political decision making, including the decision to end the federation, took place within the institutional framework set up during the communist era. As Petr Kopečky and Allison Stanger note, certain of the features of this framework, particularly the need to adopt most important legislation by a supermajority of the deputies in both the Czech and Slovak sections of the Chamber of the Nations and the requirement that constitutional amendments be adopted by a supermajority in both houses of parliament, in effect gave the numerically less powerful Slovak leadership a veto over decisions regarding the constitution. Thus, thirty-eight votes in either part of the Chamber of the Nations could block most legislation and thirty-one votes in either could block a constitutional amendment. A three-fifths majority of all deputies in each of the three parts of the Federal Assembly was also required to elect the president of the country and declare war. In some ways, these requirements can be seen as positive features, in that they prevented the adoption of major changes in the country's political structure that a significant minority of its citizens might have felt were detrimental to its interests. However, they also prevented any compromise on a new division of powers.[33]

The retention of this institutional system also had other repercussions. Operating with a constitution that was not originally set up to facilitate democratic decision making, particularly in an ethnically divided society, political leaders lacked clarity concerning procedures for dealing with unusual political events or problems. The issue of the proposed referendum on the future of the common state advocated by Václav Havel as the best means of resolving the issue illustrates the problem. Although supported by President Havel, the holding of a referendum to consider whether the common state should be maintained and if so what form it should take was opposed by many politicians from both the Czech lands and Slovakia, including Václav Klaus and Vladimír Mečiar. Although there clearly were political motives behind these positions, both leaders could base their opposition to a referendum on the fact that there was no constitutional basis for using this method to dissolve the state or resolve the question of its fate. Such legalistic objections did not, of course, deter Klaus and Mečiar from ending the state by a process of elite negotiation after the June 1992 elections, but they did help to rule out the use of other mechanisms that might have led to a different outcome.

The impact of this institutional structure was compounded by the characteristics of transition politics in Czechoslovakia. As in other postcommunist states, the new leaders of Czechoslovakia after 1989 faced multiple challenges with little experience and few resources to meet them. Despite the many important ways in which the interwar political system in Czechoslovakia, and therefore the country's precommunist political culture, differed from that of most other postcommunist states, political life in Czechoslovakia after 1989 displayed many of the same characteristics found in other postcommunist states in the years immediately after the end of communism. Briefly stated, these included a great deal of fluidity in terms of popular preferences and partisan allegiances; the lack of a stable party system capable of linking individuals firmly to the political system and mediating political conflict; new leaders with little experience in electoral politics or the art of compromise required in democracies; and the negative legacy of communist rule on the political values and attitudes of the population.

Coupled with the growing articulation of ethnic demands by Slovak leaders and the need to work within the framework of an institutional structure that facilitated the mobilization of the population along ethnic lines and hindered efforts at compromise, these features also contributed to the breakup of the state. However, it is important to be clear about one issue here: the institutions that failed to be adequate to surmount these difficulties were for the most part not newly created (although they operated in many respects in a very different way after the end of communism) but rather the same institutions that existed before the demise of communism. The situation in Czechoslovakia reflected a classic dilemma in this regard: the decision rules that governed political debate and decision making could not be changed without the adoption of a new constitution. However, it was impossible to adopt a new constitution, given the configuration of political forces in the country and its institutional structure, without a change of decision rules.

In addition to facilitating the political articulation of Slovak ethnic aims, the federal system and the impact of the politics of transition, together with underlying differences in the structure of the Czech and Slovak economies, also influenced the willingness of Czech leaders and citizens to agree to a breakup of the common state. Faced with the prospect of a continuation of conflict over the form of the state and the pace and nature of economic reform that characterized the first three years of the postcommunist period, Václav Klaus and his colleagues in the Czech leadership also had economic as well as political reasons to favor the breakup of the state.

The initial costs of the spilt to the Czech economy were greater than anticipated. But, Klaus's expectation that the Czech Republic—if freed of the need to compromise on economic policy with the Slovak leadership and of the need to absorb the cost of retooling Slovakia's inefficient heavy industry—would flourish appeared to be borne out by economic developments between 1993 and 1996. The Czech economic miracle has been called into question by the financial crisis that came into the open in the spring of 1997, and the Slovak economy has performed far better than expected. However, the contrast between the Czech Republic's inclusion among the first six countries invited to discuss membership in the EU and its invitation to be one of the first three formerly communist countries to join NATO, and the fact that Slovakia was not invited in either case, is still a telling one.

The impact of the June 1992 elections on mass as well as elite opinion regarding the wisdom of maintaining the federation is important in understanding Klaus's actions. The first real opportunity for the Slovak public to vote on the policies articulated by Vladimír Mečiar's Movement for a Democratic Slovakia showed that the largest number of Slovaks favored parties that had either cast doubt on the validity of the federation or called openly for its demise. Although most Czechs continued to oppose the breakup of the common state, the proportion of those favoring separation increased after these elections. Many Czechs, while still opposing the split, also came to feel that Slovaks should be given their chance to be independent if they were not happy within the framework of a joint Czech and Slovak state.[34] This shift in public opinion, as well as the less easily documented but important shift in the opinion of Czech intellectuals, paved the way for Klaus to begin negotiating the end of the federation.

The fact that the country was already organized into republics made this choice easier. Rather than being faced with the need to create new divisions and institutions, Czech and Slovak leaders could readily turn to the already existing republic bodies to organize political life in each region. The concentration of the population into what were for the most part mutually exclusive areas rather than ethnically mixed regions, of course, made this choice easier as well. In contrast to the situation in Yugoslavia or in parts of the former Soviet Union, the Czech leadership could agree to the breakup of the federation without stranding sizeable numbers of ethnic Czechs in Slovakia.[35]

CONCLUSIONS: NATIONALISM, INSTITUTIONS, THE "VELVET DIVORCE," AND STATE BUILDING IN THE CZECH REPUBLIC AND SLOVAKIA

As the preceding pages have demonstrated, both the development of Slovak nationalism and the institutional structure of the Czechoslovak federation contributed to the breakup of the state. These factors interacted with each other. Changes in levels of modernization and political structures allowed Slovak leaders to use ethnic identification and grievances as political tools once political life was repluralized. The institutional structure of the Czechoslovak federation facilitated this development. In turn, the increased political salience of ethnicity made it increasingly unlikely that a change in the structure that would be acceptable to both Czech and Slovak leaders would be adopted.

As in other new states that have emerged from formerly communist countries, Czech and Slovak leaders have faced the need to engage in state building while at the same time creating or re-creating democratic political institutions. The manner in which the Czechoslovak federation broke up has influenced the process of state building in both the Czech Republic and Slovakia. In contrast to situations in which states have broken up as the result of violence, citizens in both new states have been able to proceed with their lives without major disruptions. In the Czech Republic, Václav Klaus's government enjoyed a good deal of popular support until 1996. Although negative economic developments including financial and banking crises in spring 1997 have been reflected in declining support for the government, the political system had been among the most stable in the region. In Slovakia, political life has been more tumultuous, as a result of the higher degree of polarization of political elites and parties within Slovakia and the continued salience of tensions between Slovaks and the 600,000-strong Hungarian minority.

In both new states, most of the republic institutions have become national institutions. There has therefore been little need to create new institutions. The asymmetric nature of the federation during the communist era and the location of the federal capital in Prague created greater problems for Slovaks in some areas. These were most evident in those areas in which the federal government had jurisdiction prior to 1993, i.e., the diplomatic service and the army. The establishment of a Ministry of International Affairs prior to independence meant that there was an institutional basis for building a Slovak foreign ministry in 1993. However, the Ministry of International Affairs had only a rudimentary staff. The task of creating an efficient foreign service was also complicated in the Slovak case by the fact that many Slovak members of the foreign service chose to stay in Prague in 1993. The creation of a Slovak army was facilitated by the geographic redeployment of the military that took place between 1990 and 1993 but was influenced by many of the same factors.[36]

The process of building effective, legitimate states has also been influenced by the lack of mass involvement in the process by which the federation ended

and the new states were created. In both the Czech Republic and Slovakia, political elites face challenges in creating effective national symbols and myths
compatible with democratic political systems. Lacking new symbols or myths
created by mass struggle or participation in the creation of the new state, political leaders in both the Czech Republic and Slovakia have turned to the precommunist past. In the case of the Czech Republic, the leadership has attempted
to resolve this problem, with some degree of success, by appropriating the symbols and traditions of the democratic interwar Czechoslovak Republic. In Slovakia, on the other hand, making use of the past poses greater difficulties. Research conducted during the communist period and repeated since that time
demonstrates that the interwar republic is viewed very negatively by most Slovaks.[37] Many of the symbols of the Slovak national movement, however, have
been tainted by their association with the World War II Slovak state. Slovak
leaders also face the additional challenge, which many of the country's current
leaders do not admit is necessary, of finding symbols and experiences that can
include the Hungarian and other minorities found in the country. This task is
complicated by the fact that most Hungarians living in Slovakia identify figures
associated with the development of Hungarian nationalism as the most important figures in their history.

Lack of popular involvement in the creation of the new states has also meant
that the process has done little to create legitimacy for the new political entities.
For the same reason, the creation of two new states has done relatively little to influence popular satisfaction or dissatisfaction with political institutions, apart
from the somewhat greater trust of Slovak respondents in the Slovak parliament
since 1993.[38] The exclusion of the populace from the process of deciding about
the breakup of the federation has been particularly problematic in Slovakia,
where the country's sizeable Hungarian minority in large part opposed the
breakup of the common state. The association of Slovak independence with parties and leaders who present themselves as champions of Slovak national interests and have proved unwilling to reach an accommodation with the country's
Hungarian population has compounded this problem.

The breakup of Czechoslovakia, then, reflects the interaction of institutional
forms and political factors, with underlying ethnic cleavages and economic
change. In particular, it suggests the importance of decision-making rules
within political institutions and the nature of the state structure in shaping the
party system, national movements, and the issues around which political elites
can mobilize citizens. Federal systems are sometimes seen as the only viable
answer to giving diverse ethnic groups a stake in a common political system
and achieving a sufficient degree of consensus in multiethnic societies. The
breakup of Czechoslovakia and the demise of other federal postcommunist
states sound a cautionary note about this assumption, particularly in circumstances of great political, social, and economic change such as accompanied
the end of communist rule in Europe.

NOTES

1. See Jiří Musil, "Czech and Slovak Society," in *The End of Czechoslovakia* (Budapest: CEU Press, 1995), pp.77–96.

2. Mark R. Beissinger, "Demise of an Empire–State: Identity, Legitimacy, and the Deconstruction of Soviet Politics," in *The Rising Tide of Cultural Pluralism*, ed. M. Crawford Young (Madison, Wis.: University of Wisconsin Press, 1993).

3. See Michael Hechter, "The Dynamics of Secession," *Acta Sociologica*, vol. 35 (1992), pp. 2167–83.

4. This is particularly true of Hechter's elaboration of the processes of collective action necessary for secession.

5. See Sharon L. Wolchik, "Central and Eastern Europe in Transition," in *Asia and the Decline of Communism*, ed. Young C. Kim and Gaston J. Sigur (New Brunswick: Transaction Publishers, 1992). See also Valerie J. Bunce, "The Prerequisites of Liberal Democracies in Central and Eastern Europe" (unpublished manuscript).

6. See James R. Millar and Sharon L. Wolchik, eds., *The Social Legacy of Communism* (Cambridge: Cambridge University Press and the Woodrow Wilson Center Press, 1994).

7. See Mark Beissinger, "The State as Constructor of Nationalism: Nationalist Mobilization before and after the Soviet Union," paper presented at the conference on Communism, Post-Communism and Ethnic Mobilization, Cornell University, Ithaca, New York, 21–22 April 1995.

8. See Jiří Musil, "Česká a slovenská společnost. Skica srovnávací studie," *Sociologický časopis*, vol. 29, no.1 (1993), pp. 9–24. See Alena Bartlová, "Political Power-Sharing in the Interwar Period," in *The End of Czechoslovakia*, ed. Jiří Musil (Budapest: Central European University Press, 1995), pp. 159–179, for a discussion of the role that debate and disagreement over power sharing and governmental reform played in Czech–Slovak relations in the interwar period. See Zora P. Pryor, "Czechoslovak Economic Development in the Interwar Period, 1918–1948," in *A History of the Czechoslovak Republic*, ed. Victor S. Mamatey and Radomír Luža (Princeton, N.J.: Princeton University Press, 1973), pp. 188–215. See also Milan Kučera and Zdeněk Pavlík, "Czech and Slovak Demography," in Musil, ed., *The End of Czechoslovakia*, pp. 16–28, for analyses of the economic and social differences in the two regions during this period.

9. Kučera and Pavlík, "Czech and Slovak Demography," pp. 29–37; and Václav Průcha, "Economic Development and Relations, 1918–1989," In *The End of Czechoslovakia*, ed. Musil, pp. 58–75.

10. See Ivan Kamenec, *Po stopách tragédie* (Bratislava: Vydavatel'stvo Archa, 1991), p. 171.

11. See Sharon L. Wolchik, "Regional Inequalities in Czechoslovakia," in *Communism and the Politics of Inequalities*, ed. Daniel J. Nelson, (Lexington, Mass: Lexington Books, 1983), pp. 249–270. See also Carol Skalnik Leff, *National Conflict in Czechoslovakia: The Making and Remaking of a State, 1918–1987* (Princeton, N.J.: Princeton University Press, 1988.)

12. See Musil, "Czech and Slovak Society," especially pp. 79-81, for an analysis of the differences in the industrialization of the Czech lands and Slovakia, and Wolchik, "The Politics of Ethnicity in Post-Communist Czechoslovakia," in *The End of Czechoslovakia*, ed. Musil.

13. See Leff and H. Gordon Skilling, *Czechoslovakia's Interrupted Revolution* (Princeton, N.J.: Princeton University Press, 1976), pp. 49–56.

14. See Wolchik, "The Politics of Ethnicity in Post-Communist Czechoslovakia," pp. 174–184; and Sharon L. Wolchik, *Czechoslovakia In Transition: Politics, Economics, and Society* (London: Pinter Publishers Ltd., 1991), pp. 186–195, for an overview of studies illustrating these differences.

15. See Peter C. Brock, *The Slovak National Awakening* (Toronto: University of Toronto Press, 1976), for a discussion of early efforts to develop Slovak national consciousness.

16. See also Kučera and Pavlík, "Czech and Slovak Demography," pp. 15–39; and Musil, "Czech and Slovak Society," in *The End of Czechoslovakia*, ed. Musil, pp. 77–96.

17. Martin Bútora, "Reflections on the Emerging Third Sector in Slovakia," *Nonprofit Sector and Volunteering in Slovakia* (Bratislava: SAIA-SCTS and FOCUS, 1995). See also Eva Broklová, *Československá demokracie. Politický systém ČSR 1918–1938* (Prague: SLON, 1992); and Alena Bartlová, "Political Power-Sharing in the Interwar Period," in *The End of Czechoslovakia*, ed. Musil, pp. 159–179.

18. See Pryor, "Czechoslovak Economic Development in the Interwar Period, 1918–1948," pp.188–215.

19. See Vladimír Krivý, "The Parliamentary Elections 1994: The Profile of Supporters of the Political Parties, the Profile of Regions," in *Slovakia and the 1994 Elections*, ed. Sona Szomolany et al. (Bratislava: Slovak Political Science Association, 1995), pp. 114–135.

20. Yeshayahu A. Jelinek, *The Lust for Power: Nationalism, Slovakia, and the Communists, 1918–1948* (New York: East European Monagraphs, 1983), p. 67.

21. Jelinek, *The Lust for Power,* pp. 9–11. See also James Felak, "Slovak Considerations of the Slovak Question: The Ludak, Agrarian, Socialist and Communist Views in Interwar Czechoslovakia," in *The Czech and Slovak Experience*, ed. John Morison (New York: St. Martin's Press, 1992), pp. 136–162.

22. Jelinek, *The Lust for Power,* pp. 11–12.

23. See Edita Bosak, "Slovaks and Czechs: An Uneasy Coexistence," in *Czechoslovakia, 1918–88,* ed. H. Gordon Skilling (Oxford: Macmillan, 1991), pp. 74–75.

24. See Josef Rothschild, *Ethnopolitics: A Conceptual Framework* (Seattle: Washington University Press, 1981), for a discussion of the impact of these factors on elite strategies.

25. See Jaroslav Piekalkiewicz, *Public Opinion Polling in Czechoslovakia, 1968–1969: Results and Analysis of Surveys Conducted in the Dubček Era* (New York: Praeger Publishers, 1972).

26. This tendency was also evident within the republics, particularly in Slovakia, where the Hungarian community organized its own counterparts of Slovak parties, such as the Hungarian Christian Democratic Party, and the Hungarian Civic Party, Coexistence, the largest Hungarian political party, also included Ruthenian/Ukrainian members.

27. See Krivý, "The Parliamentary Elections 1994," pp. 114–135.

28. The position of Mečiar's movement prior to the June 1992 elections was not clear on the question of independence. Support for his party also derived from economic sources, as Mečiar clearly promised to change the strategy of economic reform to take Slovak conditions into account. See Center for Social Analysis, *Current Developments in Slovakia* (Bratislava, May 1992; May 1993; and December 1993).

29. Vladimír Kusý, "Slovak Exceptionalism," in *The End of Czechoslovakia*, ed. Musil, p. 143.

30. "Dnešná tvar Slovenska," *Lidové noviny* (19 September 1991), p. 3.

31. See Wolchik, "The Politics of Ethnicity in Post-Communist Czechoslovakia," pp. 174–184. See footnote 8 for an overview of studies illustrating these trends. See

also Timoracký, "Aktuálné problémy Česko-Slovenska" (Bratislava: AISA, November 1990); "Výzkum politických postojů, duben 1992" (Prague: AISA, 1992). See also the analyses of FOCUS, Center for Social Analysis, Bratislava, especially "Current Problems of Slovakia, May 1993."

32. See Irena Grudzinska-Gross, ed., *Constitutionalism in East Central Europe* (Bratislava: Czecho–Slovak Committee of the European Culture Foundation, 1994) for brief analyses for some of the people involved in these process.

33. Grudzinska-Gross, *Constitutionalism,* pp. 471–501, for a more detailed discussion of these issues.

34. See public opinion studies reported by IVVM, June and September 1993.

35. See Musil, "Czech and Slovak Society," pp. 88–89, for data on immigration between Slovakia and the Czech lands.

36. Zoltan D. Baraný, "East European Armed Forces in Transitions and Beyond," *East European Quarterly,* vol. 20, no. 1 (March 1992), pp. 3–4. See also Miroslav Purkrabek, "Politika sociální a vojenské transformace ČSA," *Sociologia,* vol. 24, no. 3 (1992), pp. 137–140.

37. From data in tables 6.1 and 6.63 found in Archie Brown, *Political Culture and Political Change in Communist States,* ed. Archie Brown and Jack Grey (New York: Holmes & Meier Publishers, 1979).

38. See FOCUS, "Current Developments in Slovakia," December 1994, for a preliminary on our comparative survey of the values and attitudes of citizens in the Czech Republic and Slovakia.

6

Electoral Rules and the Fate of Nations: Czechoslovakia's Last Parliamentary Election

František Turnovec

INTRODUCTION

This chapter presents a comprehensive analysis of the June 1992 general parliamentary elections in the Federal Republic of Czechoslovakia.[1] It examines the proportional electoral system used in the Czech and Slovak Federal Republic[2] and the political profiles of both Czech and Slovak societies and their respective representative institutions (the federal parliament as well as the Czech and Slovak republic-level parliaments). Through the use of simulation techniques, this chapter shows that while a bimodal distribution of political preferences at the federal level—which reflects the differences in political inclinations of the Czech and Slovak republics—clearly contributed to the process of separation, the electoral system adopted after 1989 also deepened the existing political crisis by producing a parliament that misrepresented public attitudes on the key issue of the common state, further exacerbating existing national tensions. Varying the electoral threshold levels in the simulation model dramatically affects the distributions of power within the Czech, Slovak, and federal parliaments. More specifically, the simulation shows that had an election taken place with pure proportional representation and no threshold of entry into parliament, the separation-friendly political formations (represented by postelectoral government coalitions) would have been unable to achieve a majority. An investigation of the Czechoslovak case suggests that while electoral systems that embrace thresholds do succeed in reducing the number of parties in parliament, their unintended consequence in multinational states may be the substantial misrepresentation of voter preferences.[3]

THE ELECTORAL SYSTEM OF CZECHOSLOVAKIA

After 1989, Czechoslovakia had a bicameral federal parliament composed of the Chamber of the People (150 seats) and the Chamber of the Nations (150 seats); it also had two republican parliaments: the Czech National Council (200 seats) and the Slovak National Council (150 seats). The Czech Republic sent ninety-nine deputies to the Chamber of the People while fifty-one deputies were sent by the Slovak Republic. The Chamber of the Nations operated under the principle of parity representation: seventy-five deputies elected in the Czech Republic and seventy-five in the Slovak Republic. The national council members were elected by the citizens of each republic.

A proportional electoral system was used with a threshold for parties and political coalitions. To enter the parliament, a party had to collect at least 5 percent of the total number of valid votes on the republican level. A coalition of two parties had to collect at least 7 percent of valid votes, and a coalition of greater than two parties had to collect at least 10 percent of valid votes.

The country was divided into twelve voting districts (eight in the Czech Republic and four in the Slovak Republic), with multicandidate lists presented by different parties. The number of seats for each district was proportional to the total number of valid votes cast in the district. Votes for the parties that did not exceed the 5-percent threshold (7 percent for two party coalitions, 10 percent for coalitions of greater than two parties) were redistributed among parties that did succeed, approximately proportionally to the received votes. Within each political party the candidates received the seats allocated to the party according to the order printed on the ballot. However, if at least one-tenth of the total of voters casting a valid vote for the respective party in the electoral district used the right to a preference vote, the candidates who received a preference vote from more than 10 percent of those voters were moved to the top of the list (in order according to the number of preferential votes). The voter was allowed to express his or her preference for candidates by circling the numbers of a maximum of four candidates listed on the ballot (an application of approval voting, since the personal votes were of equal weight and not truly preferential).[4]

The distribution of seats to parties started at the district level with a full quota allocation (a quota is defined as the total number of valid votes received by parties or coalition formations that meet the relevant threshold requirements, divided by the number of seats to be allocated plus one). The total number of votes for the party was divided by quota, and the party received the number of seats equal to the integer part of this ratio. The remainder of seats were allocated at the republican level.

Czechoslovakia's first free general parliamentary election since 1946 was held on 8–9 June 1990. The same electoral system was applied in both 1990 and 1992 (with one small but important exception: there was only a 3-percent threshold for parties to cross so as to qualify for seats in the Slovak National Council). A broad coalition of liberal-democratic Czech and Slovak civic movements that played a crucial role during the 1989 turnover of power—Civic Forum in the Czech Republic and the Public Against Violence in the Slovak Republic—won a majority of seats in the federal parliament. Only seven political formations entered the federal parliament. Only four formations entered the Czech parliament, while the Slovak parliament was composed of seven formations.

In the Czech parliament, Civic Forum won 63.5 percent of the seats, enough for the qualified majority required to pass constitutional amendments; in the Slovak parliament, Civic Forum's partner, the Public Against Violence, won 32.5 percent of the seats, and together with the Slovak Christian Democratic Movement (which captured 20.7 percent of the seats), was a member of the federal governing coalition; the latter two also formed the Slovak republican government. In contrast, the ruling party in the Czech Republic was exclusively made up of Civic Forum. However, the situation dramatically changed during 1991. The fragmentation of political parties and coalitions led to a fast expansion of political formations (i.e., both parties and coalitions) in all three parliaments. At the end of 1991, the number of factions in the federal parliament had increased from seven to sixteen, in the Czech parliament from four to eleven, and in the Slovak parliament from seven to eleven.[5] The post-Velvet Revolution euphoria had ended as the country approached its second parliamentary election, in 1992.

RESULTS OF THE 1992 ČSFR PARLIAMENTARY ELECTION

In the 5–6 June 1992 general parliamentary elections, thirty-five political formations competed for seats in the federal parliament, nineteen formations for seats in the Czech National Council and twenty-three formations for seats in the Slovak National Council. Approximately 85 percent of eligible voters took part in the election. The electoral ballot was divided into three sections: one for the federal Chamber of the People, one for the federal Chamber of the Nations (Czech Republic residents voted for their half of the chamber, and Slovak Republic residents voted for their half), and one vote for a republican parliament (Czech National Council or Slovak National Council).[6] About 26 percent of the valid votes in the federal parliament election, 19.1 percent of valid votes in the Czech National Council election, and 23.8 percent of the valid votes in the Slovak National Council election were redistributed because they were cast for political formations that did not attain the threshold. Thus only the following fourteen political formations entered the parliaments (some of them sitting only in one chamber):[7]

Czech parties and coalitions:
LBL: Left Block, Coalition of the Czech and Moravian Communist Party and Democratic Left Movement
ČSSD: Czechoslovak Social Democratic Party (after separating from the Czech Social Democratic Party of the Left Orientation)

LSU: Liberal Social Union (left-center coalition)
HSD-SMS: Movement for Self-Administration Democracy–Society for Moravia and Silesia (a Moravian regional party)
KDU-ČSL: Christian and Democratic Union–Czechoslovak People's Party (proreform centrist party)
ODS-KDS: Coalition of Civic Democratic Party and Christian Democratic Party (Václav Klaus, proreform right-center coalition)
ODA: Civic Democratic Alliance (proreform right party)
SPR-RSČ: Alliance for the Republic–Czechoslovak Republican Party (extreme rightist party)

Slovak parties and coalitions:
SDL: Party of the Democratic Left (former communist party with leftist social-democratic orientation)
SDSS: Slovak Social Democratic Party (Alexander Dubček)
HZDS: Movement for a Democratic Slovakia (Vladimír Mečiar)
SNS: Slovak National Party (the only parliamentary party with explicit program of separation of Slovakia)
KDH: Christian Democratic Movement (centrist proreform party)
MKDH-ESWS: Coalition of Hungarian parties (right orientation)

The Federal Parliament

Table 6.1 displays the results of the election to the federal parliament: the number of seats and the proportional representation of the parties. It also includes the Banzhaf–Coleman power indices in a percentage expression for simple majority voting (50 percent plus one vote) and qualified majority voting (the 60 percent required for constitutional amendments). (See Appendix, no. 1.) The calculated power indices take into account the multicameral voting rules in the federal parliament: to pass any law all three chambers of the federal parliament (the Chamber of the People, the Czech part of the Chamber of the Nations and the Slovak part of the Chamber of the Nations) had to independently vote in favor of it (Appendix, no. 2). The table shows the strong dominance of the two leading political parties—the Czech Civic Democratic Party and the Movement for a Democratic Slovakia.

From Table 6.1 we can see that the distribution of power can differ substantially from the distribution of seats; e.g., the small Slovak Social Democratic Party with a 1.67 percent representation had 2.46 percent of the power by the simple majority rule of the Banzhaf–Coleman power index, the same as the Left Block, with 11.33 percent of seats. The Movement for Democratic Slovakia, with 19 percent representation, had 37.49 percent of power, the same as the coalition of the Civic Democratic Party and the Christian Democratic Party in the Czech republic, with 28.33 percent of seats.

Table 6.1   Primary Distribution in the Federal Parliament of ČSFR after 1992 Election

Federal Parliament of ČSFR	Chamber of the People		Chamber of the Nations				Total		Power Indices	
			Slovak Part		Czech Part					
Party, Movement, Coalition	Seats	%	Seats	%	Seats	%	Seats	%	BC50	BC60
Slovak Parties										
SDL	10	6.67	13	17.33	0	0.00	23	7.67	2.54	6.95
SDSS	0	0.00	5	6.67	0	0.00	5	1.67	2.46	2.32
HZDS	24	16.00	33	44.00	0	0.00	57	19.00	37.49	30.10
SNS	6	4.00	9	12.00	0	0.00	15	5.00	2.54	4.63
KDH	6	4.00	8	10.67	0	0.00	14	4.67	2.54	4.63
MKDH-ESWS	5	3.33	7	9.33	0	0.00	12	4.00	2.54	2.32
Czech Parties										
LBL	19	12.67	0	0.00	15	20.00	34	11.33	2.46	5.57
ČSSD	10	6.67	0	0.00	6	8.00	16	5.33	2.46	3.34
LSU	7	4.67	0	0.00	5	6.67	12	4.00	2.46	3.34
KDU	7	4.67	0	0.00	6	8.00	13	4.33	2.46	3.34
ODS-KDS	48	32.00	0	0.00	37	49.33	85	28.33	37.57	30.10
SPR-RSČ	8	5.33	0	0.00	6	8.00	14	4.67	2.46	3.34
Total	150	100.00	75	100.00	75	100.00	300	100.00	100.00	100.00

Whereas the ordering in Table 6.1 follows the nationalities principle, and within the national groups, the parties are ordered from left to right, Table 6.2 presents a left-right ordering of the parties irrespective of their national background. Table 6.2 elaborates on Table 6.1, providing data about density, as well as the LR and RL cumulative distributions of seats ordered from left to right.

Based on Table 6.2, Figure 6.1 displays three curves. The first curve with two peaks, placed in the bottom of the picture, illustrates the density distribution of seats (the percentile representation of the parties in the federal parliament). The second curve, sloping down from left to right, represents the so-called RL cumulative distribution of seats: any given point on the curve shows on the vertical axis the total proportion of seats for all parties at least as right on the left-right political dimension as the corresponding party on the horizontal axis. The third curve, sloping up from left to right, represents the so-called LR cumulative distribution: any given point on the curve produces, on the vertical axis, the total proportion of seats for all parties at least as left on the left-right political dimension as the corresponding party on the horizontal axis.

Figure 6.1 can be understood as follows: The intersection of the RL and LR curves gives a location of some political equilibrium, or median position; slightly more than 50 percent of all deputies would oppose any change to the right of the

Table 6.2 Density and Cumulative Distributions of Seats in the Federal Parliament

Party, Movement, Coalition	Federal Parliament (total)				Czech Part of FP				Slovak Part of FP			
	Seats	% Seats	LR	RL	Seats	% Seats	LR	RL	Seats	% Seats	LR	RL
LBL	34	11.33	11.33	100.00	34	19.54	19.54	100.00				
SDL	23	7.67	19.00	88.67					23	18.25	18.25	100.00
SDSS	5	1.67	20.67	81.00					5	3.97	22.22	81.75
ČSSD	16	5.33	26.00	79.33	16	9.20	28.74	80.46				
HZDS	57	19.00	45.00	74.00					57	45.24	67.46	77.78
LSU	12	4.00	49.00	55.00	12	6.90	35.63	71.26				
SNS	15	5.00	54.00	51.00					15	11.90	79.37	32.54
KDU	13	4.33	58.33	46.00	13	7.47	43.10	64.37				
KDH	14	4.67	63.00	41.67					14	11.11	90.48	20.63
ODS-KDS	85	28.33	91.33	37.00	85	48.85	91.95	56.90				
MKDH-ESWS	12	4.00	95.33	8.67					12	9.52	100.00	9.52
SPR-RSČ	14	4.67	100.00	4.67	14	8.05	100.00	8.05				
Total	300	100.00			174	100.00			126	100.00		

corresponding position on the vertical axis (somewhere between LSU and SNS), while the same majority would oppose any change to the left of that position. We shall term this configuration a *political profile* of the federal parliament.

Taken as a whole, Figure 6.1 gives a diagrammatic representation of a political profile of the federal parliament (Appendix, no. 3). On the horizontal axis of the graph we use the following left-right ordering of the parties: LBL, SDL, SDSS, ČSSD, HZDS, LSU, SNS, KDU, KDH, ODS-KDS, MKDH-ESWS, SPR-RSČ. Christian Democratic Union (KDU) has been selected as representative of the center. The vertical axis represents the percentage of seats won (from 0 to 100).

We can see that the political profile of the last federal parliament of the ČSFR shows the propensity to the left center (the point of intersection of the LR and RL cumulative distribution curve in the upper left part of the diagram). At the same time we can clearly see the bimodal pattern of density distribution in parliamentary representation (two peaks—one in the left part of the spectrum and the second in the right part). The federal government coalition was formed by the Czech ODS party and the Slovak HZDS party (on the parity principle). These parties represented noticeably different political inclinations, having ironically only one unifying objective: to dissolve the common state as quickly as possible.

In Figure 6.2a and b, also based on Table 6.2, we compare the political profiles of the Czech part and the Slovak part of the federal parliament after the June 1992 elections. The political incompatibility of the Czech and Slovak representation in the federal parliament of the ČSFR, expressing the different political preferences of the citizens of the Czech Republic and the Slovak Republic, is clearly visible from the graph.

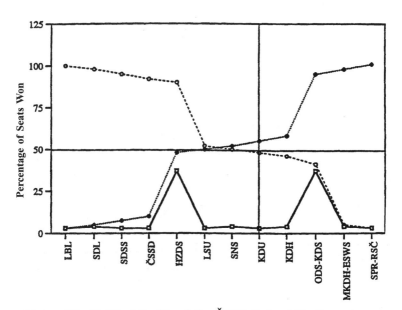

Figure 6.1   Political Profile of the ČSFR Federal Parliament

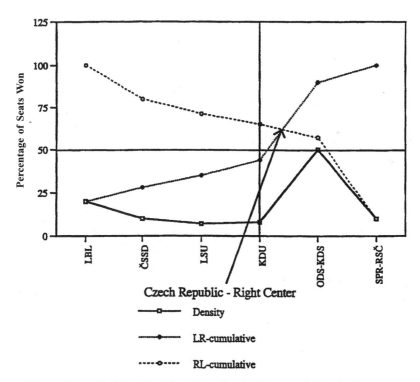

Czech Republic - Right Center

———□——— Density

·····●····· LR-cumulative

---◇---- RL-cumulative

Figure 6.2a   Political Profile of the Czech Representation in the ČSFR Federal Parliament

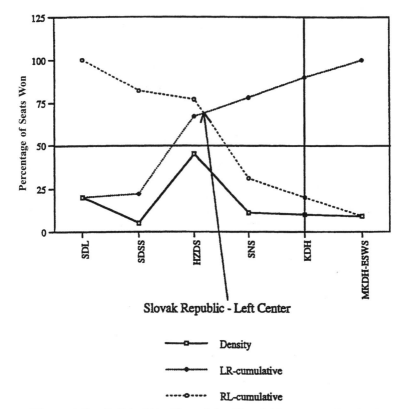

Figure 6.2b   Political Profiles of the Slovak Representation in the ČSFR Federal Parliament

One can infer from the preceding analysis that there are three factors that contributed to the (peaceful) separation of the country: first, the fundamental and substantial differences in the political profiles and preferences of the Czech and Slovak citizenry, which in turn expressed the differences in the priorities of the Czech and Slovak societies, respectively; second, the societal lack of mature democratic political experience, which did not leave much room for serious deliberation; and third, perhaps most important, the absence of the requisite goodwill on both sides to seek a mutually acceptable compromise.

The Czech National Council

Table 6.3 shows the results of the 1992 elections to the Czech National Council. Not all of the parties received enough votes to enter parliament. Parties are

Table 6.3   Results of 1992 Election to the Czech National Council

Party	% Votes	LR	RL
Left Block (LBL)	14.05	14.05	97.33
Movement of Seniors (HDZJ)	3.77	17.82	83.28
Social Democrats (ČSSD)	6.53	24.35	79.51
Movement for Social Equality (HSS)	1.08	25.43	72.98
Liberal-Social Union (LSU)	6.52	31.95	71.90
Democrats 92 (D92)	0.58	32.53	65.38
Civic Movement (OH)	4.59	37.12	64.80
Moravian Movement (HSD-SMS)	5.87	42.99	60.21
Romes Civic Initiative (RI)	0.26	43.25	54.34
Christian Democratic Union (CDU)	6.28	49.53	54.08
Civic-Democratic Party + CHDP (ODS/KDS)	29.73	79.26	47.80
Civic Democratic Alliance (ODA)	5.93	85.19	18.07
Party of Businessman (SCP)	3.15	88.34	12.14
National-Social Party (NSS)	0.15	88.49	8.99
Club of Non-Party (KAN)	2.69	91.18	8.84
National Democrats (SRNDJ)	0.17	91.35	6.15
Republicans (SPR-RSČ)	5.98	97.33	5.98
Total	97.33		

ordered from top to bottom, as per a left-right political spectrum; however, some marginal parties, with no clear economic or political program (such as the "Party of Friends of Beer" and the "New Erotic Initiative"), are omitted.

In Figure 6.3 we present the political profile of Czech society. We can see that the point of intersection of the LR and RL cumulative distribution is almost in the center.

In 1992, only seven parties succeeded in entering the Czech parliament. In Table 6.4 we give a distribution of seats and the Shapley–Shubik and Banzhaf–Coleman power indices for 50-percent and 60-percent majority rule.

The governing coalition in the Czech Republic was formed by four right-centrist parties: the Civic Democratic Party (ODS) of Václav Klaus, its coalition partner, the Christian Democratic Party (KDS), the Civic Democratic Alliance (ODA), and the Christian Democratic Union (KDU-ČSL). Statistical attributes of this coalition are given in Table 6.5 (the distribution of votes and power by the Shapley–Shubik and Banzhaf–Coleman indices). Since the government coalition did not have enough votes for the 60-percent majority (120 votes) required for constitutional amendments, it had to cooperate from issue to issue with different opposition parties in order to achieve the required level of support.

The Slovak National Council

The characteristic feature of the Slovak political spectrum was a rather overcrowded left-center with several marginal parties of both nationalist and socialist orientation. The political profile of Slovak society in June 1992 is given in Figure

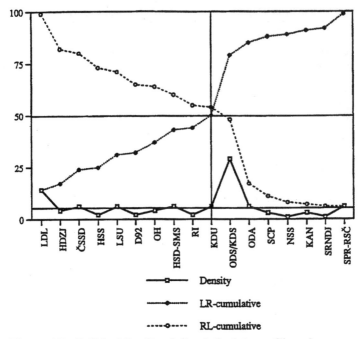

Figure 6.3 Political Profile of Czech Society as Given by Electoral Preferences

6.4. The Christian Democratic Party (KDU) has been selected as a representative of the political center. We can observe that the intersection of the LR-cumulative distribution and RL-cumulative distribution is concentrated left of center. It is interesting that the parties with explicit programs of separation (with the exception of the Slovak National Party, SNS) were not able to enter the parliament. On the other side, the leftist but profederal Slovak Social Democrats (SDSS) was also too weak to qualify for representation in the Slovak National Council.

Table 6.4 Primary Distribution of Power in the Czech National Council after 1992 Election

Party, Movement, Coalition	# of Seats	Proportional Representation (%)	SS50	SS60	BC50	BC60
LBL	35	17.50	10.71	12.14	7.45	16.16
ČSSD	16	8.00	5.95	7.38	5.32	8.08
LSU	16	8.00	5.95	7.38	5.32	8.08
HSD-SMS	14	7.00	5.95	5.24	5.32	4.04
KDU	15	7.50	5.95	5.24	5.32	8.08
ODS-KDS	76	38.00	53.57	52.14	60.64	47.47
ODA	14	7.00	5.95	5.24	5.32	4.04
SPR-RSČ	14	7.00	5.95	5.24	5.32	4.04
Total	200	100.00			100.01	99.99

Table 6.5 Government Coalition vs. Opposition

	Votes	*%*	*SS50*	*SS60*	*BC50*	*BC60*
LBL	35	17.5	0	6.67	0	7.5
ČSSD	16	8	0	6.67	0	7.5
LSU	16	8	0	6.67	0	7.5
HSD-SMS	14	7	0	1.67	0	2.5
GC	105	52.5	100	76.67	100	72.5
SPR-RSČ	14	7	0	1.67	0	2.5
Total	200	100	100	100.02	100	100

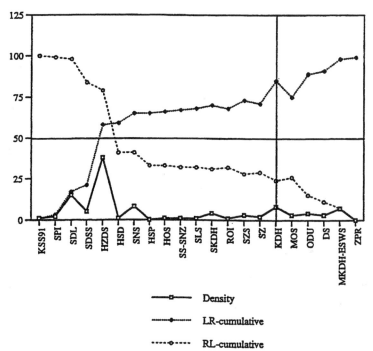

Figure 6.4   Political Profile of Slovak Society as Given by Electoral Preferences

Table 6.6 illustrates the results of the election to the Slovak National Council in June 1992.

Only the following five political formations entered the Slovak parliament after the 1992 election:

> *SDL: Party of the Democratic Left (former communist party with leftist social-democratic orientation, profederal)*
>
> *HZDS: Movement for a Democratic Slovakia (ambiguous public attitude to federation: five alternatives declared feasible, including a confederated common state and outright separation)*

SNS: Slovak National Party (the only parliamentary party with an explicit program of separation for Slovakia)
KDH: Christian Democratic Movement (centrist proreform party, with an ambiguous attitude to federation)
MKDH-ESWS: Coalition of Hungarian parties (right orientation, profederal)

In Table 6.7 we give the distribution of seats in the Slovak parliament together with Shapley–Shubik and Banzhaf–Coleman power indices for 50-percent and 60-percent majority rule. The strong dominance of the Movement for Democratic Slovakia (HZDS) is apparent.

The governing coalition in the Slovak Republic was formed by left-of-center parties: the Mečiar-led Movement for Democratic Slovakia (HZDS) and its silent coalition partner, the Slovak National Party (SNS). Table 6.8 contains data about the strength of the government coalition (distribution of votes and distribution of power by Shapley–Shubik and Banzhaf–Coleman power indices).

IMPACT OF ELECTORAL RULES
ON THE DISTRIBUTION OF POWER

While majority systems award a seat to the candidate who gets the most votes in a given constituency ("most" can mean either a plurality of tallied votes or an absolute majority of tallied votes), proportional representation systems attempt to allocate seats in proportion to overall popular voting.

The Czechoslovak electoral system was rooted in a system of proportional representation; however, the introduction of a threshold for parties and coalitions was an attempt to prevent some of the negative consequences of purely proportional electoral systems. The motivation for this modification of pure proportional representation was to try to ensure democratic stability by keeping extremist parties out of parliament.

How faithfully did Czechoslovakia's electoral system represent voter preferences, both at the federal and the republic levels? To shed light on this question, we can use the following measure of proportionality (or, better, deviation from proportionality), suggested by Taagapera and Shugart (1989):

$$D = \frac{\sum_{i=1}^{n}|s_i - v_i|}{2}$$

where

n is the number of all parties involved;
s_i is the representation of the i-th party in the parliament (ratio or percentage);
v_i is the proportional share of votes of the i-th party (ratio or percentage).

Obviously $0 \leq D \leq 1$ (or $0 \leq D \leq 100$ in percentage terms) (Appendix, no. 4).

Table 6.6 Results of the 1992 Election to the Parliament of SR

Party	% Votes	LR	RL	Party	% Votes	LR	DL
Communists 91 (KSS91)	0.75	0.75	99.71	Slovak Christian Democrats (SKDH)	3.05	70.24	32.52
Party of Labour (SPI)	0.96	1.71	98.96	Rome's Civic Initiative (ROI)	0.59	67.19	33.11
Party of Democratic Left (SDL)	14.70	16.41	98.00	Slovak Green Party (SZS)	2.14	73.46	28.39
Social Democrats (SDSS)	4.00	20.41	83.30	Green Party (SZ)	1.08	71.32	29.47
Movement for Democratic Slovakia (HZDS)	37.26	57.67	79.30	Christian Democratic Movement (KDH)	8.88	84.63	23.96
Movement for Self-Administrative Democracy (HSD)	0.12	57.79	42.04	Hungarian Civic Party (MOS)	2.29	75.75	26.25
Slovak National Party (SNS)	7.93	65.72	41.92	Civic Democratic Movement (ODU)	4.03	88.66	15.08
Movement for Freedom of Expression (HSP)	0.06	65.78	33.99	Democratic Party-Civic Democratic Party (DS)	3.31	91.97	11.05
Movement for Liberation of Slovakia (HOS)	0.23	66.01	33.93	Hungarian Coalition (MKDH-ESWS)	7.42	99.39	7.74
Party of Freedom (SS-SNZ)	0.30	66.31	33.70	Republicans (ZPR)	0.32	99.71	0.32
Slovak Peoples Party (SLS)	0.29	66.60	33.40	Total	99.71		

Table 6.7 Primary Distribution of Power in the Slovak National Council after 1992 Election

	Seats	%	SS50	SS60	BC50	BC60
SDL	29	19.33	10.00	11.67	9.09	14.29
HZDS	74	49.33	60.00	70.00	63.64	61.90
SNS	15	10.00	10.00	3.33	9.09	4.76
KDH	18	12.00	10.00	11.67	9.09	14.29
MKDH-ESWS	14	9.33	10.00	3.33	9.09	4.76
Total	150	99.99	100.00	100.00	100.00	100.00

Another, more hypothetical question to consider is: how would the Czechoslovak political spectrum change, given the electoral preferences expressed by the voters, under different electoral rules? In this final section, we shall vary the threshold levels and examine how the change in electoral rules affects the political profiles of the Czech and Slovak republican chambers, the main actors in the "separation game." In this analysis, we assume that voter preferences remain constant.

Simulation for the Czech Republic

Table 6.9 presents the effect of the simulation exercise on the structure of the Czech National Council, using the primary results of the election (distribution of votes for the parties) from Table 6.3. The "votes in election" column gives the proportional share of valid votes for the parties actually obtained in the election. The main body of the table displays the proportional share of seats for the threshold values from 0 percent to 7 percent (applying the rules of seat allocation based on corresponding thresholds). Row "NP" gives the number of parties entering the parliament and row "DP" gives (in percentage terms) the deviation from proportionality for corresponding thresholds in all particular cases. The row "profederal or indifferent" gives the total share of seats allocated (under hypothetical thresholds) to parties that were not "separation friendly." We assume that all parties participating in the Czech Republic election except ODS-KDS and ODA were ready to search for a "common state" solution to the constitutional crisis. The last row gives the percentage of votes in the actual governing coalition.

Table 6.8 Government Coalition vs. Opposition

	Votes	%	SS50	SS60	BC50	BC60
SDL	29	19.33	0.00	8.33	0.00	10.00
GC (HZDS & SNS)	89	59.33	100.00	75.00	100.00	70.00
KDH	18	12.00	0.00	8.33	0.00	10.00
MKDH-ESWS	14	9.33	0.00	8.33	0.00	10.00
Total	150	99.99	100.00	99.99	100.00	100.00

Table 6.9 Simulation of Proportional Representation in the Czech National Council

Czech National Council	Votes in Election (%)	Estimation of Proportional Representation for Different Thresholds							
		0%	1%	2%	3%	4%	5%	6%	7%
ODA	5.93	6.00	6.00	6.00	6.50	7.00	7.00	0.00	0.00
ČSSD	6.53	6.50	6.50	7.00	7.00	7.50	8.00	10.50	0.00
HSD-SMS	5.87	6.00	6.00	6.00	6.50	7.00	7.00	0.00	0.00
HDZJ	3.77	4.00	4.00	4.00	4.00	0.00	0.00	0.00	0.00
NSS-CSNS	0.15	0.00	0.00	0.00	0.00	0.00	0.00	0.00	0.00
D92	0.58	0.50	0.00	0.00	0.00	0.00	0.00	0.00	0.00
SRNDJ	0.17	0.00	0.00	0.00	0.00	0.00	0.00	0.00	0.00
KDU-ČSL	6.28	6.50	6.50	6.50	7.00	7.50	7.50	10.00	0.00
SCPZR	3.15	3.00	3.00	3.50	3.50	0.00	0.00	0.00	0.00
HSS	1.08	1.00	1.00	0.00	0.00	0.00	0.00	0.00	0.00
LSU	6.52	6.50	6.50	7.00	7.00	7.50	8.00	10.50	0.00
OH	4.59	4.50	4.50	5.00	5.00	5.50	0.00	0.00	0.00
SPR-RSČ	5.98	6.00	6.00	6.50	6.50	7.00	7.00	0.00	0.00
KAN	2.69	2.50	3.00	3.00	0.00	0.00	0.00	0.00	0.00
ROI	0.26	0.00	0.00	0.00	0.00	0.00	0.00	0.00	0.00
LBL	14.05	14.00	14.00	15.00	15.00	16.50	17.50	22.00	32.00
SPP	1.30	1.50	1.50	0.00	0.00	0.00	0.00	0.00	0.00
NEI	1.37	1.50	1.50	0.00	0.00	0.00	0.00	0.00	0.00
ODS-KDS	29.73	30.00	30.00	30.50	32.00	34.50	38.00	47.00	68.00
Total	100.00	100.00	100.00	100.00	100.00	100.00	100.00	100.00	100.00
DP%		1.27	1.58	4.91	7.60	14.52	19.11	36.89	56.22
NP		16	15	12	11	9	7	5	2
Profederal or Indifferent	64.36	64.00	64.00	63.50	63.50	58.50	55.00	53.00	32.00
Government Coalition (%)	41.94	42.50	42.50	43.00	45.50	49.00	52.50	57.00	68.00

We can see that the governing coalition obtained only 41.94 percent of the popular vote. Nevertheless, with the 5-percent threshold level in place, it obtained 52.5 percent of the seats in the Czech parliament. It is unnecessary to probe the specific positions of each party to deduce that the propensity to patient negotiation was likely to have been affected by a 19.11 percent misrepresentation in the Czech National Council.

The results of a simulation of the actual power distribution in the Czech National Council are given in Table 6.10 and Table 6.11. Table 6.10 contains the hypothetical Banzhaf–Coleman power indices for 50-percent majority rule, corresponding to the estimated proportional representation under different thresholds. The last row gives the corresponding values of power concentration measured by the Banzhaf–Coleman power index. We can see that the growth in influence of the leading Czech political formation (ODS-KDS), at the 5-percent threshold level, is substantial: from 43.33 percent in the case of 0-percent threshold to the actual 60.64 percent under a 5-percent threshold. To make the same point in slightly different fashion, we can decompose the power of any party into three components: one component is given by votes obtained, the second component depends on the structure of parliament (i.e., the difference between the power index under a zero threshold and the percentage share of votes), and the third component is dictated exclusively by electoral rules (the difference between the power index under the given electoral threshold and the power index under a zero threshold). For example, the actual power of ODS-KDS (60.64 percent) can be broken down as follows:

29.73 percent by votes
13.6 percent by structure (= 43.33 percent − 29.73 percent)
17.31 percent by electoral law (= 60.64 percent − 43.33 percent)

The 7-percent threshold in this simulation is most significant: it would have guaranteed a democratically elected one-party state, since total power would have been in the hands of the ODS-KDS coalition.

The same data for constitutionally significant 60-percent majority rule is presented in Table 6.11. Under these constraints, ODS-KDS increases its natural power, given by election, from 34.73 percent (if there were zero threshold) to 47.44 percent. Again, 7 percent is the threshold that generates 60-percent majority rule.

Simulation for the Slovak Republic

In our considerations, we use the following hypothesis: All parties participating in elections in the Slovak Republic with the exception of HZDS, SNS, HZOS, SKDH and SLS sought to preserve the common state.

Figure 6.10 Simulation of Power Distribution in the Czech National Council (50% Majority)

Czech National Council	Votes in Election(%)	Banzhaf Power Indices for 50% Majority for Different Thresholds							
		0%	1%	2%	3%	4%	5%	6%	7%
ODA	5.93	5.07	5.07	5.10	5.45	6.44	5.32	0.00	0.00
ČSSD	6.53	5.49	5.49	6.15	5.88	6.44	5.32	9.09	0.00
HSD-SMS	5.87	5.07	5.07	5.10	5.45	6.44	5.32	0.00	0.00
HDZJ	3.77	3.36	3.42	3.54	2.72	0.00	0.00	0.00	0.00
NSS-CSNS	0.15	0.00	0.00	0.00	0.00	0.00	0.00	0.00	0.00
D92	0.58	0.42	0.00	0.00	0.00	0.00	0.00	0.00	0.00
SRNDJ	0.17	0.00	0.00	0.00	0.00	0.00	0.00	0.00	0.00
KDU-ČSL	6.28	5.49	5.49	5.62	5.88	6.44	5.32	9.09	0.00
SCPZR	3.15	2.50	2.57	3.07	2.40	0.00	0.00	0.00	0.00
HSS	1.08	0.85	0.84	0.00	0.00	0.00	0.00	0.00	0.00
LSU	6.52	5.49	5.49	6.15	5.88	6.44	5.32	9.09	0.00
OH	4.59	3.80	3.81	4.01	5.34	6.44	0.00	0.00	0.00
SPR-RSČ	5.98	5.07	5.07	5.62	5.45	6.44	5.32	0.00	0.00
KAN	2.69	2.15	2.57	2.71	0.00	0.00	0.00	0.00	0.00
ROI	0.26	0.00	0.00	0.00	0.00	0.00	0.00	0.00	0.00
LBL	14.05	9.36	9.41	10.26	10.24	12.45	7.45	9.09	0.00
SPP	1.30	1.27	1.25	0.00	0.00	0.00	0.00	0.00	0.00
NEI	1.37	1.27	1.25	0.00	0.00	0.00	0.00	0.00	0.00
ODS-KDS	29.73	43.33	43.19	42.66	45.32	42.49	60.64	63.64	100.00
Total	100.00	99.99	99.99	99.99	100.01	100.02	100.01	100.00	100.00

Table 6.11 Simulation of Power Distribution in the Czech National Council (60% Majority)

Czech National Council	Votes in Election (%)	Banzhaf Power Indices for 60% Majority for Different Thresholds							
		0%	1%	2%	3%	4%	5%	6%	7%
ODA	5.93	5.48	5.48	5.47	5.77	6.29	4.04	0.00	0.00
ČSSD	6.53	5.95	5.97	6.23	6.21	6.29	8.08	9.09	0.00
HSD-SMS	5.87	5.48	5.48	5.47	5.77	6.29	4.04	0.00	0.00
HDZJ	3.77	3.65	3.53	3.59	3.24	0.00	0.00	0.00	0.00
NSS-CSNS	0.15	0.00	0.00	0.00	0.00	0.00	0.00	0.00	0.00
D92	0.58	0.45	0.00	0.00	0.00	0.00	0.00	0.00	0.00
SRNDJ	0.17	0.00	0.00	0.00	0.00	0.00	0.00	0.00	0.00
KDU-ČSL	6.28	5.95	5.97	5.91	6.21	6.29	8.08	9.09	0.00
SCPZR	3.15	2.74	2.74	3.21	3.13	0.00	0.00	0.00	0.00
HSS	1.08	0.90	0.86	0.00	0.00	0.00	0.00	0.00	0.00
LSU	6.52	5.95	5.97	6.23	6.21	6.29	8.08	9.09	0.00
OH	4.59	4.11	4.10	4.50	5.33	6.29	0.00	0.00	0.00
SPR-RSČ	5.98	5.48	5.48	5.91	5.77	6.29	4.04	0.00	0.00
KAN	2.69	2.28	2.74	2.78	0.00	0.00	0.00	0.00	0.00
ROI	0.26	0.00	0.00	0.00	0.00	0.00	0.00	0.00	0.00
LBL	14.05	14.16	14.18	15.02	14.66	13.29	16.16	18.18	0.00
SPP	1.30	1.35	1.33	0.00	0.00	0.00	0.00	0.00	0.00
NEI	1.37	1.35	1.33	0.00	0.00	0.00	0.00	0.00	0.00
ODS-KDS	29.73	34.73	34.83	35.68	37.73	42.66	47.44	54.55	100.00
Total	100.00	100.01	99.99	100.00	100.03	99.98	99.96	100.00	100.00

Table 6.12, Table 6.13, and Table 6.14 summarize the results of parallel analysis for the Slovak National Council. Table 6.12 presents an estimation of proportional representation under different thresholds. The situation is very similar to the picture from the Czech National Council: the Slovak government coalition secures a majority at the 4-percent threshold. One-party rule in this case is reached only at the 8-percent threshold; from this point of view, in June 1992, the political scene in the Slovak Republic was a bit more pluralistic than in the Czech Republic, a surprising finding. It is interesting that the power of the leading Slovak political party (HZDS) did not depend as much on the logarithm-based electoral rules as did ODS-KDS. Power decomposition in the 50-percent majority case shows that HZDS had even less power under a 5-percent threshold than it would have had under a zero threshold (see Table 6.13). But for 60-percent majority rule (see Table 6.14), the 5-percent threshold is very significant for HZDS (it led to an increase in power from 47.10 percent under a zero-threshold simulation to 61.90 percent under a 5-percent threshold).

CONCLUSION

The Czechoslovak case study does show that proportional representation with thresholds led to a significant decrease in the number of parliamentary parties and prevented the fragmentation of parliamentary representation. On the other hand, its imposition did not eliminate separatist parties. Furthermore, one of its side effects was a gross misrepresentation of individual preferences and substantial increases in deviations from proportionality. Misrepresentation was given not only due to an a posteriori redistribution of votes but also to an a priori redistribution: a rational voter tended not to vote for the party that he ranked first in terms of personal preference but rather looked for parties that were as high as possible in his ranking while at the same time had a legitimate chance of winning more than the requisite 5-percent threshold minimum. Therefore, it can be assumed that strategic voting, a strong yet unmeasurable variable, is an additional factor to consider when analyzing the June 1992 elections. In any event, the presented simulation shows that varying electoral rules can significantly influence electoral outcomes. Given the same distribution of votes among the parties, different rules can provide significantly different power distributions among the competing political formations. For the Czechs and the Slovaks, the choice of a high threshold may have enhanced "governability" but also increased the relative power of the common state's enemies.

APPENDIX

1. The distribution of votes among the parties in a committee is not a sufficient characteristic of power or influence distribution. This can be seen clearly from a

Table 6.12 Simulation of Proportional Representation in the Slovak National Council

	Votes %	Estimation of Proportional Representation for Different Thresholds								
Slovak National Council		0%	1%	2%	3%	4%	5%	6%	7%	8%
HSD-SMS	0.12	0.00	0.00	0.00	0.00	0.00	0.00	0.00	0.00	0.00
HSP-SRU	0.06	0.00	0.00	0.00	0.00	0.00	0.00	0.00	0.00	0.00
HZDS	37.26	38.00	38.67	40.00	41.33	44.67	49.33	49.33	49.33	51.33
SDL	14.70	14.67	15.33	15.33	16.00	17.33	19.33	19.33	19.33	24.00
SPI	0.96	0.67	0.00	0.00	0.00	0.00	0.00	0.00	0.00	0.00
HZOS	0.23	0.00	0.00	0.00	0.00	0.00	0.00	0.00	0.00	0.00
SS-SNZ	0.30	0.00	0.00	0.00	0.00	0.00	0.00	0.00	0.00	0.00
SKDH	3.05	3.33	3.33	3.33	3.33	0.00	0.00	0.00	0.00	0.00
MKDH-ESWS	7.42	8.00	8.00	8.00	8.00	8.67	9.33	9.33	9.33	0.00
HZSS	0.11	0.00	0.00	0.00	0.00	0.00	0.00	0.00	0.00	0.00
SZ	1.08	1.33	1.33	0.00	0.00	0.00	0.00	0.00	0.00	0.00
KDH	8.88	8.67	9.33	9.33	10.00	10.67	12.00	12.00	12.00	14.67
ODU	4.03	4.00	4.00	4.00	4.67	4.67	0.00	0.00	0.00	0.00
ZPR-RSC	0.32	0.00	0.00	0.00	0.00	0.00	0.00	0.00	0.00	0.00
NALI	0.08	0.00	0.00	0.00	0.00	0.00	0.00	0.00	0.00	0.00
SZS	2.14	2.00	2.00	2.00	0.00	0.00	0.00	0.00	0.00	0.00
ROI	0.59	0.67	0.00	0.00	0.00	0.00	0.00	0.00	0.00	0.00
SDSS	4.00	4.00	4.00	4.00	4.67	4.67	0.00	0.00	0.00	0.00
KSS 91	0.75	0.67	0.00	0.00	0.00	0.00	0.00	0.00	0.00	0.00
DS-ODS	3.31	3.33	3.33	3.33	3.33	0.00	0.00	0.00	0.00	0.00
SNS	7.93	8.00	8.00	8.00	8.67	9.33	10.00	10.00	10.00	10.00
SLS	0.29	0.00	0.00	0.00	0.00	0.00	0.00	0.00	0.00	0.00
MOS	2.29	2.66	2.67	2.67	0.00	0.00	0.00	0.00	0.00	0.00
TOTAL	99.90	100.00	99.99	99.99	100.00	100.01	99.99	99.99	99.99	100.00
DP (%)		2.35	4.03	5.11	9.37	15.73	23.76	23.76	23.76	39.11
Number of Parties		15	12	11	9	7	5	5	5	3
Profederal or Indifferent	51.29	50.67	50.02	47.76	46.67	46.01	40.66	40.66	40.66	38.67
Government Coalition (%)	45.19	46.00	46.67	48.00	50.00	54.00	59.33	59.33	59.33	61.33

Table 6.13 Simulation of Power Distribution in the Slovak National Council (50% Majority)

Slovak National Council	Votes %	Banzhaf Power Indices for 50% Majority for Different Thresholds								
		0%	1%	2%	3%	4%	5%	6%	7%	8%
HSD-SMS	0.12	0.00	0.00	.00	0.00	0.00	0.00	0.00	0.00	0.00
HSP-SRU	0.06	0.00	0.00	0.00	0.00	0.00	0.00	0.00	0.00	0.00
HZDS	37.26	64.06	63.88	67.50	65.53	67.44	63.64	63.64	63.64	90.00
SDL	14.70	5.77	6.12	5.49	6.48	6.98	9.09	9.09	9.09	0.00
SPI	0.96	0.45	0.00	0.00	0.00	0.00	0.00	0.00	0.00	0.00
HZOS	0.23	0.00	0.00	0.00	0.00	0.00	0.00	0.00	0.00	0.00
SS-SNZ	0.30	0.00	0.00	0.00	0.00	0.00	0.00	0.00	0.00	0.00
SKDH	3.05	2.16	2.15	2.07	1.97	0.00	0.00	0.00	0.00	0.00
MKDH-ESWS	7.42	5.12	5.37	5.06	5.35	6.98	9.09	9.09	9.09	0.00
HZSS	0.11	0.00	0.00	0.00	0.00	0.00	0.00	0.00	0.00	0.00
SZ	1.08	0.89	0.85	0.00	0.00	0.00	0.00	0.00	0.00	0.00
KDH	8.88	5.34	5.87	5.20	6.48	6.98	9.09	9.09	9.09	0.00
ODU	4.03	2.57	2.63	2.49	3.10	2.33	0.00	0.00	0.00	0.00
ZPR-RSC	0.32	0.00	0.00	0.00	0.00	0.00	0.00	0.00	0.00	0.00
NALI	0.08	0.00	0.00	0.00	0.00	0.00	0.00	0.00	0.00	0.00
SZS	2.14	1.18	1.26	0.78	0.00	0.00	0.00	0.00	0.00	0.00
ROI	0.?	0.45	0.00	0.00	0.00	0.00	0.00	0.00	0.00	0.00
SDSS	.00	2.57	2.63	2.49	3.10	2.33	0.00	0.00	0.00	0.00
KSS 91	0.75	0.45	0.00	0.00	0.00	0.00	0.00	0.00	0.00	0.00
DS-ODS	3.31	2.16	2.15	2.07	1.97	0.00	0.00	0.00	0.00	0.00
SNS	7.93	5.12	5.37	5.06	5.92	6.98	9.09	9.09	9.09	10.00
SLS	0.29	0.00	0.00	0.00	0.00	0.00	0.00	0.00	0.00	0.00
MOS	2.29	1.72	1.81	1.78	0.00	0.00	0.00	0.00	0.00	0.00
Total	99.90	100.01	100.09	99.99	99.90	100.02	100.00	100.00	100.00	100.00

Table 6.14 Simulation of Power Distribution in the Slovak National Council (60% Majority)

Slovak National Council	Votes %	Banzhaf Power Indices for 60% Majority for Different Thresholds								
		0%	1%	2%	3%	4%	5%	6%	7%	8%
HSD-SMS	0.12	0.00	0.00	0.00	0.00	0.00	0.00	0.00	0.00	0.00
HSP-SRU	0.06	0.00	0.00	0.00	0.00	0.00	0.00	0.00	0.00	0.00
HZDS	37.26	47.10	48.10	50.47	52.85	56.04	61.90	61.90	61.90	90.00
SDL	14.70	12.77	13.26	12.73	12.95	14.29	14.29	14.29	14.29	0.00
SPI	0.96	0.56	0.00	0.00	0.00	0.00	0.00	0.00	0.00	0.00
HZOS	0.23	0.00	0.00	0.00	0.00	0.00	0.00	0.00	0.00	0.00
SS-SNZ	0.30	0.00	0.00	0.00	0.00	0.00	0.00	0.00	0.00	0.00
SKDH	3.05	2.78	2.79	2.82	3.11	0.00	0.00	0.00	0.00	0.00
MKDH-ESWS	7.42	6.85	6.77	6.58	6.74	7.69	4.76	4.76	4.76	0.00
HZSS	0.11	0.00	0.00	0.00	0.00	0.00	0.00	0.00	0.00	0.00
SZ	1.08	1.13	1.19	0.00	0.00	0.00	0.00	0.00	0.00	0.00
KDH	8.88	7.47	8.05	7.96	7.25	7.69	14.29	14.29	14.29	0.00
ODU	4.03	3.34	3.28	3.20	3.63	3.30	0.00	0.00	0.00	0.00
ZPR-RSC	0.32	0.00	0.00	0.00	0.00	0.00	0.00	0.00	0.00	0.00
NALI	0.08	0.00	0.00	0.00	0.00	0.00	0.00	0.00	0.00	0.00
SZS	2.14	1.71	1.62	1.82	0.00	0.00	0.00	0.00	0.00	0.00
ROI	0.59	0.56	0.00	0.00	0.00	0.00	0.00	0.00	0.00	0.00
SDSS	4.00	3.34	3.28	3.20	3.63	3.30	0.00	0.00	0.00	0.00
KSS 91	0.75	0.56	0.00	0.00	0.00	0.00	0.00	0.00	0.00	0.00
DS-ODS	3.31	2.78	2.79	2.82	3.11	0.00	0.00	0.00	0.00	0.00
SNS	7.93	6.85	6.77	6.58	6.74	7.69	4.76	4.76	4.76	10.00
SLS	0.29	0.00	0.00	0.00	0.00	0.00	0.00	0.00	0.00	0.00
MOS	2.29	2.21	2.11	1.82	0.00	0.00	0.00	0.00	0.00	0.00
TOTAL	99.90	100.01	100.01	100.00	100.01	100.00	100.00	100.00	100.00	100.00

simple example of a three-member committee with 100 votes distributed among them, as in the following table:

parties	seats
1	49
2	2
3	49

With respect to the simple majority voting rule (50 percent plus one vote) all three members have the same position in the voting process (any two-member coalition is a winning one; no single member can win). In fact, under certain circumstances (if the two large members 1 and 3 have strictly opposite interests), the role of member 2 could be essential. Quite a different situation can be observed for a qualified majority, say, 70 percent. In this case member 2 has no influence on the outcomes of voting, and cooperation between members 1 and 3 is needed for approving any decision.

We can see that it is important to look for some measures that express the actual distribution of power among the members of a committee better than the data about proportional representation. Such measures do indeed exist and are called "power indices" in the literature on public choice. In this paper we use two of the most well-known measures of voting power, the so-called Shapley–Shubik and Banzhaf–Coleman power indices.

To illustrate the reasoning behind Shapley and Shubik's voting power measure (SS-power index) consider a four-member committee (with 100 votes distributed among them) characterized by the following table:

parties	seats
1	20
2	25
3	38
4	17

The committee is faced with a series of motions or bills on each of which the members will vote yes or no. Shapley and Shubik consider the process of building coalition support for a particular bill. Let us suppose that simple majority is required to pass the bill (51 votes in our case). The bill may be most enthusiastically supported by, say, member 2, second most enthusiastically by 4, next most by 1, and least by 3. Thus 2 would be the first member to join a coalition in support of the bill, followed by 4. At this point the bill would still lose, and in fact it will be able to pass only if the coalition can gain the support of the next most enthusiastic member, who would be, in this example, number 1. Gaining 1's support may require considerable modifications to the original bill, so that member 1 has a say over the form in which the bill will pass, if it passes. Thus, member 1 has crucial power in this situation.

In an abstract setting, we would not have a priori knowledge about the possible orders of coalition formation. Shapley and Shubik therefore propose that in order to measure abstract voting power, we should consider all orders equally likely. For each order, one member will be pivotal just as member 1 was above: the losing coalition will become a winning one precisely when the pivotal member joins it. The pivotal member holds the crucial balance of power. Hence, as the measure of a member's voting power we use the probability that this member will be pivotal, assuming that all orders of coalition formation are equally likely. (For a discussion of different aspects of the Shapley–Shubik power index, see Roth, ed., 1988; for applications to various voting situations and interpretation, see, Straffin 1980).

For our four-member committee with simple majority rule, there are 4! = 24 possible orders of forming the winning coalitions:

$$
\begin{array}{cccc}
123^*4 & 213^*4 & 31^*24 & 412^*3 \\
124^*3 & 214^*3 & 31^*42 & 413^*2 \\
13^*24 & 23^*14 & 32^*14 & 421^*3 \\
13^*42 & 23^*41 & 32^*41 & 423^*1 \\
142^*3 & 241^*3 & 34^*12 & 43^*12 \\
143^*2 & 243^*1 & 34^*21 & 43^*21
\end{array}
$$

We place an asterisk immediately following the pivotal member in each order for purposes of illustration. Member 3 is pivotal in 12 of the 24 orders, while each of the other members is pivotal only in 4 of the orders. The Shapley–Shubik power indices of the members are thus 4 out of 24 for 1, 4 out of the 24 for 2, 12 out of the 24 for 3, and 4 out of 24 for 4. We thus obtain the following evaluation of distribution of power among the parties: (1/6, 1/6, 1/2, 1/6).

The Banzhaf–Coleman power index (BC power index) follows a different logic. To calculate it, we have to write down all the winning coalitions and in each of them to note the "swing" voters (if such exist), those who, by changing their vote, could change the vote one way or the other. For our committee, we enumerated all of the possible coalitions:

1	2	3	4		
20	25	38	17	51	
+	+	+	+	100	W
+	+	+*	−	83	W
+*	+*	−	+*	62	W
+	+	−	−	45	L
+	−	+*	+	75	W
+*	−	+*	−	58	W

+	−	−	+	37	L
+	−	−	−	20	L
−	+	+*	+	80	W
−	+*	+*	−	63	W
−	+	−	+	42	L
−	+	−	−	25	L
−	−	+*	+*	55	W
−	−	+	−	38	L
−	−	−	+	17	L
−	−	−	−	0	L
2	2	6	2	12	

Since in each voting situation the committee splits into two parts: those who vote yes and those who vote no or abstain. We denote the yes coalitions by plus and not yes coalitions by minus. There exist exactly 2^n coalitions, 16 in our case.

By the asterisk we denote the swing members in each winning coalition. We can see that for the simple majority voting rule, we have eight possible winning coalitions. Members 1 and 2 and 4 are each twice in the swing position, while member 3 is in the swing position six times. There are exactly twelve possible swings in the committee. Assuming that in a large number of voting situations all possible coalitions are equally probable, we can evaluate the power of the members as a ratio of the number of swings the member can make to the total number of possible swings. Thus the Banzhaf–Coleman power indices of the members in our committee are (1/6, 1/6, 1/2, 1/6) (in our example, identical to the Shapley–Shubik indices).

2. To enable us to explore the former Czechoslovakia's unusual parliamentary structure, we may suppose that a committee consists of several subcommittees that vote separately and that any bill must be approved by a majority in all subcommittees. We shall call such a system a *multicameral committee*. What are the power indices in such a committee?

Consider a three-party committee consisting of three subcommittees:

parties	sub 1	sub 2	sub 3	committee
1	50	25	10	85
2	45	10	15	70
3	5	15	25	45
	100	50	50	200

Following the same reasoning as in the case of a one-cameral committee, let us suppose that the simple majority is required to pass a bill (51 votes in subcommittee 1, 26 votes in subcommittee 2, and 26 votes in subcommittee 3) and that a bill is most enthusiastically supported by party 1, second by party 2, and third by party 3. Thus, 1 would be the first party to join the coalition to support the bill, but not having a majority in all subcommittees it would look for the support of another party. Then party 2 will join the coalition. This coalition has the majority in subcommittee 1 and subcommittee 2, but the bill would still lose because of not having the majority in subcommittee 3. It will be able to win only if the coalition can gain the support of party 3. So, in this case party 3 is pivotal.

To derive an extension of the Shapley–Shubik power index, we should consider, in this case, all orders of coalition formation and look for pivotal members in the manner shown above. The Shapley–Shubik power index of a member of the committee is given by the probability that the member will be pivotal, providing that all orders of coalition formation are equally probable.

There are 3! = 6 possible orders of forming the winning coalitions in our case:

sub 1	sub 2	sub 3	committee
12^*3	12^*3	123^*	123^*
13^*2	13^*2	13^*2	13^*2
21^*3	21^*3	213^*	213^*
231^*	231^*	23^*1	23^*1
31^*2	31^*2	31^*2	31^*2
321^*	321^*	32^*1	32^*1

We marked the pivotal members with an asterisk in every subcommittee for a simple majority considered only in this subcommittee. It can be easily seen that the pivotal member for a given order of creating a winning coalition in a particular subcommittee is pivotal in our three-cameral committee only if the coalition losing in at least one subcommittee will become winning in all subcommittees precisely when the member joins it. Clearly this is the last marked member among the other marked members in all subcommittees. (For example the coalition {1,2} is winning in subcommittee 1 and subcommittee 2, but it is losing in subcommittee 3. So, without cooperation with party 3 it cannot pass a bill; in this case party 3 is pivotal). We can see that party 1 is pivotal in three of six orders, party 2 is not pivotal at all, and party 3 is pivotal in three of six orders, so we can evaluate the power of the parties by Shapley–Shubik power indices as

$$(1/2, 0, 1/2)$$

By similar argumentation we can extend the concept of a swing and modify the Banzhaf–Coleman power index for multicameral committees. In our particular case we shall obtain the same values of the BC power indices as the SS-power indices.

We receive a rather surprising result: with respect to a simple majority vote, the power of party 3 (with only 22.5 percent of deputies) in our three-cameral committee is the same as the power of party 1 (with 42.5 percent of deputies), while party 2 (with 35 percent of deputies) has no voting power at all.

3. Let $i = 1, 2, ..., n$ be the electoral parties ordered in a single left-right ideological dimension in such a way that they are numbered from left to right. Let us denote by v_1 the number of votes for the party i in the election and by s_1 the number of seats allocated to the party i after the election.

To characterize a political profile of a committee and to compare the situation in different committees, we can use concepts of density and cumulative distribution of parties' representation in the committee (see Turnovec 1995).

The political profile of a committee may be characterized by the density function

$$f(i,s) = s_i/(s_1+s_2+...+s_n)$$

(proportions of votes for the parties) and by two cumulative distribution functions: LR-cumulative-distribution function

$$F^{LR}(i,s) = f(1,s)+f(2,s)+...+f(i,s)$$

(total proportion of seats of all the parties at least as left as i including i, or the proportion of voters who would oppose any shift in policy to the right of i), and RL-cumulative-distribution function

$$F^{RL}(i,s) = f(i,s)+f(i+1,s)+...+f(n,s)$$

(total proportion of votes of all the parties at least as right as i including i, or the proportion of voters who would oppose any shift in policy to the left of i).

For the purposes of simplicity, let us suppose that F^{RL} and F^{LR} are continuous over an ideological line, then a position x_0 that solves the equation

$$F^{LR}(x,s) = F^{RL}(x,s)$$

defines some sort of political equilibrium: the proportion of votes that would oppose any shift in policy right of x_0 is the same as the proportion of votes that would oppose any shift in policy to the left of x_0. We shall call this position a political profile of the society. Since it is difficult to introduce a cardinal measure of a distance on an ideological line, but it is possible to locate a center, we shall use a diagrammatic representation of a density distribution and a cumulative distribution and visualize the political profile on the diagrams as the position of intersection of the LR- and RL-cumulative-distribution curves with respect to the center.

4. For electoral system with $q\%$ threshold let us denote by $i = 1, \ldots, n_1$ the parties that received at least $q\%$ of valid votes and by $i = n_1 + 1, \ldots, n$ the other parties. Assume that v_i and s_1 are expressed as ratios. Since

$$s_i \geq v_i \text{ for } i = 1,2, \ldots ,n_1$$

and

$$\sum_{i=1}^{n_1} v_i = 1 - \sum_{i=n_1+1}^{n} v_i$$

we have

$$D = \frac{1}{2}\left(\sum_{i=1}^{n}|s_i - v_i|\right) = \frac{1}{2}\left[\left(\sum_{i=1}^{n_1}s_i - v_i\right) + \sum_{i=n_1+1}^{n} v_i\right]$$

$$= \frac{1}{2}\left[\sum_{i=1}^{n}s_i - \sum_{i=1}^{n_1}v_i + \sum_{i=n_1+1}^{n} v_i\right] = \frac{1}{2}\left[200 - 2\sum_{i=1}^{n_1}v_i\right]$$

$$= 100 - \sum_{i=1}^{n_1}v_i = \sum_{i=n_1+1}^{n} v_i$$

Hence the proportionality measure (deviation from proportionality) in this case equals the total share of the votes for the parties that did not overcome the corresponding threshold.

NOTES

1. This research was undertaken with support from the European Commission's Phare ACE Programme 1994, project No. 94-0666-R. The author benefited from numerous discussions with Allison Stanger and Michael Kraus.

2. The Czechoslovak constitutional system was analyzed in greater detail by Lijphart (1992) and Stanger (1996); a comparative analysis of the electoral systems of Central and East European countries shortly after 1989 was attempted by Kuusela (1991).

3. The case of Czechoslovakia is quite interesting in that it seems to present a problematic trade-off: the model shows that proportional representation with a high threshold level increased the power of the "separation-friendly" forces in the parliaments, while proportional representation with a lower threshold level produces a minority government, which is, arguably, a situation where the power to dissolve the state would be much harder to harness. Put another way, high thresholds may enhance governability while misrepresenting voter preferences; low thresholds more accurately reflect voter preferences, yet make it more difficult to govern.

4. Approval voting is a comparatively modern method, suggested by Brams and Fishburn (1983). In approval voting, each voter can vote for as many candidates as he wishes,

but for each candidate he can give either one vote or no votes. While in the Czechoslovak proportional system, each voter voted for a party list, he could also, within a selected party list, apply the approval voting principle, as long as it was restricted to his or her four selected candidates.

5. For an analysis of the 1990 election results, see Turnovec (1991, 1992b), and Turnovec and Vester (1992b).

6. Interestingly enough, approximately 25 percent of the electorate voted to elect different parties to the federal and republican parliaments.

7. The results of elections are given by ordering the parties on a left–right ideological line. We are aware of the fact that the clustering may be questionable. As a basic principle we used the attitude of the parties to the speed and intensity of economic transition (left— parties that emphasize government engagement in the economy; centrists—supporters of social market economy; right—rapid economic transformation with diminishing economic role of the state). An exception, however, must be made for extreme right parties, which usually do not present clear positions on the economic transformation and emphasize national and populist topics.

REFERENCES

Banzhaf, J. F. "Weighted Voting doesn't Work: a Mathematical Analysis." *Rutgers Law Review* 19 (1965): 317–343.

Brams, S., and P. C. Fishburn. *Approval Voting*. Boston: Birkhäuser, 1983.

Coleman, J. "Control of Collectivities and a Power of a Collectivity to Act." In *Social Choice*, ed. B. Liberman. New York: Gordon and Breach, 1971.

Holubiec, J. W., and J. W. Mercik. *Inside Voting Procedures*. Munich: Accedo Verlag, 1994.

Kuusela, K. *The New Electoral Systems in Eastern Europe 1989–91*. Turku: University of Turku, 1991.

Lijphart, A. "Democratization and Constitutional Choices in Czecho-Slovakia, Hungary and Poland 1989–1991." *Journal of Theoretical Politics* 4 (1992): 207–223.

Roth, A. E., ed. *The Shapley Value (Essays in honour of Lloyd S. Shapley)*. Cambridge: Cambridge University Press, 1988.

Shapley, L. S., and M. Shubik. "A Method for Evaluating the Distribution of Power in a Committee System." *American Political Science Review* 48 (1954): 787–792.

Stanger, A. "Constitutional Change and Democracy in Post-Communist Central Europe: How Important is a Radical Break with the Past?" Paper presented at the Wissenschaft-szentrum Berlin, 28 March 1996.

Straffin, P. D. *Topics in the Theory of Voting*. Boston: Birkhauser, 1980.

"Strany, hnutí a koalice pro parlamentní volby 1992." *Hospodářské noviny*, 21 April 1992.

Taagapera, R., and M. Shugart. *Seats and Votes. The Effects and Determinants of Electoral Systems*. New Haven: Yale University Press, 1989.

Turnovec, F. "*A Priori* Power Distribution in Czechoslovak Parliaments." *Ekonomicko-matematický obzor* 27, no. 3 (1991): 289–297.

———."The 1992 ČSFR General Parliamentary Election." *Czechoslovak Journal for Operations Research* 1, no. 2 (1992a): 159–162.

————."Power Distribution in Czechoslovak parliaments." *Control and Cybernetics* 21, no. 2 (1992b): 193–205.

————."The Political System and Economic Transition." In *The Czech Republic and Economic Transition in Eastern Europe*, ed. Jan Svejnar. New York: Academic Press, 1995, 47–103.

————."1996 Parliamentary Election in the Czech Republic, Electoral Preferences and Distribution of Power." *Central European Journal for Operations Research and Economics* 4, no. 3 (1996): 231–238.

Turnovec, F., and M. Vester (1992a): "Computation of Power Indices in Multi-Cameral Quota Majority Games." *Czechoslovak Journal for Operations Research* 1, no. 3 (1992): 228–232.

————."Differentiation and Changes in Power Distribution in the Federal Parliament of ČSFR." *Czechoslovak Journal for Operations Research* 1, no. 1 (1992): 57–60.

"Úřední přehled volebních výsledků vydaných Ústřední, Českou a Slovenskou volební komisí." *Hospodářské noviny*, 11 June 1992.

"Ústavný zákon o Československej federácii z 2. októbra 1968, č. 143 Zb."

"Zakon č. 47/1990 Zb. o volbách do Federálného zhromaždenia" v znení zákonného opatrenia FZ č 208/1990 Zb. a zákona č. 59-92 Zb. (úplné znenie č. 60/1992 Zb.).

"Zákon SNR č. 80/1990 Zb. o volbách do SNR" v znení zákona SNR z, 26 February 1992.

7

The Price of Velvet: Constitutional Politics and the Demise of the Czechoslovak Federation

Allison Stanger

INTRODUCTION

Regardless of their disciplinary homes, scholars of those lands where communism once reigned are, in some sense, all transitologists now. One consequence of the collapse of communism in Europe, therefore, has been the swelling of the literature on democratic transitions to voluminous proportions. Social scientists East and West, however, have largely neglected the comparative study of "the contexts in which constitutional formulas are adopted or retained."[1] Yet the study of constitutions and the political struggles that accompany their promulgation and institutionalization provide a window on the way in which key actors in any transition perceive themselves and their relationship to rivals for power in both the new regime and in the external world. Constitutions are more than narrow legal documents; as Robert Sharlet aptly puts it, they are "meta-policy on the rules of the game," and the politics of constitution crafting are a revealing mirror of the state's past, present, and future.[2]

To investigate and assess the constitutional choices that Václav Havel and his compatriots made in the early days of postcommunism, it is helpful to begin by placing these developments in larger comparative perspective. The opponents of communism in power all faced a common and immediate problem once it became clear that the old regime was on its last legs: What was to be done with the abundant legal inheritance from the totalitarian era, especially the constitutions, which all paid lip service to democracy and the rule of law but had functioned in practice as the tools of the one-party state?

While the actual range of choice was circumscribed by the balance of political power in each state, aspiring democratizers in the postcommunist context could follow three basic paths to constitutional reconstruction. First, the custodians of the transition could restore precommunist constitutions, where they existed. Second, postcommunist elites had the option of pursuing a strategy of "radical continuity," whereby the communist constitution would be accepted as the law of the land only to be amended beyond recognition following its own amendment rules, in this way pursuing a "revolution by constitutional tinkering."[3] The path of radical continuity, in short, consists of grafting revolutionary amendments onto an undemocratic constitutional base. Third, proponents of change could renounce the constitution of the ancien régime and concentrate their efforts on drafting a brand new charter, either adopting an interim basic law to govern politics until that task was completed or promulgating a new constitution concurrently with the retirement of the old.

The third option is the one most familiar to citizens of the West, especially Americans, yet the transition to democracy in Poland, Hungary, and the former Czechoslovakia followed the second path. Each of these countries embraced the method of radical continuity as a stopgap measure until a new constitution could be drafted and ratified. Each found the task of agreeing on a new constitutional framework to be more rather than less difficult as the initial revolutionary euphoria evaporated.[4] In the former Czechoslovakia, the unintended consequences of early constitutional decisions were arguably most profound. The ultimate price of adopting the communist legal framework as a point of departure for regime change in Czechoslovakia was the death of the common state itself.

In maintaining that communism's legal legacy was a contributing factor to Czechoslovakia's demise, I do not mean to suggest that there were easy and obvious means to resolving the postcommunist constitutional crisis that were not properly exploited. With the benefit of hindsight, it is tempting enough to pronounce the dissolution of Czechoslovakia inevitable, but leaping to this conclusion has the unfortunate consequence of obscuring more than is likely to be revealed. This chapter argues that if the potential for Czechoslovakia to survive communism's demise indeed existed, the negotiation and implementation of new constitutional first principles for a democratic life were a necessary condition for the common state's continued viability. It begins with the assumption that Czechoslovakia's partition may have been probable but was not inevitable and then explores the range of alternative courses of action that existed, and the tradeoffs among them, in an attempt to ascertain whether the road not taken might have led to a different ultimate destination.

The remarks that follow are divided into four principal sections. In the first part of my chapter, I lay out Civic Forum's early constitutional choices and attempt to account for them. I then turn to a discussion of the impact of those choices on the quest for a new federation and demonstrate how inherited concepts and institutions exacerbated rather than ameliorated ethnic tensions. In the penultimate section, I use Bruce Ackerman's conception of the "constitutional moment" to consider the significance of timing and sequence in Czechoslovakia's transition and in the former communist federations more generally. I conclude by framing the critical events this chapter examines with their proper historical context in an effort to shed further light on the causes of Czechoslovakia's dissolution.

CIVIC FORUM'S APPROACH TO
CONSTITUTIONAL TRANSFORMATION

In contrast to its neighbors, Czechoslovakia had a slumbering democratic tradition, which was at least a potential weapon in the hand of communism's opponents. After all, the 1920 constitution had framed twenty years of uninterrupted parliamentary democracy earlier in the century. In early discussions in dissident circles, the idea of utilizing the 1920 constitution as a point of departure for recasting the totalitarian order was proposed but never received any serious consideration.[5] In all likelihood, the reason that restoring the interwar constitution of 1920 was never an option that was seriously entertained was that it was based on the obsolete notion of Czechoslovakism (its opening lines, for example, read "We the Czechoslovak people"), which in 1989 had for some Slovaks become a euphemism for Czech chauvinism. As such, Czechoslovakia's "usable past" with respect to constitutional considerations was less usable than it might initially appear.

Another distinctive feature of the Czechoslovak revolution is found in the character of the transition process itself. The governing coalition that emerged from the Czechoslovak Round Table talks differed from its Polish and Hungarian counterparts—both of which had taken place before the fall of the Berlin Wall—in one critical respect: when the dust had cleared, the opposition had effective control of both domestic and foreign policy. While the interim Government of National Understanding formed by Marián Čalfa on 10 December 1989 looked like a power-sharing arrangement on paper because of communist premier Ladislav Adamec's prior attempt to stack the first interim government (which forced his resignation), in practice, it was not.[6] With respect to matters of constitutional import, therefore, the makers of the Velvet Revolution had unprecedented potential power to remake the institutions of the communist regime.

Even though the Czechoslovak communist regime was of the hard-line variety when compared with its reforming Warsaw Pact allies (the Czechoslovak Communist Party's initial reaction to *glasnost* in the Soviet Union, for example, was to stop selling *Pravda* in Prague), its minions had nonetheless been hard at work on a new constitution that might incorporate the Gorbachev agenda. The Communist Party member who was to eventually lead the Government of National Understanding, Marián Čalfa, had served the old regime since 1988 as the federal minister for legislation. In that capacity, he had headed the committee in charge of drafting a new constitution, which had been scheduled to go into force in

1990.[7] The Čalfa commission had produced a draft in the fall of 1989, which mentioned neither the leading role of the Communist Party nor Marxism-Leninism.[8] Consequently, Civic Forum's request early on in its negotiations for the removal of the party's leading role from the constitution was immediately acceptable to the communist government in principle, as long as the changes were implemented according to existing legal procedures.[9]

What is striking about the Czechoslovak roundtable talks, however, is the extent to which the opposition treated the existing constitution with greater reverence than did its communist creators; for example, it was future prime minister Václav Klaus, not a member of the government negotiating team, who urged that President Gustav Husák appoint the members of the interim government before resigning, so as to adhere to the letter of the law.[10] Although in December 1989 the party's representatives proposed holding immediate direct elections to the presidency, which would have enabled the opposition to appeal over the heads of the Federal Assembly that had been "elected" in 1986 directly to the Czech and Slovak people, Civic Forum's leadership insisted that Czechoslovakia's new caretaker president be elected by the parliament, as specified in the old regime's constitution.[11]

The cautious behavior of Civic Forum's leadership on matters of constitutional import cannot be explained as an effort to buy time to formulate a clearly defined position. Civic Forum already had a professionally elaborated draft federal constitution in hand at the roundtable talks.[12] Civic Forum's December 1989 draft, in turn, was not entirely a creation of revolutionary times but built on the dissident community's earlier work on democratic first principles. When in January 1989, the Husák regime announced that it had begun work on a new constitution (proclaiming that a public discussion on the matter should commence, which of course never took place), the members of the coordinating committee of the Movement for Civic Freedom (HOS) launched a parallel project. Their first move was to ask then-dissident and future Czech premier Petr Pithart to organize a group of lawyers to work on an official alternative charter. According to Pithart himself, the group never dreamed that their creation might one day function as the basic law of the land. Their principal motive in drafting a new constitution was to have a rival document of their own in hand when the communist regime announced the successful completion of its own constitutional initiative. To appear to be outflanked on constitutional matters by an undemocratic government was clearly problematic.[13]

Unfortunately, this expert initiative was slow to bear fruit, and in June 1989, the members of HOS decided to issue a more general statement of first principles instead. Future Slovak prime minister Ján Čarnogurský, a member of HOS, wanted both republics to be equal before the law, to have their own constitutions, symbols, and flags, and for the federative union to be formed out of the free will of the constituent republics; the Moravian representative also requested that his region be recognized in the constitution.[14] In the wake of the Velvet Revolution, these ideas would spring to life in myriad forms in the debate on the form and content of Czechoslovakia's democratic refounding.

The task of formally elaborating and codifying the principles expressed in the HOS declaration, however, remained incomplete until the events of November 1989 jump started the process. With the communist regime collapsing and the job not yet completed, Havel turned to a fellow dissident with legal expertise, Pavel Rychetský, and asked him to draft a new constitution.[15] Havel thought it important for Civic Forum to have a formal codification of its vision for Czechoslovakia's future, despite the fact that others—such as the lawyer Zdeněk Jičínský, who was one of the authors of the 1960 socialist constitution as well as a key architect of constitutional reform during the Prague Spring—did not share Havel's sense of urgency.[16] Rychetský promised Havel that he could have a draft in two days, provided he did not sleep, and was able to deliver on this promise.[17]

In the midst of the unfolding revolution, however, the Civic Forum draft constitution appears to have had neither generated controversy nor received sustained attention.[18] Although Havel initially found it imperative for Civic Forum to have its own rival draft in hand as it negotiated with the outgoing order, he postponed addressing the constitutional issue until after the first free and fair elections had been held in June 1990.[19] Despite the existence of alternative courses of action, then, both opposition and government were in tacit agreement that the existing point of departure for the transfer of power would be the communist constitution, albeit for different reasons.[20] Given that their demands for constitutional amendments were all accepted with little resistance and that the balance of power was in their favor, why did the makers of the Velvet Revolution from the outset embrace a conservative approach to the necessary transformation of the country's basic law, especially when they had a draft of a new constitution that they might have proposed as a provisional replacement?

In framing an answer to this question, there are at least four factors that are of importance. First, the hard-line nature of the Czechoslovak communist regime certainly must be taken into account. It was difficult, at the time, to imagine that the apparatus would accept substantive change without a fight, and the outgoing order still had all the instruments of repressive power in its hands.[21] While the fear level at the Polish and Hungarian roundtable talks was also palpable, given that both sets of negotiations took place before the fall of the Berlin Wall, this must be weighed against the mitigating factor that the price of a crackdown was higher for reform communists than it was for unreconstructed party members of the Czech and Slovak variety.

Second, in many respects, Civic Forum was understandably wholly unprepared for the breathtaking pace of change. In Timothy Garton Ash's oft-cited phrase, it took ten years to make the revolution in Poland, ten months in Hungary, and ten days in Czechoslovakia.[22] Czechs and Slovaks did not have the luxury of self-consciously reflecting on the course that the revolution was taking while they were negotiating; there simply was not enough time in the day.[23] Viewed in this context, it is perhaps unsurprising that when in round two of the negotiations Ladislav Adamec unexpectedly asked the opposition to propose candidates for ministerial positions, Civic Forum at first refused to do so, only to present the regime with a list of names a full week later.[24]

Third, the method of radical continuity had been deployed previously in Czech history. The declaration of Czechoslovak independence on 28 October 1918 explicitly stated that the empire's laws would remain in force until new ones could be enacted. Upon seizing power in February 1948, even the communists had not formally abrogated the 1920 constitution.[25] Although this does not seem to have been a conscious element in the opposition's early legal decision making, at the risk of sounding Hegelian I mention it here, for the weight of history is sometimes capable of making itself known even when its principal agents are not fully aware of its influence. Put another way, in constitutional terms the regime change in 1989 Czechoslovakia mirrored those that had preceded it.

Finally, and perhaps most important, Civic Forum's indisputable leader does not seem to have initially believed that a new constitution belonged at the very top of the democracy movement's list of priorities. While Havel had requested the drafting of an alternative federal constitution, he did not press for its immediate implementation as a provisional replacement, nor did he spearhead an initiative to refine the Rychetský draft. Instead, he waited until after the June 1990 elections to take up in earnest the task of constitutional renewal. Why was this the case?

One obvious response is that the new president and leader of Civic Forum surely had plenty of other things to think about. It also bears mentioning that Havel's tendency to insist on the moral purity of means made him unlikely to adopt the less than wholly democratic tactics of someone such as General Charles de Gaulle, who, deploying extraconstitutional means, personally orchestrated France's transition from the Fourth to the Fifth Republic.[26] Yet these commonsense explanations do not tell the whole story. In his dissident writings and early presidential speeches, Havel repeatedly stressed that laws or systems, in and of themselves, can really guarantee nothing of value at all. Good laws alone can never create the quality of life on which human dignity relies, for democracy is more than a collection of formal rules. A well-crafted constitution, by extension, is not the key to establishing democratic principles, for getting things right on paper is less important than individuals making a personal choice to live in truth.[27] With these long-held beliefs shaping Havel's initial approach to politics in practice, the dissident strategy of simply demanding that the laws be upheld—in Havel's 1978 words, "an act of living within the truth that threatens the whole mendacious structure at its point of maximum mendacity"[28]—carried the day. What is interesting is that it continued to do so even after the balance of power between government and opposition had dramatically changed, empowering the dissidents to recast the very mendacious structure they had long struggled to bring down.

THE CONSEQUENCES OF THE VELVET
CONSTITUTIONAL REVOLUTION

Three parliaments (the Federal Assembly and the Czech and Slovak national assemblies, respectively) were elected in the first free elections on 8–9 June 1990. Each body was elected for two years, half the normal term, with a mandate to adopt a new constitution.[29] The hope was that these newly elected bodies might swiftly negotiate and ratify a new democratic constitution for postcommunist Czechoslovakia and that elections two years hence would then take place under the auspices of this new document. While the Czechoslovak Assembly was successful in passing a series of significant amendments to the federal constitution in 1990–1991, its efforts to draft a new constitution, ironically, were undermined by voting rules inherited from the communist era.

Communism's Institutional and Legal Legacy

The 1968 Law on the Federation, an amendment to the 1960 constitution that transformed Czechoslovakia from a unitary state to a federal one, provided for a federal assembly with two chambers. Representatives were elected to the upper chamber (the Chamber of the People) by the entire population on a proportional basis. In contrast, the lower chamber (the Chamber of the Nations) was comprised of seventy-five representatives elected in the Czech lands and seventy-five representatives elected in Slovakia. In voting on any bill, both houses were governed by the antimajority principle (*zákaz majorizace*), which translates literally as the prohibition of majoritarian rule.[30] Ostensibly designed to protect the rights of the Slovak minority, it stipulated that the ratification of any extraordinary legislation—constitutional amendments, declarations of war, and the election of the president—required a three-fifths majority (supermajority) of both the Czech section and the Slovak section in the lower chamber.[31] What this meant, in practice, was that a mere thirty-one Slovak deputies in the Chamber of the Nations could block any proposed constitutional amendment, even if the bill had the unanimous support of all the other 269 deputies in both chambers.[32] There was, while it existed, no democratic government anywhere else in the world "in which comparable minorities of legislative bodies have as much blocking power."[33]

To complicate matters still further, Czechoslovakia's communist constitution was a curiosity even among other federal systems of the Soviet variety. It proclaimed a federal state that presupposed the existence of republic-level constitutions to govern its functions, yet the Prague Spring reform process had stopped short of actually promulgating these documents for the constituent states.[34] Although the 1968 Law on the Federation had outlined the powers for two republic-level parliaments, the Czech and Slovak national councils, only the Slovak National Council survived normalization, its actual power retracted and restored according to the whims of the communist ruling elite.[35] The Czech National

Council was formed in May 1968,[36] in quite undemocratic fashion, with a mandate to work with its already existing Slovak counterpart on preparing the new federal constitution, until elections could be held, but it had withered away after the Soviet invasion. As a result, 1969–1989 Czechoslovakia continued to have the same asymmetrical institutional structure that the 1945 and 1968 Slovak movement for federalization had sought to remedy; Slovakia had its own republic-level institutions, while the Czech lands did not.

Civic Forum's decision to accept temporarily the legitimacy of this legal framework meant that in 1989, Czechoslovakia's democratic forces inherited one existing republican parliament (the Slovak National Council) and a federal constitution that called for another that would have to be created (the Czech National Council). Neither the actual nor the nascent body had a constitution to guide its operations, yet the federal constitution already in place presupposed such. Upholding the communist constitution, consequently, required the immediate drafting of republican constitutions, yet this aim had to be pursued at the same time that the Federal Assembly was laboring to retire the old constitution. Put another way, demanding that the laws be upheld meant in practice that no less than three new constitutions had to be worked on simultaneously. It also entailed the resuscitation of a long-dormant institution, the Czech National Council.[37]

Building the Federation from Below

Who was to tackle the task of refounding the federation initially seemed at least relatively straightforward. The Federal Assembly would work on drafting a new federal constitution, while coordinating its endeavors closely with the efforts of deputies in the Czech and Slovak national councils, which were charged with the simultaneous creation of the Czech and Slovak republics' first constitutions.[38] The Slovaks immediately after the revolution began work on their own constitution, having a first draft ready in April 1990, well before the Czechs had even begun.[39] Clearly, from the outset, the need to define republic-level rights and responsibilities was felt more keenly in Slovakia than it was in the Czech lands.

Though it was uncontroversial to delegate the drafting of a new federal charter to the Federal Assembly, the question of how that document, once devised, was to become the legitimate law of the land presented a major stumbling block. Using the communist constitution as a guide to ratification procedures raised more questions than answers. Article 1 of the 1968 Law on the Federation begins by proclaiming the sovereignty (*suverenita*) of the Czechoslovak state's constituent nations, which of their own free will had joined together to form the federation.[40]

To complicate matters, the Czech language has two words for "sovereignty": *suverenita*, which was used to describe the status of the Czech and Slovak republics vis-á-vis one another from the vantage point of constitutional law, and *svrchovanost*, which refers to sovereignty from the perspective of international law.[41] This notion of dual sovereignty—that of the working class on the one hand

and that of the nation on the other—was a feature in all the communist variants of federalism.[42] While Czechoslovakia was ruled by the Communist Party and had effectively surrendered its sovereignty (svrchovanost) through membership in the Warsaw Pact, declaring the Czech and Slovak nations sovereign amounted to little more than rhetoric; with a multiparty system in the making and Soviet troops heading back home, the designation acquired practical significance.

Possessing suverenita surely implied, at the very least, that any new federal framework would require the explicit approval of each sovereign republic to be rendered legitimate. And if the Slovak nation's sovereignty was enshrined in the federal constitution to begin with, wouldn't any subsequent declaration of sovereignty made by Slovakia simply be a ceremonial confirmation of adherence and allegiance to Czechoslovakia's basic law?[43] It is easy enough to see how when Slovak politicians such as Vladimír Mečiar began to deploy these two ambiguously defined terms to describe Slovak aspirations, a recipe for miscommunication and conversation at cross-purposes was in the making, especially when deliberate obfuscation in pursuit of political ends became part of the equation. For many Czechs and some Slovaks, Mečiar seemed to be speaking in a series of logical contradictions.[44] Many of the controversies in post-1989 Czech–Slovak relations can be traced back to contradictions embedded in the document that both sides were forced to use as a point of reference for guidance on how to transform the political order in legal fashion.

The notion that the federation derived its legitimacy from the consent of the republics was further institutionalized in the December 1990 power-sharing agreement between federal and republican institutions, which after lengthy negotiations was passed in the form of a constitutional amendment by the Federal Assembly. The power-sharing agreement built on the understanding reached in August 1990 at earlier meetings of republican and federal representatives in Trenčianské Teplice that a strong federation is comprised of strong republics.[45] It devolved most economic powers to the republics, with the federation retaining control of foreign policy and financial strategy. It also tacitly further confirmed that the ratification of a new federal constitution for Czechoslovakia would of necessity require the approval of both the Czech and Slovak national councils. At a subsequent meeting in Kroměříž, representatives of the federal and republican governments formally agreed that the new federal constitution should be ratified by the national councils.[46]

In retrospect, the endorsement of the notion that a strong federation is comprised of strong republics was a fateful step, for involving republican legislatures in the ratification of a federal constitution would likely be a recipe for conflict, even in an ethnically homogeneous state. No republican parliament is likely to authorize the curtailment of its own power, which any federal system by definition entails. Further, it is extraordinarily difficult, if not impossible, to establish the supremacy of the federal constitution over its constituent parts when the latter have rendered the former legitimate. These are two of the

reasons that James Madison insisted that state legislatures not be directly involved in the ratification of the American constitution.[47] Handing over the responsibility for forging consensus to the national councils also made it less
likely that agreement would be reached for another simple reason: representatives of the Czech and Slovak national councils, unlike their federal counterparts, had no experience working together.[48]

   While President Havel endeavored to keep all the negotiating parties focused
on the urgent task of drafting a new federal constitution, for the majority of leading Slovak politicians in early 1991, this now amounted to putting the cart before
the horse. Accordingly, the new Slovak prime minister, Ján Čarnogurský, for example, argued that if the Czech–Slovak relationship was to be placed on a new
footing, and the common goal was to build a federation from the bottom up, then
a treaty (*smlouva*) between the two republics, consistent with international law,
must first be forged. Once this treaty was established and Czech–Slovak equality
was therefore officially inscribed in law, only then could the task of adopting a
new federal constitution be tackled.[49] In June 1991, after the Kroměříž talks,
Havel astutely described this Slovak approach as one of dissolving the existing
federation temporarily and refounding it on a new ground, which the president
saw to be dangerous, since the legal continuity of the common state would be destroyed in the process.[50] Past experience, quite understandably, made the Slovaks
suspicious of any federal structure that had links with the past, however tenuous.

A Dialogue of the Deaf

   A seemingly insurmountable impasse had been reached as 1991 began to wind
down. A series of high-level negotiations seeking to resolve Czech–Slovak constitutional deadlock had already taken place. Despite the president's valiant effort
to mediate between opposing views, the fault lines in the Czechoslovak political
landscape were now crystallizing and hardening along ethnic lines. In an attempt
to jump start a negotiating process that had sputtered to a near halt, Havel invited
key representatives from both federal and republican governing bodies to his
summer house in Hrádeček in November 1991. The transcript of this Hrádeček
meeting—the only publicly available stenographic record of the series of meetings between Czech, Slovak, and federal representatives on the future of the common state—is an important primary source and merits careful study. Not only
does it provide a window on the Czech–Slovak discussions at a critical point in
time, but it also sheds light on the course of earlier negotiations that are still
shrouded in secrecy.

   The 3 November 1991 meeting at Hrádeček began with a solemn toast from a
bottle of *slivovice* that a neighbor had buried in 1968 and unearthed after the November 1989 revolution, bestowing it upon Havel as a gift.[51] After informing the
gathering that they would break at 7:30 P.M. for the news and a dinner of home-
made goulash that he had spent the entire afternoon preparing, the president pre-

sented a proposal for action to serve as a point of departure for subsequent discussion. Havel's opening statement focused on two interrelated problems: (1) the content of the smlouva[52]—i.e., the actual division of powers that the smlouva should delineate, and (2) the procedure through which the smlouva should be adopted, including the relationship of that document to the three constitutions that were presently in the process of being formalized.[53]

With respect to the content of the smlouva, Havel envisioned a document consisting of five chapters. In general, the smlouva should present a statement of shared basic principles, with the details of the division of competencies reserved for elaboration in the new constitutions. The smlouva should preserve the zákaz majorizace in a single-chamber federal assembly. Most important, the smlouva and the Slovak, Czech, and federal constitutions must not only be in legal harmony one with the other but must also all come into effect simultaneously to avoid a dangerous state of dual law.[54]

On the topic of procedure, Havel envisioned an eight-step process:[55]

(1) The participants in the present meeting should form an expert commission, with appropriate representation, to review drafts of the smlouva.

(2) Their preliminary work complete, the commission would then present a consensus draft to the Slovak National Council for comment (note the exclusion of the Czech National Council from this step).

(3) Incorporating the Slovak National Council's suggestions, a revised text of the smlouva would then be sent to both national councils for ratification by the end of November 1991.

(4) At the beginning of December, the ratified smlouva would be presented to the Federal Assembly, which would approach it as a legal initiative, originating in the national councils. The definition of the smlouva as a legal initiative should not be included in the smlouva itself but instead should be conveyed in the remarks of the presenting chairs.

(5) In the winter of 1991–1992, both national councils should draft and ratify constitutions that would be in harmony with the smlouva; the smlouva and the new republican constitutions must all have an identical effective date.

(6) In the spring of 1992, the Federal Assembly would ratify a new federal constitution that should not contradict the spirit and letter of the smlouva.

(7) Once accepted by the Federal Assembly, the new federal constitution would then be ratified by the national councils.

(8) All four documents—the smlouva, the two republican constitutions, and the new federal constitution—would go into effect simultaneously before the June 1992 elections. The elections would then take place under the new laws of the born-again federal regime.

In his concluding remarks, Havel stressed the importance of accomplishing the tasks described above in timely fashion; it was especially critical that the new elections take place under the new constitutional arrangements. As far as a referendum on the future of the common state was concerned, Havel maintained that, depending on its results, it could either grease the wheels of the process of federal transformation he envisioned or derail it entirely.[56]

The Havel proposal was acceptable to the Slovak participants at Hrádeček. It appealed to the predominant Slovak view that the existing federation was irreparable, that it was necessary to clean the slate and start anew, doing things the right way this time around. In short, the Slovaks at this point in time were not interested in anything less than a complete refounding of the existing political order. As deputy chair of the Slovak National Council Ivan Čarnogurský put it at Hrádeček, "If everyone at this point does not realize... that we are attempting to build a state that is different from the ČSFR as it previously existed, then we can meet, ten, twelve times, and never agree on anything."[57] In chair of the Slovak National Council František Mikloško's words: "when we left Kroměříž...it seemed that everyone thought there could be a new Pittsburgh Agreement."[58] Havel's Hrádeček plan was an attempt to satisfy the Slovak need for a symbolic new beginning while accomplishing such without acts of blatant illegality. The president even expressed willingness to include the right to secede in the federal constitution as a sign of goodwill, even though no Slovak participant at Hrádeček asked for it.[59]

It was representatives from the Czech delegation rather than the Slovak—especially deputy chair of the Czech National Council, Jan Kalvoda—who served as the principal obstacle to consensus in November 1991. While the meeting at Kroměříž had produced mutual understanding that a smlouva was necessary,[60] the ensuing discussion of the Havel plan foundered on the question of the smlouva's legal significance, or put another way, what both parties had earlier actually agreed upon. Though much of the time at Hrádeček was spent attempting to define the principal points of dispute, the clash of views, with the benefit of some distance from actual events, can be summarized quite simply. For most Czech politicians, the locus of refounding, the most significant imminent legal act, was the adoption of a new federal constitution, the smlouva being something akin to a symbolic gesture without the force of law. From their point of view, the Slovak proposal sought to end Czechoslovakia and refound the Czech–Slovak union on new ground, a move that they were not legally empowered to take. For Slovaks, it was the smlouva—or *statní smlouva* (state treaty), as they preferred to refer to it[61]—which they perceived to be a legally binding act between two equal and sovereign nations, that would shape and define the constitutions that emerged from it, both federal and republican.

Building on this understanding of the state treaty's significance, Ivan Čarnogurský informed those assembled at Hrádeček that from the Slovak point of view, there was no difference between the smlouva and an agreement between Czechoslovakia and Germany.[62] When pressed later on in the discussions to justify his understanding of the smlouva, Čarnogurský explained that the existing constitution, in place for over twenty years, named the national councils as the highest legislative organs of the Czech and Slovak nations, and that Slovakia was not about to surrender this right.[63] The logic of Čarnogurský's argument, in turn, was not something that the Czech side could easily accept, since they viewed Slovakia as a member of the Czechoslovak federation rather than as a sovereign state. Further, the Czech National Council had existed only in the realm of theory during the same period of time from which Ivan Čarnogurský derived the rights of its Slovak counterpart. In short, both sides agreed that they needed to conclude a smlouva, but there was an enormous gulf between their respective understandings of its significance.

While Czech politicians expressed exasperation at the peerless Slovak notion that citizens of the same country could forge something akin to an international agreement, at another level, Slovak demands followed logically from the spirit of the power-sharing constitutional amendment, that is, from the supposition that it was not for the federation to devolve powers to the republics but rather that it was only the republics who could delegate authority to the federal government. Whenever Slovak politicians felt that this basic principle had been compromised, they threatened to declare the supremacy of Slovak laws over federal ones, a move that their Czech counterparts almost uniformly interpreted as tantamount to dissolving the state. The clash of perceptions was further fueled by communism's legal legacy. The reader will recall that Slovakia's sovereignty (suverenita) had been enshrined in Article 1 of the 1968 Law on the Federation, at a time when Czechoslovakia did not possess svrchovanost. Frictions were bound to arise when svrchovanost was restored to the Czechoslovak state, yet suverenita of the republics remained. In the presence of svrchovanost, what did suverenita actually mean in concrete political terms? The divergent conceptions of the smlouva's meaning in November 1991 might be interpreted as differing views of suverenita's significance for the Czech and Slovak republics in light of Czechoslovakia's restored svrchovanost.

Havel's position heretofore reflected an enduring belief that any transition to parliamentary democracy must take place in legal fashion. However, at this stage in the game, faced with an escalating crisis in Czech–Slovak relations, he was willing to turn a blind eye to actions that adherence to full legality might not permit—his proposal being one prominent example—if they promised to contribute to the preservation of the common state. Others, such as Jan Kalvoda, continued to cling to the existing legal order as a sine qua non condition for legitimate political action. In the discussion that took place at Hrádeček over the significance of the smlouva, for example, the president argued with those who criticized his proposal on the grounds that it was illegal, maintaining that strict adherence to the letter of existing law would logically prohibit the adoption of *any* new constitution. The smlouva could not help but be in contradiction with such, maintained Havel, since it bore the seeds of three new constitutions and was to serve as a catalyst for the remaking of the federal order.[64] With this position, Havel had traveled some distance from the dissident strategy of simply demanding that the laws be upheld.

The resultant Hrádeček communiqué would camouflage the full gravity of the widening gap between Czech and Slovak views. Shortly before midnight at the Hrádeček meeting, Havel asked both sides to break for a few minutes and attempt to summarize their differences. Speaking for the Slovak delegation (even though some Czechs and Slovaks were present in a federal capacity, they presumably met along ethnic lines), the opening line of František Mikloško's summary statement was that the parties present were "not going to be able to overcome the basic difference." The Slovak side, Mikloško continued, was willing to convey agreement with the president's perspective but realized that act would isolate him on the Czech political scene. The Slovak National Council, he concluded, would invite the president to explain his views to that body, but he "has the feeling that no further agreement will be reached."[65] Speaking for the Czechs, chair of the Czech National Council Dagmar Burešová cited conflicting interpretations of the smlouva as the principal stumbling block.[66]

With the prospects for attaining a new constitution before the June 1992 parliamentary election all but gone, in early 1992 President Havel made a final attempt to break the constitutional deadlock by proposing several constitutional amendments for reform of both the antimajority principle and the federal assembly structure.[67] All of Havel's proposals were blocked by the Slovak nationalist opposition. Though a good portion of Slovak deputies seemed to vote against the proposals simply because they were President Havel's, their voting behavior can also be explained by simple self-interest: Why should a minority with extraordinary power voluntarily vote it away, particularly when that power might be used as a bargaining chip in unrelated negotiations?[68] In February 1992, a last-chance compromise draft of the smlouva was successfully negotiated in Milovy, but the presidium of the Slovak National Council by a one-vote margin prevented the treaty from ever being submitted to the body as a whole for ratification.[69] The institutionalized impasse reached its logical point of culmination in June 1992, when a minority of deputies blocked the reelection of Havel as president. In a very real sense, then, the prospects for Czechoslovak democracy were undermined by the initial adoption of legal procedures that were never designed to govern a liberal democracy.

The method of radical continuity, therefore, had the largest unintended consequences in the former Czechoslovakia. Abiding by the communist legal rules of the game, even against the backdrop of an ongoing series of significant amendments to the old constitution, had the unfortunate byproduct of underscoring and encouraging what divided rather than united citizens of the common state. Attempting to draft and agree on ratification procedures for the basic charter for three new political orders—Czech, Slovak, and Czechoslovak—with the zákaz majorizace in full force was an invitation to constitutional deadlock even had all three legislative bodies been comprised of angels.

THE CONSTITUTIONAL MOMENT
AND THE CZECHOSLOVAK TRANSITION

Bruce Ackerman has argued that the immediate aftermath of revolution provides liberal democrats with a unique opportunity, what he calls "the constitutional moment," where circumstances are optimal for laying the legal foundations
for a democratic order and mobilizing the requisite broad popular support for the
constitutional initiative. Timing in tackling major constitutional controversies is
critical, for the opposition to authoritarian rule will only remain united for a fi-
nite amount of time after it has become clear that a new order is in the making.
The gains of liberal revolution need to be locked in early on, before more self-interested factions are able to hijack constitutional politics and exploit it to secure
their own ends. If the constitutional moment passes in vain, therefore, it is very
difficult to recreate.[70]

The case of the former Czechoslovakia supports Ackerman's hypothesis. As
Ackerman might predict, the decision to follow the letter of communist constitutions never designed to function in conditions of genuine liberty facilitated the
bracketing of the more difficult constitutional questions for resolution at a later
date. While postponing these hard tasks allowed democratizing elites to focus on
other pressing problems, it also meant that fundamental constitutional questions
would have to be confronted after the salient cleavages dividing postcommunist
societies had fully crystallized into rival political groupings. Once those new divisions had clearly emerged, the goal of securing a new constitution to replace interim arrangements was rendered all the more elusive.

Ackerman's framework highlights the potential significance of early constitutional choices for future political development. With respect to the case of
Czechoslovakia, it is important to realize that the decision to defer action itself
constituted a significant choice. As we have seen, the makers of the Velvet Revolution decided to postpone tackling the task of devising a new constitution until
a freshly elected Federal Assembly was in place, and that newly democratic body
was then issued a two-year timetable for getting the job done. Regardless of how
one assesses the likelihood that a Czech–Slovak compromise might have been
reached had the relevant issues been confronted earlier rather than later, the subsequent two-year deadline, which was established primarily because Václav
Havel could not envision himself serving as president for much longer than that
amount of time, had implications all its own.[71] Meant to focus attention on the
critical task at hand—forging a constitutional compromise that might preserve the
common state—it instead had the unintended effect of increasing the probability
that the negotiations necessary to sustain that common enterprise would break
down. In this way, the desire to "settle things once and for all" prior to the June
1992 elections became an unfortunate self-fulfilling prophecy. Things were indeed settled once and for all, but not at all in the manner that those who had set
the deadline in the first place had envisioned. One is left to wonder whether the

ultimate outcome might have been different had Czechs and Slovaks instead agreed to an ongoing conversation without deadlines on the shape of their shared future, rather than reaching a final agreement within two years or going their separate ways.[72] With the benefit of hindsight, once Ackerman's constitutional moment had passed, the two-year timetable seems to have been a mistake for a two-member federation.[73]

Events following the Velvet Revolution also suggest an extension of Ackerman's conceptual framework. What Ackerman does not anticipate, since his approach presupposes enduring agreement among democratizing elites on how the state itself is to be defined, is the likely emergence of state-challenging forces in a multinational state after the constitutional moment passes in vain. Looking back from the present, it is all too easy to conclude, mistakenly, that the Czech–Slovak conflict was a direct factor in early constitutional choices. In reality, the causal arrow actually points the other way. The initial acceptance of federal norms and institutions devised by nondemocrats encouraged the development of the political cleavages that would ultimately spell Czechoslovakia's demise—not the other way round.[74] The Czech–Slovak case suggests that bracketing vexing constitutional issues is particularly risky business for multinational democratizing states, especially in an era when a powerful external military threat no longer exists to facilitate unity.

CONCLUSION

The unique version of federalism delineated in the constitution that Czech and Slovak democrats inherited in 1989 had two distinctive features. First, the sweeping zákaz majorizace, which applied to ordinary as well as extraordinary legislation, transformed the practice of democracy into an exercise in political gridlock and constitutional deadlock. Second, the simple fact that the Czechoslovak federation was comprised of but two members only rendered the potential manifestations of the zákaz majorizace all the more pervasive.[75] In an organization with more than two members, the polarizing effects of the minority veto can be ameliorated by the threat of exclusion; cooperation can be forged out of conflict, because a dissenting member poised to deploy the minority veto fears the future consequences of being the party responsible for derailing the initiative in question. In a two-member federation, this threat of exclusion does not exist. Negotiations on any agenda issue are a zero-sum game, with a clear winner and a clear loser. The cumulative effect of this system over time in circumstances of real democracy is likely to be the triumph of discord over cooperation, as the Czechoslovak case amply illustrates.

In making this point, I do not mean to suggest that the tensions in Czech–Slovak relations after the Velvet Revolution were the creation of inherited institutions alone. The legacy of the past obviously involves not only words on paper and their institutional incarnation. In many ways, after all, the events of 1990–92 can be portrayed as a replaying of the 1968 Czech–Slovak drama. It is important to bear in mind that the original 1968 Slovak initiative for a symmetrical constitutional system was based on federal proposals advanced by the Slovak National Council in 1945. In 1968, the Slovak National Council's expert committee had proposed an essentially confederal scheme, with both the federation and the republics possessing sovereignty. As in 1990–91, this proposition was viewed by Czech lawyers and politicians to be a dangerous threat to the common state. The title of the new federal state was a point of conflict in 1968, just as it was in 1990. In 1991, Czechs and Slovaks battled over the meaning of the smlouva; in 1968, Czechs and Slovaks quarreled over the content of the constitutional act that would federalize the country. Czech communist reformers wanted it to be a statement of principles, with the specifics to be filled out in subsequent ordinary legislation, while the Slovaks tended to be suspicious of any abstract declaration of intentions and wanted the details to be spelled out in the constitutional act itself.[76]

In short, one of the principal barriers to reaching an agreement that might have staved off Czechoslovakia's dissolution was the fundamental mistrust that had been generated by years of Slovak demands being either misconstrued or ignored, as well as the damage done by the political manifestations of Slovak frustration at crisis moments in the common state's history.[77] The survival of the Czechoslovak federation after communism's collapse was contingent on a joint commitment to begin anew, on a common effort to refound both the political regime and its institutional manifestations. The method of legal continuity, arguably itself a Czech tradition, preserved the velvet character of the Czech/Slovak revolution but was at direct cross-purposes with this aim. Put another way, there was an inherent conflict between the desire to maintain the common state and the strategy of forging democracy in Czechoslovakia on a legal foundation that had been built by the communist regime. The latter only served to infuse latent points of misunderstanding with new life, rendering impossible the consummation of the former.

As the transcript of the meeting at Hrádeček analyzed in detail in this chapter indicates, the situation in Czech–Slovak relations had already reached a crisis point in November 1991. At one particularly tense moment in those proceedings, Havel himself maintained that the participants gathered there had a stark choice: they could either hammer out some sort of agreement, or "Slovakia will vote for independence, Mečiar will become Slovak premier, and all of you here will be emigrating to the Czech lands."[78] When the conversation on a shared future entered the "agree—or else" phase, the negotiations had been transformed into a zero-sum game, with clear winners and losers. Securing Czech–Slovak cooperation in this context became only all the more elusive. Czechs could no longer meet Slovaks halfway without feeling that they had succumbed to blackmail. Slovaks could not compromise without fearing a repeat of history. Though the June

1992 election winners, Klaus and Mečiar, played their part in the partition of Czechoslovakia, a close examination of the effort to arrive at a new federal constitution indicates that the stage for the dissolution of the country was essentially set by constitutional deadlock well in advance of the June 1992 elections that brought Klaus and Mečiar to power.

In the end, postcommunist Czechoslovakia's fate provides an indisputable instance where the actual content of the laws mattered, and mattered enormously. Laws in and of themselves may guarantee nothing, as Havel argued in his dissident days, but this maxim inevitably takes on a different meaning in a democratic context. The same words on paper that were of little significance in a communist one-party state proved to be an enormously significant force in shaping the stage on which political action would take place in the newly democratic Czechoslovakia. Demanding that the laws be upheld, that the party abide by its own constitution, helped to bring the totalitarian system crashing down in remarkably nonviolent fashion. But the persistence of that same strategy in an era when the previously powerless had become powerful had the unintended effect of mortally wounding the Czechoslovak federation.

NOTES

For helpful comments on earlier drafts of this chapter, the author would like to thank Benjamin Block, Damjan de Krnjevic Miskovic, Murray Dry, Michael Kraus, Carol Skalnik Leff, and participants at the IREX Seminar, Czech Academy of Sciences, 28 May 1996, and the Conference on Czechoslovakia's Dissolution, CERGE-EI, 28 June 1996, Prague. Vital financial support from the National Council on Soviet and East European Research (contract 810-30, with Michael Kraus) and the International Research and Exchanges Board (IREX) is also gratefully acknowledged. This chapter draws from and elaborates on work I have published elsewhere. See Allison K. Stanger, "The Unintended Consequences of the Velvet Constitutional Revolution," *East European Constitutional Review*, vol. 5, no. 4 (Fall 1996).

1. This gap is noted by Juan Linz and Alfred Stepan in their recent study, *Problems of Democratic Transition and Consolidation: Southern Europe, South America, and Post-Communist Europe* (Baltimore: Johns Hopkins University Press, 1996); the quote comes from page 81. Jon Elster has also noted this neglect. See Jon Elster, "Ways of Constitution-Making," in Axel Hadenius, ed., *Democracy's Victory and Crisis* (Cambridge: Cambridge University Press, 1997), p. 123.

2. Robert Sharlet, "Post-Soviet Constitutionalism: Politics and Constitution-Making in Russia and Ukraine," in Michael Kraus and Ronald D. Liebowitz, *Russia and Eastern Europe after Communism: The Search for New Political, Economic, and Security Systems* (Boulder: Westview Press, 1996), pp. 16–17. The quoted passage is from page 16.

3. The former phrase is Andrew Arato's, the latter, Stephen Holmes's and Cass Sunstein's. See, respectively, Andrew Arato, "Constitution and Continuity in the East European Transitions," *Journal of Constitutional Law in Eastern and Central Europe*, vol. 1, no. 1 (1994), p. 110 (footnote 25); and Stephen Holmes and Cass Sunstein, "The Politics of Constitutional Revision in Eastern Europe," in Sanford Levinson, ed., *Responding*

to Imperfection: The Theory and Practice of Constitutional Amendment (Princeton: Princeton University Press, 1995), p. 286.

4. For a detailed comparative analysis of constitutional politics in postcommunist Central Europe, see Allison Stanger, "Institutional Inertia, Democratic Consolidation, and the Politics of Constitutional Renewal in Post-Communist Central Europe," Program on Central and Eastern Europe, Working Paper Series #44, Center for European Studies, Harvard University, January 1998.

5. See, for example, the February 1989 set of discussion points, "Než bude zahájena diskuse o novém návrhu čs. ústavy," document #30, in *Hnutí za občanskou svobodu 1988–89: dokumenty* (Praha: Ústav pro soudobé dějiny AV ČR, 1994), pp. 94–95.

6. Michael Kraus, "Settling Accounts: Post-Communist Czechoslovakia," in Neil J. Kritz, ed., *Transitional Justice: How Emerging Democracies Reckon with Former Regimes,* vol. 2, *Country Studies* (Washington, D.C.: United States Institute of Peace Press, 1995), pp. 542–544. That the Czecho–Slovak communists had minimal actual power in the interim government is one of the reasons they did not find it necessary to immediately rename their party, as their counterparts in Poland and Hungary (whose role in shaping the transition was more substantive) were compelled to do.

7. Miloš Čalda, "The Roundtable Talks in Czechoslovakia," in Jon Elster, ed., *The Round Table Talks* (Chicago: University of Chicago Press, 1996), p. 148.

8. See Návrh Ústavy Československej socialistickej republiky, Českej socialistickej republiky, a Slovenskej socialistickej republiky (October 1989, with comments). The accompanying comments, while unidentified, are presumably Čalfa's, since they are written in Slovak, like the draft constitution itself. Archives of the Center for the Study of Constitutionalism in Eastern Europe, University of Chicago Law School, Constitutions, Constitutional Drafts, Laws & Acts (filed by country in first file cabinet top drawer). The reader should note that the Center for the Study of Constitutionalism in Eastern Europe ceased operations in June 1997. Its archive is now maintained by the University of Chicago Libraries. This means that the filing system may have changed since my visit in summer 1995.

9. Vladimír Hanzel, *Zrychlený tep dějin* (Prague: OK Centrum, 1991), pp. 62ff. This text provides edited transcripts for nine meetings between the government and opposition from 26 November to 9 December 1989. Newly available parliamentary documents reveal the low priority that the Communist Party attached to devising a new constitution and that the original proposals from within the party to remove the party's leading role and references to Marxism–Leninism from the restructured constitution initially met with considerable resistance. It is also clear from this record that Čalfa was an early advocate of movement toward the rule of law. See František Cigánek, "Předlistopadový parlament ve světle archivní dokumentace," in *Dvě desetiletí před listopadem 89: Sborník* (Prague: Ústav pro soudobé dějiny AV ČR, 1993), pp. 66–68.

10. Hanzel, *Zrychlený tep dějin,* pp. 323–324.

11. For an elaboration of Civic Forum's position on this issue, see "The Position of the Coordinating Center of Civic Forum, 14 December 1989," and "Václav Havel's speech, 16 December 1989," both documents from the Archives of the Center for the Study of Constitutionalism in Eastern Europe, University of Chicago Law School.

12. "Občanské Forum předkládá československé veřejnosti a ústavním orgánům republiky první návrh nové ústavy," 5 December 1989. Document in author's possession, thanks to Rudolf Battěk.

13. Petr Pithart, comments at the Conference on Czechoslovakia's Dissolution, CERGE–EI, Charles University, Prague, Czech Republic, 28 June 1996.

14. *Hnutí za občanskou svobodu 1988–89: dokumenty* (Praha: Ústav pro soudobé dějiny AV ČR, 1994), introduction, p. 14. The 26 June 1989 HOS statement of first principles is included in this collection (see document #62, pp. 148–51). Among the thirteen signatories were Ján Čarnogurský, Rudolf Battěk, Václav Benda, and Jan Ruml.

15. Interview with Rudolf Battěk, Prague, Czech Republic, 26 February 1996.

16. See Zdeněk Jičínský, *Charta 77 a právní stát* (Brno: Doplněk, 1995), p. 11.

17. Petr Pithart, remarks at the Conference on Czechoslovakia's Dissolution, CERGE–EI, Charles University, Prague, Czech Republic, 28 June 1996. For a critique of the Civic Forum alternative constitution, see Francis Delpéreé, "Belgie a Československo: úvahy o federalismu," *Právník*, ročník 130, číslo 1, rok 1991, pp. 31–32.

18. To the best of my knowledge, the democratic opposition in Poland and Hungary, for example, did not have draft constitutions in hand at their respective roundtable negotiations with the communist regime.

19. Petr Pithart, remarks at the Conference on Czechoslovakia's Dissolution, CERGE–EI, Charles University, Prague, Czech Republic, 28 June 1996.

20. Čalda, "The Roundtable Talks," p. 48.

21. See Václav Havel's 1992 New Year's Day Address, "Novoroční projev (Praha, 1.1.1992)," in Václav Havel, *Vážení občané: Projevy červenec 1990–červenec 1992* (Praha: Lidové Noviny, 1992), pp. 134–135.

22. Timothy Garton Ash, *The Magic Lantern* (New York: Random House, 1990), p. 78.

23. On Civic Forum's initial lack of an explicit program and the requisite internal organization to implement it, see Jiří Suk, "Vznik Občanského fóra proměny jeho struktury (19. listopad–10. prosinec 1989), *Soudobé dějiny*, II/1/95, pp. 28–31.

24. Hanzel, *Zrychlený tep dějin,* pp. 70–72; pp. 158 ff. Interestingly, no Slovaks were present at round four of the negotiations, which was the meeting where Havel first proposed candidates for cabinet positions, initiating the negotiations over the composition of the federal government. There, Adamec cautioned Civic Forum that Slovaks were underrepresented in its first proposed government. See Hanzel, *Zrychlený tep dějin,* pp. 161 ff.

25. For a lucid review of Czech and Slovak constitutional history, see Vratislav Pechota, "Czechoslovak Constitutionalism," *Czechoslovak and Central European Journal*, vol. 10, no. 2 (Winter 1991), *Zrychlený tep dějin,* pp. 1–19.

26. For a comparative investigation of De Gaulle's strategy and tactics in the transition from the Fourth to the Fifth Republic, see Allison K. Stanger, "Refounding by Referendum: DeGaulle and Yeltsin," *The Oxford International Review* (Winter 1994/95).

27. See, for example, Václav Havel, "The Power of the Powerless" (1978) and "Politics and Conscience" (1984) in Václav Havel, *Living in Truth* (London: Faber and Faber, 1989), especially pp. 95–100 and 153–57, respectively. See, also, President Havel's speech to the first freely elected Federal Assembly, 29 June 1990, in Václav Havel, *Projevy: leden–červen 1990* (Prague: Vyšehrad, 1990), pp. 151–183.

28. Václav Havel, "The Power of the Powerless," p. 98.

29. Katerina Mathernova, "Czecho?Slovakia: Constitutional Disappointments," in E. Dick Howard, ed., *Constitution Making in Eastern Europe* (Washington: Woodrow Wilson Center Press, 1993), p. 63.

30. See "Ústavní zákon o československé federaci, z 27. října 1968, c. 143 Sb.," especially articles 41 and 42. This act can be found in the Archives of the Center for the

Study of Constitutionalism in Eastern Europe and in Jiří Grospič, *Československá Federace* (Prague: Orbis, 1972), pp. 139–263.

31. Mathernova, "Czecho? Slovakia," pp. 64–65. All other (i.e., ordinary) legislation required a simple majority of both the Czech section and the Slovak section in the Chamber of the Nations.

32. Vojtech Cepl, "Constitutional Reform in the Czech Republic," *University of San Francisco Law Review*, vol. 28 (Fall 1993), p. 30. For further details on how the minority veto operated in Czechoslovakia, see Petr Kopecky's contribution to this volume.

33. Lloyd Cutler and Herman Schwartz, "Constitutional Reform in Czechoslovakia: E Duobus Unum?" *The University of Chicago Law Review*, vol. 58 (Spring 1991), p. 549. Civic Forum's alternative constitution was noteworthy in one particular respect: it restricted the ban on majority voting to extraordinary legislation only, bringing voting procedures in the Federal Assembly closer to those of other multinational democracies.

34. On the establishment of the federation in 1968, see Jozef Žatkuliak, *Federalizacia Československého Štátu 1968–1970: Vznik česko–slovenskej federacie roku 1968* (Praha–Brno: Ústav pro soudobé dějiny AV ČR, 1996), which includes the key documents; see also Žatkuliak's "Realizacia ústavného zákona o československej federacii od oktobra 1968," *Historický časopis*, vol. 40, no. 3 (1992), pp. 356–369.

35. H. Gordon Skilling, *Czechoslovakia's Interrupted Revolution* (Princeton: Princeton University Press, 1976), p. 476; Josef Žatkuliak, "Deformacie ústavného zákona o československej federacii po oktobri 1968," *Historický časopis*, ročník 40, čislo 4/1992, pp. 473–486.

36. On the short-lived 1968–1969 Czech National Council, see Zdeněk Jičínský, *Vznik české národní rady* (Prague: Svoboda, 1990).

37. This would be a daunting agenda even in the best of circumstances. It is instructive to recall, for example, that the American states had both constitutions and legislatures in place when the new federal constitution was under debate.

38. President Havel's speech to the first freely elected Federal Assembly, 29 June 1990, in Václav Havel, *Projevy: leden–červen 1990* (Prague: Vyšehrad, 1990), pp. 155–157.

39. "Návrh Ústavy Slovenskej Republiky (1. pracovna verzia)," Komisia Slovenskej národnej rady pre prípravu Ústavy Slovenskej republiky pod vedením Prof. JUDr. Karola Planka, predsedu Najvyššieho súdu Slovenskej republiky, Bratislava, April 1990. Archives of the Center for the Study of Constitutionalism in Eastern Europe.

40. "Ústavni zákon o československé federaci, z 27. října 1968, č. 143 Sb.," čl. 1.

41. Vratislav Pechota, "Československé ústavní dějiny," *Právník*, ročník 130, číslo 4, rok 1991, p. 281.

42. On the concept of dual sovereignty in the confederal 1974 Yugoslav constitution and its pernicious implications after communist ideology had collapsed, see Robert Hayden, "Constitutional Nationalism in the Formerly Yugoslav Republics," *Slavic Review*, vol. 51, no. 4 (Winter 1992), especially p. 665.

43. Representatives of HZDS deployed this argument. See, for example, the 25 June 1992 article by Milan Čic in *Národná Obroda*, where Čic maintained that "a possible declaration of Slovakia's sovereignty would be nothing but a ceremonial declaration of a fact already embedded in the Czechoslovak constitution. In the HZDS concept, sovereignty does not mean breaking the continuity of the Czechoslovak legal system." Press Survey, CTK News Wire, 25 June 1992. Available: NEXIS Library: Europe File: All Europe.

44. Petr Pithart et al., Conference on Czechoslovakia's Dissolution, CERGE–EI, Charles University, Prague, Czech Republic, 29 June 1996.
45. In a public statement in August 1990, Czech premier Petr Pithart referred to the agreement reached at Trenčianské Teplice as "the only alternative to the disintegration of the state." See Czech premier's statement on need for national consensus, 18 August 1990, BBC Summary of World Broadcasts (1990, August 22). Available: NEXIS Library: Europe File: All Europe.
46. See Václav Havel's characterization of the outcome of the Kroměříž meetings in the transcript of the November 1991 negotiations at Havel's summer home, published as a series in *Slovenské Listy*, 1994, "Poločas rozpadu: Přepis stenografického záznamu ze setkání nejvyšších ústavních činitelů u prezidenta Václava Havla na Hrádečku dne 3. listopadu 1991," pp. 25, 29–30. These page references and those that follow refer to the prepublication manuscript in its entirety, a document in the author's possession, and hereafter referred to as "Poločas rozpadu."
47. See Max Farrand, ed., *The Records of the Federal Convention of 1787* (New Haven: Yale University Press, 1966), vol. 1, pp. 122–123, Federalist #43, and Herbert J. Storing, *What the Anti-Federalists Were For* (Chicago: University of Chicago Press, 1981), pp. 12–13. I am indebted to Murray Dry for this citation.
48. On this point, see Zdeněk Jičínský, "Ke Ztroskotaní Československého Federalismu," in Rüdiger Kipke and Karel Vodička, eds., *Rozloučení s Československem: Příčiny a důsledky československého rozchodu* (Prague: Patriae, 1993), pp. 78-79.
49. David Franklin, interview with Pavel Rychetský, May 1991. Rychetský provided written answers to questions that Franklin had submitted. Archives of the Center for the Study of Constitutionalism in Eastern Europe.
50. DSee President gives views on constitutional talks and Sudeten German issue, 23 June 1991, BBC Summary of World Broadcasts (1991, June 26). Available: NEXIS Library: Europe File: All Europe.
51. D"Poločas rozpadu," p. 3.
52. DBecause the debate that ensued, to a large extent, turned on semantics, for purposes of clarity, I use the word *smlouva* throughout this section rather than varying my word choice and using its several English equivalents. The smlouva, as we shall see, was an international or state treaty for the Slovaks, a mere interrepublican agreement for the Czechs.
53. D"Poločas rozpadu," p. 3.
54. D"Poločas rozpadu," pp. 3–5.
55. DHavel's eight-step process is delineated in "Poločas rozpadu," pp. 5–6.
56. D"Poločas rozpadu," pp. 6–7.
57. D"Poločas rozpadu," pp. 12–13.
58. D"Poločas rozpadu," p. 19. The Pittsburgh Agreement was the 1918 document that mobilized Slovak support for the First Czechoslovak Republic.
59. DThis is an example of another constitutional proposal that was grounded in misunderstanding of practice abroad. Havel erroneously asserted at Hrádeček that the right to secede was not much of a concession, since all federal constitutions, including the Soviet one, included it. See " Poločas rozpadu," p. 24.
60. See President Havel's comments on page 22 of "Poločas rozpadu."
61. At the Hrádeček negotiations, Federal Premier Marian Čalfa described the Slovak side as having "fallen in love with the idea of a state treaty." Having watched Yugoslavia

and the Soviet Union fall apart, Čalfa there maintained, Slovakia feels that it, too, must now somehow express its statehood (*státnost*). See "Poločas rozpadu," pp. 72–73.

62. "Poločas rozpadu," p. 39.

63. "Poločas rozpadu," p. 68.

64. "Poločas rozpadu," pp. 63–64.

65. "Poločas rozpadu," p. 76.

66. "Poločas rozpadu," pp. 76–77.

67. Cutler and Schwarz, "Constitutional Reform," pp. 549–551.

68. Mathernova, "Czecho? Slovakia," pp. 73–75.

69. Václav Žak, "The Velvet Divorce—Institutional Foundations," in Jiří Musil, ed., *The End of Czechoslovakia,* ed. Jiří Musil (Budapest: Central European University Press, 1995), pp. 261–262.

70. Bruce Ackerman, *The Future of Liberal Revolution* (New Haven: Yale University Press, 1992), especially pp. 46–50. Ackerman also acknowledges that it is possible for the constitutional moment to be seized and subsequently co-opted by members of the old regime, as he argues was the case in Bulgaria and Romania. Both countries have new constitutions, but because they were produced and ratified before fully free elections had been held, they were initially viewed to be illegitimate by democratic forces in these two countries. See Ackerman, *The Future of Liberal Revolution,* p. 60 and note 19 on pp. 132–133.

71. On this point, see Petr Pithart's contribution to this volume.

72. In a remarkable essay on the present Canadian constitutional crisis, Simone Chambers has argued that constitutional negotiations that focus on maintaining a certain type of discourse over time rather than on reaching an agreement that settles things once and for all are more likely to prove successful. See Simone Chambers, "Contract or Conversation? Theoretical Lessons from the Canadian Constitutional Crisis," *Politics and Society,* vol. 26, no. 1 (March 1998), pp. 143–172.

73. Petr Pithart has made this argument; see his chapter in this volume.

74. While important, it is beyond the scope of this paper to take up the question of whether the breakdown of larger states into their constituent parts is a phenomenon the West should encourage or strive to prevent.

75. Jon Elster has rightly pointed out that a two-member federation is inherently unstable, but he does not emphasize the degree to which a minority veto can compound that instability. See Jon Elster, "Consenting Adults or the Sorcerer's Apprentice? Explaining the Breakup of the Czechoslovak Federation," *East European Constitutional Review,* vol. 4, no. 1 (Winter 1995), especially p. 36.

76. Skilling, *Czechoslovakia's Interrupted Revolution.* pp. 454, 479–80, 861, 865.

77. For the best treatment of the history of Czech–Slovak elite relations presently available in English, see Carol Skalnik Leff, *National Conflict in Czechoslovakia: The Making and Remaking of a State, 1918–1987* (Princeton: Princeton University Press, 1988).

78. "Poločas rozpadu," p. 70.

Part III

Media, Economic, and International Factors

8

Failing Democracy: Journalists, the Mass Media, and the Dissolution of Czechoslovakia

Owen V. Johnson

INTRODUCTION

Of all the factors that might have contributed to the breakup of Czechoslovakia, the mass media are perhaps the most difficult to study. It is possible to measure what was in the media; it is harder to measure the effect. At best, public opinion polls taken at the time of media activity can measure awareness of the broadcast or publication of news or opinion. Proving, however, that opinion or knowledge gained through the media motivated individuals to act is far more complicated. Despite this difficulty, it is important to examine the mass media role so that facile understandings of the impact of the press can be avoided.

Many people believe in the considerable power of the media to influence decisions and events, when in reality the media are much more likely to reinforce existing attitudes than to change them.[1] The general populace, for example, bathed every day in pictures on the TV screen and newsprint in the press, presumes that such an omnipresent institution must be a major player in public affairs, but such people have confused memory with effect. Politicians, raised in a political culture that ascribes immense power to the media, assume that mass communication must have such influence. This belief has been particularly widespread in East Central Europe, where in the past many politicians spent part of their early careers in journalism. Scholars who use the media to document political change too often presume that the media therefore have the power to move people and events.

Some Czech and Slovak politicians believe that journalists and the media in Czechoslovakia were strongly committed to national perspectives and thus contributed to the worsening of national relations after the end of communism. Pavel

163

Rychetský, a former vice premier, even holds the media responsible for the country's breakup:

> The [politicians] carried out this elimination of the state without the citizens, without a referendum, and that could happen only because the mass media began to support it, because the mass media, especially the right-wing newspapers, stirred up nationalism, racism, [and] xenophobia.[2]

This influence should be questioned, because the press was still only moderately trusted by the public. Further, right-wing tabloids, the most widely read print medium in the early postcommunist years, were not politically influential.

Political scientist Carol Skalnik Leff shares Rychetský's view, seeing the media as exacerbating discord between Czechs and Slovaks:

> The media atmosphere of charge and countercharge, and the historical experiences that generated such heated exchanges, undermined the constitutional negotiations and impeded reconciliation. In the course of negotiations, the Czech press accused Slovaks of pursuing a "secret strategy" of independence; of trying to "break up the federation" with their economic demands. Mečiar was a "country bumpkin," a police informant, or an authoritarian demagogue. Slovak journalists protested their "demonic image" as "neofascists, neocommunists, and anti-Semites" in the Czech media and countered with charges of "Pragocentric" colonization of Slovakia, "secret Czech strategies" of restoring Czechoslovakist ideology, and robbing from the Slovak economy to build Czech prosperity.[3]

But this was merely the media following the politics of the parties in the fashion of the interwar Czechoslovak Republic, with little evidence that readers or viewers were changing their minds.

Jeremy Druker says the split of the country came about because of a failure of the journalism profession in Slovakia:

> If much of the mainstream media did not support outright secession and did not generate separatist sentiments among the majority of the public, how then did an independent Slovakia arise? The answer lies in the failure of the media to look with a penetrating eye at, and educate the public about, the political course Mečiar's MDS was plotting in Slovakia in the second half of 1992. . . .
>
> Many factors contributed to these shortcomings. Slovak journalists educated under communism had no tradition of pressing government leaders. . . . Journalists who came of age after the fall of communism were largely young and inexperienced. Many journalists were unfamiliar with the new terminology. . . . Mečiar's MDS was effective at intimidating some journalists with threats while seducing others with promises. . . . Most Slovak media never explored the impact that separation would have on the Slovak economy and standard of living.[4]

Druker is unfair in expecting Slovak journalists to meet standards that even few U.S. journalists would meet, but he is right in observing that Slovak journalists were rarely independently active.

In contrast to the conclusions of Rychetský, Leff, and Druker, in a book devoted to an analysis of the "social, economic and cultural forces which in the seventy-year-long history of Czechoslovakia worked either for its integration or for its disintegration," hardly mention any media institution.[5] The summary of one of the contributors in that book shows a country whose citizens no longer saw eye to eye not because they had been persuaded of anything by the media but because of longer-term historical reasons and shorter-term experience:

> [T]he values and orientations of citizens of the Czech and Slovak republics differed in many important ways prior to the creation of two independent states. These differences, which were not limited to views concerning the organization of the state, reflect the influence of each people's history and levels of economic development, as well as the legacy of the communist period. They also reflect the different impact of the transition to the market in the two regions.[6]

Throughout modern Czech and Slovak history, leading journalists and politicians were partners in the political process. In Vladimír Kusin's words, "The press, still largely tied to political parties or causes, set . . . greater store [in] advancing opinion and conducting polemics than [in] purveying and analyzing news."[7] During the period of communist rule in Czechoslovakia, the mass media were ascribed considerable powers in advancing the cause of party and state. Struggle over the maintenance of control of the mass media was a major issue in the Prague Spring.[8] After the communist collapse, many journalists sought to regain their imagined influence, but if they did so, they found that what they said was little different from what politicians were saying. If they sought to follow the more Western model of objectivity and balance, they were reduced to transmitting the messages of politicians. This produced journalistic "schizophrenia," with journalists wanting the right to be independent and professional but also to be active advocates of party positions. The result was the kind of journalism most U.S. journalists practiced in the nineteenth century.[9] On those occasions where journalists had the chance to talk among themselves about their work, they sounded professional.[10] Both Czech and Slovak journalists founded professional syndicates to defend their professional and social interests. But independent professional attitudes less often emerged in print—much of which remained allied with political parties—and even less on the air. Instead the press specialized in rumors and petty politics.

According to one study completed in late 1991, politicians were, generally speaking, "rather unhappy with the manner they [were] being covered by media and journalists. They often accuse[d] media of partiality, anti-government bias, superficiality and sensationalism."[11] The media thereby preserved the place they defined for themselves in public life: a substitute for mass democracy. Even in the postseparation Czech Republic, no media institution or individual has secured significant independent influence on public affairs, a trend not improved by the significant pressures of commercialization and the gradual depoliticization of the media, and a process supported by the high degree of foreign ownership that seeks to avoid involvement in Czech domestic political affairs.[12] That is not true in Slovakia, where efforts by the Vladimír Mečiar regime to bend the media to its will has forced some of the media to take on an independent role in the public arena in order to avoid losing their influence.[13]

This chapter argues that the media role in the breakup of Czechoslovakia was minimal in the last few years before the split, an outcome that preserved the political control of the elite (including journalists) and thus was welcomed by them. First, from the founding of Czechoslovakia in 1918 until the collapse of the country nearly three-quarters of a century later, media development in the Czech lands and Slovakia took place along similar paths, but the amount of media interaction between the two parts of the country was limited, except at a few crisis periods. The only shared media experience was television, increasingly in late communism an entertainment medium whose function was to distract people from politics. Second, except for the reform period of the mid- and late 1960s, media under communist control were not trusted by a substantial portion of the population. It was not possible for the media, in the relatively short period from 1989 to 1992 to regain the people's trust. A statewide survey in late 1991 found only 34 percent of the population had confidence in television, 48 percent in the press, and 56 percent in radio (figures similar to or higher, however, than in the federal government, the army, and the church). More than half thought stories on TV and in newspapers were inaccurate, a view perhaps related to their belief that the media were not independent but were often influenced by political organizations or people.[14] Together, this lack of trust and lack of media-developed knowledge and opinion meant that the picture in the Czech mind about Slovakia and the picture in the Slovak mind about the Czechs were conditioned by the folklore of experience and the publicists of the past who nurtured these ideas; e.g., of Slovak pot menders coming to Prague in the interwar period and of Slovak fleecing of the Czech lands in the communist period, or of Czech influence in Slovakia in the interwar period and during the worst times of communist rule. Without independent media activity, Czechs did not know well the mind-set and agenda of Slovaks in 1992, and vice versa. Third, politicians were successful in preventing the development of an independent media role in postcommunist politics, primarily by a policy of nonresponse to journalistic activity. Finally, journalists proved unable to carve out an independent role for themselves in the postcommunist period, for both historical reasons and the absence of established political patterns and institutions.

The direct role of the media in the breakup, therefore, must be seen as subtle. Most important, after 1968 both Slovak society and Slovak development stayed rather hidden from Czechs because of the more tightly controlled Czech media and the very small circulation of Slovak media in the Czech lands. As Maria Todorova explains more broadly about East Central and Southeastern Europe, under communism, "there was a lid on nationalist discourse, but this is not the same as saying there was a lid on nationalism."[15] Katherine Verdery suggests that "the organization of socialism enhanced national consciousness."[16] The Slovak media, then, far less affected by personnel removals after the Soviet invasion in 1968 than were the Czech media, contained sustained national—though rarely nationalist—discourse until the end of the communist era. The inability of the Czech media in the Husák years to report the changing national outlook in Slovakia meant that after the Velvet Revolution, the depth of Slovak national feeling surprised most Czechs and played on the prejudices established by relative Slovak backwardness in the interwar period, the division of the country in 1939, and the belief that Slovak concern with national equality in 1968 had contributed to the downfall of the Prague Spring. In this way, the legacy of the precommunist period combined with the legacy of communism was the end of Czechoslovakia.

The role of the media in the breakup, then, was not so much in telling people what to think after 1989, but in what the media, following the cues of political leaders, told or did not tell people to think about, beginning in 1969. They provided both the agenda and—for the respective populations of the Czech lands and Slovakia—the frames through which the agenda was to be viewed. While the Czech media focused on democratic and economic reform, the Slovak media concerned themselves with national issues.[17] In one important case to be discussed here, political leaders sought to influence the frames: a momentary coalition of Slovak prime minister Vladimír Mečiar and journalists who would eventually oppose him succeeded in significantly reducing the influence of federal TV news, beginning in mid-1992.

HISTORY

From the time Czechoslovakia was founded in 1918 until its first breakup in 1939, there were virtually no statewide media in the country. Czech knowledge about Slovakia was abysmal.[18] A small number of Slovak intellectuals, mostly based in Prague, evidently read the interwar *Lidové noviny*, the intellectuals' newspaper that generally reflected the perspectives of the Hrad group that gathered around President Thomas G. Masaryk.[19] In the last years of the First Republic, commercial imperatives drove some Czech publishers to begin to serve the Slovak market, primarily from Žilina and Bratislava in the west of Slovakia. Statewide radio broadcasting began only in 1926, and even by the end of the First Republic, radio receivers were still not universal in Slovakia. Slovak newspapers in the First Republic were distinctly provincial publications. Rarely did they have any correspondents abroad, and then usually only in Vienna or Budapest. No more than one or two newspapers had Prague correspondents. Instead, coverage of events in Prague consisted of rewriting or commenting on news that occurred in the Czechoslovak capital. Most Slovak newspapers were rather modest in size and focused their coverage on events in Slovakia. With the exception of *Sloven-*

ská politika, Slovak newspapers were associated with political parties, further separating them from the public at large.

Czech attention, in contrast, was focused on the relationship with Germany, not surprisingly, given the large German population in Bohemia and Moravia, particularly in the Sudetenland. Slovakia was viewed generally as an extension of Czech territory, much in the fashion that northern Italians have tended to view southern Italians as less developed and not worthy of extended attention. A 1946 survey showed that half of the Czechs had never visited Slovakia, and another one-fifth had been there only once, hardly a sign of a well-integrated populace.[20] Even the Czech and Slovak elite sat at separate tables: almost all of the Czech elite in the mid-1960s were educated in the Czech lands and worked there. Similarly, a substantial proportion of the Slovak elite studied and worked only in Slovakia.[21] When Václav Havel came to Bratislava for the first time after the communist regime was overthrown, he remarked that he had been in Slovakia only twice before: once on a skiing holiday and once for a meeting of dissidents. Migration between the two parts of the country steadily diminished under communist rule. According to Jirí Musil, "Both parts of the Republic became more closed and the interaction between them steadily decreased."[22] In spring 1989, eight months before communist rule collapsed, a Czech historian remarked to this author how Czech historians hardly ever went to Slovakia anymore and that the few Slovak historians who came to Prague were totally focused on Slovak national issues.

The different outlooks of the population in the two halves of the republic are best demonstrated by surveys of popular opinion about the history of the Czechs and Slovaks. Surveys of the most important historical individuals in 1968 showed that while there were significant differences in ranking, five of the same names appeared in both Czech and Slovak top-ten lists (T. G. Masaryk, Jan Hus, J. A. Komenský, Ludvík Svoboda, and Alexander Dubček). In 1989 there were still five (but with Klement Gottwald replacing Dubček). By 1992, there were only three (Masaryk, Komenský, and Václav Havel).[23]

REPLACING COMMUNISM

An earlier study of the role of the Czech and Slovak media in the development of the Velvet Revolution found them increasingly ineffective in the 1980s and suggested that word of mouth was the primary factor in 1989 that called people to come and demonstrate in the main squares of Prague and Bratislava and other cities in the republic. The revolution broke out without benefit of domestic media, which had been marginalized and was "only babbling incoherencies."[24] When some television employees succeeded in transmitting five minutes of one of the great Wenceslas Square rallies, it simply confirmed that the monopoly of communist power had been broken; it did not break that monopoly.

The postcommunist governments moved quickly to eliminate a substantial part of the state's control over the mass media. The co-opted parliament that served until the June 1990 elections made only a few changes in the still valid 1966 press law. It eliminated censorship and gave any individual or organization the right to start up a publication. For a variety of reasons, no further action was taken on a press law during the life of the Czechoslovak Federal Republic. Prime Minister Marian Čalfa, presenting the Czechoslovak government's program in July 1990, remarked that the media's responsibility was to inform the public promptly and truthfully. The state, he said, would avoid direct editorial control.[25] The Slovak government was more activist, a response in part to more nationalist Slovaks who argued Czech and federal media represented Czech-controlled institutions trying to exert influence in Slovakia.[26] A resolution adopted 6 March 1991 promised funds to those newspapers whose prospects for long-term success were good.

REPORTING CZECHS AND SLOVAKS

Jan Jirák and Otakar Šoltýs, in their examination of the portrayal of Czech–Slovak relations in the Czech mass media from November 1989 to December 1991, point out that in the absence of a visible justification for the existence of a Czech–Slovak state, media reporting and discussion employed language in which the idea and conception of national feeling was "coded." Further, they argue that the Czech mass media were very slow to pay attention to the Slovak independence movement. In part this represented the fact that open discussion on the subject had been taboo for two decades, but it also represented a realization that some Slovak complaints had been valid and that they desired not to endanger the federation by discussing them. Celebrations of the life of Andrej Hlinka, the Slovak autonomist priest of the interwar period, in September 1990 finally awakened the Czech press. Jirák and Šoltýs are not bothered by the strong evidence that, at best, the media only followed politics, seeing this as a considerable improvement over the previous single-view communist system. They also acquit the press because they say the media are drawn primarily to news, and so much of the material relating to the question of splitting the state had to do with longer-term issues and discussions.[27] One Czech newspaper, *Lidové noviny*, whose roots were more in analysis than in day-to-day news coverage, paid perhaps the greatest attention to Slovakia, but its focus was mostly on Slovak nationalism. A Slovak newspaper found that 157 of the 191 articles on Slovakia that appeared in *Lidové noviny* through the end of May 1990 dealt with Slovak nationalism.[28]

The performance of media in Slovakia also left something to be desired. A study of Slovakia through mid-1991 suggests that the emergence of democratic values was hindered by "the unfavorable structure" of the Slovak press, "unprofessional" editorial staff on Slovak radio and television, and intellectuals who failed in efforts to address the Slovak public.[29]

A December 1992 study by Ondrej Dostal, Zuzana Fialova, and Michal Vasecka showed how strongly national in form the Slovak mass media were. The authors established six categories for the daily and weekly press: extreme nationalism, radical nationalism, moderate nationalism, nationally oriented, nonnationalism, and antinationalism. The category with the largest circulation was the nationally oriented one:

> Because these periodicals with the largest circulation have not resolutely countered nationalism and failed to condemn nationalist excesses, because they leniently offered space also to extreme views, which needed unequivocal challenge, they indirectly participated in significant shifts in public opinion. Their endeavor to offer space to all made possible a gradual dominance of the most aggressive, least constructive, and intolerant opinion so that, in consequence, they pushed one side of the dialogue into the background.[30]

The study despaired that "the antinationalist press . . . perished precisely because the dominant Slovak press failed to react to the outburst of nationalism, thereby relegating the antinationalist position to the role of marginal intellectual extremism."[31] The study shows clearly how much the national Slovak frame succeeded in pushing alternative frames out of the picture. This process was aided by the "financial and journalistic incompetence" of profederal papers.[32]

It was also aided by what Elisabeth Noelle-Neumann has called the "spiral of silence." She says that interpersonal opinion and mass media content are the two primary sources of public opinion. When people in the minority refrain from publicly expressing their opinions, perceptions of the climate of opinion are distorted. Expression on the losing side is curtailed because people fear they will be socially isolated, so the public believes there is less support for the minority position than there really is. She concludes, "What does not get reported does not exist, or stated more cautiously, its chances of becoming part of ongoing perceived reality are minimal."[33] At the same time, a bandwagon effect occurs as people increasingly favor what they believe will be the winning side because they want to benefit from the social rewards of being on the winning side.[34] The media power in Czechoslovakia resided not in their transmission of political views, but in rooting those definitions in popularly accepted frames of reference.[35] What complicated the matter in Slovakia was that the bandwagon and spiral of silence were driving majority opinion to the Slovak side, but the content of the Slovak side was not clearly defined.

READING ABOUT THE OTHER

Widely conflicting data surround the question of how extensively Czech newspapers circulated in Slovakia and Slovak newspapers in the Czech Republic. The question is important because it addresses the issue of the print integration of

Czechoslovakia. In the 1960s there had been an effort to publish a Slovak edition of the Czechoslovak Communist Party organ, *Rudé právo*, but it had failed.[36] When Jiří Seydler visited Bratislava in early 1969 he was struck by the absence of Czech publications and by how the Slovak press had practically no significant news about the Czech lands.[37] One detailed 1991 survey reported not even 1 percent of Slovaks read *Lidové noviny*, then still the liberal successor to the samizdat publication and the most widely circulated Czech newspaper in Slovakia.[38] A study by the Journalism Research Institute in October 1991 found that 0.6 percent of the Slovak population read Czech newspapers daily and an equal number read them three times a week.[39] Another survey the previous winter showed that 21 percent of Slovak citizens read the Czech periodical press, including 32 percent in Bratislava. Another 26 percent of Slovak citizens wanted to read the Czech press but were unable to obtain it. Readers of the Czech press were not typical Slovaks, however. Highly represented were high school and university graduates, white-collar workers, and people in larger cities and towns. Only the newspapers *Lidové noviny* and *Rudé právo* had significant numbers of readers in Slovakia. The other Czech publications with significant readerships were magazines, such as the popular *Mladý svět*, the women's magazines *Vlasta* and *Květy,* and the humor magazine *Nový dikobraz*. Particularly telling was that 57 percent of readers of the Czech press in Slovakia thought news coverage was unsatisfactory, compared to 27 percent who were satisfied.[40] In contrast, 50 percent of those who read Slovak dailies thought the information there was truthful and adequate. Sixty-four percent of the consumers of Slovak mass media thought they were in general objective and unbiased about events in the Czech lands. More serious was the general failure of most Czech newspapers to maintain correspondents in Slovakia, and vice versa. By far the favorite Slovak publication in the Czech Republic in September 1990 was the weekly *Dorka* (119,670 copies), followed by several other general-interest magazines. The most widely available dailies were *Práca* (650 copies), *Smena* (530), *Verejnost* (329), and *Národná obroda* (232).[41] A later survey of Prague newsstands by PNS showed *Pravda* (684 copies), *Práca* (263), *Smena* (249), *Sport* (195), *Verejnost* (170), *Rol'nícke noviny* (96), *Národná obroda* (75), the Hungarian-language *Új Szó* (43), and a handful of others. But some of these went unsold.[42] The situation improved in the second half of 1992, thanks to concentrated action by four Slovak dailies that engaged a new distribution network resulting in more timely delivery, but also raised total Slovak circulation in Prague by 2,000 copies and began distribution also to Brno, with plans for wider circulation in Moravia.[43] Although there are no data on the subject, it is quite likely that many of the copies were purchased by Slovaks who lived in Prague. In sum, there was more interest in Slovakia about the Czechs than there was in the Czech Republic about Slovaks (where interest was confined mostly to Prague). There was practically no interest in communication between the two parts, except in crisis. "When something happens in Slovakia, then I watch it on TV in the evening," said a Prague shop clerk.[44]

Part of the reason for the lack of Czech interest in Slovak thinking is the point of view. "If the Czech press writes of 'our place' in the world, of returning to Europe, it means this for all of [Czechoslovakia]," one observer noted. "Things are different in Slovakia. . . . where the geographic position is accentuated, where the connecting Danube River is stressed, as is the national viewpoint, their own way, and self-justification."[45]

THE CENTRALITY OF TELEVISION

Because television was the only media institution available to both Czechs and Slovaks, it deserves special attention, particularly as to its integrative role. Television news is also more likely to be supportive of the government line.[46] Television became a mass medium in Czechoslovakia during communist rule. For nearly thirty-five years, from the day it went on the air in 1955 (November 1956 in Slovakia), it had no competition. It was the mass medium that most closely touched the lives of citizens. The audience, prompted by other signals from the regime, increasingly saw television's subtext as a national institution. While communist rulers may thus have repressed outwardly visible political expressions of ethnic or national goals, communist mass media policy indirectly encouraged the strengthening of ethnic or national identities through its emphasis on language as the primary form of national expression.

The symbolic significance of television in the national sphere was recognized alongside the federalization of the country in 1968. The main evening news program henceforth alternated reports in Czech with reports in Slovak, a practice that would continue until the breakup of the country.[47] One of the results of the depoliticization of television was the virtual disappearance of any critical consideration or even news of Czech–Slovak relations. One night of television a week was given over to "Slovak night," a practice many Czechs found annoying, seeing it merely as quotaism and adding nothing to the quality of the broadcast. From the early 1970s on, television also provided the platform through which rulers could most easily reach large audiences, making its journalism the most politicized of any mass media institution. At the same time, as the regime increased the amount of available entertainment on television, it depoliticized society. The regime was torn, however, between its commitment to politics in journalism and its recognition that the audience rejected the regime's politics. If the regime tried to soften its political stance, it risked losing the justification it had enunciated since the invasion, that the Communist Party leadership would guarantee social and economic growth as well as prevent a repeat of the 1960s liberalization that had blossomed into the Prague Spring, which would surely produce another invasion. Politics on radio and television became either "'a libation to the ideological gods' before and after the main broadcast, or in the form of speeches of various representatives of 'party and state.'"[48] As long as social and economic growth was steady, as it was in the 1970s—except for some setbacks caused by the increase in world oil prices—the communist message, while not necessarily welcomed, seemed reasonable. As the regime stumbled into the 1980s, however, the successes stopped coming, and the regime had to turn to alternative ways of gaining popular acceptance or tolerance. In television, it meant stretching the boundaries in entertainment programs, not news. Corruption in the state football (soccer) league was not dealt with in a news or sports report but in a feature film, *Zelená je tráva*. Other programs examined in fictional form problems of medical care and the challenges of daily life in an economy of shortages.

Even before 1989, Slovak television had limited autonomy and its own separate budget. Fees paid by TV-set owners in Slovakia were used to fund the Slovak part of Czechoslovak television. A similar situation applied in the Czech lands.[49] During the long years of political stagnation that followed the end of the Prague Spring, increasing Slovak complaints were heard about the lack of overall balance in programming between Czech and Slovak productions, the complaints reaching even into the main Slovak Communist Party newspaper, *Pravda*. The Velvet Revolution did not, therefore, produce a revolution in broadcasting in Slovakia but simply accelerated trends already in progress. The residues of the communist past were combined with the political and national imperatives of the present. The broadcast media of the past were pluralized politically in varying degrees but with the depth of national feeling limiting the extent of that pluralization. After the collapse of communist rule, the director of Czechoslovak television in Slovakia openly demanded that federal television carry Czech and Slovak programming on a one-to-one basis.[50] For the leaders of Czechoslovak federal television, who had been so sensitive in trying to avoid any slighting of Slovaks, these demands must have been surprising.[51] In March 1991, under strong public pressure led by the Union for Independent Radio and Television Broadcasting, the government officially ended the state monopoly on land-based broadcasting and established separate Czech and Slovak television systems. The Slovak system was partially subsidized by the Slovak government, while the federal system remained in place, with responsibility for coordinating federal news. The solution was a compromise between those who wanted to maintain a federal monopoly and those who wanted the federal system eliminated, since it was seen as a symbol of centralized communist control. About 70 percent of its programming was in Czech, with the remainder in Slovak.[52] Three broadcasting councils were established as regulatory bodies, one federal, and the Czech and Slovak ones responsible for their respective republics. As an indication of the devolution of the control of television, the federal council in its one year of existence made no decision on policy, awarded no broadcasting license, and imposed no fines but was concerned only with Czech–Slovak controversies and eventually the complete division of federal holdings.

In Slovakia, viewership of the federal program held steady while that of Slovak TV rose dramatically.[53] Viewers in both the Czech Republic and Slovakia increasingly trusted their national television far more than the federal one.[54] *Denník ČST*, the daily evening news program of federal Czechoslovak television, remained a potentially significant player in statewide affairs. Seventy percent of viewers in Slovakia trusted the program.[55] This was just behind the later evening Slovak television news program, *Aktuality*, which was trusted by 73 percent.[56] At the beginning of 1992, nearly three-quarters (72 percent) of the Slovak population watched *Denník ČST* daily, while another 17 percent watched it regularly. In contrast, only 25 percent watched *Aktuality* daily, and 34 percent watched it regularly. The survey also showed that people in Slovakia favored a statewide Czechoslovak television network that would carry federal, Slovak, and Czech programs.[57] The rapid growth in the number of local radio stations rapidly diminished the importance of central Czechoslovak radio. For instance, in Slovakia, 57 percent listened to Bratislava *Rádiožurnál* daily, while only 24 percent listened to the Czechoslovak station.[58]

The role of federal television became a subject of controversy during the 1992 parliamentary campaign. Political and government leaders represented groups and sought office in one or the other of the two parts of the country. Federal television potentially could provide the forum where the two sides could speak to each other. By and large, this did not happen. Would the voters of Indiana want to hear a debate between the candidates for governor of Ohio? Some people thought so: the Slovak Election Commission vigorously attacked Jiří Kantůrek, the director of the federal channel, for failing to allow five Slovak political parties running candidates for the Slovak parliament (*Slovenská národná rada*) to present their programs on the channel even though it had given U.S. "Czechoslovaks" time to air their views.[59] The deputy editor in chief of federal TV news said the problem was with the Slovak side, which he alleged refused to send political news, claiming it was prevented from doing so by the election law.[60] When Czech Prime Minister Petr Pithart tried to advance the interests of the entire country, he was shouted down.[61]

The election results changed the boundaries of the public arena represented by communications. Slovak politicians supported efforts by some Slovak journalists to advance national interests by actively building up a separate Slovak public sphere, thereby undermining common federal positions. The old communist structure of television with its recognition of national television structures, even if not fully developed, facilitated this effort. Slovak television, complaining that the news it had been sending to federal television had been selected and edited to meet Czech and federal perspectives, set up its own early evening news program to be broadcast just before the federal news. STV also reported that it no longer had the resources to provide material to the federal channel.[62] Federal television responded by hiring staffers to open editorial offices in Bratislava.[63] Viewership of the main Slovak TV news was initially strong, starting out at 51 percent but dropping to 34 percent in December 1992.[64] It was Mečiar's strong support for a Slovak television presence that may have been his most canny move on the road to Slovak independence.[65] At his first meeting with Václav Klaus following the parliamentary elections, he demanded the immediate disbanding of federal radio and television.[66] The demand became part of the new Slovak government's program.[67] Peter Duhan, the director of the federal Czechoslovak radio, objected strongly, saying that his station was the most listened to in the Czech lands and the second most popular station in Slovakia, so that any decentralization would be against the wishes of the listeners.[68]

Not only did Mečiar want to eliminate federal television, but he also sought to bring as much of the Slovak media as possible under his control. Against the wishes of Slovak TV News Director Ján Füle, Mečiar demanded regular time to speak to the people of Slovakia. Mečiar's supporters put pressure on Füle to accede to Mečiar's wishes by sending observers to watch how he would edit Mečiar's meeting with the pro-Mečiar "Journalists for a Truthful Picture of Slovakia." [69] Mečiar's supporters said Slovak television was insufficiently professional, was not objective, and was spreading disinformation, anxiety, and fear, meaning it was not backing Mečiar strongly enough.[70] Mečiar's attitude can be summed up by saying that he did not object to criticism, so long as he could provide his "truthful" side of the issue.[71] Within two months of these actions, Slovak support for a common state had dropped precipitously, even though the citizens of Slovakia were not optimistic about the improvement of broadcast news in an independent Slovakia.[72]

UNDERSTANDINGS, ALTERNATIVES, AND CONCLUSIONS

Benedict Anderson has suggested that people create imagined communities through their use of the media.[73] Instrumentalism is left somewhat vague in this matter. Do people participate in a national community through sharing the same media rituals and messages, or do those media help shape the identity? If Slovak media were placing the political agenda in a clearly Slovak national frame, how should one explain the considerable increase in Slovak national discontent registered between 1990 and 1992 without reference to the independent media role?[74] Three explanations can be offered. First, the actions and speeches of Slovak political leaders on these matters were duly carried in Slovak media, giving the media the role of transmission belt. Public opinion is extremely responsive to elite discourse generally.[75] In a society with limited opportunity for individual choice for forty years, this is even more likely to be the case. Second, the Czech response was available only through federal television, while the federal response through the same source was gradually withering away. Finally, each individual's insecurity about the future of the state, the economy, and democracy reflected heightened individual sensitivity based on general attention to the public arena, not something created independently by the media. Supporters of Mečiar's Movement for a Democratic Slovakia came to believe that these problems could be solved outside the common state framework.[76] This occurred even when mass media support for Mečiar was relatively weak. On the Czech side, national issues were well down in the list of issues for public debate.

What may not be clear from the preceding is what alternative paths the media might have followed that might have provided them with greater independent influence. One would have been the building of a new meaning for the existence of Czechoslovakia. What was abundantly clear from the hyphen debate over the new name of Czechoslovakia in March 1990 until the end of the country's existence in 1992 was the inability of anyone—journalist, politician, or thinker—to formulate the purpose of Czechoslovakia. Given that the media, except for television, were fundamentally national, i.e., Czech or Slovak, it would have been impossible for them to create a supranational meaning. Television could not do so because it is fundamentally an entertainment medium and because its news, opinion, and information programs could not, for all practical purposes, follow a different agenda than that of the print media.

No referendum was ever held on division of the state; voters had little chance of influencing the decision. Prime Ministers Václav Klaus and Vladimír Mečiar—both more populist than democratic because they claimed to speak for their peoples more than to represent them—made the division decision for political, not national, reasons. Without a specific referendum proposal, it was much harder for the media to play an informational and organizational role on the issue. This was particularly true for television, whose news is organized in time rather than space. Journalism and journalists in the modern world react to specific events and proposals because they are the stuff of focused stories. Without a specific referendum proposal, journalists were unable to ask specific questions and provide the exact information that might have helped the many undecided readers and viewers to make meaningful choices. Because many journalists, and the media they represented, held a variety of views on the efficacy of a referendum and which question should be asked, the media could not have independently united in favor of a referendum. Even if they had, they would have faced a public that did not yet fully trust the media. The result was that "hardly any significant and influential public political debate occurred."[77] Given this situation, without a specific proposal, journalists were left with theater to report. Both Mečiar and Klaus engaged in angry shouting matches with journalists, although Klaus usually chose his words better than did his Slovak counterpart, and both often simply ignored journalists.[78] They both inherited a communist tradition in which the media could be used to help carry out a policy, but they were not the source of "the flow of information on which sound policy decisions are made."[79]

U.S. journalism philosophy is based on a rationalist eighteenth-century system that focuses on the individual yet recognizes that we live in communities and must be responsible to the general good of those communities. European journalism, in contrast, grows more out of the nineteenth-century sense of collectivity, in which the collective bore certain responsibilities to the group. People are members of a nation or class first of all, and it follows that the media must represent those groups. Prior to communist rule, the Czech media had a historical tradition initially national but later more class oriented, while the Slovak tradition was primarily national. Communist rule artificially substituted the proletariat as the group focus, later broadening this niche focus to represent a wide range of groups. The end of communist rule raised anew consideration of media philosophy. Almost immediately, Slovak mass media strengthened their old national tradition, a reflection of the direction of Slovak politics. The Czech media, in contrast, were divided among a devoutly political ethic that sees journalism as playing a major role in influencing public policy debates; an individual, serve-the-public ethic, in which providing information to help people make up their minds is the highest priority; and an aphilosophical, bottom-line ethic, focused on increasing the media organization's profit margin by giving the public what it wants. The national focus, such as that which characterized the Slovak media, was most effective in opposition. Its influence was not by persuasion but by its agenda, which defined most issues in their national context and thus gave their resolution national importance. There was little or no room for matters of the larger federal state.

To elucidate the significance of the media role in Czechoslovakia, it is useful to recall two critical junctures in American history: the antislavery movement in the 1830s and the civil rights movement in the 1950s and 1960s. The appearance of millions of copies of abolitionist newspapers and tracts in the 1830s met with widespread protests in both the South and the North. The protest meetings were led by "gentlemen of property and standing" who recognized that "news in print . . . was an invitation to citizens assigned no political role in the normal course of Whig or Democratic campaigns." Mass circulation would bring the public at large into politics independently. In the 1950s, dozens of journalists from major northern media institutions streamed to the South to report on civil rights demonstrations. They were attacked, often physically, by southerners, not because they were reporters but because the attackers believed that their side of the story was not being told. The southerners began to ask northern newspapers to examine black–white relations in their own backyards, the inner cities. Some southern politicians, such as George Wallace, also learned that they could use the press to advance their own causes.[80]

Postcommunist Czech and Slovak journalists—whether or not they had worked as journalists under communism—were drawn more to politics than to journalism. They did not seek to change the frames and the context of the political agenda so that news could be read another way. The more they brought the public into the process by providing independent news about the other republic, the more they would have diminished their own expectations of leadership and decision making. Conditioned as they were by the decades-old frames of the "other," both Czech and Slovak journalists failed to project an adequate picture of the people in the other republic. The weakness of the federal idea made this even harder to accomplish. Slovak political leaders, especially Mečiar, recognized that if federal media, especially television, had the opportunity to report a detailed picture of Slovakia to Slovakia, the public, empowered by this alternative information, might no longer so willingly support them. On this, they saw eye to eye with Václav Klaus. Unlike George Wallace, however, who developed support across the United States, Mečiar never attempted to expand his political base to the rest of Czechoslovakia.

Journalists, drawing on a tradition of their influence that stretched back from communism through the interwar republic to the nineteenth century, shared the desire of Klaus, Mečiar, and other politicians to maintain their power and not to yield a significant civic and democratic role to the public. Hence they largely did not seek to serve the public. Nor did they play an independent role. That the public had limited trust in the news media only made it easier for journalists and politicians to act the way they did. These decisions of journalists and politicians to leave the public outside the policy arena surely must raise questions about the nature of democracy in both the Czech Republic and Slovakia.

NOTES

1. Joseph T. Klapper, *The Effects of Mass Communication* (New York: The Free Press, 1960).

2. Andrew Yurkovsky, "The Voracious Readers in Czechoslovakia," *Editor and Publisher* 128:2 (14 January 1995), p. 25.

3. Carol Skalnik Leff, "Could This Marriage Have Been Saved? The Czechoslovak Divorce," *Current History* 95:599 (March 1996), p. 132.

4. Jeremy Druker with Jon Vanden Heuvel, *Continuity and Change: The Media in Slovakia* (New York: Freedom Forum Media Studies Center, 1994), p. 7.

5. Jiří Musil, ed., *The End of Czechoslovakia* (Budapest: Central European Press, 1995). Quotation is from Musil's introduction, p. ix. The media are also ignored in Rüdiger Kipke and Karel Vodička, *Rozloučení s Československem: Příčiny a důsledky česko–slovenského rozchodu* (Prague: Český spisovatel, 1993).

6. Sharon L. Wolchik, "The Politics of Transition and the Break-Up of Czechoslovakia," in *The End of Czeckoslovakia,* ed. Musil, pp. 238, 240.

7. Vladimir V. Kusin, "Media in Transition," *Report on Eastern Europe* 2:18 (3 May 1991), p. 5.

8. Frank L. Kaplan, *Winter into Spring: The Czechoslovak Press and the Reform Movement 1963–1968* (Boulder: East European Quarterly, 1977).

9. Michael E. McGerr, *The Decline of Popular Politics: The American North, 1865–1928* (New York: Oxford University Press, 1986).

10. E.g. "Novinári všetkých krajín, klepte politikom po prstoch!" *Slovenský denník,* 20 December 1991, p. 5.

11. Rudolf Prevrátil et al., *Communication in the Transition to Democracy in East Europe* (London: World Association for Christian Communication, 1993), p. 26.

12. Steve Kettle, "The Czech Republic Struggles to Define an Independent Press," *Transition* 1:18 (6 October 1995), pp. 4–6.

13. Sharon Fisher, "Slovak Media Under Pressure," *Transition* 1:18 (6 October 1995), pp. 7–9.

14. Lisa Ellis and Martha MacIver, "Czechoslovaks Becoming More Open to Private Media," *USIA Report* M-13-92 (6 February 1992), pp. 4–5.

15. Maria N. Todorova, "Ethnicity, Nationalism, and the Communist Legacy in Eastern Europe," in James R. Millar & Sharon L. Wolchik, eds., *The Soviet Legacy of Communism* (Washington, D.C.: Woodrow Wilson Center, 1994), p. 101.

16. Katherine Verdery, "Nationalism and National Sentiment in Post-Socialist Romania," *Slavic Review* 52:2 (Summer 1993), p. 180.

17. Otto Ulč, "The Bumpy Road of Czechoslovakia's Velvet Revolution," *Problems of Communism* 41:3 (May–June 1992), p. 31, labels the Slovak media "vigorously nationalist," thus confusing topic with point of view.

18. Jiří Beránek, "Spolek Československá jednota v meziválečných česko–slovenských vztazích," *Acta Universitatis Carolinae* 1991—*Philosophica et Historica* 5, p. 65.

19. The Hrad group was an informal "brain trust" of politicians and democratic intellectuals who met with Masaryk from time to time. Masaryk used the group to promote a generally progressive policy that placed state interests over those of party, profession, or religion. Alena Gajanová, "K charakteru první republiky," *Historie a vojenství* 1968, no. 5, p. 799; See also Vera Olivová, "Hradní buržoazie," *Dějiny a současnost* 7:4 (1965), pp. 39–42; and Karl Bosl et al., eds., *Die "Burg": Einflussreiche politische Kräfte um Masaryk und Benes*, 2 vols. (Munich: R. Oldenbourg Verlag, 1973–1974).

20. Čeněk Adamec, Bohuš Pospíšil, and Milan Tesař, *What's Your Opinion: A Year's Survey of Public Opinion in Czechoslovakia* (Prague: Orbis, 1947), p. 17.

21. Carol Skalnik Leff, *National Conflict in Czechoslovakia: The Making and Remaking of a State, 1918–1987* (Princeton: Princeton University Press, 1988), pp. 287–294.

22. Jiří Musil, "Česká a slovenská společnost," *Sociologický časopis* 29:1(1993), p. 19.

23. Ján Mišovič, "Opinions on the Personalities of the Czech and Slovak History in the Past and Today," in Dusan Kováč, ed., *History and Politics* (Bratislava: Czecho–Slovak Committee of the European Cultural Foundation, 1993), p. 25.

24. Owen V. Johnson, "Mass Media and the Velvet Revolution," in Jeremy D. Popkin, ed., *Media and Revolution* (Lexington: University Press of Kentucky, 1995), pp. 220–31.

25. "Programové prohlášení vlády ČSFR," ČTK, 3 July 1990, as cited in Rudolf Převrátil and Stanislav Perkner, "Nach der Euphorie der Freiheit die ganz normalen 'schwierigen Zeiten'," *Media Perspektiven* 2/91, p. 79.

26. See "Co s televizí," *Lidové noviny*, 12 November 1991, p. 3; and "Co budeme počúvat' v rozhlase: Pýtame sa riaditel'a Slovenského rozhlasu Vladimíra Štefka," *Verejnost*, 28 March 1991, p. 5.

27. Jan Jirák and Otakar Šoltýs, "Zobrazení česko–slovenských vztahů v tisku v období 17.11.1989 až 31.12.1991—státoprávní uspořádání," in Fedor Gál et al., *Dnešní krize československých vztahů* (Prague: Sociologické nakladatelství, 1992), pp. 40–67; Převrátil and Perkner, Nach der Euphorie, p. 82.

28. "Mutné vody," *Práca*, 19 October 1990.

29. Martin Bútora, Zora Bútorová, and Tatiana Rosová, "The Hard Birth of Democracy in Slovakia: The Eighteen Months Following the 'Tender' Revolution," *Journal of Communist Studies* 7:4 (December 1991), p. 454.

30. Reported in Peter Brhlovič, "Noted in Passing," *Slobodný piatok*, 26 March 1993, p. 2, as translated in JPRS-EER-93-037-S of 4 May 1993, p. 23.

31. Brhlovič, "Noted in Passing," p. 2.

32. Milan Žitný, "The New Slovak Market of Ideas," *East European Reporter* 5:3 (May–June 1992), pp. 30–31.

33. Elisabeth Noelle–Neumann, *The Spiral of Silence—Our Social Skin* (Chicago: University of Chicago Press, 1984), quote from p. 150.

34. Michael W. Traugott, "The Impact of Media Polls on the Public," in Thomas E. Mann & Gary R. Orren, eds., *Media Polls on the Public* (Washington, D.C.: The Brookings Institution, 1992), pp. 125–49.

35. This thinking is influenced by Stuart Hall et al., *Policing the Crises: Mugging, the State, & Law & Order* (London: Macmillan, 1978).

36. Antony Buzek, *How the Communist Press Works* (New York: Praeger, 1964), p. 121, indicated the "obvious intention" was to slowly replace the Bratislava *Pravda* as the Slovak communist organ. The change in Slovak communist leadership in 1963 probably signaled an end to this project.

37. Jiří Seydler, "Čím žije hlavní město slovenské socialistické republiky," *Reportér* 4:5 (6 February 1969), pp. 8–10.

38. "Dnešná tvár Slovenska: Masmédia," *Lidové noviny*, 20–21 September 1991.

39. Vladimír Holina, "Čitatelia a čítanie," *Otázky žurnalistiky* 35:1 (1992), p. 10.

40. "Twenty-Seven Percent Satisfied," *Lidové noviny*, 5 April 1991, p. 2, as translated in JPRS-EER-91-051 of 22 April 1991, pp. 2–3; Dana Soucová, "O objektivite masovej komunikácie," *Národná obroda*, 13 April 1991.

41. "Pár výrecnych čísel," *Národná obroda*, 20 December 1990.

42. Ivan Sobotka, "Kupte si slovenské noviny," *Roháč*, 21 January 1991, p. 11.

40. "Budu čítat' po slovensky?" *Pravda*, 14 July 1992, as reprinted in *Lidové noviny*, 16 July 1992, p. 9.

44. Sobotka, "Kupte si slovenské noviny," p. 11. Petr Pithart discusses the reasons for this mutual lack of interest in "Před a za zrcadlem," *Střední Evropa* 12:62 (September 1996), pp. 65–80.

45. Jiří Svítek, "The Press through the Eyes of Political Scientists," *Reportér*, 10 July 1991, as translated in JPRS-EER-91-110 of 26 July 1991, p. 7.

46. Limor Peer and Beatrice Chestnut, "Deciphering Media Independence: The Gulf War Debate in Television and Newspaper News," *Political Communication* 12:1 (January–March 1995), pp. 81–95.

47. Frederic Wehrle, *Le divorce tchéco–slovaque: Vie et mort de la Tchécoslovaquie 1918–1992* (Paris: Éditions L'Harmattan, 1994), p. 122.

48. Alexander Langer, "Elektronická masmédia a stabilita střední a východní Evropy," *Mezinárodní vztahy*, 1993/1, p. 65.

49. Milan Šmíd, "The Czech and Slovak Republics," in Jeremy Mitchell and Jay G. Blumler, eds., *Television and the Viewer Interest: Explorations in the Responsiveness of European Broadcasters* (London: John Libbey & Co., 1994), pp. 68–69. An additional channel, 0K3 (in the Czech lands) and TA3 (in Slovakia), broadcast retransmission of satellite programming on the channel formerly used for Soviet TV programming.

50. *Rudé právo*, 7 March 1990, p. 2.

51. During a visit to Czechoslovak TV studios in March 1989, I was told of several instances where the lack of a tape or script in the appropriate language had caused great consternation and fear that the party leadership would take disciplinary action against those responsible for the shortcomings.

52. Šmíd, "The Czech and Slovak Republics," pp. 68–69.

53. Zora Bútorová et al., *Aktuálne problémy Česko-Slovenska januar 1992* (Bratislava: Centrum pre sociálnu analýzu, spol. s.r.o., 1992), p. 124.

54. "Dôverujeme národnému rádiu," *Národná obroda*, 17 October 1992.

55. "Dnešná tvár Slovenska: Masmédia," *Lidové noviny*, 20–21 September 1991.

56. Pavol Frič et al, *Aktuálne problémy slovenskej spoločnosti maj 1991: Správa zo sociologického prieskumu* (Bratislava: Ustav pre sociálnu analýzu Univerzity Komenského, 1991), p. 69.

57. Pavel Filip, "Sledují Slováci federální a českou televizi?" *Sociologické aktuality*, 20 September 1992), p. 9.

58. "Dnešná tvár"

59. "Trest pro Kantůrka?" *Lidové noviny*, 4 June 1992, p. 2.

60. "Do šotu jsme nezasahovali," *Lidové noviny*, 27 June 1992, p. 2.

61. Carol Skalnik Leff, *Czech and Slovak Republics* (Boulder: Westview Press, 1996), chap. 4.

62. "Vlastní informace," *Lidové noviny*, 30 June 1992, p. 16.

63. Martin Vadas, chief editor of Czechoslovak television, observed that even before the establishment of the separate Slovak newscasts, Slovaks in Bratislava "were reluctant to ask certain questions." Robert Sobota, "The Instantly Born 'STV News': CST is Seeking Editors for Its Bratislava Operation," *Mladá fronta Dnes*, 1 July 1992, pp. 1–2, as translated in JPRS-EER-92-097 of 28 July 1992, p. 8.

64. Ernest Páleník and Ervín St'ava, "Televízne spravodajstvo v nových podmienkách," *Informačnýbulletin—Syndikát slovenských novinárov* 4:34 (1993), p. 18.

65. Jacques Rupnik, "Společnost se musí bránit," *Respekt*, 15–21 June 1992, p. 14.

66. Leszek Mazan, "Splitting at the Seams," *Warsaw Voice*, 21 June 1992, p. 5.

67. "Charakteristika návrhu programového vyhlásenia vlády SR," *Národná obroda*, 9 July 1992.

68. "Právo na život," *Lidové noviny*, 25 June 1992, p. 2.

69. "Slovak Television Issues a Strong Protest," *Telegraf* (Prague), 13 July 1992, p. 2, as translated in JPRS-EER-92-074 of 22 July 1992, p. 22.

70. *Report on Czechoslovakia* 3:9 (September 1992), p. 6.

71. Owen V. Johnson, "Whose Voice? Freedom of Speech and the Media in Central Europe," in Al Hester & Kristina White, eds., *Creating a Free Press in Eastern Europe* (Athens: University of Georgia, 1993), pp. 23–28.

72. V. Krivý, *Trvanie a zmena na Slovensku - september 1992* (Bratislava: ISS FM Uko, 1992), as cited in Bútorová, "Premyšlené," pp. 99–101. Samuel Brečka and Zdena Cupiková, "Slovensko a česko–slovenské vzt'ahy vo federálnych médiach," *Otázky žurnalistiky* 36:1(1993), pp. 19–26, blame one-sided federal TV news for this shift in opinion, but the evidence they provide is not persuasive.

73. Benedict Anderson, *Imagined Communities: Reflections on the Origin and Spread of Nationalism* (London: Verso, 1991).

74. Among other places, data measuring this discontent are summarized by Zora Bútorová, "Premyšlené 'áno' zániku ČSFR: Image stran a rozpad Česko–Slovenska očami občanov Slovenska," *Sociologický časopis* 29:1(1993), pp. 88–103.

75. Benjamin Page, Robert Y. Shapiro, and Glenn R. Dempsey, "Television News & Changes in America's Policy Preferences," *American Political Science Review* 83 (1987), pp. 23–44.

76. Bútorová, "Premyšlené," p. 95.

77. Martin Palous, "The Czechoslovakian Divorce: 'Velvet' Settlement, or Muted Coexistence?" in Crawford D. Goodwin and Michael Nacht, eds., *Beyond Government: Extending the Public Policy Debate in Emerging Democracies* (Boulder: Westview Press, 1995), p. 199.

78. Ivan Lamper, award-winning editor of *Respekt*, observed, "Our new politicians quickly learned to take a dismissive and patronizing attitude toward the press." "The Death of Czecho–Slovakia," *Uncaptive Minds* 5:3 (Fall 1992), p. 88.

79. Beverly Crawford and Arend Lijphart, "Explaining Political and Economic Change in Post-Communist Eastern Europe: Old Legacies, New Institutions, Hegemonic Norms, and International Pressures," *Comparative Political Studies* 28:2 (July 1995), p. 192. This reference to the totally utilitarian concept of the press and the obliteration of vital flows of information under communism is also made by Prevrátil and Perkner, Nach der Euphorie, p. 78.

80. Thomas C. Leonard, "Antislavery, Civil Rights, and Incendiary Material," in Popkin, ed., *Media and Revolution* pp. 115–35.

9

Explaining Czechoslovakia's Dissolution: Assessing Economic Performance before and after the Breakup

Jan Svejnar

INTRODUCTION

In this chapter, I examine the economic performance of the Czech and Slovak republics before and after the dissolution of Czechoslovakia on 1 January 1993.[1] A rigorous analysis of the economic impact of the dissolution would require estimating a model that would isolate the effect of the split while controlling for the effects of other relevant factors on the economic performance of the two countries. There is no doubt that factors such as the disintegration of the Council for Mutual Economic Assistance (CMEA) and the collapse of the Soviet market may have affected the two countries differently in the short run. However, as it has only been a short time since the demise of Czechoslovakia, a relatively complex multivariate analysis cannot yet be adequately carried out. In this chapter, I have therefore decided to analyze the issue by comparing time series of various performance indicators in the Czech and Slovak republics with those of other Central and Eastern European countries that were implementing a transition from plan to market and were exposed to the same external shocks. Whenever possible, I also draw on more complex comparative analyses of particular issues.

My main finding is that, with the exception of unemployment, the economic performance of the two republics-turned-states has been quite similar in the few years immediately preceding and following the partition of Czechoslovakia. In terms of economic performance, the Slovak Republic caught up remarkably with the Czech lands between 1950 and 1989. As a result of this similarity of their ini-

tial (1989) conditions and post-1989 economic policies, the economic performance of the two countries between 1989 and 1998 was also relatively similar, although the Slovak economy declined more in the early 1990s and grew faster in
the mid-1990s.

An interesting aspect of the dissolution of Czechoslovakia is that perceived
economic differences contributed significantly to the dissolution. In a nutshell, in
view of the more rapidly rising unemployment and the slightly faster rate of decline in the Slovak economy as compared to the Czech one, many Slovak leaders
advocated a more gradual approach to the economic transition from plan to market. The same statistics, together with the historically less-developed nature of the
Slovak economy, compelled many Czech leaders to perceive the Slovak economy
as the weaker partner who would slow down the Czech engine of growth. The in-
troverted nature of the Czech–Slovak debates was so intense that the policymakers did not fully appreciate the enormous similarities between the Czech and Slovak economies in comparison to the other economies in the region.

1918–1989

At Czechoslovakia's creation in 1918, there was by all accounts a major gap between the levels of economic development of the Czech and Slovak parts of the
country. As discussed by Václav Průcha (1995), 1921 figures indicate that Slovakia was primarily an agrarian country, with 61 percent of its working population
engaged in agriculture and forestry. The comparable figure for the Czech Republic was 32 percent. Similarly, 40 percent of the Czech working population was in
1921 employed in manufacturing, construction, and crafts, while only 17 percent
of the Slovak working population was located in this sector. Another way to look
at the same situation is to note that in 1918, Czechoslovakia inherited over 60
percent of the entire industrial production of the Austro–Hungarian Empire. Yet,
Slovakia, with 21 percent of the Czechoslovak population, accounted for at most
8.5 percent of Czechoslovakia's industrial production (see Kotrba and Kříž 1992;
and Dědek et al. 1996, p. 8).

The above figures yield a somewhat surprising result, namely, that at the time
of the founding of Czechoslovakia, industrial productivity of labor was on average quite similar in the Czech lands and in Slovakia.[2] In contrast, statistics related
to productivity differences in agriculture indicate that the yield per hectare on a
Slovak farm was about 40 percent of the yield on a Czech farm (Průcha 1995, p.
42). Since land is fixed and population was relatively immobile, the different
agricultural productivities of land are a plausible outcome.

Between the two world wars, the Czechoslovak government adopted a fairly
laissez-faire attitude toward the two republics. During this period, the Czech
lands advanced quite rapidly, while Slovakia underwent a significant but uneven
economic development. Immediately after 1918, Slovakia allocated significant

resources to reorienting its economic infrastructure and activity away from Hungary and toward the Czech lands. Its development was further hampered by the economic recession of 1921–23. As a result, it was only in the second half of the 1920s that Slovakia started benefiting from new infrastructure developments (especially electrification and construction of railways) and was able to begin developing new industries. This process was restarted after the Great Depression of 1929–33, and it continued during the first part of the war years (1939–43), when Slovakia launched a major development of its armaments industry.

The development of Slovakia's armament industry was temporarily slowed down between 1945 and 1948, but it was resumed after the communist coup d'état in 1948, since the Soviet strategy stressed the rapid industrialization of Slovakia, including its armament industry. More generally, in the forty years from the 1950s to the 1980s, the incremental capital-output ratio (defined as the change in capital stock divided by the change in output, and denoted as ICOR) was consistently about 10 percent higher in Slovakia than in the Czech lands. Thus the percentage differential in Slovak versus Czech ICOR was 11.2 percent in the 1950s, 9.3 percent in the 1960s, 7.8 percent in the 1970s, and 10.9 percent in the 1980s (Kotrba and Kříž 1992).[3] When examining the gross investment/ national income ratio, one finds that during the 1950s and 1960s gross investment, expressed as a five-year average, represented 35–38 percent of national income in Slovakia, as compared to 21–27 percent in the Czech lands. In the 1970s and 1980s the corresponding ranges were 37–39 percent and 30–31 percent.[4] Similarly, investment in education is reported to have been 52 percent higher in Slovakia than in the Czech lands between 1950 and 1990 (Kotrba and Kříž 1992), resulting in higher educational levels in Slovakia than the Czech lands by the late 1980s (Dědek et al. 1996, p. 24).

Calculations by Krovak and Zamrazilova, reported in Oldřich Dědek et al. (1996, p. 25), indicate that the rapid development of Slovakia was accompanied by a significant transfer of resources from the Czech lands to Slovakia. In particular, when expressed as a share of the Slovak national income, the calculated transfers amounted to 14.7 percent in the 1950s, 14.1 percent in the 1960s, 10.3 percent in the 1970s, and 6.8 percent in the 1981–88 period. These calculations are naturally subject to numerous caveats, as prices were administratively set and flows of goods and services were hard to evaluate at their scarcity values.

1989–1998

The communist regime's special effort to develop Slovakia resulted in a significant narrowing of the historically large Czecho–Slovak economic gap. Josef Kotrba and Karel Kříž (1992) report that the relative per capita income differential between the Czech Republic and Slovakia was still 47 percent in 1953 but only 9 percent by 1990. Similarly, Dědek et al. (1996) show the Slovak national income per capita to have been 88 percent of the Czech level in 1989. However, Ivan Sujan (1993) reports a larger (25 percent) differential in gross domestic product (GDP) per capita for 1992, which may be accounted for by a somewhat larger GDP decline in Slovakia than in the Czech Republic immediately after the Velvet Revolution (Table 9.1) but which is probably mostly due to some discrepancy in the data used in the different studies.[5]

Using microdata on all industrial firms in the Czech and Slovak republics, John Ham, Jan Svejnar, and Katherine Terrell (1995) find that the average gross wage paid by these firms was essentially identical during the first, third, and fourth quarters of 1989, with the second-quarter average Slovak wage being 15 percent below the Czech wage. Ham et al. (1995) also show that in 1989 the relative distribution of the labor force across principal sectors was very similar. In particular, the proportion in agriculture was 11 percent in the Czech Republic and 14 percent in Slovakia, while the proportion in industry was 39 percent and 33 percent, respectively.

Finally, Dědek et al.'s (1996, pp. 54–56) analysis suggests that in terms of (a) production and use of raw materials and semifinished goods, and (b) integration into CMEA, the two republics were remarkably similar in the late 1980s. In particular, an earlier analysis by the Economics Institute of the Slovak Academy of Sciences (1990) suggested that in the mid-1980s only 21 percent of Czech industrial output was semifinished goods used in Slovakia, while the corresponding number for Slovakia was 56 percent. Dědek et al. (1996) in turn claimed that at the end of the 1980s, sixteen out of thirty Czech industries produced more semifinished goods than did their Slovak counterparts and that 64.1 percent of the Czech exports to Slovakia were semifinished goods, as compared to 52.4 percent of Slovak exports to the Czech Republic. Moreover, using the 1987 input-output table, Dědek et al. (1996) found that Slovak exports to the Soviet bloc constituted

Table 9.1 Growth in Real GDP in Selected Transition Economies

	1990	1991	1992	1993	1994	1995	1996	1997	1998
Czech Republic	−1.2	−11.5	−3.3	0.6	3.2	6.4	3.9	1.0	−2.5
Slovak Republic	−2.5	−14.6	−6.5	−3.7	4.9	6.9	6.6	6.5	4.5
Slovenia	−4.7	−8.9	−5.5	2.8	5.3	4.1	3.1	3.8	3.6
Poland	−11.6	−7.0	2.6	3.8	5.2	7.0	6.1	6.9	4.8
Hungary	−3.5	−11.9	−3.1	−0.6	2.9	1.5	1.3	4.6	4.7
Bulgaria	−9.1	−11.7	−7.3	−1.5	1.8	2.1	−10.9	−6.9	1.0
Romania	−5.6	−12.9	−8.8	1.5	3.9	7.1	3.9	−6.6	−5.0
Ukraine	−3.4	−11.6	−13.7	−14.2	−23.0	−12.2	−10.0	−3.3	−1.7
Russia	−4.0	−5.0	−14.5	−8.7	−12.7	−4.1	−3.5	0.8	−4.6

Data Sources:
1990:   Taken from a table from the European Bank for Reconstruction and Development, *Transition Report 1997* (London: EBRD, 1997), p. 115.
1991–1996:   Taken from tables from the European Bank for Reconstruction and Development, *Transition Report 1998* (London: EBRD, 1998), pp. 211–230.
1997:   Data from DataStream (Economist Intelligence Unit).
1998:   Estimates from DataStream (Economist Intelligence Unit).

13 percent of exports of the thirty industries, which was only marginally higher than the 11.8 percent figure for the Czech Republic.

In sum, while different measures point to somewhat different magnitudes in the two countries, there is no doubt that since 1918 (and especially in the 1950–90 period) Slovakia experienced economic progress relative to the Czech Republic and that by 1989 the two republics were remarkably similar from an economic standpoint.

The period 1990–98 was a period of economic transformation in both republics as well as in all other Central and East European countries. The statistical evidence that I present below indicates that, except for unemployment, the evolution of the Czech and Slovak economies was very similar, especially in comparison to the developments in the other countries in the region, which were exposed to similar external shocks. Moreover, while the initial similarities could in part be accounted for by the unified economic policy emanating from the federal government, the similarities persisted for a number of years after the dissolution and appear to have been grounded in other factors such as the similar initial (1989) conditions created by a common economic policy and the similar post-1992 policies of the two governments.

Inflation

Unlike most Central and East European countries, Czechoslovakia maintained virtual price stability until 1989. Indeed, the officially measured consumer price index recorded average inflation of less than 1 percent a year during the 1985–89 period, and even unofficial estimates of economists critical of the communist government policies put annual inflation at less than 3 percent (see Dyba and Svejnar 1993 for a discussion of this issue). Both the Czech and Slovak republics experienced modest inflation of about 10 percent as central planning was lifted in 1990. As can be seen from Table 9.2, prices jumped in the two republics by 52–58 percent when most prices were liberalized in 1991, 9–13 percent in 1992, 18–25 percent when the value-added tax was introduced in 1993, 10–12 percent in 1994, 7–8 percent in 1995, 5–9 percent in 1996, and 6–8 percent in 1997. In some years (1991, 1993, and 1994) inflation was somewhat higher in Slovakia, while in the other years it was somewhat higher in the Czech lands.[6] In contrast, the figures in Table 9.2 indicate that in the early 1990s all the other countries in the region experienced high inflation and some of them even hyperinflation. Moreover, in the mid-1990s most of them struggled to reduce inflation below 30 percent and some, such as Slovenia, Poland, Hungary, and Russia, succeeded in reducing inflation significantly in the 1996–97 period.

Unit Labor Cost

The dollar unit labor cost figures in Table 9.3 indicate that firms in both the Czech Republic and the Slovak Republic were less successful than those in

Table 9.2   Inflation in Selected Transition Economies (*Change in the Year-End Retail/ Consumer Price Level, as a Percentage*)

	1991	1992	1993	1994	1995	1996	1997	1998
Czech Republic	52	13	18	10	8	9	8	11
Slovak Republic	58	9	25	12	7	5	6	7
Slovenia	247	93	23	20	9	9	8	8
Poland	60	44	38	29	22	19	16	12
Hungary	32	22	21	21	28	20	18	14
Bulgaria	339	79	64	122	33	311	1,082	22
Romania	223	199	296	62	28	57	155	59
Ukraine	161	2,730	10,155	401	182	40	16	11
Russia	161	2,506	840	204	129	22	15	28

Data Sources:
1991–1996:   Taken from tables from the European Bank for Reconstruction and Development, *Transition Report 1998* (London: EBRD, 1998), pp. 211–230.
1997:   Data from DataStream (Economist Intelligence Unit).
1998:   Estimates from DataStream (Economist Intelligence Unit).

Poland and Hungary in controlling the rise in labor cost as a percentage of total cost of production (expressed in dollars). The Czech and Slovak republics were thus gradually becoming less competitive in international markets, primarily on account of the real appreciation of their currencies[7] and the slow restructuring of firms. Note, however, that until 1995 Slovakia was losing competitiveness more slowly than the Czech Republic. This difference was brought about primarily by the slower rise of wages in Slovakia and by the 1993 devaluation of the Slovak crown relative to other currencies. In contrast, during 1995 and 1996, Slovakia's dollar unit labor costs rose faster than those in the Czech Republic.

Government Budget

Unlike most other economies in the region, between 1990 and 1998 the Czech and Slovak governments for the most part pursued restrictive budgetary policies. As can be seen from Table 9.4, Czechoslovakia ran a balanced budget in 1990 and

Table 9.3   Annual Percentage Change in Dollar Unit Labor Cost

	1990	1991	1992	1993	1994	1995	1996 Q1–Q3
Czech Republic	−17.3	−14.8	32.8	25.8	13.2	6.9	3.9
Slovak Republic	—	—	13.0	12.4	5.9	19.3	11.0
Bulgaria	−37.8	−35.1	85.4	21.5	−31.4	17.3	−15.2
Romania	3.5	−18.9	−22.6	13.1	−4.7	5.0	−6.3
Russia	—	—	—	134.5	89.3	12.0	49.3
Hungary	14.4	29.4	7.6	−9.6	−1.0	−8.7	−7.8
Poland	−8.9	66.5	−8.7	−8.8	−7.3	15.1	−7.8

Source: Taken from a table by the European Bank for Reconstruction and Development, *Transition Report Update, April 1997* (London: EBRD, 1997), p. 14.

Table 9.4   General Government Balances[a] as a Percentage of GDP in Selected Transition Economies

	1990	1991	1992	1993	1994	1995	1996	1997	1998
Czech Republic	na	−1.9	−3.1	0.5	−1.2	−1.8	−1.2	−1.0	−1.6
Slovak Republic	na	−2.0	−11.9	−7.0	−1.3	0.2	−1.9	−3.8	−4.0
Slovenia	−0.3	2.6	0.2	0.3	−0.2	0.0	0.3	−1.1	−1.0
Poland	3.1	−6.7	−6.7	−3.1	−3.1	−2.8	−3.3	−2.8	−2.5
Hungary	0.4	−2.9	−6.8	−5.5	−8.4	−6.7	−3.1	−4.0	−3.7
Bulgaria	na	na	−5.2	−10.9	−5.8	−5.6	−10.4	−3.1	0.0
Romania	1.0	3.3	−4.6	−0.4	−1.9	−2.6	−4.0	−3.6	−3.3
Ukraine	na	na	−25.4	−16.2	−9.1	−7.1	−3.2	−6.7	−2.5
Russia	na	na	−4.1	−7.4	−9.0	−5.7	−8.3	−7.1	−4.8

[a]General government includes the state, municipalities, and extrabudgetary funds. Balances reported on a cash basis except for Poland.

Data Sources:

1990:   Data is taken from tables from the European Bank for Reconstruction and Development (EBRD), *Transition Report 1997* (London: EBRD, 1997), p. 120, except the Czech and Slovak republic data, which is from the EBRD, *Transition Report 1996* (London: EBRD, 1996), pp. 191 and 204.

1991–1996:   Data is taken from tables from the European Bank for Reconstruction and Development, *Transition Report 1998* (London: EBRD, 1998), pp. 211–230, except Slovak Republic data for 1991–1992, which is from the EBRD, *Transition Report 1996* (London: EBRD, 1996), p. 204.

1997:   Data is taken from DataStream (Economist Intelligence Unit), except Slovak Republic data, which is from European Bank for Reconstruction and Development, *Transition Report 1998* (London, EBRD, 1998)

1998:   Estimates from DataStream (Economist Intelligence Unit), except the estimate for the Slovak Republic, which is from European Bank for Reconstruction and Development, *Transition Report 1998* (London, EBRD, 1998).

a mild 2 percent deficit (as a percentage of GDP) in 1991. In 1992, the year immediately preceding the dissolution of the country, Slovakia ran a large budget deficit of 12 percent, while the Czech deficit was 3 percent. The Czech Republic had a budget surplus of 0.5 percent in 1993 and deficits of 1.2 percent and 1.8 percent in 1994 and 1995, while Slovakia still ran a significant deficit of 7 percent, as it was incurring independence-related adjustment costs in 1993. However, Slovakia reverted to a trivial 1 percent deficit in 1994 and recorded a slight surplus in 1995. During this period, Poland, Hungary, and many other economies in the region struggled with major budget deficits without incurring the costs of building new government institutions as was the case in Slovakia (Table 9.4). After 1995, the Czech and Slovak republics started running budget deficits, and their behavior in this area began to resemble that of several other Central and East European countries.

Income Distribution

The Czech and Slovak republics entered the transition with a pair of the most equal distributions of income in the world. Moreover, unlike other countries in the region, they maintained remarkably equal distributions of income during the transition. One of the most widely used measures of income inequality is the Gini coefficient, which equals zero when income is distributed equally among all members of the population and takes on the value of unity when one individual appropriates all income. As Thesia Garner and Katherine Terrell (1997) show, in the Czech Republic the per capita Gini coefficient increased marginally, from .183 in 1989 to .187 in 1993. During the same period, the corresponding Slovak coefficient rose slightly, from .176 to .185. Comparable figures for other countries in the region are reported by Branko Milanovic (1997). He shows that Hungary's per capita Gini coefficient rose from .207 in 1987 to .229 in 1993, Slovenia's coefficient increased from .198 in 1987 to .223 in 1995, Poland's coefficient rose from .250 in 1987 to .320 in 1995, and Russia's coefficient jumped dramatically from .219 in 1989 to .455 in 1994. Hence, compared to other countries in the former Soviet bloc, the Czech and Slovak republics started with and maintained very equal distributions of income. As Garner and Terrell (1997) show, the two countries achieved this outcome by pursuing aggressive social transfer policies.

Investment

While investment figures may be particularly unreliable in the transition economies, the official figures reported in Table 9.5 indicate that, unlike other countries, the Czech and Slovak republics have been able to maintain relatively high rates of investment. In the last few years, both countries have invested over 30 percent of GDP, which greatly exceeds the 18–20-percent rate in Hungary and the 7–10-percent rate in Poland. The Czech and Slovak investment rate falls within the bottom part of the 30–40 percent range observed during this period in the rapidly growing Southeast Asian economies.

Table 9.5 Investment and GDP Growth in Central Europe

Date	Czech Republic I/GDP	Hungary I/GDP	Poland I/GDP	Slovak Republic I/GDP
1991	0.22	0.21	0.15	0.25
1992	0.25	0.19	0.12	0.30
1993	0.28	0.18	0.09	0.28
1994	0.31	0.20	0.09	0.28
1995	0.34	0.18	0.10	0.31
1996	0.36	0.20	0.12	0.42
1997	0.35	na	0.07	0.43

Source: Excerpted from Lubomír Lízal and Jan Svejnar, "Enterprise Investment during the Transition: Evidence from Czech Panel Data," *Davidson Institute Working Paper 60a,* December 1997, Table 1. Data from CESTAT (Statistical Bulletin of Czech, Hungarian, Polish, Slovak, and Slovenian Statistical Offices). 1996 and 1997 data updated from CESTAT (Statistical Bulletin of Czech, Hungarian, Polish, Slovak, and Slovenian Statistical Offices) 1998 first quarter.

Note: Comparable methodology is used across countries. Investment includes tangible and intangible fixed assets (except for the Czech republic, where it includes only tangible fixed assets). With the exception of Poland, all investment data are for the entire economy, including estimates for entities not directly monitored by the statistical offices. In Poland, investment reflects entities with more than twenty (fifty in industry) employees.

Foreign Trade

As mentioned earlier, the slower rise in real wages and the 1993 devaluation of the currency enabled Slovakia to maintain a more competitive foreign trade position than that of the Czech Republic in the mid-1990s. As a result, Slovakia managed to maintain relatively balanced trade (until 1996), while the Czech Republic incurred increasingly severe trade deficits from 1995 to 1997. However, the tendencies were the same in both economies, especially when one considers a broader measure, such as the current account, which includes services—especially tourism. In 1997, both the Czech Republic and Slovakia ran high current account deficits, resulting in an attack on the Czech currency and its devaluation in May 1997. Slovakia may have to follow suit in the near future.

In their approach to exchange-rate policy and foreign trade, the two republics again displayed remarkable similarities in comparison to other countries in the region. In 1990, Czechoslovakia embarked on a policy of fixed exchange rates, with limited but gradually broadening convertibility of the Czechoslovak crown. Apart from the Slovak devaluation in 1993, both countries adhered to the fixed exchange-rate policy until 1997, when the Czech Republic was forced by speculators to abandon this policy and allow its currency to float. Hence, in contrast to Slovenia, which used a floating exchange rate from the start, and Poland and Hungary, which switched from fixed to flexible exchange-rate policies in the early 1990s, the Czech and Slovak republics jointly maintained the longest record of fixed exchange rates in the region.

GDP

Since the various indicators examined above have taken on similar values in the Czech and Slovak republics, one would naturally expect the dynamics of GDP also to be similar in the two countries. As can be seen from Table 9.1, the Czech and Slovak economies indeed recorded a similar dynamic in the decline and growth of GDP between 1990 and 1997, with Slovak GDP declining more precipitously in the early 1990s and rising more rapidly in the mid-1990s. In particular, Slovakia's slower GDP growth (1 percent versus 4.5 percent) in 1989 turned into a slightly steeper (2.5 percent versus 1.2 percent) decline in 1990. Both countries experienced a significant fall in GDP in 1991, with the Czech republic registering 11.5 percent and Slovakia 14.6 percent. The two economies declined by 3.3 percent and 6.5 percent, respectively, in 1992. In 1993, the year of dissolution of the country, the Czech Republic arrested its GDP decline (+.6 percent), while Slovak GDP still fell almost 4 percent. However, from 1994 to 1998 the Slovak Republic recorded a faster rate of growth of GDP than the Czech lands. In 1994 GDP rose by 5 percent in Slovakia but 3 percent in the Czech lands. In 1995 and 1996 Slovakia grew at 7 percent, while the Czech economy recorded a 6 percent growth rate in 1995 and a 4 percent increase in 1996. Finally, preliminary figures for 1997 suggest that the Czech Republic grew at a mere 1 percent, while Slovakia registered a 6.5 percent growth rate.[8]

The reasons for the somewhat different rates of decline and rise of GDP in Slovakia and the Czech Republic in the early versus mid-1990s are not yet fully understood, but several factors may play a part. The steeper decline in Slovak GDP in the early 1990s has often been attributed to Slovakia's weaker economic structure and slower economic transformation. As I discuss later, Slovakia had a significant share of its economy tied to export-oriented military production, which started declining in the late 1980s (Ivanek 1994; and Milivojevic 1995). Moreover, in the early 1990s, the growth of small firms was stronger in the Czech lands than in Slovakia. This coincided with a greater inflow of foreign direct investment and faster privatization in the Czech lands—by 1993, over 53 percent of workers were in private firms in the Czech Republic, as compared to only 32 percent in Slovakia.

The faster growth of the Slovak economy since 1994 is in part attributable to a naturally stronger rebound from a deeper depression but is possibly also attributable to other factors, most of which have not yet been carefully analyzed. First, as mentioned earlier, the Czech Republic experienced a faster rise in the unit labor cost in the early to mid-1990s (Table 9.3), mostly as a result of a faster growth of wages and real appreciation of the exchange rate. This resulted in a greater loss of international competitiveness in the mid-1990s. Second, the Slovak government pursued a more active industrial policy, including a greater push for trade with Russia and the other Soviet successor states. Finally, there is the aforementioned issue of whether the structure of Slovak exports does have a greater base in raw materials and semifinished goods, which could make these products more competitive than the more high-tech but also relatively more obsolete Czech products on world markets. Overall, it remains to be seen whether Slovakia will maintain its faster rate of growth in the late 1990s. Its current account deficit has been rising rapidly, and the economy is showing some of the same strain as the Czech economy did in late 1996 and in 1997.

As is the case with other performance indicators, the striking aspect of the Czech–Slovak comparison is the fact that the GDP dynamics in the other transition economies, except perhaps for pre-1996 Romania, have been quite different. Poland was the first country to launch the transition, experiencing an early GDP downturn and the fastest return to rapid growth. In contrast, Hungary went through a similar decline but did not succeed in achieving a fast rate of economic growth in the mid-1990s. Finally, Russia and other Soviet successor states only started recovering in the late 1990s.

Unemployment

Unemployment is one indicator on which the two republics differed from the start of the transition. In particular, in terms of unemployment statistics, the Slovak Republic resembled all the other transition economies in the region, while the Czech Republic was an outlier. Outside of Yugoslavia, open unemployment was basically nonexistent in the communist economies. As can be seen from Table

9.6, unemployment emerged as a new phenomenon in the late 1980s or early 1990s, and by 1993 the unemployment rate reached double digits in all countries except the Czech Republic, Ukraine, Russia, and Slovenia. In the Czech Republic, the unemployment rate in fact declined from over 4 percent at the end of 1991 and early 1992 to under 3 percent in 1995, rising gradually to 5 percent by the end of 1997. Compared to the 6–7 percent average unemployment rate observed in the OECD countries, the Czech Republic was thus well below the other transition economies and performed well above the OECD average.

Numerous analyses have tackled the question of the unemployment differential between the Czech lands and the rest of Eastern Europe (see, e.g., OECD 1993; Ham, Svejnar, and Terrell 1995, 1996; Munich, Svejnar, and Terrell 1995; and Svejnar, Terrell, and Munich 1995). The basic mechanics underlying the unemployment difference is the fact that at the start of the transition the inflow rate into unemployment was slightly lower and the outflow rate of individuals from unemployment was much higher in the Czech Republic than in the other countries in the region. What accounts for these differences in inflow and especially outflow? The studies point to a mixture of factors.

One important factor appears to be differences in demand conditions. Daniel Munich, Jan Svejnar, and Katherine Terrell (1995) for instance document that nationally, as well as at the level of individual districts, the Czech Republic tended to have many more advertised vacancies (job openings) than Slovakia, both in absolute numbers and relative to the number of employed and unemployed individ-

Table 9.6 Unemployment in Selected Transitional Economies

	1990	*1991*	*1992*	*1993*	*1994*	*1995*	*1996*	*1997*	*1998*
Czech Republic	0.8	4.1	2.6	3.5	3.2	2.9	3.5	4.6	6.4
Slovak Republic	1.5	11.8	10.3	12.2	13.7	13.1	11.1	11.6	14.0
Slovenia	4.7	7.3	8.3	9.1	9.0	7.4	7.3	7.1	na
Poland	6.3	11.8	13.6	16.4	16.0	14.9	13.2	11.2	10.1
Hungary	1.9	7.4	12.3	12.1	10.4	10.4	10.5	8.9	8.2
Bulgaria	1.5	11.1	15.3	16.4	12.8	11.1	12.5	13.7	12.0
Romania	na	3.0	8.2	10.4	10.9	9.5	6.6	7.4	na
Ukraine	0.0	0.0	0.3	0.4	0.4	0.5	1.1	2.8	na
Russia	0.0	0.0	4.8	5.3	7.1	8.3	9.2	10.8	11.8

Data Sources:

1990–1996: Data is taken from tables by the European Bank for Reconstruction and Development (EBRD), *Transition Report 1996* (p. 204), *Transition Report, 1997* (pp. 214–239), *Transition Report 1998* (pp. 211–230).

1997: Czech Republic, Poland, and Hungary are from DataStream (OECD Economic Outlook). Slovak Republic, Romania, and Russia are from DataStream (International Financial Statistics). Slovenia is from EBRD, *Transition Report 1998* (London: EBRD, 1998), p. 234. Bulgaria and Ukraine are from DataStream (WIIW).

1998: Czech Republic, Poland, and Hungary: Estimates from OECD Economic Outlook. Slovak Republic, Bulgaria, and Russia: Estimates from Economist Intelligence Unit, Country Reports.

Notes: Czech and Slovak data 1990–1992 are based on registry data; 1993 is based on labor force surveys consistent with ILO methodology. Slovenia data based on estimation from registry data based on labor force surveys consistent with ILO methodology. Hungary and Romania data are based on registry data. Russia data are not end of year, but are annual averages.

uals. Hence, to the extent that vacancies signal demand for workers, the Czech Republic had more favorable demand conditions. The more rapid creation of small private firms that tend to engage in labor-intensive production as well as the more significant inflow of foreign direct investment are plausible product market causes of this labor market phenomenon.

A specific demand factor that was often mentioned in the popular press was the greater exposure of Slovakia to declining military production.[9] Interestingly, much of the differential decline occurred before rather than during the transition, but the artificially maintained full employment under central planning brought about greater labor redundancy in this sector in Slovakia than in the Czech lands and delayed the labor market adjustment. Indeed, the peak in Czechoslovak military production occurred in 1987, when military production is estimated to have accounted for 3 percent of total industrial production and generated seventy-three thousand direct and fifty to seventy thousand indirect jobs. At this time the value of Slovakia's military production was 50 percent above that of the Czech Republic.[10] In 1988 military production started to decline in both republics, but the decline was much faster in Slovakia. In the 1988–90 period the value of military production in constant prices dropped by 48 percent in Slovakia and 35 percent in the Czech Republic, resulting in identical values of production in both republics in 1990. The production continued to decline at a similar rate in 1991 and 1992, with some estimates suggesting that the rate of decline was slightly faster in Slovakia than the Czech lands (Ivanek 1994). The decline in 1991–92 was dramatic, with the constant price value of military production dropping by an estimated two-thirds between 1990 and 1992. Most of this drop occurred in 1991, when unemployment rose dramatically in Slovakia.[11] Despite the fact that military and total industrial production decline in 1990–92 was similar in the two countries, Slovak military producers entered the transition with a much more pent-up problem of redundant labor, which became apparent and coincided with the rise of unemployment in 1990–92.

Ham, Svejnar, and Terrell (1995) also note that working in a neighboring Western country has been easier for the Czechs than for the Slovaks. The Czech Republic has a longer border with Austria than Slovakia does and, unlike Slovakia, it has a border with Germany. Both countries pursued relatively lenient policies toward guest workers, and the Czechs could presumably take better advantage of these opportunities.[12] Ham, Svejnar, and Terrell (1996) also analyze the reasons for different outflow rates of the unemployed from unemployment and note that the two countries differ in the reactions of individuals and institutions to labor market and institutional phenomena.

Finally, one should mention the possibility that the official statistics underreport the extent of economic activity in the service and small-manufacturing sectors of the transition economies (see Svejnar, Terrell, and Munich 1995). After the revolution, these sectors developed faster in the Czech Republic than in Slovakia. To the extent that their underreporting is an important phenomenon, it may cause a systematic bias in that the Czech growth indicators would be undervalued relative to those in Slovakia. This hypothesis is consistent with the observed difference in the unemployment rate between the two republics.

CONCLUSION

When the Austro–Hungarian Empire disintegrated in 1918, Slovakia was economically much less developed than the Czech lands. While Slovakia built up considerable infrastructure and some industrial might in the interwar and World War II period, the Slovak economy still lagged markedly behind that of the Czech lands immediately after World War II. The Soviet-led effort of the Czechoslovak communist government to develop Slovakia was launched in the 1950s and it resulted in a forty-year investment boom that virtually closed the output and income gap between the two republics. Indeed, Slovakia is a rare example of successful economic development from a low- to middle-income country under central planning.

In comparison to other economies in Central and East Europe, the Czech and Slovak republics recorded similar economic performance in the predissolution 1989–92 as well as in the postpartition 1993–98, period in virtually all areas except for unemployment. At the time of the debates that led to the breakup of Czechoslovakia, this remarkable overall statistical similarity in performance was largely unrecognized. The emphasis was usually placed on the actual and likely future differences in the performance of the two economies. Similarities in performance were usually regarded as a temporary result of the unifying policies of the federal government. Focusing on the high unemployment rate and somewhat steeper economic decline in Slovakia relative to the Czech Republic, Czech and Slovak leaders both expected the Slovak economy to be the weaker performer in the future. The dissolution of Czechoslovakia was often viewed as a solution to this very problem, permitting the Slovak leaders to proceed with more gradual and socially oriented policies, while allowing the Czech government to complete a rapid economic transformation.

The faster growth of the Slovak economy and the overall similarity in the economic performance of the two countries in the five years since the separation has surprised most Czech and Slovak policymakers. The similarity points to the importance of initial conditions (similar levels of economic development achieved by 1989) and the similarity of government policies pursued in the two countries during the 1989–92 as well as the 1993–98 periods. The fact that the 1993–98 outcome came as a surprise indicates how little the political decision makers knew about the similarities in the relative structure, potential, and responsiveness of the two economies. In the context of this retrospective volume, the interesting question of course is whether full knowledge of the economic similarities between the two countries and the growth potential of Slovakia would have prevented the breakup. As a political-economic analyst who observed the events at the time, I sense that it would not have forestalled the split. The real struggle was elsewhere.

NOTES

1. The paper was originally prepared for the Conference on the Dissolution of Czechoslovakia, held at CERGE-EI, Prague, Czech Republic, on 28–30 June 1996. I would like to thank Josef Kotrba and other participants of the conference, as well as the editors of this volume, for many useful suggestions on the earlier draft. In preparing the paper, I benefited from NSF Grant No. SBR95-12001. I am solely responsible for any remaining errors.

2. To understand this, note that with the Slovak population being 21 percent of the total Czechoslovak population, the Slovak population amounted to 17.4 percent (= .21/1.21) of the Czech population. Now, with 17 percent of the Slovak and 40 percent of the Czech population being in industry (defined as manufacturing, construction, and crafts), the Slovak population in industry represented about 7 percent of the total Czechoslovak population in industry (.174*.17/.4 = .075 and .075/1.075 = .07). Slovakia's 7 percent labor share is of course very similar to its (at most) 8.5 percent share in total industrial production. With labor productivity in industry defined as industrial output per industrial worker, labor productivity appears to have been similar in the two parts of the country.

3. Within the Soviet-type statistical measures, ICOR was defined as investment per unit of increase of net material product. The denominator was thus defined more restrictively than in the Western statistical measures of total output.

4. See Dĕdek et al. (1996, p. 26). The figures for the 1980s refer to 1981–88.

5. As in the Soviet Union, neither GDP nor Western-style national income data were collected by the Czechoslovak communist authorities. As a result, they had to be calculated de novo from GMP and other data after the revolution. The calculation of these measures for the Czech and Slovak republics was further complicated by the fact that many statistics were traditionally assembled at the Czechoslovak level rather than separately for the two republics. Jaroslav Jílek (1995) provides a detailed discussion of the problems encountered by the statistical authorities after the Velvet Revolution.

6. The statistical offices have issued so many corrections of statistical figures during this period as to make minor differences across the years for all practical purposes insignificant.

7. The real appreciation of the Czech and Slovak currencies was brought about by the governments' continued adherence to a fixed exchange rate while incurring higher domestic inflation than that in the Western world.

8. The similarity between the Czech and Slovak GDP figures is also reflected in the data on industrial and agricultural production.

9. In the late 1980s, the Visegrad countries (Czechoslovakia, Hungary, and Poland) were collectively the fifth largest arms exporter in the world. In 1989, their exports equaled $600 million (Milivojevic 1995).

10. Since the Slovak labor force is almost exactly one-half the size of the Czech labor force, the extent of military production relative to the size of the economy was clearly much larger in Slovakia than in the Czech Republic.

11. An offsetting factor was the fact that the Czechoslovak federal government contributed significantly to the conversion efforts of the military producers—about $50 million in 1991 and $35 million in 1992. The orientation of these subsidies tended to mitigate the relative unemployment problem in the two republics, as three-fourths of the subsidy in each year went to producers in Slovakia.

12. In the southern German state of Bavaria, the Czechs were reportedly often allowed to work even without a work permit.

REFERENCES

Boeri, Tito. "Labor Market Flows and the Persistence of Unemployment in Central and Eastern Europe," in OECD (ed.), *Unemployment in Transition Countries: Transient or Persistent*, Paris, OECD, 1993.

Dědek, Oldřich et al. *The Break-up of Czechoslovakia: An In-depth Economic Analysis*. Brookfield,VT: Avebury-Ashgate Publishing Co., 1996.

Dyba, Karel, and Jan Svejnar. "Stabilization and Transition in Czechoslovakia," in O. Blanchard, K. Froot, and J. Sachs (eds.), *The Transition in Eastern Europe*, Chicago, University of Chicago Press, 1993.

Economic Institute of the Slovak Academy of Sciences. "Strategy of the Economic Development of Slovakia." Publication No. 81, 1990.

Garner, Thesia, and Katherine Terrell. "Changes in Distribution and Welfare in Transition Economies: Market vs. Policy in the Czech Republic and Slovakia." The William Davidson Institute Working Paper No. 77, June 1997.

Ham, John, Jan Svejnar, and Katherine Terrell. "Czech Republic and Slovakia" in S. Commander and F. Coricelli (eds.), *Unemployment Restructuring and the Labor Market in Eastern Europe and Russia, Economic Development Institute*, The World Bank, 1995, pp. 91–146.

Ham, John, Jan Svejnar, and Katherine Terrell. "Unemployment, the Social Safety Net and Efficiency in Transition: Evidence for Micro Data on Czech and Slovak Men." The William Davidson Institute Working Paper no. 34, May 1996.

Ivánek, Ladislav. "Ekonomické problémy konverze zbrojní výroby." *Mezinárodni vztahy*, no. 1 (1994), pp. 42–49.

Jílek, Jaroslav. "The Quality and Availability of Official Statistical Data," in J. Svejnar (ed.), *The Czech Republic and Economic Transition in Eastern Europe*, New York: Academic Press, 1995, pp. 103–118.

Kotrba, Josef, and Karel Kříž. "The Common State in Economic Perspective." *East European Reporter*, September-October 1992, pp. 3–5.

Milanovic, Branko. "Explaining the Growth in Inequality during the Transition." World Bank, Mimeo, 1997.

Milivojevic, Marko. "Uncertain Future: Armaments Production and Exports in Central and Eastern Europe." *Army and Defense Quarterly Journal*, 125, no.1 (1995), pp. 77–79.

Munich, Daniel, Jan Svejnar, and Katherine Terrell. "Regional Skill Mismatch in the Czech and Slovak Republics," in OECD (ed.), *The Regional Dimension of Unemployment in Transition Countries*, OECD: Paris, 1995.

Průcha, Václav. "Economic Development and Relations, 1918–89," in J. Musil (ed.), *The End of Czechoslovakia*, Prague: Central European University Press, 1995, pp. 41–76.

Sujan, Ivan. "Hospodárske a socialne dosledky Česko–Slovenskeho Rozchodu," in *Rozluceni s Československom*. Patriae Foundation, 1993, pp. 163–172.

Svejnar, Jan, Katherine Terrell, and Daniel Munich. "Explaining Unemployment Dynamics in the Czech and Slovak Republics," in *The Czech Republic and Economic Transition in Eastern Europe*, ed. J. Svejnar. New York: Academic Press, 1995, pp. 285–316.

10

The End of Czechoslovakia: International Forces and Factors

Michael Kraus

Studies of the dissolution of Czechoslovakia typically emphasize internal forces and factors, such as economic disparities, constitutional deadlock, differentiated levels of modernization, different political cultures, the role of political elites, or the mass media. To be sure, the impact of such factors—as other contributions to this volume amply demonstrate—must be taken into account and may well have been decisive. Yet politics in Central or Eastern Europe has never taken place in an international vacuum. Changes of regimes in this region in general, and in Czechoslovakia in particular, were shaped by the outside powers or variations in the international environment. This was the case at Czechoslovakia's birth at the century's beginning, and, as this chapter contends, it was also the case at the point of the country's expiration on 1 January 1993. Moreover, the historical fact that Czechoslovakia, Yugoslavia, and the Soviet Union, which all emerged simultaneously as offspring of the First World War, disappeared from the map at the same time forces us to search for the wider significance of the disintegrative forces at work, for it seems unlikely that the causes of such disintegrations are unique to each case.

This chapter seeks to assess the role of external forces in Czechoslovak politics during 1989–1992 in the broadest sense of the word "external." For analytical purposes, it is useful to separate their impact in terms of three levels of influence: one, changes in the interstate system that have provided the historical setting for crises in Czech–Slovak relations; two, external factors that shaped the nature of Czechoslovakia's political system, in which the post-1989 developments were initiated; and three, those specific outside influences that informed the perceptions and actions of the key Czech and Slovak political actors after 1989.[1] Since the actions and inactions of political elites were decisive in shaping the fate of Czechoslovakia, the lion's share of this chapter is devoted to the latter

set of influences. While an exhaustive analysis of these levels of influence is beyond the scope of this essay, it is possible to sketch at least some basic patterns
and reflect on their significance.

SPHERES OF EXTERNAL AND INTERNAL INFLUENCE

Transformations of the international (interstate) system have historically occurred
in the wake of major wars. The First World War is a case in point, for it not only
fundamentally recast the prewar balance of power, supplying the preconditions for
the Russian Revolution, but it also provided the impetus for the quest for a new
world order based on the principles of self-determination. The latter, informed by
the Wilsonian vision of self-determination, contributed mightily to the rise of new
states in East–Central Europe, including Czechoslovakia and Yugoslavia.

States come into being, at least in part, in response to external dangers that
unify peoples across class and ethnic boundaries. This sense of external vulnera-
bilities certainly played a role in the shared history of the Czech and Slovak peoples. At times, as in the very founding of the state, it acted as a tie that cemented
the relationship. Tomáš Garrigue Masaryk's founding vision was informed by the
notion that the Czech and Slovak peoples, closely related in terms of their Slavic
ethnicity, were bound together by the surrounding sea of German peoples, who
also vastly outnumbered them. Masaryk took his point of departure from the relative vulnerability of each partner in this union to their more powerful neighbors,
Germany and Hungary, who had historically dominated the less numerous
Czechs and Slovaks, respectively. Or as Masaryk stated it in 1916, "Together [a
Czechoslovak alliance] would raise the Slav majority of the population to almost
nine million, and be much stronger vis-à-vis the minority."[2] In short, the very notion of a Czechoslovak nation, which would later serve as a legitimizing doctrine,
was rooted in the less than congenial security conditions of the new state.

Concerns about the collective political power of the German minority also reinforced Czech–Slovak cohesion in the First Republic. As far as government stability was concerned, Carol Skalnik Leff has noted that "Czech and Slovak politicians were particularly anxious not to depend on German parties for a majority."[3]
In another respect, though Prague's failure to accord autonomy to Slovakia in the
interwar period is frequently singled out (especially on the Slovak side) as a case
in point of promises unfulfilled, this fact was not unrelated to the geopolitical circumstances of the First Republic. To grant autonomy to one people inside the
multiethnic state would have meant at the same time to invite demands for the
same prerogatives from other minorities, especially the Germans and Hungarians.

Moreover, their substantial ethnic diasporas inside the new Czechoslovakia (as
well as in the neighboring lands) made Germany and Hungary de facto actors inside Czecho–Slovak politics as well—all the more so, as the young Czechoslovak republic, much like Yugoslavia, though born out of the embrace of the prin-

ciple of national self-determination, did not live up to its logic. But the very creation of these states was to remain in the interwar period a thorn in the side of the defeated powers, Germany and Hungary. Conversely, both new actors on the international scene eagerly sought external allies to fortify their positions against increasingly revisionist neighbors, and at the same time, they themselves were sought after by France and Great Britain for similar reasons. For all these reasons, in the minds of Prague's decision makers, the political aspirations of Czech Germans and Slovak Hungarians could not be separated from those of ethnic conationals across the border. Indeed, after Hitler's rise to power, such a separation was made increasingly impossible—by both the words and the actions of the Czech Germans themselves. So geopolitical factors and, as the 1930s drew to a close, growing security concerns linked in many ways the plight of the Czechs and the Slovaks. At the same time, inasmuch as they fortified Czech unwillingness to entertain Slovak demands for autonomy, Prague's centralizing policies swelled the ranks of the more radical and nationalist Slovak voices, which toward the late 1930s found a common cause with German radicalism.[4]

Yet it must also be noted that external threats can be a source of internal cohesion only up to a limited point, beyond which they are perceived as a mortal danger to the survival of a nation's way of life and become a source of political divisions rather than unity. Further, where several nations coexist within a single state, their respective leaders will tend to define political situations in different ways and adopt differentiated responses to perceived threats on that basis. Such was the case with the emergent nationalist German, Hungarian, and Slovak leaders in Czechoslovakia in the late 1930s.

From the perspective of the outside powers, the Czech–Slovak differences and divisions served as valuable assets for divide and conquer strategies that only too often proved effective. The story is much too familiar to need full recounting, so here we only need to note in passing that Hitlerite Germany used national cleavages in the late 1930s to the same ends—though with more dire consequences for the Czechoslovak state—as did Stalin in the 1940s and the 1950s and Brezhnev in the 1970s and the 1980s.

Where Hitler prodded the hapless Slovak leadership in 1939, albeit with its own grievances against Prague, to choose "independence or else," the Soviet strategy of divide and rule relied successively and successfully on Edvard Beneš's unwitting assistance and that of the Czech democratic parties, first in the mid-1940s in circumscribing the scope of Slovak autonomy, and later in the decade in undercutting the Slovak anticommunist forces. Moreover, the postwar expulsion of the German minority (as well as the Soviet annexation of Ruthenia) not only paved the way for the advent of communist power but also—as Stalin was quicker to grasp than Beneš—bound Czechoslovakia more tightly into the Soviet orbit. But the expulsion also removed one interwar element of cohesion between the Czechs and Slovaks, shifting the internal balance of power in the bipartite direction. The trials of "bourgeois nationalists" in the 1950s and the tribulations of the "normalization" era in the 1970s and the 1980s also played on and accentuated the conflicts between Czechs and Slovaks by implicating the representatives of one ethnic group in the eyes of the other.[5] Consistently, the Czech–Slovak national conflict served as a potent resource in the hands of cunning dictators, contributing mightily to Czechoslovakia's periodic submissions to hostile powers. This is not to say that internal circumstances played no role here; on the contrary, such external actors typically linked up with willing collaborators on the domestic front. But were it not for the outside influence, the shape of the past—instead of serving as a source of mutual recriminations after 1989—would have acquired a different and perhaps less divisive character.

Sweeping changes in the structure of the international system after the First World War were matched by similarly dramatic changes after the Second World War. The bipolar Cold War system was characterized by Soviet and American military, economic, and ideological domination, thereby reducing the role of Europe as an independent actor. While the quest for self-determination in Asia and Africa led to the undoing of British and French colonial influence, the last of the modern empires rose in East–Central Europe. The subordination of bloc countries, including Czechoslovakia, to Moscow was effected via ideological, political, and military instruments of bloc cohesion. As Alexander Dubček has pointed out, at the level of bloc elites even in the late 1960s, the "main criterion of one's relationship to the Soviet Union" was "only blind and unconditional obedience."[6] Dubček's admission indicates, among other things, the difficulty involved in separating domestic politics from external influences in the communist era.

Though its demise in the late 1980s did not take the form of a major war, the military, economic, and ideological exhaustion of one of the antagonists, the Soviet Union, had similar consequences for the international system as wars had had in the past. Since East–Central Europe was an integral part of the Soviet system of power, the weakening of communist power at the center not only caused the collapse of communist regimes at the periphery but also undermined the ties that bound East–Central Europe to Moscow. As a result, the contemporary international system has been in the midst of major restructuring.

The sense of euphoria surrounding the altogether unexpected collapse of communism and the end of the Cold War temporarily eliminated any sense of external threats to Czechoslovakia. In 1990, surrounded by a democratic and newly unified Germany, a democratizing, and soon to be disintegrating, Soviet Union, and a newly free Poland and Hungary, Prague's decision makers initially dreamed of a new Europe, free of military blocs, including the Warsaw Pact and NATO. The purported "end of ideology," the declining utility of military power, the emergence of new supranational organizations in Europe—these assumptions and trends seemed to lend substance to Havel's and his foreign minister Jiří Dienstbier's vision. Few could foresee in 1989–1990 that the end of superpower domination would accelerate the seemingly contradictory impulses toward (West) European integration and (East) European disintegration.

In the broadest sense, then, the impact of the changes in the international system was twofold: first, it provided the necessary preconditions for any changes in the Czechoslovak political regime, the sine qua non for the opening of the political system to democratic politics; and second, by eliminating external domination and removing threats to the integrity of the Czechoslovak state, the end of the Cold War also served to diminish a shared sense of Czech–Slovak vulnerability, thereby severing perhaps one of the last common bonds.

LEGACIES OF "FEDERALIZED TOTALITARIANISM"

As we know today, the communist era bestowed an immensely difficult set of challenges upon the democratic elites emerging from free and contested elections after 1989. Broadly speaking, postcommunist transformations have entailed political, economic, and security dimensions. In the case of the three socialist federations (and Russia today), the additional challenge included the search for a new basis upon which to organize their multiethnic societies. Setting out to create institutions of a market economy and political democracy, the new regimes had to contend with legacies of the past, such as the violations of human rights under the predecessor regimes, property restitutions, or the institutions of coercion, including the secret police. Yet there is another set of legacies that stemmed much more directly from the character of the communist political system. This set of legacies is of greater interest to us insofar as it structured many of the points of Czech–Slovak friction and collision after 1989. These generally center on the dependent character of the communist regime, but include the precommunist phase as well.

Czech and Slovak historians, especially since 1989, have made much of the 1945–48 agreements concerning Czecho–Slovak relations, by means of which "Prague" increasingly circumscribed the scope of Slovak autonomy.[7] The point of departure for such assessments was the formulations of the so-called Košice program of the government, which stipulated the principle of a Czech–Slovak partnership on an "equal with an equal" basis, thereby bringing "all old quarrels to an end."[8] The current mainstream view of these negotiations is that because such agreements were only understandings between Czech and Slovak representatives and were not rooted in constitutional laws, "the Czech side took advantage of, and abused, these agreements."[9]

Yet the unspoken supposition of such assessments is that they took place in a democratic setting, in which all parties bargained independently and shared the same language of politics. But the Košice program was actually written in Moscow and, as recent evidence reveals, under the full supervision of Soviet advisors, who acted as mentors of the Gottwald leadership, providing detailed guidance on the program provisions before submitting them to President Beneš and his allies.[10] Following Soviet mischief during the Slovak National Uprising and the annexation of Ruthenia (Carpathian Ukraine), the London exiles in a defeatist mood accepted the Soviet (Košice) program, which included a thinly veiled blueprint for sovietization of the Czechoslovak armed forces, and which was deliberately later unveiled publicly only in Košice, a city in Slovak territory. But its proper name should be the Moscow program, not only because that is its proper pedigree but also because it had to fully conform to Soviet preferences.

Given that one of the architects of Soviet federalism was Stalin, and considering that his notions of "equality among nations" were fully compatible with deportations of entire ethnic groups, the supposition that the Soviet understanding of federalism can be taken at face value is simply unwarranted. And the same applies by extension to the Czech and Slovak communist leaders of Stalin's generation. As his role in the 1947 coup in Slovakia demonstrated, those would-be-ardent supporters of federation among Czech and Slovak communists, such as Gustav Husák, were not prepared to tolerate the results of contested elections, which in 1946 had brought unwelcome news of communist defeat in Slovakia. In short, for traditional Soviet, Czech, or Slovak communist elites, questions of constitutional arrangements were always secondary matters, duly subordinated to what Lenin called, in Klement Gottwald's paraphrase, "the main question of every revolution—the question of power."

Such constitutional architecture accounts for the clearly anomalous "asymmetric model," which endured for more than two decades, whereby Slovak institutions of party and government existed side by side after 1945 with no equivalent Czech institutions (or theoretical justification for the arrangement). "Closely tailored to Soviet specifications," notes Leff, it served—like so many Soviet-inspired formulas—to make no one happy. In institutional terms, it supplied a conflict-intensifying factor, for in the eyes of Slovak critics, the asymmetry "inevitably put central institutions into the position of defending Czech interests."[11]

The instrumental approach also goes a long way in explaining why the 1968 federalization, even in its emasculated version of subsequent years, was the only reform of the Prague Spring to survive the Soviet intervention. As long as the content of federation provisions did not encroach upon the party's monopoly rule, their form could hardly matter. Thus it was possible to endow both Soviet and Slovak republics with constitutional provisions of "sovereignty," for the fundamental subordination of the republics to the center was ensured by democratic centralism and the *nomenklatura* system.

Along the same lines, the 1968 provisions concerning the prohibition of majority voting (the minority veto) in the federal parliament could be enacted, because the exercise of genuine parliamentary rule was never to be tested in fully democratic practice.[12] But in the post-1989 context of democratic politics, such Soviet-era formulas acquired an immense (and, even by their architects, never-intended) significance. Where, for example, the prohibition of majority voting was concerned, it empowered thirty-one determined deputies in the 300-member Federal Assembly to paralyze parliamentary politics and the critical deliberations on the constitutional setup by their sheer absence from the assembly.[13]

The holders of power in Czechoslovakia after 1948 (with the brief and partial exception of 1968) were either imposed from the outside or so beholden to Moscow for their power and privilege that they identified more or less fully with Soviet interests. In short, they formed the political elite of a dependent regime that was fully penetrated by the outside power through well-known mechanisms and methods. By definition, the extent of such penetration and the degree of dependency are also measures of external influence.

Former deputy premier and foreign minister Jiří Dienstbier takes the view that the possibilities for autonomous Czech and Slovak politics in the communist era were narrowly circumscribed by Moscow. He has argued that a series of critical issues faced by the first postcommunist government, such as the future of Slovak tank factories or dams such as Gabčíkovo—which adversely affected Czech–Slovak and republic–federal relations—were a function of outside influence, of decisions "often made in the context of pressure by foreign powers, such as the Warsaw Pact."[14] It is significant (and surprising) that the post-1989 leaders rarely pointed out the complex nature of the external influences on Czech–Slovak relations.[15] This pertains not only to the well-known facets of the communist subsystems, epitomized by the monopoly of party rule as well as "regional" organizations such as the Warsaw Pact and Comecon, but also to the entire mechanism of centralized allocation of resources, which was still in place after 1989.

Judging by the 1990–92 debate concerning state subsidies and perceptions of economic inequality, it appears that few Czech and Slovak commentators fully appreciated the critical role of the Soviet experience in shaping patterns of resource allocation in communist Czechoslovakia. That experience, in a very different setting, mandated a highly centralized state, in which mainly central authorities "determined the level and geographical allocation of economic resources."[16] Since Marxism-Leninism embraced the notion that social and economic inequality gives rise to tensions and conflicts, including interethnic conflict, the goal of reducing social and economic disparities across its territory was one of the deeply held tenets of successive Soviet regimes. The state budget served as a vehicle for reallocation of resources among republics and regions in accordance with the national economic plan. To meet that objective, Soviet planners embraced "dual development goals—'equalizing' the productive capacities of Soviet regions and living standards of the population and attaining maximum economic growth."[17] But the twin goals of equalizing and growth were contradictory, for investments, guided by the former imperative, went to less productive regions, typically generating slower growth in return.

This developmental pattern, also in evidence in communist Czechoslovakia, not only generated tensions and conflicts along national lines but also required its own system of economic, political, and administrative structures as well as fiscal arrangements. Designed along national lines, it endowed the socialist "pseudofederations" with the facade of a federal administrative system, which was in reality driven by the authoritarian institutions of the Communist Party, concentrating power and resources in the hands of the central authorities. One of the causes (in the Soviet case) and one of the consequences (in the Czechoslovak and Yugoslav cases) of the fall of communism was the mounting pressure for a redesign of the entire architecture—in Havel's apt phrase—of "federalized totalitarianism."[18]

In this sense, the view that "the breakup of the Czechoslovak federation in 1992 was brought about from within, although it was influenced by the international environment,"[19] is in need of a qualification. Owing to the previous four decades of Sovietization, the "international" element was by 1989 also very much imbedded in the internal institutional and administrative arrangements themselves. Whether it had more to do with the institutional underpinnings with which the new political elite had to contend, or with the system of resource allocation, or with a sense of mutual betrayal emanating from the past episodes of Czech–Slovak discord—which typically also had the imprimatur of outside influence—the role of external factors and forces in setting the stage for the latest, and final, chapter in the Czech–Slovak coexistence and conflict was considerable.

RETURNING TO EUROPE, SEPARATELY

After four decades of Soviet domination, postcommunist Czechoslovakia set out rapidly to establish autonomous foreign policy. During 1989 to 1992, Czech and Slovak political orientations toward foreign issues were as much a function of historical influences and changes in the international system as a reflection of the wide-ranging debate concerning the present, the past, and the future of the common state, including the relationship of the constituent parts of that state to the outside world.

Soon after November 1989, domestic collisions along national lines began increasingly to reflect different geopolitical concerns, stemming from historical experience with one's neighbors. What also tended to differentiate Czech and Slovak perspectives were regional crises, which had a different meaning for different political constituencies. Another source of conflict centered on the relationship of the federation but especially that of the republics with Europe and the outside world. Ultimately, these Czech–Slovak diverging outlooks on various matters of foreign policy crystallized in the form of demands for new institutional underpinnings of foreign policy, which would allow for a distinctive expression of Slovak interests. In combination, all these factors and trends tended to polarize the Czech–Slovak relationship inside the federation and to overload the domestic political agenda.

One of the early measures undertaken by the new leaders, which divided the political elite along national lines and which placed the question of the foreign policy role of the republics squarely on the agenda, was the January 1990 announcement that Prague would ban weapons sales. Historically, Czechoslovakia had been a leading arms producer, ranking seventh in the world as arms exporter from 1984 through 1988. Thus it was newsworthy when in the course of a January 1990 interview with *The New York Times*, Dienstbier announced that Prague's role as one of the arms merchants of the world would come to an end immediately: "Czechoslovakia will simply end its trade in arms without taking into account what the pragmatists will say, that it will be a blow to the state coffers, that those people will get arms from somebody else anyway if we don't supply them." The foreign minister also divulged that the new policy "hasn't been officially announced" yet, "but it will simply be done and weapons just won't be sold anymore."[20]

But banning weapons production and arms trade could not "simply be done" as Dienstbier had predicted. For one thing, in March 1990, one of Dienstbier's deputies backpedaled on the new policy, explaining that Czechoslovakia would honor the existing contracts of arms deliveries.[21] Moreover, given the considerable influence of the arms manufacturers as a political lobby and the very different economic impact on the Czech and Slovak republics of any ban on weapons production, ending arms exports would turn out to be a far more complicated, politically divisive, and protracted process than had originally been envisaged by the foreign minister.

The Czech Republic's arms industries specialized in light planes, avionics, and radar equipment that were more readily convertible to civilian uses. By contrast, Slovakia, with some 60 percent of the total Czechoslovak defense industry production, had inherited the more obsolete tank factories that were also more dependent on increasingly scarce spare parts from the Soviet Union. In the face of declining weapons orders in the late 1980s, the arms industry had already suffered its greatest losses in earnings during 1988 and 1989, when military production had dropped to a third of the 1987 level.[22] But Slovakia, where the defense sector relative to the size of the overall economy was at least twice the size of that of the Czech lands, with over 80,000 employees in the arms industry, was especially hard hit by the declining markets. Because the state had continued to subsidize the industry in the late 1980s, thereby postponing the day of reckoning, the rising unemployment in this sector did not become a factor until 1991–92. Since Slovakia's unemployment rate by then was three times as high as that in the Czech republic, a growing number of Slovak government officials opposed the new federal policy.[23] That is why in January 1991 the Slovak government—in a forceful display of its newly acquired autonomy—disclosed its decision to continue with weapons production, "so long as the enterprises have customers."[24] While the decision underlined the lack of policy coordination and the growing conflict on the federal–republic level, it also indicated the absence of a coherent federal strategy in foreign security policy.

Arms sales issues, however, never went away. They flared up again in the spring of 1991, when it was disclosed that a Slovak manufacturer was scheduled to supply Syria with 250 tanks and that the projected sales were meeting with high-level protests from the U.S. government and Israel. Other reports of weapons contracts and deliveries continued to receive a great deal of attention by the media, putting the foreign policy objectives of disarmament, as stressed by Dienstbier and Havel, representatives of the federation, on a collision course with Slovak economic needs and interests.

Threatened with a major loss of jobs, Slovak leaders of all political persuasions defended their republic's right to produce weapons and to continue arms deliveries. To them, Dienstbier's (and Havel's) policy appeared particularly galling, given the very different impact such a measure would have upon the Czech and the Slovak republics, making Slovakia bear the brunt of the decision's economic costs. Moreover, since Prague was fully capable of such indifference to Slovak interests, the affair also raised questions about foreign policy formulation in general.

The absence of a coordination mechanism for security, trade, and foreign policy among various government agencies charged with responsibilities in these areas compounded the problem. The inexperience of the new political elite on the world stage often manifested itself in foreign policy pronouncements that appeared to disregard international conventions. Along these lines, Marián Čalfa, the federal prime minister, did not help matters much when he explained during a May 1991 official visit to Israel (at the invitation of the World Jewish Congress) that "tanks are goods just like any others, and in addition one of the few products that we are able to sell in the world. This is why we will sell them to anyone."[25]

As a result, Czechoslovakia first promised to deliver the tanks, then postponed the decision, and finally, under mounting Slovak pressure, and despite vehement American protests, carried out the deliveries. The confrontation left a bitter aftertaste in Bratislava, the Slovak capital. Though motivated by the moral resolve to part with the old way of doing things, to demonstrate, as Dienstbier put it, that things "can be done if people want to do them," in the eyes of many Slovaks, the weapons ban was a barometer of "federal," Pragocentric lack of consideration for Slovak interests.

Concurrently, the Slovak weapons industry also figured prominently in the most serious political crisis of postcommunist Czechoslovakia. On 23 April 1991, after six weeks of political instability in Slovakia, the Slovak parliament ousted seven members of the Slovak cabinet, including prime minister Vladimír Mečiar, member of the governing party, the Public Against Violence. The latter had in the course of the previous weeks divided into a profederal and a more nationalist/populist wing, headed by Mečiar, which argued that the strategy of economic transformation as designed at the federal level was ill suited for Slovak needs. But Mečiar's fate was sealed when parliamentary investigations in April concluded that during his official visit to the Soviet Union at the end of March, he had held secret talks with Soviet generals about arms sales without prior consultation with his government or parliamentary colleagues. These disclosures paved the way toward Mečiar's removal in April. Though President Havel hailed his ouster at the time as "a triumph of democracy," Mečiar, a former boxer, was down but not out. Riding a wave of popularity as the leader of a new party, Movement for Democratic Slovakia, he would return to the same office again, sweeping the June 1992 elections. But the second time around, Prime Minister Mečiar would be neither a friend of the federation nor an ally of Havel.[26]

Undoubtedly, economic hardships stemming from the difficulties in the Slovak arms industry, further exacerbated by Prague's actions, provided fertile ground for the radicalization of Slovak demands for autonomy of decision making. But there were bitter feelings in Prague as well. Czech foreign policy specialists portrayed the reversal of the federal government's original decision as a product of an "intrapolitical dictate," in which the alliance of Slovak politicians with arms manufacturers and the Slovak-led ministry of foreign trade had reshaped the course of Czechoslovak foreign policy.[27] Significantly, the first major and successful challenge to foreign security policy of the federation came from Bratislava and resulted in the reassessment of Czechoslovak interests and, eventually, of federal policy as well. Even more fundamentally, the tanks imbroglio testified to the growing divergence of definitions of Czech and Slovak interests at home and abroad and to the absence of institutional structures capable of mediating the ensuing conflicts. After 1990, in both the domestic and foreign policy spheres, the Slovak political elite would increasingly feel empowered to assert Slovak interests separate from those of the federation. As we shall see later, this foreign policy divergence would eventuate in the creation of institutional underpinnings, i.e., ministries, for separate foreign policies, Czech and Slovak.

Geopolitical considerations also shaped—and reflected—the divergence in Czech and Slovak perspectives. This was particularly notable in regard to relations with the neighboring states, which were informed by age-old historical enmities and new apprehensions. Given the history of domination by their larger neighbors, the Czechs tended to show greater sensitivity toward Germany, and the Slovaks toward Hungary. Yet the distinctive Czech and Slovak perceptions of their neighbors impinged upon and complicated their mutual relationship inside the federation as well.

After 1989, Czechoslovak–German relations improved considerably, culminating in the 1992 adoption of the friendship and cooperation treaty, which endorsed the inviolability of the existing borders, declared the 1938 Munich Agreement "null and void," and expressed German support for Czechoslovakia's integration into the European Community. Yet the deliberations leading up to the treaty agreement reopened the wounds of the past. Many Czechs, for example, displayed heightened nervousness over the future status of the 3 million Sudeten Germans, who had been expelled from postwar Czechoslovakia, where (largely in the Czech lands) they had resided for generations. Fueling such apprehensions, the German-based representatives of the Sudeten Germans demanded, unsuccessfully, that the treaty language address their "right of return" as well as the return of their property, which had been expropriated by the postwar government. Czech communists, social democrats, and nationalists played up this prospect, and emphasized the threat of "Germanization," symbolized by the penetration of

German capital—by far the largest source of foreign investment in Czechoslovakia. Protracted negotiations with Germany over the treaty text kept the German question at the center of public attention during 1991–92.

Public opinion polls conducted on the question of the postwar German expulsion in the spring of 1992 point to differences in Czech and Slovak attitudes about the past. In March, some 58 percent of Bohemian Czechs and 49 percent of Moravians approved the postwar "transfer" of the Germans, but only 30 percent of Slovaks (who would be less affected than the Czechs by any German property restitution claims) shared that view.[28] But when the treaty with Germany came up for approval, a crossnational coalition of Czech left-of-center parties and Slovak nationalists made common cause in a failing effort to defeat it. While in their opposition to the treaty, Czech communists, socialists, and nationalists vented their fear of Germanization, they—like the governing coalition—argued that the treaty had to include references to Czechoslovakia's uninterrupted existence since 1918, rendering the wartime German Protectorate of Bohemia and Moravia illegal. By contrast, Slovak nationalists, as well as the leaders of the governing Christian Democrats, including Slovak premier Jan Čarnogurský, attacked the same treaty language, protesting the notion of the "uninterrupted existence" of Czechoslovakia from 1939 to 1945, thereby defending the "legal" existence of the wartime Slovak state, which had marked the first instance of Slovak statehood. This stance, however, won them no applause from the mainstream Czech public, in whose eyes the wartime Slovak state was an ugly offspring of Hitler and symbolized the years of betrayal. In short, because the past had a different shape and meaning for the Czechs and the Slovaks, the resurrection of its ghosts even in relation to third parties such as Germany produced newly divisive effects upon Czech–Slovak relations, loosening the bonds of the federation.

Parallel, though unequal, was the Slovak relationship with Hungary. In fact, the Hungarian factor complicated relations with the Czechs on several levels. During 1990 to 1992, Slovakia's Hungarian minority consistently supported the preservation of Czechoslovakia's federation as the best guarantor of the protection of its rights in the wake of rising Slovak nationalism. This stand, of course, made the Hungarian political parties doubly suspect in the eyes of Slovak nationalists. The incipient profederalist Czech–Hungarian alliance inside Czechoslovakia was clearly a factor with international dimensions, linking up as it did with relations with Budapest. Slovak officials complained frequently that Prague was much too soft on irredentist Hungarian claims, such as the provocative statement of Budapest's prime minister Jozsef Antall in August 1990 that he was "in spirit" the leader of all 15 million Hungarians in the world, including, by implication, some 600,000 Hungarians inside Slovak borders.

Evidently, what Bratislava perceived as lukewarm Czech support for Slovak official protests on such Hungarian transgressions gave rise to the notion in some Slovak circles that Prague was trying to play the "Hungarian card" to keep Slovak demands for a restructuring of Czech–Slovak relations in line. Conversely, internal Czech–Slovak debates over the future of the federation had the tendency to spill over into issues involving Hungarian interests as well. A case in point was the argument presented by federal premier Marián Čalfa in November 1991 to the effect that independent Slovakia would face uncertain borders because Budapest's position on that issue was wide open. Čalfa's suggestion that Hungary might have territorial designs on Slovak territory elicited official protest from Budapest.[29]

On another level, the Czechs were forced to defend the Slovak view against the Hungarians on the Gabčíkovo-Nagymaros dam project on the Danube. For environmental reasons, Hungary chose to abandon the project, but for Slovakia, the completion of the dam had become a symbol of national pride. By obtaining the authority to negotiate directly with Hungary over the Gabčíkovo-Nagymaros, the Slovak government played on Czech apprehensions that the federal government in Prague bore full responsibility for the consequences of Slovak intransigence, while at the same time it was increasingly powerless to influence Bratislava's pattern of negotiations and bargaining terms. As the 1992 elections drew near, the federal government had virtually given up trying to influence Bratislava in this realm.

Different Czech and Slovak responses to regional crises illustrate both internal and external linkages and the growing gap in Czech and Slovak perspectives. In August 1991, the Soviet coup transformed, if temporarily, the security environment in East and Central Europe. The sudden vulnerability of the new Central European democracies prompted President Havel on 19 August to declare that though Czechoslovakia was "not directly endangered," Czech and Slovak leaders should reassess their internal disputes in the wake of the Soviet crisis.[30] While the Czech government took the view that the interests of the Czech Republic were not immediately threatened, Čarnogurský, then Slovak prime minister and the leader of the Christian Democratic Party, took a more ambiguous stand. On the one hand, he advocated that, if the situation deteriorated any further, Czechoslovakia should seek to coordinate its Soviet policies with Hungary and Poland. On the other hand, a few days after the coup failed, he also stressed that the developments in the Soviet Union validated his view that Maastricht should serve as the model for Czechoslovakia: "What is on the level of the European Community could belong to the federation, and what belongs to the member states would fall under the competence of the national republics."[31] From early 1991 on, the notion that a Czechoslovak Maastricht represented a viable solution to the problems of the federation became the preferred coin of Slovak political discourse.

The crisis in Moscow also engendered declarations from national parliaments and statements from individual political parties. On 20 August, the anniversary of the 1968 Soviet invasion, both republic parliaments condemned the coup. But where the Czech parliament rejected outright the new "unconstitutional" Moscow leaders, the Slovak National Council merely registered its hope that the Soviets would "return to democratic reforms." Moreover, while several Czech and Slovak parties, except for the Communist Party of Bohemia and Moravia, also issued condemnations of the coup and echoed Havel's call to resist the temptation to engage in internal disputes, the separatist Slovak National Party complained loudly that Czechoslovak federalists would take advantage of the Soviet crisis to discount the " justified aspirations [for independence] of the Slovak nation."[32]

By contrast, the Public Against Violence, a member of the Slovak governing coalition, issued a statement on 19 August linking democratic forces in the Soviet Union with the party's stand "against the breaking of the common federal state, in which we see the guarantee of a secure home, the guarantee of our dignified place in Europe and the world, of our future prosperity."[33] Both Havel's and the Slovak parties' perspectives indicate the growing tendency on the part of Czech and Slovak political elites and groups to view external relations and crises in terms of regionally defined domestic issues and internal crises.

The years 1990–91 were also a turning point in the disintegration of Yugoslavia and the Soviet Union, which by 1992 had transformed the international context in which the debate concerning the redefinition of Czech–Slovak relations took place. Yet the impact of the rapidly changing external environment was mixed. On the one hand, the centrifugal tendencies in the multiethnic neighboring states reinforced those Slovak voices arguing for a greater measure of Slovak autonomy. The 1990–1992 avalanche of declarations of "sovereignty" by Soviet republics, for example, was a source of inspiration for Slovak nationalists and separatists. Similarly, among the Czech pessimists, the same trends strengthened the perception that the days of Czechoslovakia were numbered. But at the same time, the increasingly violent transition in Yugoslavia limited the appeal of a precipitous secession and pointed to the high costs of state dissolution. Public opinion polls conducted in September 1991 indicated a difference in Czech and Slovak perspectives in regard to the proposition that "we are now facing the same danger as Yugoslavia," but did not reveal a widespread fear. While a majority of Czechs (66 percent) and about 49 percent of Slovaks disagreed with this opinion, only 22 percent of Czechs and 33 percent of Slovaks agreed.[34] Undoubtedly, these results reflected the fact that for all their disagreements, top Czech and Slovak decision makers—unlike their Yugoslav counterparts—agreed that Slovakia had the full right to self-determination, and if the majority of Slovaks wished to create an independent state, both Czech and Slovak governments had no choice but to work together on a peaceful, constitutional separation.

Nonetheless, the Soviet and Yugoslav disintegrations and the rise of the successor states provided further ammunition for the arguments of Slovak confederalists and separatists that national self-determination required the creation of an independent Slovak state. Slovak prime minister Čarnogurský in July 1991 disclosed his belief that an independent Slovakia would emerge by the year 2000. As he put it, "I believe the events in Yugoslavia and the Soviet Union will find their echoes here, too. The Slovaks have a sense of national solidarity. But the Czechoslovak federation is not a priority for them, on the contrary."[35] The same month, Mečiar, the former prime minister, argued that "the struggle of Slovenes for their identity is a model for the struggle of Slovakia to solve many of its painful problems."[36]

In early September 1991, after months of fruitless discussions, Czech and Slovak parliamentary leaders initialed a basic agreement on the constitutional drafting process, envisaging a step-by-step approach that would avoid unconstitutional means. But the agreement was rejected by Mečiar out of hand, because, in his view, Slovakia had "an inalienable right to adopt its own constitution" without consulting the Czech authorities. "Considering the international situation and the efforts of many nations of Central and Eastern Europe to emancipate themselves, the time has come," Mečiar argued, "for the Slovak Republic to demand its right to self-determination and achieve sovereignty. Postponing this matter is a grave political mistake that will leave Slovakia outside an integrated Europe."[37] Along these lines, the disintegrative influence of the developments in the neighboring countries made itself felt in the Czecho–Slovak context. Fedor Gál, writing in early 1992, expressed his belief that as far as Czechoslovakia was concerned, "an immediate danger of the disintegration of the state no longer exists." But he also noted in the aftermath of Soviet dissolution that the "only country that views the disintegration of the former Soviet empire with a sense of worry-free euphoria, as a part of the process of the self-determination of nations, is Slovakia, specifically its separatistically inclined part of the media and population."[38]

In the course of 1990–92, the negotiations that sought to redefine the Czech–Slovak relationship focused ostensibly on the internal nature of the common state, including political and administrative decentralization, economic strategy, and resource allocation. But the relationship of the new federation and its constituent parts to the outside world was also a major issue. Characteristically, the Czecho–Slovak debates over the future of the federation blurred the distinctions between domestic institutional arrangements and the process of European integration.

As early as March 1990, Čarnogurský, then a deputy prime minister in the federal government, explained that the Slovaks "would rather meet the challenge [of pan-European or central European] integration as an autonomous entity than through Czechoslovakia's mediation."[39] He reiterated the goal of the "gradual dissolution of the Czechoslovak federation" in April, and his Christian Democratic Movement reaffirmed in July 1990 its advocacy of a Czecho–Slovak confederation that would enable the Slovaks to enter Europe "as a sovereign and equal entity."[40] Still more separatist platforms were propounded by the Slovak National Party and the Movement for Independent Slovakia, which called for outright independence.

Sharing Čarnogurský's long-term vision, but going beyond it in some respects in the short run, then-former Slovak premier Mečiar had enunciated his own conception of a confederation by June 1991. It embraced the demand for a new, loose union of "a common market, the freedom of movement and capital, similarly as it is in the European Community. Then we can speak of common interests in the area's defense and coordination of foreign policy and monetary policy."[41] Given that Mečiar also endorsed demands for Slovak sovereignty and international recognition of the Slovak government, his idea of confederation was barely distinguishable from the creation of two independent states—something he never spelled out in full, however, preferring to pay lip service to the idea of a common state.

By July 1991, Čarnogurský's vision had become even more explicit. Regarded as a leading Slovak defender of the "go slow approach" to independence, Čarnogurský explained to the French daily *Liberation* that Slovak independence was inevitable. Slovakia's goal was to gain full independence by the end of the century and then join the European Economic Community as a sovereign state. In his words, Slovakia's goal "will not be realized by the simple disintegration of Czechoslovakia. It will come by way of a detour, through the integration with Europe." He suggested that Czechoslovakia could not survive another international crisis and indicated that Slovakia was constitutionally free to secede, and might do so, if the European Community did not open its doors to it.[42]

In Čarnogurský's perspective, then, the prospect of Slovakia's joining Europe as an independent state by the end of the decade was to act as a brake on Slovak "national impatience" and to take the wind out of the sails of the separatists, who wished to obtain independence immediately. But in embracing this approach, Čarnogurský in fact blurred the line between his party's goals and that of the Slovak separatists, for the only difference between the governing Christian Democratic Movement, the separatist opposition, and the confederalists led by Mečiar now appeared to be one of tempo. That, in any event, is the way his *Liberation* interview was received by the wider Czech public. One of the spokesmen of the Civic Democratic Party, the Czech political party with the largest following, for example, replied that "if the Slovak premier does not abandon this goal . . . then we have no choice but to recommend speedy dissolution."[43]

When President Havel paid an official visit to the Slovak parliament in June 1991 to discuss the conduct of foreign policy, the subject of foreign affairs hardly came up, for (as Havel himself noted in his concluding remarks) most of the discussion centered on questions concerning the future of Czech–Slovak relations.[44] What Havel may not have realized at the time, however, was that for many of the Slovak parliamentarians in the audience, relations with the Czechs had increasingly come to assume the character of interstate relations. In November 1991, during the crucial negotiations between the federal and republic government leaders behind closed doors, one of the main stumbling blocks became the question of the prerogatives of the republics vis-à-vis the outside world. When Čarnogurský demanded the right of the Slovak government to ratify the future accession to the European Community and to acquire international stature as a government "subject to international law," Petr Pithart, the Czech premier, described such shaky foundations for common statehood as "making a snow man out of April snow—it will melt before our eyes." Pithart finally objected: "we pretend we are discussing a common state, but in reality, we are discussing two states."[45]

CONCLUSIONS

By January 1992, the Czechs had accepted the Slovak proposal that the republics could, with the approval of the federation, enter into treaty relationships with other countries. That move, as much as the expanding scope of activity and influence of the Slovak Ministry for International Relations, finally led the Czech parliament to authorize in March 1992 the establishment of the Czech Ministry of International Affairs, effective as of June 1992. Though Pithart publicly denied that the step was being taken in reaction to the creation two years earlier of the Slovak ministry, such was clearly the case. To quote his own earlier words, the Slovak ministry's activities were "placing into question the existence" of Czechoslovak "statehood in the eyes of the world."[46] Czechoslovakia's foreign policy had acquired two faces by 1991: federal and Slovak. In this sense, it is difficult to sustain the proposition that "the process of Czech–Slovak separation in the early 1990s took place . . . without foreign policy playing a major part in it."[47] Soon after the June 1992 elections, in fact, both republic-level ministries would inherit the full responsibility for the conduct of their government's foreign policies—as independent states.

In hindsight, it seems that a vicious circle of sorts came to envelop Czech–Slovak relations. The country's precarious existence in a hostile external environment provided the rationale for the Czech elite's inclinations to centralize power, yet the policy of centralization repeatedly incurred resistance and protest, eventually spurring on the Slovak quest for allies abroad "to compensate for the unequal balance of power within the state." Yet such forays for "compensations" were fraught with problems of their own, for Slovak attempts to reach out would tend to land them in the hands of the perceived and real enemies of the Czechs, prompting another round of recriminations. Thus, as Leff has so aptly put it, "Slovak nationalism . . . appeared to Czech opinion, successively, as the cat's-paw of Magyar irredentism, German imperialism, and Soviet hegemony."[48]

As the developments surveyed here suggest, Slovak national assertion in both domestic and foreign policy crystallized in 1990–92. As we have seen, after 1990, Slovak political elites tended to view national interests through the prism of nation building. Clearly, the legacy of very different historical experiences informed the Czech and Slovak self-perceptions, their views of their respective neighbors, and their attitudes toward each other. The search for national identity in both republics was fraught with a sense of mutual grievances from the past, which tended to overload current issues with historical baggage.

The process of differentiation of Czech and Slovak national interests internally had its counterpart in the emergence of separate and increasingly divergent perspectives on international affairs as well. While the creation of an independent Slovak ministry of international affairs was originally motivated by the need to increase Slovak visibility abroad, it soon began to play a more active role in advocating Slovak interests and redefining Slovakia's international identity. The fact that the Slovak side led the way in both creating the new institution and expanding its realm of responsibility was also a partial measure of the Czech and Slovak political elites' relative identification with federal foreign policy. In hindsight, the establishment of the Slovak ministry of international affairs has come to be seen as the first step toward full Slovak independence.[49]

Slovak (and to some extent, Czech) spokesmen tended to overestimate the pace and the scope of the Maastricht process. The quest for ever greater Slovak autonomy was informed by the proposition that the new Czechoslovak state would, as Mečiar proposed, occupy "a common economic and defense space," with international recognition conferred upon both the Czech and the Slovak republics, each with its own seat in the United Nations and European institutions, yet somehow still loosely tied together. Clearly, Maastricht encouraged the illusion in the Slovak ranks that the hard choices between national sovereignty and supranational institutions were fast losing their salience. But by 1993, when Czechoslovakia had ceased to exist, Western Europe's drive toward economic and political integration had slowed down considerably, and the bloody war in the Balkans and on the periphery of the former Soviet Union pointed to the high and still-rising costs of dissolution.

Much like its Yugoslav counterpart, Czecho–Slovak conflict after 1989 was a function of both the postcommunist transition from totalitarianism to pluralism and of the revolutionary transformation occurring in the international system. Domestic conflict ultimately became inseparable from the international context.

NOTES

1. To students of Kenneth Waltz's *Man, the State, and War* (New York: Columbia University Press, 1959), these levels of analysis will be all too familiar.

2. Karel Pichlík, *Zahraniční odboj 1914–1918 bez legend* (Prague: Svoboda, 1968), p. 214.

3. Carol Skalnik Leff, *National Conflict in Czechoslovakia: The Making and Remaking of a State, 1918–1987* (Princeton, N.J.: Princeton University Press 1988), p. 63.

4. Josef Harna, "Česká politika a její vklad do politického systému první Československé republiky," in *Slovensko v politickom systéme Československa*, ed. Valerián Bystrický ed. (Bratislava: Predsedníctvo Slovenskej národnej rady, 1992) p. 19.

5. For evidence, see Leff, *National Conflict*, esp. ch. 8; Petr Pithart, *Osmašedesátý* (Praha: Rozmluvy, 1990), pp. 83 & ff.

6. Dubček is quoted in Jindřich Pecka, "Záznam telefonického rozhovoru L. Brežněva s A. Dubčekem 13.8. 1968, *Soudobé dejiny*, 4–5/1994, p. 578. The document, a transcript of a 1968 telephone conversation in which Brezhnev on the eve of Soviet intervention demanded of Dubček censorship of the media, personnel changes, and strengthening of the repressive organs of the ministry of the interior, provides ample evidence of Brezhnev's fraternal imperiousness, dutifully lived up to by Dubček's comradely servility.

7. For a recent study, see for example, Jiří Kocian, "Ústavněprávní poměr Čechů a Slováků v návrzích politických stran při přípravě Ústavy ČSR v letech 1946–1948," *Soudobé dějiny*, 2–3/1995, pp. 399–471.

8. Quoted in Kocian, "Ústavněprávni pornér Čechů a Slováků," p. 401.

9. See the report on an October 1995 conference of Czech and Slovak historians, "Renewal of the Common State of the Czechs and Slovaks in 1945," in which these "well-known realities" are noted. Jan Měchýř, "Cizí s cizím aneb znovu o Česku, Slovensku a ČSR," *Soudobé dějiny*, 4/1995, pp. 655–658.

10. These observations are based on the author's own recent research in Russian archives.

11. Leff, *National Conflict in Czechoslovakia*, pp. 98 and 123.

12. It is significant that some of the architects of the federal provisions believe to this day that "the constitutional law on Czechoslovak federation was being prepared in 1968 in a relatively democratic fashion," even though such preparations took place exclusively under the auspices of the Communist Party, which invited no input from nonparty channels, even in 1968, the most relaxed period of its rule. Zdeněk Jičínský, *Charta 77 a právní stát* (Prague: Doplněk, 1995), p. 145.

13. For a well-informed discussion of this issue, see Jan Rychlík, "The Development of the Consciousness of the Czechs and Slovaks and Its Political Consequences," in Armand Clesse and Andrei Kortunov, *The Political and Strategic Implications of the State Crises in Central and Eastern Europe* (Luxembourg, 1993), pp. 276–277.

14. *Jana Klusáková a Jiří Dienstbier rozmlouvají Nadoraz* (Prague: Primus, 1993), p. 29.

15. When in the course of the same interview, Dienstbier was asked why political leaders like himself failed to emphasize more frequently the role of external legacies, his reply was: "I don't know." *Klusáková a Dienstbier*, p. 30.

16. See Ronald D. Liebowitz, "Russia's Center–Periphery Fiscal Relations during Transition," in Michael Kraus and Ronald D. Liebowitz, eds., *Russia & Eastern Europe after Communism: The Search for New Political, Economic, and Security Systems* (Boulder: Westview Press, 1996), p. 160.

17. Liebowitz, "Russia's Center–Peripheny Fiscal Relations," p. 162.

18. See *Klusáková a Dienstbier*, p. 25.

19. Jacques Rupnik, "The International Context," in *The End of Czechoslovakia*, by Jiří Musil (New York: Central European University Press, 1995), p. 271.

20. *The New York Times*, 25 January 1990. This section draws on my "Returning to Europe, Separately: International Factors in Czechoslovakia's Dissolution, 1989–1992," in Michael Kraus and Ronald D. Liebowitz, eds., *Russia & Eastern Europe after Communism*, pp. 223–245.

21. Jan Obrman, "Czechoslovakia and the Arms Trade," *RFE/RL Report on Eastern Europe* (hereafter cited as *RFE*), 20 April 1990, p. 22.

22. See "Buyers, please: Czech arms," *The Economist*, 6 November 1993, p. 90.

23. "Buyers please," p. 90.

24. Federalní ministerstvo zahraničních večí, *Československá zahraničí politika* [hereafter *CZP*], *Data*, 1/1991, p. 25.

25. *CZP: Data*, 1/1991, p. 25.

26. For background and analysis of this episode, see Jiri Pehe, "Political Conflict in Slovakia," *RFE*, 10 May 1991, pp. 1–6.

27. See the essays by Jan Wenner, "Oblast Středního východu v širším kontextu orientace ČSFR," p. 164; and Jiří Valenta, "Československé zájmy z pohledu roku 1992," p. 229, in Jiří Valenta et al., eds., *Máme Národní Zájmy?* (Prague: Ústav mezinárodních vztahů, 1992).

28. Jan Obrman, "Czechoslovak Assembly Affirms German Friendship Treaty," *RFE*, vol. 1, no. 21, 22 May 1992.

29. For an articulate expression of Slovak reservations about Prague's foreign policy, see Roman Zelenay, *Dialog o národních zájmech* (Prague, 1992). Zelenay, the deputy head of the Foreign Relations Committee of the Federal Parliament and cofounder (with Vladimír Mečiar) of the Movement for Democratic Slovakia, criticized Prague's policies on account of what he saw as the Czech tendency to play the "Hungarian card."

30. My discussion draws on Jan Obrman, "Czechoslovakia," in "The Attempted Coup in the USSR: East European Reactions," *RFE*, vol. 2, no. 35, 30 August 1991, pp. 5–8.

31. *CZP: Data*, 8–9/1991, p. 550.

32. CZP: Data, 8–9/1991, p. 550.

33. *CZP: Data*, 8–9/1991, p. 540.

34. See Michael Deis, "A Study of Nationalism in Czechoslovakia," *RFE*, 31 January 1992, p. 11.

35. See his remarks in *Liberation*, reprinted in *CZP: Dokumenty*, 7/1991, pp. 812–813.

36. Quoted in "Weekly Record of Events: Czechoslovakia," *RFE*, 12 July 1991, p. 31.

37. Quoted in Jan Obrman, "Further Discussions on the Future of the Federation," *RFE*, 20 September 1991, pp. 8–9.

38. Fedor Gál et al., *Dnešní krize československých vztahů* (Prague: Sociologické nakl., 1992), pp. 109–110.

39. Quoted in Peter Martin, "The Hyphen Controversy," *RFE*, vol. 1, no. 16, 20 April 1990, p. 17.

40. Quoted in Peter Martin, "Relations between the Czechs and the Slovaks, *RFE*, vol. 1, no. 7 September 1990, p. 4.

41. See Mečiar's interview in *Die Presse*, 12 June 1991, reprinted in *CZP: Dokumenty* 6b/1991, p. 653.

42. His interview is reprinted in *CZP: Dokumenty*, 7/1991, pp. 812–813.

43. *Rudé právo*, 20 July 1991.

44. For a transcript of Havel's discussion, see *CZP: Dokumenty*, 6a/1991, pp. 487–513.

45. *Poločas rozpadu: Přepis stenografického záznamu ze setkaní nejvyšších ústavních činiteů u prezidenta Václava Havla na Hrádečku dne 3. listopadu 1991* (Prague: Sloven-ské listy, 1994), pp. 15–16, 72. The confidential record of these discussions provides rich insight into the bewildering confusion on the part of the plenipotentiaries, especially Slo-vak, as to what constitutes a common state.

46. *CZP: Data*, 6/1991, p. 377.

47. Rupnik, "The International Context," p. 272.

48. Leff, *National Conflict in Czechoslovakia*, p. 275.

49. See Jan Obrman, "Perspektivy nezávislého Slovenska," *Medzinárodné otázky*, vol. 2, nos. 1–2, 1993, p. 79.

Part IV

The View from the Ground: Czech and Slovak Perspectives

11

A Retrospective Look at the Dissolution of Czecho-Slovakia

Ján Čarnogurský

In 1989, the American futurologist Francis Fukuyama published an essay, "The End of History." He argued that the world was witnessing the end of ideologically colored conflicts and that the transcendant benefits of international trade, exchanges of cultural values, and, simply put, communications among peoples in accordance with the laws of reason would triumph. With a good deal of imagination, one could conclude that these predictions came true in the former Czecho-Slovakia, although in paradoxical fashion. After the fall of communism, the ties that bound the Czechs and the Slovaks in a common state collapsed as well. The overall stability of international relations, which in Europe is represented by the European Union, rid the Czechs and the Slovaks of their old fears of their neighbors. The will to live independently and abide by the rational rules of international relations was expressed at the level of nations rather than of individuals. The peaceful division of Czecho-Slovakia is compatible with such an explanation.

But let me return to the Velvet Revolution. The final phase of the struggle against communism concentrated all opponents of communism into one front; no national, religious, or other conflicts played any significant role in Czecho-Slovakia at the time. Resistance against communism was the source of solidarity, which obscured and overwhelmed all other possible differences. No sooner had communism fallen than all of the other conflicts surfaced in accordance with the principle of pluralism, especially the national ones. The legacy of supranational solidarity from the communist era carried on inside dissident circles, so long as they were in power in Slovakia and in the Czech lands. The long-standing ties between these former dissidents were the last bond maintaining the common state. After the June 1992 elections, when they did not receive a sufficient number of votes and left the governments or parliaments, there was no force that could hold Czecho-Slovakia together.

Slovak–Czech relations had one dominant theme on the Czech side and another on the Slovak side. On the Czech side, the dominant theme was the demand that financial resources no longer be redistributed via the federal budget—i.e., that each republic should pay its own way. On the Slovak side, the dominant theme was the demand for formal equality with the Czechs within the framework of the republic and the prospect of equality with other nations in international relations.[1] After the Velvet Revolution, the same theme in more subtle form resurfaced in the meeting of the Slovak and Czech governments in Lnáře in April 1990.* It came up annually in a very concrete form during budget preparation.

I recall the budget-making process for fiscal year 1992. First, the federal minister of finance and the finance ministers of both republics met and approved the basic parameters of the budget. The Czech government then did not approve the previously agreed-upon parameters and demanded five billion crowns more for the Czech budget. That is why in early December 1991, in Brno, the premiers of both governments met in the presence of President Havel. The eventual agreement reflected the relative influence of each republic vis-à-vis the federation: the federal budget received 4.5 billion crowns less, the Czechs 4 billion more, and the Slovaks half a billion more, to keep them quiet. This agreement was possible only because there were friendly political forces in all three governments. Even if the division of Czecho-Slovakia had not taken place, it is unlikely that the budget for 1993 could ever have been put together, because those friendly political forces had largely lost their leadership positions in the June 1992 elections.

On the Slovak side, the demand for formal equality was predominant. It was visible for the first time in the so-called hyphen war in March 1990. The Slovak National Council demanded that the name Czecho-Slovakia be written with a hyphen and with a capital S, instead of as Czechoslovakia. The Czech side rejected this proposal, because it was reminiscent of the form in which the republic's name was written after the Munich Agreement and before the first dissolution of the country in March 1939. The problem was solved again in a fashion characteristic of the balance of power within the republic. Both republics retained the right to write the name of the republic in the way each deemed appropriate. And so in the Czech Republic they wrote Czecho-Slovakia without the hyphen and in Slovakia with the hyphen.

In the election campaign prior to the first free elections of June 1990, President Havel openly supported the Public Against Violence (VPN), fearing that the Christian Democratic Movement (KDH), which was at first leading in the public opinion polls, would possibly initiate the division of the country. After the elections, the Public Against Violence presented Vladimír Mečiar as the premier of the Slovak government. Immediately, it became apparent to all that communications

---

* These negotiations between republic governments took place without the participation of the federal government. It was the consensus at Lnáře that each republic should live off taxes collected from inhabitants of its territory, with the federation receiving only a fixed amount of these receipts to cover administrative expenses.

between Prague and Bratislava would be difficult. In October 1990, Premier Vladimír Mečiar convened the presidium of his government on short notice and informed us that we would fly to Prague to meet the presidium of the Czech government and possibly the entire Czech government. None of us knew the likely substance of these deliberations or the immediate impetus for the journey to Prague. The meeting with the Czech government in Prague was chaotic, without a specific agenda, and without any specific results. During the meeting, however, Vladimír Mečiar informed the Czechs that they would have to reckon with the Slovak National Council's forthcoming declaration of Slovak sovereignty. Although the Slovak National Party had spoken previously in favor of such a declaration, neither it nor any other party or group of deputies had any sense what a declaration of Slovak sovereignty would actually mean. As we know from the publication of Petr Pithart*, Vladimír Mečiar's statements led the Czech government to convene an extraordinary session of the presidium of the Czech National Council and to initiate contingency planning for the division of Czecho-Slovakia.

In April 1991, differences inside the Public Against Violence led to the recall of Vladimír Mečiar. Mečiar then founded a new party, the Movement for a Democratic Slovakia (HZDS), which proceeded to wage an open campaign against Czecho-Slovakia. The political program of HZDS, however, never gave a clear explanation of its desired constitutional framework for Czecho-Slovakia. Prior to the elections of 1992, HZDS promised the citizens a referendum, in which they would be able to choose among five constitutional forms, from independent Czech and Slovak states to confederation, from federation to a unitary state.**

After the elections of 1990, a commission headed by Alexander Dubček was created in the federal parliament, which was supposed to prepare a new Czecho–Slovak constitution. The commission barely did any work, so President Havel in January 1991 launched a personal initiative and began to invite party leaders from both republics to a series of discussions on the future constitution. These meetings with the president were followed by deliberations between the presidiums of the Czech and Slovak national councils. From the beginning, these negotiations suffered from excessive democratic pluralism. On the Czech and Slovak sides, the presidiums of both national councils were comprised of representatives from different political parties, each advocating a different political platform for constitutional design and ratification. The deliberations did not have a unifying idea on either the Czech or the Slovak side. Instead, what often happened was that in the each round of negotiations, we had to come back to matters we had already discussed in preceding sessions. These negotiations eventuated in the Milovy accord of February 1992, which neither the Czech nor the Slovak National Council ratified. The Slovak side demanded a state treaty (*smlouva*) between the Slovak and Czech republics; this state treaty would then serve as a

---

* See his contribution in this volume.
** Although promised, no such referendum ever took place.

foundation for the new Czecho–Slovak constitution. The Czech side at first rejected this treaty in principle. Somewhat later, it showed willingness to accept an agreement of this sort only as a legislative initiative offered within the framework of the existing federation.* As a result, all negotiations ended with the Milovy accord.

The roughly 2:1 population ratio between the Czech and Slovak republics was the fundamental hurdle in Czech–Slovak deliberations on the future constitutional arrangements of democratic Czecho-Slovakia. This ratio enabled neither side—not the Czech and even less so the Slovak—to force its political will on the other. Given that there was no third force or external threat that might have compelled both sides to reach an agreement, an agreement was, from the beginning, highly unlikely. On the Czech side, there was a conceptual contradiction; in its economic arrangements it was reaching for a confederal model, while in its constitutional stance it demanded a federation. During the deliberations, the Czech side never ceased to take the stand that we would either agree on a federation or let each republic go its own way. In contrast, during the same deliberations, the Slovak side never proposed the independence of Slovakia as a viable alternative in the event that the negotiations failed. Both parties to the conflict believed that if the negotiations failed, the other side would not have the courage to cross the point of no return and choose the division of the country.

The Public Against Violence also contributed to Czech misperceptions of the Slovak stance on constitutional arrangements. At the top, the VPN was comprised of the liberal intelligentsia, which had very good rapport with the leadership of Civic Forum in Prague. In this fashion, the VPN created the impression that it was an ideal partner for the Czech side in any dialogue on constitutional forms. Under the liberal leadership of VPN, however, hid a radical underside, which propelled Vladimír Mečiar into the spotlight. After the splintering of the VPN in early 1992, what the actual balance of power inside the party had been became clear. HZDS, which came out of the VPN, won the election, while the original VPN did not even make it into the Slovak parliament.

My assessment of the role of the Christian Democratic Movement in deliberations with the Czech side is of necessity subjective. From its inception, KDH inherited Slovak ethnic politics. We were familiar with the national mood in Slovakia, and we knew that the old constitutional arrangements could not survive. Further, we knew—or at least we suspected—the problems that would emerge in the event of Slovak independence. And finally, we were a part of the larger European Christian Democratic movement. These three components led us to see the completion of the Slovak process of emancipation in the framework of European integration. As it turned out, our vision was far too idealistic for most Slovaks as well as for the Czech side.

---

* That is, as an intrastate agreement and not as an interstate treaty, which is how the Slovak representatives conceived of it. For further details on the substance of this dispute, see the contribution by Allison Stanger in this volume.

Our platform for future constitutional forms was expressed symbolically by the slogan "For a little seat and a little star in the European Union," as well as by the political demand for a state treaty between Slovakia and the Czech Republic. In 1990–92, however, political development in the constitutional area was determined by radicals. KDH could not be successful in such an environment. But thanks to our political orientation at that time, we have retained the ability to be a stabilizing force on the contemporary Slovak political scene. During the constitutional deliberations, KDH was conscious of the fact that the dark shadows of past Slovak ethnic politics, particularly in the years 1939–45, was also its legacy. We viewed this inheritance as a source of learning so as to ensure that we did not again lead Slovakia into a blind alley as had happened back then. At the same time, we were conscious that if we were ultraradical on the national question, we could have easily been accused of continuing the Lud'ak separatism of 1939, which would have been a bad omen for any reborn Slovak republic.

This brings us to the present situation: Czecho-Slovakia divided in a peaceful manner, and all those who had prior to the division begged us to stay together were later to commend our peaceful means. We see that development in both republics since the partition has proceeded in different directions. The deterioration of relations between the two republics provides an ex post facto justification for the division. Simply put, we were nations too different to comprise one state. But if in time it will be shown that despite independence, we are connected by certain elementary strategic interests, it might be the beginning of qualitatively new relations between the Slovak and Czech republics. Elements of a common approach to certain questions of international relations are quite apparent. Perhaps future international crises will test this. But that is a topic for another paper.

Translated from Slovak by Michael Kraus and Allison Stanger

NOTES

1. In the 1980s, this theme appeared in the samizdat publications of Rudolf Slánský, Jr. In 1988, Ladislav Adamec also mentioned Czech Republic subsidies for Slovakia when he replaced Lubomír Štrougal as federal prime minister.

12

The Division/Dissolution of Czechoslovakia: Old Sins and New Forms of Selfishness

Petr Pithart

In this chapter, I will attempt to answer several questions while at the same time deliberately leaving other questions aside. I will not attempt to answer the question of whether the Czech or the Slovak side was more responsible for the division/dissolution of Czechoslovakia nor whether what happened at the close of 1992 could have been prevented.

In my judgment, both sides were undoubtedly responsible for the end result, and it is not so important which was more responsible. It is important, however, to recognize specific Czech and specific Slovak motives for the division/dissolution. The dissolution probably could have been prevented, but this proposition tells us very little of value: one would have to specify more precisely the cost of keeping the state intact, yet that price would almost certainly have been unacceptable for one or the other or both sides. So one has to conclude with the counterpoint that preserving the state might have been possible, but the price would have been unacceptable, and therefore it was in actuality impossible.

I have to begin by clarifying why I was an opponent of dividing the state until the very end. Spelling out the reasons for my politically suicidal stand will perhaps make it possible to understand better my sense and understanding of the causes of the whole process.

1. States are maintained by the ideas on which they were founded. This (paraphrased) dictum of Tomáš Masaryk's is repeated by everyone, but only a few believe in it seriously. At the very least, with the division of Czechoslovakia, the Czechs abrogated the founding idea of the independent state of the western-most Slavs and thereby endangered the existence of even its successor formations. This is not affected by the fact that this danger may become apparent only at a later

time. But something has already become evident: Czech fears of Germany have grown markedly since the split, but not only because the Czech state is smaller and the German state larger. Apart from other things, by dividing Czechoslovakia, we have, in the eyes of some Germans, questioned the heretofore unquestioned unacceptability of the Munich Agreement—as if we had given credence to that agreement and absolution to our Germans.

2. States and their integrative agglomerations rest, among other things, on the principle of solidarity: the Czech economic motive for the division was antisolidarity. The pejorative word *penězovod**(money pipeline) has captured this motive well. We wanted to be closer to Europe, which is in fact itself enmeshed in a web of money pipelines. The division of Czechoslovakia and the factual abrogation of Visegrad had a common denominator. The underlying motives were similar—to be as far away as possible from the poor postcommunist partners and as close as possible to rich Western Europe. A reasonable European Union (EU), however, should first and foremost reward goodwill and the ability to integrate even before one enters the gates of the EU. Consideration of specific macroeconomic indicators of a given country should be a secondary factor.

3. Ethnically homogeneous state units throughout history have been the exception. Ethnic homogeneity was more often a characteristic of state formations that were on the periphery, barbaric. The great centers of all world civilizations have always been a rich mixture of nations, cultures, faiths, and ways of life, and that is why they were not just centers of spiritual activities. Only in recent times has Western Europe moved toward greater homogeneity, but that is balanced by its receptiveness toward newcomers. Homogeneity spiritually and culturally impoverishes. It sets limits on self-reflection as the highest degree of knowledge—self-knowledge.

4. It was evident that the division of the state would not enhance Czech and Slovak democracy, although the effects would be different in each instance. The "founders" of new states, whose actions were celebrated as "peaceful" (as if there existed a viable nonpeaceful alternative), reaped rewards, which artificially improved their positions of power. Elements of authoritarianism—and I emphasize, not to the same extent—became evident in both countries.

5. Since the division in the end took place legally but not legitimately—after a great effort and at the price of unkept promises—legitimacy would have to be bestowed upon the partition after the fact. This was (and still is) accomplished in two ways. First, relations between the Czech and Slovak republics are maintained below the standard of ordinary neighborly relations. Second, the governments of each new republic periodically carry out acts of ill will against each other. These acts would eventually win over those who were originally against the division:

---

* *Penězovod* is a Czech term that was coined after 1989 in reference to the purported transfer of financial resources from the Czech lands to Slovakia.

subsequently they too would see that "you really cannot work with them." In short, as long as the proponents of the division are in power, there is no hope for better mutual relations.

6. The division of Czechoslovakia undermined the fragile stability of Central Europe because the Czech and the Slovak republics, alone or together, are not what Czechoslovakia was. Owing to our elongated shape, we were the East–West clamp of this rather unstable space. We light-heartedly exchanged the complexities of Czech–Slovak relations for far more complicated and above all far more dangerous Czech–German and Slovak–Hungarian relations. It does not seem to me to have been a good bargain.

Now that I have explained my motives, ideas, and fears, I will try to answer the following question: what on the Czech side, led, above all, to the division of the state, the agreement to do so, and the reluctant acceptance of this outcome? What were the motives, the ideas, the fears? I will, once again, grossly generalize and speak of "we," i.e. "the Czechs." As for Slovak motives, let the Slovaks first speak for themselves, and then we can say how we understood them from the Czech side. I am convinced that such generalizations are not unjustified. In my view, our motives, our ideas and fears were not the result of some purportedly in-born national character but instead stem from both common and individual Czech and Slovak historical experiences.

In addition, I am convinced that what was decisive and decided the issue was precisely these generally shared attitudes, not concrete mistakes or omissions on the part of those in power, nor defects in the constitution, nor failures of the economic transformation. All these other factors, of course, played a role, but for the most part, our generally shared attitudes were decisive.

1. Bohemia—I am leaving out Moravia here—did not in the least think in a regional fashion but instead thought of itself in centralist terms throughout its entire history. Its center was and is Prague and only Prague. The Czechs do not even understand Moravian regionalism, which they regard as some sort of an irrational quirk or as the invention of ambitious local politicians. So how could they possibly grasp Slovak strivings for autonomy or federalism? For the Czechs, the kingdom could never be anything but a unitary state. They would reluctantly accept another state structure only if they had no other alternative. They were pleaded with for a long time, and once they were talked into it (1968). The principle of federation as an element in the division of powers was and is alien to the Czechs. It is comprehensible to them only as an act of stubbornness, of childishness. The whole state, however large and however constituted, was fixated on Prague, just as the Czech Kingdom was always fixated on Prague. This was a deeply held Czech conviction, one that is really akin to a deeply rooted prejudice. It was always shared by practically everybody: politicians, the media, and millions of people. In the early years, more than 40 percent of the Czechs always voted for the unitary state as the best configuration. Furthermore, in the context of the unitary principle, the Czechs were very tolerant of centralism.

2. We also tolerated the so-called real socialism more than any of the other So-viet bloc countries. Perhaps as a result of the disillusionment stemming from the Prague Spring—and here I have in mind its protagonists after the 1968 occupa-tion—we were able to develop effective adaptive mechanisms. In essence, a "sec-ond" unofficial society of sorts was created, a network of connections ever less dependent on belonging to the ruling party. Back then, a "privatization of social-ism" took place through the creation of structures such as the "fortress house-hold," as sociologists have dubbed it. People largely withdrew from the public sphere and oriented themselves toward short-term economic interests, which were satisfied, thanks to the gray economy. After November 1989, these orienta-tions could not have changed overnight. On the contrary, for then-capitalist pri-vatization had begun in earnest. For these reasons, not only before November but even after, the public sphere significantly atrophied. From the protracted privati-zation of socialism straight into shock capitalist privatization without a transi-tion—this could not have transpired without repercussions.

Short-term material interests were therefore not only the most easily under-stood but also the most powerful argument for the division of the state: We will be better off, the Czechs alone, without the Slovaks! That was the lowly voice of the people, even though it was not the dominant voice at the beginning. Decadent socialism and rapacious frontier capitalism were good preparation for an over-simplified perspective in which the common state appeared as a frivolous and un-necessary luxury.

3. It may seem like a paradox, but as much as the Czechs were basically fond of the Slovaks, they knew very little about them. This holds true for the past, both distant and recent, not to mention the future. Slovak dreams, aspirations, con-cerns, and fears—these the Czechs did not really know, or if they did, understood only superficially. They had no idea how the Slovaks experienced cohabitation with the Czechs, nor did they feel guilty about this, for they so much enjoyed vis-iting and traveling in Slovakia. Some even saw in the Slovak character something complementary to the Czech character. To be sure, it was something more prim-itive but also something more spontaneous, more generous, more heartfelt, some-thing comparable to lost innocence. But when all was said and done, the Czechs knew nearly nothing about the Slovaks, nor did the politicians who had to decide the "what" and the "how" after 1989. I was an everyday witness to this situation. It gave rise to an unending series of small and large misunderstandings, conflicts, and embarrassments, which must have irritated the Slovak side a great deal. Czech haughtiness was sky high—not only did they know nothing about the Slo-vaks, but they didn't even know that they knew nothing. This ubiquitous and pa-tronizing Czech ignorance could not but be apprehended beyond the Morava River* as a lack of interest, as an aura of superiority, as paternalism. As a result, the Slovaks were in a state of permanent alert: while they read Czech newspapers

---

* The Morava River divides the Czech lands from Slovakia.

and books, the Czechs, for example, did not read Slovak newspapers and books. That is how it was, is, and most likely will be.

I would argue, however, that this Czech ignorance does not concern only the Slovaks but actually applies to relations with all our neighbors. Nonetheless, I realize that this could not be a source of comfort to the Slovaks. We have always known more about France and today about America than about the Poles, the Austrians, or the Slovaks. But our relationship with the Slovaks was nevertheless special, in some respects even more ignorant. After all, this was a relationship with a younger brother who would one day grow up. The younger brother is always only of peripheral interest to us, even though we basically like him, because he bores us: we are going to dancing lessons, into the EU, and he is only beginning to smoke and to build basic institutions.

4. In the twenty years leading up to November 1989, the Czechs and the Slovaks lived in an entirely different social, political, and cultural climate. The Czechs stormed the heavens of communism immediately after the war, then again at the end of the 1960s, and yet again in a quite sunken fashion in the era of normalization. The Slovaks were always considerably cooler toward these ideological hallucinations and furies. In the seventies and the eighties, it was as if things had turned around. The Czechs waged a destructive cold civil war, while the Slovaks themselves pragmatically took advantage of normalization without great scruples. The Slovaks, who were initially less enamored of socialism, experienced the normalization years favorably (in Slovakia, the process of modernization had yet to be completed), while the Czechs lived through the same period as the most repulsive of times. After November 1989, the Czechs imagined that they were reawakening into freedom as right wingers, which to an extent was the case, while the Slovaks were concurrently the most receptive to socialism. This would give rise to a host of misconceptions and misunderstandings.

Bear in mind that 80 percent of the Czechs, not the Slovaks, voted for socialism in 1946. The Slovaks eventually grew used to it, since the Czechs wouldn't have it any other way. In 1989, when the ideologically zealous Czechs started to build genuine capitalism, the ideologically cooler and more conservative Slovaks were not too keen on abandoning socialism. The era of normalization had put a greater distance between us than we had suspected: after November 1989, we hardly knew each other.

Is this a paradoxical story of missed opportunities? It is a story about how the objective differences between our nations had always been there. Unfortunately, when they had diminished the most, both nations did not realize that this was the case. On the contrary, they felt intensely that they did not understand one another. This is a story of how objective reality need not mean anything. Instead, what is decisive is the actual experience and the capacity for empathy, the ability to put oneself in the shoes of another.

From my perspective, these four basic conditions/motives for the Czech and Slovak parting of ways were merely replicated by the media, and the politicians then exploited and abused them (unless their thinking was no different from that of the man on the street). In short, I would not single out for blame either the journalists or the politicians. A distinction needs to be made, however, between politicians and statesmen. Statesmanlike deliberations and responsibility never came to the fore, because there were no statesmen here. Václav Havel did not want to divide the state over which he presided. He learned relatively quickly to think and to act like a statesman, but it was hopelessly too late.

It is my deep conviction that the processes leading toward the dissolution of the state had begun long ago and had long been under way, but these processes were hidden from those who either did not want to or could not see them because they did not want to admit such problems existed. Indifferent toward the cohabitation of the Czechs and the Slovaks, they did not want to acknowledge the disagreements. By this, I do not mean that they wished to divide the state. On the contrary; they wanted the state to endure and remain unchanged: Czechoslovakia as the Czech lands writ large.

While it may have been possible to anticipate such developments, what was evidently lacking was a sense of responsibility. In 1977, I wrote a book, *Osmašedesátý (Sixty-Eight),** and devoted an entire quarter of it to Czech–Slovak relations. Many of the passages could not be understood as anything else but a warning against the most serious problems that awaited us. In fact, the likelihood of the division of the state is implicit in my book as one that threatened to become a self-fulfilling prophecy unless we acknowledged it as a real possibility.

From my perspective, no genuinely new phenomenon in Czech–Slovak relations appeared after 1989. Today there is nothing that we could identify as the decisive moment in the process of division, whether it has to do with the responsibility of the media or of the politicians. What is generally involved are the same old sins. Real socialism and our adaptation to it had equipped us—although the Czechs quite differently than the Slovaks—with new forms of selfishness. And the latter in relation to the old sins gave us something new after all: a new form of blindness.

Perhaps only one post-November 1989 error was fundamental, even though quite unprecedented: the two-year deadline for the drafting of a new constitution was clearly irresponsible, from whatever point of view. This deadline, however, was rooted in the choice of the two-year term for the first elected post-1989 parliament, whose task it was to draft the constitution. That choice, in turn, had nothing whatsoever to do with either Czech–Slovak relations or the constitution. Rather, Václav Havel's initial hesitation to assume the presidency and his insistence that nothing longer than a two-year presidential (and therefore parliamentary) term was acceptable determined the short duration of the first parliamentary term. I was against it, but I did not protest vehemently enough. I regret it to this

---

* Originally published in *samizdat* and abroad under the pseudonym J. Sládeček, *Osmašedesátý* was published in Prague in 1990 (Rozmluvy).

day. The goal of drafting a new constitution within two years meant that once we were midway through the term, we started feeling very nervous, for we knew we were already running out of time. That the two-year term was born accidentally and that we linked the continued existence of the state to it testified to the short-comings of our legal and constitutional culture, which enabled Civic Forum to accept these stipulations so light-heartedly.

In the final analysis, the state fell apart, above all, because neither the Czechs nor the Slovaks showed at any time enough will to create a common political na-tion. As Czechs and as Slovaks, we helped each other, harmed each other, ex-plained ourselves, and reproached each other, while we attempted, for better or for worse, to build a common state. As citizens of this single state, we incurred too many debts. And that is why today we are citizens of neighboring states.

Translated from Czech by Michael Kraus and Allison Stanger

13

A Comment on Čarnogurský and Pithart

Daniel Kroupa

I see these developments very differently. I would like to begin by making some brief comments about the contributions of Jan Čarnogurský and Petr Pithart. In my view, both papers conflate two distinct perspectives. On the one hand, there is an objective sociological perspective, which analyzes social processes only to predict the dissolution of the state. On the other hand, both contributions contain very subjective elements; both authors attempt to deal in some way with the problem of who is to blame for the division. While Čarnogurský strives to shift the blame away from the Slovak side and himself, Pithart in a very democratic fashion attempts to assign blame to both sides in a just manner. That is perhaps the reason why Pithart made an error with the notion of *penězovod* (money pipeline) on the Czech side. The term was introduced by the economist Karel Kříž in response to statements by Vítězslav Moric, a leader of the Slovak National Party, who argued that the milk milked in Slovakia should remain there. In response, economists countered that it was not the Czechs who were ripping off the poor Slovaks but instead that more money flowed into Slovakia from the Czech lands than the other way round. I remind you of this because it is only with the benefit of hindsight that we can see clearly the distorted perceptions held by some political forces—especially in Slovakia—about the nature of the Czechoslovak state.

I prefer to reserve judgement about the sociological perspective, for it is beyond my immediate area of expertise. While clearly a legitimate approach, it cannot explain much about the division of Czechoslovakia. The division, in my view, was a result of the more or less free deliberations of a very narrow group of politicians who attempted to deal with a very specific political situation after the 1992 elections. Those elections took place in a constitutional setting first created in 1969 and inherited directly from the communist regime. In post-1992-elections Czechoslovakia, the constitutional framework made it impossible to establish an effective governing majority in the federal parliament and thereby a government capable of governing and maintaining social order.

From a sociological point of view, what may seem the most mysterious is the behavior of the Czechs. From 1989 to 1992, they defended themselves against all efforts on the Slovak side to divide the federation or to devolve powers in such a way that the federation would disintegrate on its own. For example, during the early 1990 hyphen war in the federal parliament, the Czech side was initially horrified to discover that there were nationalist forces in Slovakia seeking to divide the country. Yet after the June 1992 elections, the Czechs ultimately became the most passionate proponents of the division. In contrast, the Slovaks, who had previously promoted the country's division, were suddenly taken aback, appearing as if they had never wanted the split in the first place. When I say "the Slovaks," I mean those people who in some fashion took an active part in these developments. In reality, the greatest mystery on the Czech side is precisely the ease and the lightness with which the partition was accepted.

There were two kinds of nationalism in Slovakia: one I would call emancipatory, and here I refer to the nationalism of Jan Čarnogurský, who never made any secret of it.[1] He spoke of the need for the Slovak nation to undergo a process of emancipation. In his view, part of this process involved the creation of an independent national state, and in all likelihood, this emancipation would later result in a subsequent movement toward reintegration. Even before the fall of communism, Čarnogurský gave an interview to the underground bulletin of *Hnutí za občanskou svobodu* (Movement for Civic Freedom), in which he was incredibly open, given the communist setting, about declaring his political goals.[2] Clearly, in the dissident environment, at least as far as some dissidents were concerned, Čarnogurský's views did not represent anything surprising or novel. What was surprising, however, was how quickly the effort to stir up nationalist feelings in Slovakia succeeded.

I have yet to see a compelling explanation of why these two types of nationalism—the emancipatory nationalism of Čarnogurský, which was nonconfrontational, and the nationalism of the Slovak National Party, which was confrontational vis-à-vis the Hungarians and the Czechs—acquired such great political influence, despite the fact that every sociological survey suggested that they were the preference only of marginalized social groups. My personal hypothesis is that nonnationalist forces had already attempted at the beginning of 1990 to take the wind out of the nationalists' sails. For example, the election program of the Public Against Violence fits this pattern. They chose the wrong political tactic, coopting the nationalist agenda as one of the pillars of their program so as to take away votes from the nationalists instead of taking a firm stand against them. In my view, this was a misguided political tactic, for it only enhanced the initially negligible appeal of nationalist groupings. Something similar would have happened in the Czech Republic, for example, if Czech political parties had attempted to co-opt the anti-Romany rhetoric of the Republican Party so as to win the votes of their supporters. This would undoubtedly have only exacerbated the Romany problem in the Czech Republic.

All of the nationalist forces that continue to play a role in Slovakia today have not yet, in my view, been clearly identified. For example, take the role of the Canadian Slovaks. I remind you that many of these individuals were shaped by the environment of the wartime pro-Nazi Slovak state. Because the documents concerning their wartime behavior wound up in KGB hands, these individuals could subsequently be manipulated by the Soviet intelligence apparatus. I do not wish to overestimate the influence of these factors and circumstances, but I am deeply convinced that they played some kind of a role and that, at the very least, they should be explored.

Another element worth examining in the rapid rise of Slovak nationalism in early 1990 is the source of funding for some nationalist newspapers and journals as well as nationalist parties. I would like to remind you that some of these parties openly declared their warm relations with certain Sudeten German organizations. Examining the content of some key Slovak journals and newspapers, such as *Zmena*, would also be revealing. Unlike most Czechs, who did not read Slovak newspapers and journals and who were not interested in developments in Slovakia, I paid a great deal of attention to the Slovak press, and I was taken aback by the radical expressions of nationalism there. It is my impression that there were certain social groups that were particularly active in fomenting nationalist sentiment.

I mention these aspects of the situation despite my opening statement that the division of the state was largely a freely taken decision seeking to resolve a specific political situation after the elections. While I am arguing that there were specific social factors that shaped the political situation, I must emphatically reject the notion that it was the different characteristics of the Czech and Slovak nations that led to the dissolution of Czechoslovakia. I dare say that within the Czech Republic there are far greater differences between some of its constituent parts than those that exist between the Czech and Slovak republics. What I have in mind are the differences, for example, between Southern Bohemia and Northern Moravia, which are great, even though they are both Czech regions. In my view, we should not overstate the influence of Czech and Slovak social differences on the division of the state, which was first and foremost a *political* act.

In contrast, I believe that what facilitated the division of the state was Czechoslovakia's constitutional framework, which emerged in 1969 from the ideology of 1968. The latter found expression in the preamble to the 1969 constitutional law on the federation, which stated that the nationality question could only be resolved in a system of democratic socialism. With a reference to this principle, a new, federal, constitution was born, one that contained elements that in all likelihood would have led to the dissolution of states more ethnically homogeneous than was Czechoslovakia. A number of Western constitutional experts who advised our parliamentary constitutional commission (of which I was a member) pointed this out in 1990. They noted that the presumed federation in our country

actually contained confederal elements, which under certain political constella-
tions could lead to the breakup of the state. For a parliament that abides by the
minority veto, different election results in each republic mean that one cannot create a parliamentary majority at the federal level that would support a cabinet. In
such a context, policymakers face a choice: between an escalating crisis that
might lead to anarchy at the federal level—in which unconstitutional actions at
the level of the republican parliaments would have to be tolerated (in fact, those
parliaments may have no choice but to behave unconstitutionally in such a situation)—and attempting to find a procedure for dividing the state so as to allow for
the preservation of minimum social order in both republics. Contending with this
stark choice explains the rapid change of positions on the part of the political
elite, who prior to the 1992 elections had battled for the preservation of the federation but after those same elections opted for the fastest and most effective
strategy for dissolving the state.

At the same time, I do not mean to suggest that the differences between the
Czechs and the Slovaks were insignificant. Needless to say, such differences
made themselves felt in the divergent results of the elections in the two republics.
But such results could have brought on the dissolution of the state only under certain concrete and specific circumstances. It is my thesis that they could not have
brought on the dissolution of the state without the federal constitution's minority
veto. Those states who have constitutional systems free of confederal elements
(the minority veto being an example of such) are far more stable. Our federal parliament, as it functioned with the minority veto, promoted Slovakia's nationalist
forces, because it gave a disproportionately large influence to miniature political
parties that would have been quite insignificant in a normal parliament. Given the
existence of minority veto power, many laws could be passed only with the support of such small parties. These circumstances caused some political parties in
the federal parliament to propose a constitution devoid of the minority veto.

From a practical point of view, opinions varied on how to effect the dissolution. The Slovak National Council chose not to wait for the outcome of the search
for constitutional solutions at the federal level. Instead, it adopted a declaration
of sovereignty, thereby placing the Czech side in a situation where it had to respond in some fashion. One possible solution was for the Czech and Slovak national councils to agree on procedures for dissolving the state and then to ratify
this agreement in a constitutional manner in the federal parliament. This is the solution that was eventually accepted.

In my opinion, there was another solution, which even though it was not anticipated by the federal constitution, was not in conflict with it. For lack of better
words, I call it an extraconstitutional solution. With this approach, the remaining
political representatives at the federal level would have declared the Slovak National Council's unilateral secession to be a violation of the federal constitution,
thereby upholding legal continuity. This would have meant the preservation of the
Chamber of the People and the dissolution of the Chamber of the Nations of the

federal parliament. The Chamber of the People would have continued to function, passing laws necessary for further development. By means of this procedure, however, the division of Czechoslovakia, effected by the Slovak side, would have been rendered illegitimate, and all elements of state continuity would have belonged to the Czech side. This idea, perhaps a bit too fantastic from today's perspective, would have had the benefit of leaving open the possibility for political forces in Slovakia one day to resuscitate a federal Czechoslovakia. In the event of a change in the political situation in Slovakia, such forces could have retroactively declared the unconstitutionality of the Czechoslovak dissolution, thereby renewing their allegiance to the Czechoslovak federation. The division of Czechoslovakia by mutual agreement made the breakup definitive, however, and since then, developments in both republics have proceeded in different directions. In my view, this is not a function of different mentalities or cultures but of differences in the victorious political forces.

In conclusion, I would like to reiterate my main point: the differences between the Czechs and the Slovaks are far smaller than allowed by the proponents of the theory that Czechoslovakia broke up because of these differences. Such disparities did not prevent the existence of a common state, and such differences are often far greater within each individual republic than between them. In my view, the main cause of the dissolution was the inherited constitutional framework, which narrowed considerably the range of options after the 1992 elections.

Translated from Czech by Michael Kraus and Allison Stanger

NOTES

1. I do not use the word *nationalist* in a pejorative sense but in a technical sense, i.e., any attempt to legitimize political behavior through reference to national ideas or the need for national emancipation.

2. For a text of the March 1989 interview, see *Hnutí za občanskou svobodu, 1988-89: dokumenty* (Praha: Ústav pro soudobé dějiny, AV ČR, 1994), pp. 98–105. Editors' note: *Hnutí za občanskou svobodu* was a dissident movement in the communist era headed by Rudolf Battěk. Kroupa was a participant in this movement.

14

Fragments from the Dividing of Czechoslovakia

Miroslav Macek

INTRODUCTION

I do not deny that I have always been among the active proponents of and actors in the dissolution of Czechoslovakia. I had and still have many reasons for this, but I have always considered two of them fundamental.

The first is the general history of Bohemia and Moravia, and Slovakia. Here one can focus on distant history, which contained very little in common for Bohemia and Moravia on the one hand and Slovakia on the other. During this period, the future constituent parts of the federation lived very different economic, political, legal, sociocultural, and intellectual lives, which were to determine future opinions, moods, and actions. One can also refer to more recent common history, which fulfilled neither federative nor unifying aspirations but for a short time only connected the unconnectable.

The second reason for my political stance was the nonsensical but constitutionally determined point of departure: the two-member federation. This federation was by its very nature dysfunctional and unstable. Lacking external or internal cohesive force, it proved incapable of further existence.

THE HYPHEN WAR IN THE FEDERAL ASSEMBLY

As in other instances, the man who stood at the apparent beginning of this hyphen war was Zdeněk Jičínský, who blocked approval of a simple deletion of the word *socialist* from the name of the republic in the then–Federal Assembly through classic delaying tactics of parliamentary procedure. The hyphen war sparked one of the most tragicomic conflicts in this institution.

I recall vividly the incredible transformation of some Slovak deputies, who had acted rationally and matter-of-factly up to that point but suddenly were turned into fanatical and intolerable nationalists. One example stands out above all others: Dr. Pavol Balgavý from Senice, who was transformed in a second from a soft-spoken intellectual into a passionate fanatic.

Disagreement about the name of the state was, understandably, a mere pretext to pursue more fundamental demands, which if they had been accepted, would soon have inexorably led toward a confrontational and chaotic breakup of the state.

These continuing and escalating demands were perfectly captured in a tongue-in-cheek text of the representatives of Civic Forum from Southern Bohemia, which they presented at a meeting of Civic Forum in Olomouc on 9 December 1990. I have taken the liberty of quoting from the text at length:

The Historical Demands of Southern Czechs

1. We demand that those carps raised in Southern Bohemia* must also be consumed there.
2. We demand that the energy networks that go through Southern Bohemia should be exclusively under our control.
3. Since we have traditionally had the highest rate of savings in our region, we are justified in demanding the creation of our own department of the treasury.
4. In the event that the Federal Assembly and the Czech National Council do not accept our demands, we will declare the supremacy of local regulations over republic and federal laws.
5. From the above, it follows that the optimal solution in this situation is the creation of an independent Federation of Bohemia-South.
6. We are willing to negotiate the aforementioned demands with you without a single change in the text in the neutral village of Sudomerice u Tabora—the border of the Central Bohemian and Southern Bohemian region.
7. If you want to show goodwill toward the preservation of Czech unity, you can get in touch with our Ministry of Exclusively Internal Relations in Geneva, Switzerland.
8. By this declaration, we have shown our goodwill. Now it is your turn.

I have nothing to add.

KLAUS'S MISSION TO SLOVAKIA: SPRING 1992

This concerned a spring 1992 visit to Košice, Michalovce, and the Chemko Stražské enterprise. It was an exploratory foray, whose task it was to map the mood in Eastern Slovakia, known for its less than cordial attitudes toward nationalism, on the one hand, and the policies of Vladimír Mečiar, on the other. On location, we wanted to assess the influence of various political parties.

---

* Southern Bohemia is a region traditionally associated with carp and trout raising.

The small helicopter, which took us from Bratislava to Košice, flew low over the landscape, and the visit to Chemko Strážské provided tangible evidence for something of which I had already been convinced.

We flew over a landscape in which a majority of the industrial enterprises and state buildings, as well as public housing, were built after 1945, even after 1948. This rapid development occurred in a region that had never experienced a comparable pace of development or the same degree of political repression as the Czech lands, but where friendship or family ties were decisive.

The village in the vicinity of Michalovce—a region that prior to the war was the poorest of them all—from which the largest numbers had emigrated across the ocean, was full of split-level family houses, garages, and goods from Tuzex shops.* The heart of Chemko Strážské belonged to a chemical unit, which the Red Army had seized in postwar Germany and imported to the USSR. In the early 1950s, they presented it to the town as a newly built factory. The vicinity of Chemko was so soaked with phenol that to clean up the subsurface water would have cost billions. Infrastructure and services in this region lagged very much behind those of the developed world.

Put yourself in the shoes of the politician who has to explain to the local people that for forty years they had lived on credit and had been subsidized by other parts of the country. Imagine telling them that this development had blinded them, so that they had neglected all those things that their eyes did not see as pressing concerns. Imagine telling them that a wise proprietor would not have managed his property in this fashion, that a part of what they had spent on construction, food, drink, and living in general might have been better invested in the modernization of the enterprise, the protection of the ground water supply, the construction of communication networks, and so on.

Now realize that this same politician would have to say all of the above, knowing full well that his antagonist is a demagogue, one who will merely step in front of the voters and declare: If you elect me, you will live just as well and perhaps better than you have up until now. Our politician might attempt to stand up to the demagogue, but surely he could not succeed. Regrettably, there were no such politicians to seriously attempt this in Slovakia.

Ján Čarnogurský and his Christian Democratic Movement constantly vacillated between nationalist and federalist postures, attempting to collect points on both sides, and eventually lost with both. The Public Against Violence was an amalgam perpetually seeking to define itself and never succeeding.

Attending the latter's republic-level congress in Poprad as a representative of the Civic Democratic Party (ODS), I wrote a short piece entitled "Kočkopes" (The Cat-Dog), which was published in the Czech and Slovak press. The word itself became a political label used to this day. I think that the text of this piece speaks clearly about the situation, and not only inside the Public Against Violence.

---

* Tuzex was the network of state-sponsored hard currency stores under communist rule in the former Czechoslovakia.

THE CAT-DOG

Cat-Dog is precisely the word that came to my mind when I reflected on the half-baked deliberations during the convention of the Public Against Violence. The final result only confirmed my intermediate impressions. Everything followed quite smoothly: it all fell into place quite nicely. Strong applause and shows of support for the representatives of the Civic Democratic Party and the Civic Democratic Alliance equaled the applause and shows of support for the representatives of Civic Forum. The presentation of the members of the Social Democracy Club of the Public Against Violence was immediately followed by words from someone from the rightist Liberal Conservative Party. There was endless debate on whether the old members of the Communist Party should be prohibited from holding positions in the Public Against Violence. And there was action: the election of Marián Čalfa as deputy chair; the changing of the party name while at the same time keeping the old name; a clear expression of support for the common federative state, followed by the declaration of extension of the coalition with the Christian Democratic Party. Ultimately, a new chair (Martin Porubjak) was elected, and a lot of old names resurfaced in the new presidium, including the sworn supporter of all movements, Fedor Gál.

It is my impression that this cake, baked by a cat and a dog, will not appeal to the voters' palate.*

It did not.

THE FIRST NEGOTIATIONS WITH THE MOVEMENT FOR DEMOCRATIC SLOVAKIA (HZDS) IN BRNO, 8–9 JUNE 1992

The first postelection negotiations between ODS and HZDS took place at a beautiful round table designed by Ludwig Mies Van der Rohe for the villa of the Tugendhat family. An incident that took place before the formal negotiations had a major impact on the discussions that followed. This incident led relatively quickly and inexorably toward the division of the state. At the request of Václav Klaus, a meeting of the "chiefs" took place in another room before the commencement of the actual negotiations, presumably so that they could feel each other out and agree on a basic agenda. Instead of the projected five to ten minutes, their meeting lasted longer. While waiting, I wanted to break the ice with the other side, so I asked Michal Kováč, whom I knew very well from the federal parliament, what they were bringing to the table. Michal Kováč beamed, took a stack of papers out of his briefcase, and proceeded to explain sincerely and with enthusiasm that they had dusted off the 1968 notion of an economic and defense union.

---

* This reference to a cake baked by a cat and dog alludes to a well known Czech book for children, *Povídání o pejskovi a kočičce*, written by Josef Čapek. In the story, a cat and a dog bake a cake out of all of their favorite foods. It appeals to no one.

Several additional questions were sufficient for me to see clearly that this notion, which I subsequently referred to on television as "Slovak independence with Czech insurance," could not and must not be accepted by the Czech side.

After the return of Klaus and Mečiar, Klaus took the floor and proceeded to introduce in general terms the next steps in the negotiations, which were to lead to a mutually acceptable form of federation. After several minutes, I interrupted Klaus, letting him know that while we had waited, we had actually traveled a lot further. I repeated the basic theses of the economic and defense union as they had been enthusiastically presented to us by Kováč just a short while ago: two governments with a very thin federal shell, a common currency with two treasuries, two independent armies supervised by a joint defense committee, two coordinated foreign policies, and so on.

While speaking, I was looking directly at Vladimír Mečiar, so I could see how he turned pale, then ashen, apparently crumbling on the inside. In just several minutes of conversation, Kováč had divulged his side's ultimate goals. This was something that Mečiar had wanted to reveal only gradually, over the course of the negotiations in the weeks to come. During such Mečiar-style negotiations, yesterday's concession is presented as today's starting point, whereupon further concessions are demanded.

The battle was over before it had begun. It was time to haggle and to sign a peace treaty.

A document had by then reached me of the text of an agreement on a common defense between the Czech and Slovak republics. And even though the Slovak side has never admitted its authenticity, it did not depart in the least from what Michal Kováč had revealed to us at the beginning of the negotiations.

Here for illustration are several articles from the treaty on a common economic and defense union.

Article 6. The parties to the agreement create an open common military-political defense union, whose role is to secure the common defense of both parties to the agreement. Its scope of activity is based on a common defense doctrine.

Article 8. The parties to the agreement create the Council of Common Defense, with representation from each party, which will negotiate all questions concerning the implementation of this agreement. The Council will be organized in such a way that it will be able to assemble swiftly. The Council will create the administrative bodies it deems necessary. Above all, it will immediately appoint the Defense Committee.

Article 9. The Defense Committee will develop a strategic concept of joint deployment of the Armed Forces of the parties to this agreement: it presents to the Council of Common Defense its recommendations for the development and training of the Armed Forces; it coordinates the standardization of weaponry and weapons systems, the preparation of command and special units, and on the basis of the approval of the Council of Common Defense, it implements the supervision of the training of the designated forces. It recommends to the Council of the Common Defense additional measures necessary for the implementation of this agreement.

Article 10. To secure territorial integrity, political independence, and security in the event of threats, the parties to this agreement will designate common armed forces with the necessary command units. The Council of Common Defense will establish the size and structure of the designated units and will authorize their deployment. The joint forces are under a command, which in a given territory of the parties to this agreement directs military operations. The expenditures relating to the activity of the Council of Common Defense, its Defense Committee, and other joint bodies created for the implementation of this agreement will be shared equally by the parties to this agreement.

It was symptomatic of the situation that, compared to negotiations with Mečiar and the Movement for Democratic Slovakia, dealing with colleagues in the parliamentary club of the ODS in the Federal Assembly seemed much more complex and difficult. The ODS parliament deputies did not trust Mečiar and his people in the least. They lived in constant fear that after the federation had begun to unravel, Mečiar would cease to negotiate and be satisfied with his accomplishments. They also had limited trust that Václav Klaus, faced with the prospect of a dysfunctional federation, would refuse to accept it. Fortunately, they were wrong on both counts.

CONCLUSION

I am glad that the developments after 31 December 1992 vindicated the proponents of Czechoslovakia's division and their arguments for it. The speed with which both republics of the former Czech and Slovak Federative Republic proceeded to separate politically, economically, and socioculturally is only further proof of the weakness of the bonds that had connected them in the short history of twenty interwar and forty-seven postwar years of the common state's existence.

Translated from Czech by Michael Kraus and Allison Stanger

15

Domestic and International Aspects of the Czechoslovak State's Crisis and End

Milan Zemko

All reflections about the historical second demise of the Czechoslovak state are reminiscent of postmortem meditations of surviving relatives. What was he like? Why did he die? Why did he die when he did? None of the survivors, however, are likely to consider seriously the possibility of resurrection. The deceased is only a subject of emotional remembrances; his life story, including possibly his end, might perhaps be a source of some lesson for the future or an inspiration for some of the surviving relations. And so it is with the second demise of Czechoslovakia, in contrast to the first demise in 1939.

Today's deliberations concern something that is impossible to revive, in contrast to the World War II years, when no one except hopelessly compromised collaborators regarded the protectorate and the Slovak state as a permanent state formation. These attitudes were not only a function of the uncertain wartime conditions. More important, above all for the Czechs, was that the wartime end of Czechoslovakia be rightly identified with the loss of freedom. For the Czechs and for freedom-loving Slovaks, this meant that the new quest for the return of freedom was unthinkable without the renewal of Czechoslovakia. Here we see the principal difference in the consequences of the two demises of the same state.

Instead of a common Czechoslovak state, two independent states of two free nations exist today, each responsible for its own well-being. And what is no less important, both nations and their political elites no longer feel the need for the existence of a common state as a fundamental premise of a secure future, as was the case at the time of the founding of the Czechoslovak state in 1918, as well as during the struggle for its renewal after World War II.

Let us recall, first of all, the fundamentally different international circumstances in the case of the first and the second demise of the Czech and Slovak common state. The international situation at the end of the 1930s made it possible for the *Diktat* of the totalitarian great powers, with the assistance of several smaller authoritarian regimes, to triumph over the "island of democracy" in East–Central Europe. At the beginning of the 1990s, that very same part of Europe was liberated from another—this time communist—dictatorship, which had bound the East European states and nations, both internally and internationally. At a stroke, relatively small states could make decisions about their internal social order and international orientation without the intervention of one of the great powers. Just as freedom was being born, however, all the multiethnic states of postcommunist Europe found themselves in the midst of a complex of interethnic problems. In the circumstances of a collapsing old regime, the citizens and especially the political elites of the Baltic republics and the Yugoslav republics had to decide under what type of state-administrative arrangements they would cohabit with other nations, and what to do if they could not find a mutually satisfactory arrangement in a common state or in several separate states.

THE RISE OF UNACKNOWLEDGED NATIONALISM

In related fashion, Czechoslovakia's two nations and its ethnic minorities found themselves suddenly and unexpectedly caught in a revival of particular national interests, accompanied by nationalist emotions. Czech politicians and journalists especially did not like to admit to such. On the contrary, they emphasized Czech Western rationality, which supposedly informed Czech steps even in the search for new solutions to the constitutional crisis. In my view, all deliberations concerning the new administrative arrangements after November 1989—from the first conflict, which involved new state symbols, including the new name for the common state, all the way to the final deliberations, in which the victors of the 1992 parliamentary elections agreed to divide and end the Czechoslovak federation—show that both parties to the conflict approached the problem from a nationalist perspective, even though both refused to see it as such.

The absence of any recognition of one's own nationalist orientation led to our most difficult obstacle: the lack of empathy for the other. This precluded the participating parties from grasping in depth the attitudes and reasoning of the other side and from attempting to define possible common interests. Our lack of empathy also made it impossible to gauge when and how to make concessions so that a compromise might be reached. That is why whatever tenuous compromises were reached, they never encouraged the feeling of a shared future; they tended to leave bitter feelings and a sense of continuing injustice. Feelings of deepening disharmony would then lead both partners to a new confrontation.

With the benefit of hindsight, I have come to conclude that the political deliberations concerning the new name of the state in the spring of 1990 and the results of the parliamentary elections of June 1990 foreshadowed the subsequent stance and approach of the political actors, as well as the reactions of the mass media and public. The first conflict over the name of the state already conveyed a certain lack of political experience on the part of President Havel, who attempted to launch an initiative without first vetting the matter with the key political players. This conflict also conveyed the limited sensitivity on the part of the Czech political representatives and wider public to the Slovak attitudes on this question. In addition, it showed an equally limited Slovak understanding of the significance of tradition, including the attachment of Czech society to the official name of the interwar Czechoslovak Republic.

The apparently spontaneous proposal of President Havel on 23 January 1990 to renew the original name of the common but unitary state, the Czechoslovak Republic (*Československá republika*), was countered by a proposal from the Slovak National Council on 1 March 1990 for a brand new name, the Czecho-Slovak Federation (*Federácia Česko-Slovensko*). On 6 March 1990, the Czech National Council rejected the latter idea and endorsed the president's vision. Not only did the name with the hyphen remind the Czechs of the post-Munich republic, it also signaled something for which Czech society was unprepared—namely, that the Slovaks in the new political circumstances also expected to place the Czech–Slovak relationship on a new basis.[1] Only after a sharp exchange, in which the Czech side deployed philological arguments, did the president offer a compromise: the Czecho-Slovak Republic (*Republika Česko-Slovenska*). After considering the president's proposal in mid-March, Czech deputies in the federal assembly rejected it. On 29 March 1990, on the crest of the first big wave of erupting Czech–Slovak nationalism, the Federal Assembly finally accepted a compromise solution—the Czech and Slovak Federative Republic (*Česká a Slovenská Federatívna Republika*). It belonged to the doubtful category of hollow compromises. The new awkward name satisfied no one, and its provisional nature signaled the provisional nature of the state so named. On 30 March 1990, a joint declaration of the government of the Slovak republic and the presidium of the Slovak National Council criticized the federal assembly for its failure to adopt the name Czecho-Slovak Federation.[2]

While the battle over the state's name raged, and the Czech media pronounced the debate to be over "minutia," there were other voices heard in the international arena signaling the movement of Lithuania and Estonia toward independence. After many years, the freely elected representatives of two small nations actualized their political will, despite the wishes of the great powers. The Lithuanian parliament declared independence on 11 March 1990, and the next day, the Estonian congress declared the supremacy of Estonian laws over those of the Soviet Union, as well as condemning as illegal the Soviet annexation of Estonia in

1940.[3] Similar political tendencies simultaneously made themselves felt in Yugoslavia. In July 1990, the Slovenian parliament passed a declaration of Slovenian sovereignty.[4] This development led to a search for confederative arrangements within the multinational state, which failed with the disintegration of Yugoslavia the following year.

CZECH POWER PLAYS

In Czechoslovakia, political elites and the wider public viewed the new division of powers between the federation and the republics of December 1990 as a temporary solution; the definitive resolution was to be found only in new republic and federal constitutions. But even before the acceptance of the competency law, a new conflict had erupted over differing Czech and Slovak perspectives on the role of federal and republic organs. Even Czech politicians admitted that the Husák normalization following the events of 1968 had reduced the powers of the republics in favor of the federation, deforming therefore the original federal arrangements. Despite this fact, during the negotiations on the restoration of powers to the republics, the Slovak side could not rid itself of the feeling that the Czech politicians and public regarded this particular legacy of Husák's normalization as the least problematic of all communism's legacies. Following the August 1990 negotiations in Trenčianské Teplice, for example, several commentators in Czech papers warned against "significant movement toward the division of the country" and against the growing "separatist tendencies of some members of the Slovak political elite."[5] Petr Pithart, then the prime minister of the Czech government, noting the dissatisfaction on the part of the Czech public with the preparations to devolve powers to the republics, singled out the media coverage of these same events as "not the best work of our journalists in this area."[6] So on the merry-go-round of politics, on the Czech and above all on the federal side, there was an effort to retain federal powers, and on the Slovak side, an attempt to return powers to the republic level. Throughout the negotiations on the distribution of powers, the power play of the federal and Czech representatives against the Slovak political representatives was in evidence. I myself was a witness to this phenomenon.

In the fall of 1990, when the working commissions dealing with the distribution of powers were wrapping up their activities and the surrounding polemics had reached a new height, Marian Čalfa, the premier of the federal government, gave a speech on Czechoslovak television. He presented an inventory of the minimal powers that the federal government required to function effectively, but the scope of such powers would have left the republics with only secondary powers and roles.[7] The Slovak premier, Vladimír Mečiar, responded in mid-November with a threat that in such circumstances, the Slovak side would not coordinate its work on the new constitution with the federal and Czech governments.[8] And when some committees of the Federal Assembly proposed to amend the previously agreed upon draft law on the federation, Mečiar warned in early December that the Slovaks might insist on a state treaty (*statní smlouva*) with the Czechs.[9] Immediately prior to the parliamentary vote on the federation law, President Havel warned against legal chaos and the adoption of unconstitutional measures.[10] On 12 December 1990, after a stormy debate, the parliament approved the new law, arriving at practically the last significant compromise on constitutional matters. Characteristically, Prague viewed this law as having gone too far, while Bratislava believed that the same law did not go far enough in giving the republics their due.[11]

In connection with this process, another significant factor that would play a major role in the quest for new constitutions made its first appearance. This was the phenomenon of the so-called federal Slovaks or Prague Slovaks—i.e., politicians and highly placed state officials of Slovak origin working in the federal government. Many had spent most of their lives in Prague. They were connected with the Czech environment not only through their work but also through their family ties. They supported a federation with a strong Prague center, in which they had influence and position, as the optimal constitutional form. Perhaps the most typical representative of this group of Slovak politicians in Prague after November 1989 was the 1990–92 premier of the federal government, Marián Čalfa. A graduate of Prague's Charles University, Čalfa's entire career was wedded to the central state organs in Prague, in both communist and postcommunist regimes and all the way up to the elections of 1992, when his political party (ODU) failed to obtain enough votes to win seats in parliament.

THE SEARCH FOR ALTERNATIVES

The deliberations (as well as the media commentaries on those deliberations) made it clear that neither the federal nor the Czech republic-level politicians saw any compelling reason for a fundamental change in the distribution of powers between the federation and the republics. During the September 1991 negotiations between the Czech and Slovak national councils (I was at the time a member of the presidium of the latter), Dagmar Burešová, chair of the Czech National Council, pointed out that in the Czech lands there was no equivalent sense of a need to attain Czech statehood, as there was on the Slovak side.[12] The negotiating posture of the Czech political representatives implied that they would be quite content if their republic occupied the same constitutional place as the *länder* in Germany or Austria. I myself encountered these attitudes at all joint sessions of the leadership of the Czech and Slovak national councils. Along the same lines, František Mikloško, the chair of the Slovak National Council, reported to us that in the informal discussions with Moravian ČSL-KDU deputies from the Czech Republic, in which I took part, they had repeatedly proposed a transformation of the

Czechoslovak federation into federal arrangements on the German model. In this fashion, the Moravian deputies wanted to strengthen the constitutional position of Moravia and Silesia, while Slovakia would, if it wished, be granted special status, somewhat akin to Bavaria's place in Germany. Such proposals, however, never went beyond informal consideration, and Slovak participants rejected them as unrealistic.

In contrast to Czechoslovakia, the German länder were and are states within one linguistic–cultural commonwealth, in which the acceptance of a higher level of subsidiarity fully satisfies the regions that comprise the länder. Slovak political representation at the republic level took the view that both Slovakia and the Czech Republic comprised separate nations, and hence should have a different constitutional position than do, for example the Hessians in Germany or the Korutans in Austria. This view was shared by a large segment of Slovak society. These contrasting perspectives on Czech–Slovak relations were a feature of all the deliberations during 1991 and 1992.

From the very first gathering of the federal and republic-level representatives at the invitation of President Havel on 4 February 1991, two important processes accompanied the deliberations that were to lead to the new republic and federal constitutions. First, the country's economic transformation had a different impact on the Czech and Slovak economies. Second, different political opinions crystallized within the two hegemonic movements of the Velvet Revolution, Civic Forum in the Czech lands and the Public Against Violence in Slovakia. With respect to the first process, the economic transformation resulted in rates of unemployment three times higher in Slovakia than in the Czech lands. This unemployment was accompanied by a growing distrust of the federal government's economic reforms on the part of the Slovak public. With respect to the second, after the fragmentation of Civic Forum and the Public Against Violence, the most fervent supporters of the federation became members of the politically weaker and less influential political offspring of these two movements. In public opinion surveys in Slovakia, after the departure of Mečiar and his supporters in April 1991, support for the Public Against Violence dropped to less than 5 percent, and never improved. In the Czech lands, Civic Movement (OH), one of the successors of Civic Forum, was in a similarly weak position, as the elections of June 1992 would show. In Slovakia, support for the Christian Democratic Movement (KDH) was also waning. The representatives of the foregoing political groupings of declining popularity, however, continued to play the decisive role in the deliberations on constitutional matters.

At the February 1991 opening meeting, Ján Čarnogurský, the chair of KDH, raised the subject of a state treaty between the Czech and Slovak republics for the first time. He thought it was essential to adopt new republic-level constitutions first and then to agree on a treaty between the two republics defining the future of the common state. Representatives of Civic Forum rejected this approach at the same meeting.[13] The content of the state treaty, the related procedural question as to how and when new republic and federal constitutions were to be ratified, as well as the substantive question of the division of powers became central and key themes of the subsequent formal and informal negotiations on the future shape of the common state.

These negotiations took place against an international backdrop of deepening crisis in the other multinational postcommunist states. Related and equally lively discussions on similar themes were also taking place in established democracies, such as Belgium and Canada, and in the much younger Spanish democracy. The struggle for independence by the Baltic republics in the USSR and by the non-Serbian republics in Yugoslavia had a dual impact on Slovak society. Armed interventions by Moscow and Belgrade against secessionist republics evoked great concern about a similar confrontation in Czechoslovakia. At the same time, the resolve of small nations, numerically even smaller than the Slovaks, to obtain independence despite the sacrifices and risks involved inspired a small segment of the Slovak population and its political representatives.

But with the deepening Czech–Slovak conflict, that portion of the electorate that on principle rejected the notion of Czech and Slovak independence dwindled. According to public opinion surveys, support for the division of the federation became predominant only after the June 1992 elections and after the unsuccessful negotiations between the election's victors. In November 1992, when the division of the common state was being planned, according to the Prague-based IVVM, 50 percent of respondents in the Czech Republic and 40 percent of respondents in Slovakia agreed with these steps, while 43 percent of respondents in the Czech Republic and 49 percent of those polled in Slovakia were opposed. According to another poll conducted by the Slovak Statistical Office, 47 percent of respondents in Slovakia were for the division and 40 percent were against it.[14]

While in the USSR and Yugoslavia dramatic political changes were occurring and new states were emerging, negotiations in Czechoslovakia, while often sharp, were always peaceful. These negotiations sought to establish a new constitutional foundation for a common Czech–Slovak state. That is also why the emergence of an independent Slovakia and Czech lands, which meant the end of the federation, was not at all straightforward or unambiguous. In the course of twelve months of formal and informal deliberations—whether they were bilateral (comprised of representatives of the two republics) or trilateral (comprised of representatives of the republics and of the federation) in form—all sorts of constitutional alternatives were presented and considered. A broad spectrum of alternatives was considered. At one end, there was (if we exclude the sporadic proposals to renew a unitary state) the image of a "functioning" federation. For the Slovaks, this was very reminiscent of the federations that had existed prior to 1989. In particular, the proposals to abolish the minority veto in the federal parliament evoked the specter of pre-1968 constitutional arrangements. At the other end of the spectrum was the project of a "loose" federation, which in terms of the distribution of powers for the republics, as well as in terms of the proper procedure for its imple-

mentation, appeared to the Czechs as a confederation or some kind of a commonwealth, in which they were not interested. In such a state formation, the
Czechs saw a fundamental discontinuity with the common state founded in 1918,
which they found objectionable. They also did not see how such an entity could
function in practice.

A HOUSE DIVIDED

Czech and Slovak negotiators could rely only in part on public support to guide
them, for surveys of public opinion pointed in contradictory directions. In the fall
of 1991, 39 percent of respondents in the Czech lands and 20 percent of respondents in Slovakia supported a unitary state. Twenty percent of respondents in the
Czech lands and 6 percent of respondents in Slovakia supported "cooperative federalism" on the German model. Confederation had the support of 27 percent of
respondents in Slovakia, but only 4 percent of respondents in the Czech lands.
Fourteen percent of respondents in Slovakia and 5 percent of respondents in the
Czech lands endorsed full independence. Only the existing federation received
relatively high support in both republics: 30 percent in the Czech lands and 26
percent in Slovakia.[15] Public opinion had not changed fundamentally when the
same agency carried out a survey in March 1992, i.e., only a few months prior to
the June elections. In the Czech Republic, support for a federation had gone down
by 4 percent (to 26 percent), while in Slovakia, support for independence had
gone up by 5 percent (to 19 percent).[16] Broadly speaking, the preferences running
in favor of the unitary state and federation in the Czech Republic meant support
for Czech politicians in their efforts to implement a functioning federation, while
significant support for federal and confederal conceptions in Slovakia led Slovak
politicians (with the exception of ODU and DS) to prefer the loosest sort of federation, one with confederal elements.

   While the entire Slovak political elite could not accept constitutional proposals aiming at the status quo ante of November 1989, opinions on optimal alternative arrangements varied dramatically. On these questions, Slovak political leaders were far less united than their Czech counterparts. In fact, during the
deliberations, Slovak perspectives became even more differentiated and divided.
This was in evidence, for example, at the Bratislava gathering of the presidia of
the Slovak and Czech national councils on 5–6 September 1991. Here the representative of the Slovak National Party supported an independent state. Mečiar's
HZDS was in favor of a confederation. Čarnogurský's KDH preferred to ratify a
new Slovak constitution first and then negotiate a state treaty between the two republics. The Public Against Violence was in favor of first concluding the state
treaty, which would then give rise to new republican constitutions. In contrast, the
presidium of the Czech National Council embraced a united platform, whereby
the treaty containing the principles of the federal constitution would be accepted

first. Both national councils would then view the treaty as a legislative initiative, which would be binding for the Federal Assembly and would simultaneously guide the development of republic constitutions. As a legislative initiative the agreement would not have the binding character of a state treaty, as originally proposed by the KDH.[17]

What further complicated the position of the Slovak political representatives was their mandate to secure constitutional changes, while the Czech political representatives, along with the Slovaks in the federal government, de facto defended the status quo in constitutional terms. At the Bratislava negotiations of the presidia of the Czech and Slovak national councils in September 1991, Dagmar Burešová, the chair of the former, emphasized that the common state had existed since 1918. Her Czech colleagues defended the point of view that the foundation of the federation must be, as it had been heretofore, a constitution ratified by the Federal Assembly.[18] After these meetings, Jan Kalvoda, the deputy chair of the Czech National Council, reiterated his view that an agreement to preserve the constitutional continuity of the common state had already been reached; therefore, two sovereign republics would not be permitted to emerge in order to create the new federation.[19] This view—the defense of legal continuity—reaffirmed the existing federation from above via a constitutional law to be passed by the Federal Assembly. It was propounded by the Czech leadership in the presidium of the Czech National Council, in the Czech government, and in the federal government until the very end of all common constitutional negotiations. Petr Pithart's conception of a looser federation as expressed in his concept of the "duplex" (*dvojdomek*) was the one major exception to this rule. But Pithart's conception never found supporters on the Czech side, and it wound up hurting him politically.

In February 1992 in Milovy, under great time pressure, a joint commission of the two national councils agreed on a compromise draft of the state treaty. The Milovy compromise, however, did not find majority support in the presidium of the Slovak National Council. As a member of the presidium at the time, I voted, along with nine other members, against the Milovy draft. I did this because the draft did not make the constitutional positions of the republics as the new constituent elements of the federation sufficiently clear, leaving many of the republic and federal powers for later deliberations. Had it been adopted, this would only have established new sources of constitutional conflict. Therefore, there could be no expectation that such a treaty would win the support of the majority of the Czech and Slovak national councils.[20]

The end of constitutional deliberations was marked by the approaching parliamentary elections and by the fact that the main participants, especially on the Slovak side, were now representatives of parties that had lost the support and respect of the public. This would, in very drastic fashion, be made evident in the June 1992 elections. In Slovakia, KDH suffered great losses, while ODU and DS failed to win any seats in the parliament. In the Czech Republic, OH also failed to obtain a seat in the parliament, while ODA, which had adopted hard-line positions on constitutional questions, failed to meet the threshold for seats in the Federal Assembly, and only narrowly made it into the Czech parliament.

THE TRIUMPH OF THE SECOND-BEST SOLUTION

After the June 1992 elections, the new governing coalitions in the two republics did not bring any new ideas on the form of a future common state to the negotiating table. On the Slovak side, HZDS, supported by SNS, embraced a platform of confederative arrangements with international recognition for both republics, a position they had already signaled during the election campaign. At the second congress of HZDS on 22 March 1992, Vladimír Mečiar offered five constitutional alternatives: (1) federation; (2) confederation; (3) "real union"; (4) an arrangement on the Benelux model; or (5) the creation of two independent states.[21] On the Czech side, ODS and its coalition partners maintained that only a "functional federation" was acceptable, i.e., sufficiently strong federal powers, with the federation as the sole subject of international law. When nobody offered a compromise, the Czech representatives headed by Václav Klaus swiftly ended negotiations on the future form of Czechoslovakia and initiated new negotiations on the peaceful dissolution of the common state. In comparison with the division of other states, it was very successful. Observers of Czechoslovakia's last days have called this the second-best solution for both sides.[22]

That partition was the second-best solution for both sides is probably the reason why neither the Czech nor the Slovak publics protested the division but instead peacefully accepted it. According to surveys of public opinion carried out after the division of the state, a majority of the population would have opposed the partition in a referendum, if there had been one. But the same surveys also indicate that there was no consensus on how this common state was to have been constitutionally organized. A significant segment of Slovak society saw the future common state, which they did not want to see divided, as existing in some other form besides the unitary or federal state, i.e., as a confederation or a union. According to an October 1993 survey of public opinion in Slovakia, for example, 60 percent of respondents opposed the division, while 32 percent wanted an independent state. Twenty-seven percent were for confederation or union, and only 7 percent were in favor of a federation.[23] But these alternative constitutional forms were unacceptable to the Czech public and its political elites. So when the second-best solution appeared, a majority of the population in both republics accepted it, if not with satisfaction, then at least without major protest. With the breakup of Yugoslavia and the Soviet Union, the subsequent dissolution of Czechoslovakia represented the last attempt in Central Europe of this century to have two or more nations coexist in one state.

Translated from Slovak by Michael Kraus and Allison Stanger

NOTES

1. Though the name Czecho-Slovakia was depicted in the Czech media as the "name with the dash," in reality, it contained a hyphen, which is a grammatical sign connecting two words, not dividing them.
2. *Pravda* (Bratislava), 31 March 1990.
3. *Pravda* (Bratislava), 13 March 1990.
4. *Pravda* (Bratislava), 2 July 1990.
5. *Lidové noviny*, 18 August 1990 and 11 August 1990.
6. *Lidové noviny*, 5 September 1990.
7. See L. Kubín et al., *Dva roky politickej slobody* (Bratislava: Nadacia RaPaMaN, 1992), pp. 91–94.
8. *Národná obroda*, 14 November 1990.
9. *Národná obroda*, 8 December 1990.
10. *Národná obroda*, 11 December 1990.
11. This disparity in feeling could not be disguised, even with the gesture of František Mikloško, the chair of the Slovak National Council, who immediately after the passage of the law, treated the deputies and ministers of the Federal Assembly to the traditional Slovak dish, *halušky* (potato dumplings).
12. *Národná obroda*, 6 September 1991.
13. Kubín, *Dva roky politickej slobody*, p. 101. This subject was broached previously by Mečiar, but only tactically, to put negotiating pressure on his Czech counterparts.
14. *Národná obroda*, 21 and 27 November 1992.
15. *Rudé právo*, 22 November 1991.
16. *Národná obroda*, 28 April 1992.
17. Kubín, *Dva roky politickej slobody*, pp. 110–111.
18. *Národná obroda*, 6 September 1991.
19. *Národná obroda*, 7 September 1991.
20. See the various reactions of the parliamentary clubs on 11 and 12 February 1992 to the draft treaty in Kubín, *Dva roky politickej slobody*, pp. 92–95.
21. Kubín, *Dva roky politickej slobody*, p. 44.
22. Michael Kraus, "Returning to Europe, Separately: International Factors in Czechoslovakia's Dissolutions, 1989–92, in Michael Kraus and Ronald Liebowitz, eds., *Russia and Eastern Europe after Communism: The Search for New Political, Economic, and Security Systems* (Boulder: Westview, 1996), pp. 240, 245.
23. Zora Bútorová et al., *Slovensko styri roki po...* (Bratislava: Focus, 1993), p. 3.

16

Czechoslovakia after 1989: The Reasons for the Division

Peter Zajac

The unending search for the reasons and causes of the division of Czechoslovakia on 1 January 1993 has causes of its own. The common denominator is, above all, the indefinite nature of the causes and the questionability of the dissolution.

In contrast to Yugoslavia and the Soviet Union, where referenda witnessed a great majority of citizens voting in favor of dissolutions, in Czechoslovakia, the division did not enjoy the support of the majority of the population even at the very end of the state's existence. No such referendum ever took place in Czechoslovakia, and the division was largely the result of political agreements between the Movement for a Democratic Slovakia (HZDS) and the Civic Democratic Party (ODS) after the elections of 1992. While the insistence of HZDS on certain political demands—above all, on full international recognition of Slovakia—led to the actual division, ODS was the dynamic actor, making the division reality by pressing for a speedy dissolution.

Negative memories of the division of Czechoslovakia in 1939 were very much alive throughout 1990–92. In the 1930s, the external pressure and violence from Nazi Germany, combined with the failed resolve of the Western democracies, produced the trauma of the protectorate and the Slovak wartime state. By contrast, in the 1990s, the division of Czechoslovakia did not take place in the circumstances of external pressure. On the contrary, all Western European institutions strongly warned against the dissolution, pointing to the negative repercussions for the country as a whole as well as for the international position of both newly emerging states. This attitude changed only against the backdrop of the bloody developments in Yugoslavia and the Soviet Union, when it was replaced by an attitude that welcomed the peaceful nature of Czechoslovakia's dissolution.

The division of Czechoslovakia was also contrary to pan-European processes. While Western Europe was in the throes of integration, Czechoslovakia's disintegration, as well as that of other states, was seen as a historical paradox of sorts. Czech–Slovak relations were not weighted down by historical traumas of the type that influenced the conflict among the nationalities of the former Yugoslavia or Soviet Union. Nor were they under the sway of negative historical memories, such as those that divide the Czechs and the Germans, or the Slovaks and the Hungarians.

In short, one could list numerous reasons for maintaining Czechoslovakia as a common state. They range from relevant economic, social, familial, and cultural factors to security and foreign policy concerns—even though perhaps the most important of these, geopolitical factors, never played a very significant role in the debate as a whole. The only commentators who emphasized geopolitical issues were historians—Jan Křen and Jan Rychlík.

Despite the absence of compelling reasons for doing so, Czechoslovakia dissolved anyway at the end of 1992. As a result, the division from the beginning posed many questions. The fundamental, even if not always explicitly formulated, question was: Why? Austrian journalist Karl Peter Schwartz at the end of his book writes that Czechoslovakia disintegrated because the reasons for her existence had lost their meaning. His claim is a paraphrase of a well-known statement by Masaryk that states are maintained by the ideas that gave them rise.[1] Schwartz's claim is one of the many explanations of the division of the Czechoslovak state. The official political version was born during the deliberations between ODS and HZDS after the elections of 1992. Its major architect was the political leadership of ODS, which presented the reasons for the division as "ODS's acceptance of and respect for the emancipation process in Slovakia." This romantic constitutional image of the national emancipation process was co-opted by the official ideology of HZDS and incorporated into the new constitution of the Slovak Republic.

Jon Elster has argued that the dissolution was the so-called second best solution. In this view, the conflict between either maintaining or dividing the state was resolved by each party securing its second choice outcome, which doesn't speak directly about dividing the state but instead hides behind more moderate, gradualist formulas, such as confederation or international recognition. These half-way-house obfuscations led to the dissolution.[2]

Another argument has to do with the view that the division of Czechoslovakia was caused by the internal dynamic of the negotiations concerning future constitutional arrangements. The ceaseless escalation of demands for further devolution of powers led to a situation in which the defenders of the common state were increasingly on the defensive. In this version, the will for division was ultimately stronger than the forces of state cohesion, where cohesion sometimes stood for the unifying idea and at other times for the unwillingness of the post-November 1989 elite to defend the common state.

Still another version, born only ex post facto, argues that Czechoslovakia was a mistake from the very beginning, that its division only corrected this historical error, which was comprised of the lack of Slovak gratitude on the one hand, and the colonial attitudes of the Czechs on the other.

Karel Vodička lists the following causes for the division: (1) cracks in the foundation of the Czechoslovak state, which the seventy-four years of common existence did not fill; (2) the economic and social crises, which inevitably accompany the structural changes in moving from a centrally planned to a market economy; (3) insufficient experience of the citizens with democracy; (4) the deformations and deep distortions in the political culture caused by communist indoctrination; (5) insufficient responsibility of the political elites; (6) insufficient political experience of the new political elites after November 1989, on the part of both sincere democrats and former dissidents as well as the far more numerous revolutionary opportunists; and (7) the interests of the new Slovak power elite in the division of the state.[3]

Michael Kraus and Allison Stanger have presented similar reasons in the introduction to this volume. The collapse of the Czechoslovak federation might be seen as the product of (1) the legacies of the communist and precommunist eras (the inevitability thesis); (2) the rational and/or erratic actions of postcommunist political elites; (3) demonstration effects (international factors fostering separatism); (4) constitutional deadlock; (5) regional economic disparities; (6) the absence of political parties as well as other associations and groupings that unite people across ethnic lines; and (7) the role of the mass media.

I have presented elsewhere my own reasons for Czechoslovakia's dissolution: (1) the asymmetry and asynchronicity of the historical development of the Czech lands and Slovakia; (2) the divergent behavior of the political elites, media, and the general public in the Czech and Slovak republics after 1989; (3) the insufficient and slow realization of the seriousness of Czech–Slovak problems on the part of the Czech and Slovak post-November 1989 political elites; (4) time pressure, which demanded the immediate solution of all problems that had accumulated over the previous fifty or sixty years; (5) the obfuscation and conscious manipulation of the whole constitutional problem on the part of some political elites and mass media, which stemmed also from the poor grasp of legal issues by post-November political elites, journalists, and the general public; (6) geopolitical pressure from the national liberation movements and disintegrative processes in the Baltic states, Soviet Union, and Yugoslavia (in the final analysis, these trends did not lead toward the strengthening of Czechoslovak statehood, but to the reformulation of the problem so that the "positive nature" of Czechoslovakia's division was emphasized); (7) the historical redefinition of the condition of Czechoslovak statehood after 1945, on the basis of the homogenization of Czech ethnicity in the Czech Republic that resulted from the transfer of the Sudeten Germans; (8) the radical processes of national emancipation in the postcommunist countries, evoked by the long-term suppression of such tendencies (paradoxically, the emphasis on Slovak emancipatory strivings facilitated Czech national emancipation).[4]

In parallel fashion, but apparently independently of each other, we have reached similar conclusions. At this point, I am not interested in comparison but in something else. While listing particular causes, we might lose sight of the manner in which these factors were interdependent. In the evolution of the constitutional framework after 1989, the solution of one problem only created another problem. Similarly, the interdependence of various issues sometimes became surprisingly clear only in their new context. For example, the question of military conversion, particularly sensitive in Slovakia, was linked to the growing unemployment problem.

From yet another perspective, the debate about the constitutional framework problem unfolded in a greatly condensed time and space. It was a historical turning point, at first engulfing only Central and Eastern Europe but gradually changing the configuration and coordinates not only of all of Europe but also of other continents. As the German sociologist Claus Offe puts it, the key to the successful transformation of postcommunist countries is democratization, the creation of a market economy, and territorial policy. In essence, different states must solve three fundamental problems: the problem of economic transformation, the problem of the creation of a state based on the rule of law and civil society, and the problem of the transformation of the state, which is often connected with the creation of a new state.[5]

Czechoslovakia, during and after November 1989, faced two key problems: economic transformation and the transformation from totalitarianism to a state based on the rule of law. The two were obviously connected, for the transformation of the economy required an appropriate legal framework. That is why I believe that it is justified to speak in the Czechoslovak case not about a coup but about a constitutional revolution, in the same sense that Tocqueville contrasted the French social and American political revolutions.[*]

Constitutional reform was seen as a prerequisite for the creation of a state based on the rule of law. But at the outset, nobody emphasized this. As early as the first message from Civic Forum (OF) to the Public Against Violence (VPN), Havel emphasized that although these were two sister organizations, a democratic federation needed to be built in Czechoslovakia. This term was later modified into "authentic federation," "partnership federation," or "federation from below." In other words, the leadership of OF and VPN recognized from the very beginning the problem of the constitutional framework. In the general revolutionary euphoria, however, neither movement fully appreciated that the problem of Czech–Slovak relations had played a critical role at all turning points of the Czechoslovak state and that it would play it again after 1989.

---

[*] See Alexis de Tocqueville, *Democracy in America*, trans. George Lawrence, ed. J. P. Mayer (New York: Harper & Row, 1988), pp. 13, 18, 72, 432, 508–509.

The problem first appeared after 1918, when the concept of one Czechoslovak nation confronted the formulation of two autonomous nations, and it lasted practically for the entire duration of interwar Czechoslovakia. One of the consequences was the establishment after 1939 of the Slovak state, which emerged as a result of external pressure but also as a function of an enduring quest for autonomy. After 1945, the federal model that had been proposed by the Slovak political leadership, which was a product of the Slovak national uprising, lost out again. On the one hand, as a consequence of the Beneš tradition, Slovakia distrusted federalism, and the Czech democratic forces feared Slovak separatism. On the other hand, the power aspirations of Slovak communists led them to swap their quest for national equality for power, so that the institutional embryo of the federation was turned into an empty shell.

Similarly, in 1968, the creation of the federation became entwined with the Soviet occupation of Czechoslovakia and the regime of normalization, which proceeded to render the federation a formality, an asymmetric structure underpinned by the Communist Party. In short, after 1968, the Czechoslovak federation could not function as a normal federation; such is possible only in a democratic system. Therefore, prior to 1989, Czechoslovakia had no previous experience with a functioning federation of the modern type, whether it be a federation based on the American or on the German model. In addition, there was the problem that Czechoslovakia was a two-member federation based on ethnicity.

Bringing up the problem of constitutional arrangements, moreover, has had a one-sided and one-dimensional character throughout Czechoslovak history: the Slovaks made "demands" and the Czechs always had to make "concessions." Thus, in a dual sense, the resolution of the constitutional conflict was asymmetrical throughout Czechoslovak history. First, Czechoslovakia never had ample time and opportunity to experiment with a federative solution based on partnership. Second, the Czechs often understood Slovak demands for institutional change as blackmail, even after 1989. This asymmetry was the point of departure for Czechoslovakia in November 1989, and this perceived pattern of Slovak demands and Czech concessions informed the views of most Czechs.

With the exception of the Movement for Czechoslovak Understanding, which played only a marginal role on the Slovak political scene, all political forces in Slovakia demanded a federation, if not more. At first, the main issue was the form of the federation and what type of political strategy would lead toward a realization of this goal. On the one side, there was VPN, with its platform of "partnership federation." On the other, there was the Slovak National Party (SNS) and the Christian Democratic Movement (KDH) with their platforms of a looser relationship or even a confederation (first advanced in the spring of 1990 by the postcommunist Party of Freedom). The demand for independence appeared in the platform of the SNS only after the 1990 elections. Between 1990 and 1992, according to surveys of public opinion, SNS was supported by 8 to 17 percent of those surveyed.

Given that the VPN had no interest in a confrontation with OF and that OF had no clear conception of future constitutional arrangements for Czechoslovakia, it was small wonder that soon after November 1990, both of these political forces found themselves on the defensive. Their proposals were often one step behind actual developments. This was the case with the proposal for a referendum, which still had a chance of being adopted in October 1990, when the leadership of VPN and OF first discussed the proposal with Havel. By December of that same year, however, when President Havel actually presented it to the Federal Assembly, it was already too late. The antireferendum forces—SNS, SDL, KDH and soon HZDS—had realized that any referendum would only support the continued existence of Czechoslovakia, which led each to oppose it for different reasons.

Moreover, from the very beginning, inside OF and VPN, there were well-intentioned but naive notions of transforming the federation. J. Vavroušek, for example, wanted to create a federal parliament from the representatives of the republic-level parliaments. This proposal would have been in fundamental conflict with the standard model of the division of labor between the federation and its constituent republics, which was based on the premise that members of one body cannot simultaneously hold responsibilities in another.

Similar confusion reigned where the definition of federation was concerned. Only in this fashion could it have happened that a typical demarcation of federal sovereignty vis-à-vis the republics, as stipulated in the 1990 electoral program of VPN, was understood by some leaders of OF—for example, Alexander Vondra—to be an expression of separatism. This led to an unbelievable paradox. In Slovakia, VPN was often regarded or viewed as pro-Czechoslovak, while at the same time it was perceived in the Czech lands as separatist.

In other words, the general absence of proper legal training and familiarity with constitutional law played quite a destructive role, both at the public and the elite levels. This was especially the case in the third round of the constitutional negotiations between March 1991 and February 1992, which culminated in the "constitutional fundamentalism" of Jan Kalvoda, then chair of the Civic Democratic Alliance (ODA). Kalvoda rejected the notion of a "state treaty" between the two member republics, while he was accepting of a "treaty between peoples or national councils," even though there was no fundamental conflict between these solutions. Czech and Slovak constitutional lawyers, lacking familiarity with five decades of postwar legal scholarship, were ill equipped to address questions concerning federalism and the division of powers.

The lack of preparation of OF and VPN, which prevented them from tackling the problem at the outset and retaining political initiative throughout, therefore, played no small role. What started off in early 1990 as a seemingly innocent quarrel over the name of the state turned into a "dash war," which framed the issue in accordance with the traditional model of Slovak demands versus Czech concessions. In the fall and winter of 1990, the second round took the form of deliberations about the division of powers, eventuating in the December 1990 compromise. These negotiations already signaled confrontational attitudes on both sides, although the issues were still being considered in the context of a common state. The third round, also known as "the tour of castles and chateaux,"* brought together the relevant political forces and President Havel, and culminated in the joint sessions of the Czech and Slovak national councils at the end of 1991 and the beginning of 1992. The record of these negotiations makes it quite evident how the political will of the post-November 1989 political elites to find a compromise solution progressively weakened through each round of deliberations.

Simply put, it was impossible to solve the problem once and for all while at the same time maintaining a functioning common state. What was lacking was a certain sense of perspective that only time could provide. Also missing was an effective referendum law, which was only being drafted. Instead, the federal structures and institutions ceased to function: at the beginning of 1992, both chambers of the federal parliament were in disharmony; the same was true of the relationship between the Federal Assembly and the Czech National Council on the one hand and the Slovak National Council on the other, as well as the relations between the two national councils. It was precisely the dysfunctionality of the parliamentary institutions that led to growing skepticism about the possibility of preserving the common state. Precisely at the time when a petition supporting the common state had secured more than a million signatures, the Czech and Slovak national councils paradoxically were incapable of agreeing on practically anything.

One additional aspect should be singled out: on the Slovak political scene, several parties exchanged roles during 1990–92, of which the most relevant was the position swap between KDH and HZDS. In the summer of 1990, when KDH began considering various confederative arrangements, premier Mečiar was resolved to break his party's coalition agreement with KDH (at least he pretended that this was the case). Subsequently, on the eve of the 1992 elections, with KDH fragmented and hesitatingly embracing the federal solution, HZDS came to prefer a confederation, which it presented in the public domain as a variant of the common state.

Moreover, there was a strange and growing gap between rhetoric and reality. On the level of rhetoric, there was still much talk about the need to "loosen the federation," or "confederation as a common state," during 1990–92. In practice, the state was gradually ceasing to function, becoming ungovernable, and ultimately reaching the crisis stage.

Another key obstacle to the resolution of the constitutional impasse was encroachment of problems from other areas. The best example of this is the issue of economic transformation. Slovakia's economic transformation had a different character from the very beginning because of its higher level of unemployment. The resistance to the "Klaus reforms" in Slovakia was often linked to resistance to the federal government in principle. This was especially the case in two areas,

---

* It was known as such because castles and chateaux were the settings for these meetings.

beginning in January 1991, following the conflict over the power-sharing law: (1) the conversion of military industries, whose problems were blamed on the federal government; and (2) issues surrounding the liquidation of cooperatives. Both problems were highly sensitive in Slovakia and practically the entire population had a wholly negative orientation toward them.

With the launch of the economic transformation in 1991—liberalization of prices, restitution, and privatization—there was a palpable growth of nostalgia for the old regime in Slovakia. This nostalgia stemmed largely from the prior asynchronous processes of modernization in the Czech and Slovak lands. Modernization in the Czech lands took place in the second half of the nineteenth century and resulted in an advanced, highly differentiated bourgeois society in interwar Czechoslovakia. In contrast, the main modernizing force in Slovakia was the communist regime, which produced economic growth but fostered neither the development of a modern infrastructure nor the rise of a democratic political culture. From 1991 on, Slovakia diverged from the general strategy of transformation, which was quite naturally identified with the federation. The engines of transformation were the organs of the federation, whether the Federal Assembly in the legislative sphere, the federal government in the executive, or federal television.

The situation with the media illustrates the growing abyss between the federation and the Slovak public. For the majority of Slovak viewers, federal television became the incarnation of "federal evil." By early 1991 at the latest, much of the Slovak political elite and media were aware of the Slovak public's growing distrust of Prague. At that time, the notion that Czechoslovakia would have to be divided was still not a dominant conviction, yet confrontational approaches toward the Czechs received ever growing degrees of support, especially in the Slovak media. Vladimír Mečiar's popularity in Slovakia during 1991–92 stemmed from the fact that he personified the mainstream Slovak vision of the need to defend Slovak interests. None of the other conciliatory and consensus-seeking parties could compete with his hard-nosed posture.

Concurrently, other multiethnic states of East and Central Europe were dissolving. The violent form of these breakups did not lead Czechs and Slovaks to reject dissolution but instead to search for half-baked solutions, which, willy-nilly, led to the peaceful dissolution. In this entire matrix of problems, two additional elements played a role on the Czech political scene. After the Second World War, the transfer of the Sudeten Germans eliminated one of the pillars of the Czech conception of Czechoslovakia. In this conception, the Czechs, with the support of the Slovaks, would numerically outnumber the Germans on Czechoslovak soil. With the expulsion of the Sudeten Germans, even though it was never defined this way, the Slovaks ceased to be the glue that held the state together and therefore ceased to be indispensable for the continued existence of the Czechs.

On the territory of Czechoslovakia proper, however, six hundred thousand Hungarians remained. After 1989, the nationalities problem, as well as the Gabčíkovo Dam issue,* generated a sense of helplessness in the Czech political arena. The Czechs never properly understood the problem, and the Slovak post-November elite could not find the key to unlock it. Such elements contributed to the centrifugal tendencies in the Czech Republic and enabled the Czech political elite to dissolve the state more easily.

Evidently, the compression of particular problems in time and space and the creation of accelerating centrifugal forces, in the end, led to the dissolution of Czechoslovakia. Undoubtedly, the emancipatory element connected to the entities seeking independence in other postcommunist lands also played its role. This process was also under way in the Czech Republic.

The result of this struggle can only be one of two outcomes for Slovakia: authoritarian or democratic government. The idea of Slovak independence has so far taken shape as a function of power. Only the end of this struggle will reveal which side will win out.

One can view the dissolution of Czechoslovakia from two perspectives. The first is a historical–teleological one, where the event is seen as a historical inevitability. The second argues that Czechoslovakia might have been preserved as a common state if only it had been capable of changing, to quote Tomáš Masaryk, "the ideas that gave rise to it," and, after 1989, there was neither opportunity nor time for that.

In considering the causes of the split, the Slovak sociologist Soňa Szomolányi examined three sets of issues, which both sides used to argue in favor of partition: economic differences, differences in the perspectives of the political elites that were victorious in the 1992 elections, and the problem of national emancipation as historical inevitability. She raised ample doubts about each of these explanations.[6] Today, it is evident that even in the economic sphere, the differences are by no means as great as they appeared in 1992. What lurked behind emancipation were, above all, power and economic interests. Despite all the major differences in the political situations of the Czech and Slovak republics, there is one common characteristic of all postcommunist political elites: the arrogance of *nomenklatura* capitalism, which leads to the eventual loss of support from the wider public. In 1992, both Czech and Slovak political representatives appeared self-satisfied. Today, only five years after the dissolution of Czechoslovakia, they have no good reasons to feel that way.

Translated from Slovak by Michael Kraus and Allison Stanger

---

* For a brief explanation of this issue, see Jan Rychlík's chapter in this volume.

NOTES

1. Karl Peter Schwartz, *Česi a Slováci: Dlhá cesta k mierovému rozchodu* (Czechs and Slovaks: The Long Journey to the Peaceful Dissolution) (Bratislava: Odkaz, 1994), p. 233.

2. Author's conversation with Jon Elster.

3. Karel Vodička, *Rozloučení s Československem* (Praha: Patrie, 1993), pp. 113 ff.

4. *Rozdelenie Československa* (Trnava: Trnavska univerzita, 1993), p. 90 and ff.

5. Claus Offe, *Der Tunnel am Ende des Lichts* (The Tunnel at the End of the Light) (Frankfurt/Main: Campus Verlag, 1994), p. 57ff.

6. Soňa Szomolányi, "Was the Dissolution of Czechoslovakia Inevitable?" *Scottish Affairs*, Summer 1994.

17

Notes on the Role of Television in Czechoslovakia's Dissolution

Martin Vadas

INTRODUCTION

This chapter reflects on the mass media situation after the Velvet Revolution—especially on developments in the news division of Czechoslovak Television during 1991–1992—and assesses its role in Czechoslovakia's dissolution. My contribution is based on documents, interviews, and personal experience from my short tenure as the editor in chief of the news division of Czechoslovak Television. For nine months, between 1 April and 31 December 1992, I supervised some 240 employees and was responsible for about three hours of daily programming, both news and commentary, broadcast on the federal channel F1 and watched by some five to nine million viewers each day.[1]

After I was chosen for the position of editor in chief in an open competition at the close of 1991, the general director of Czechoslovak Television, Jiří Kantůrek, a fellow Czech, met with me only to express his disappointment that the commission had not chosen his favored Slovak candidate, Ladislav Karásek. Kantůrek had hoped that the presence of a Slovak in a significant programming post of Czechoslovak Television would have complemented his presence as a Czech and the general director of federal television, thereby preempting some of the criticism from Slovakia.

Could another choice for the position of editor in chief of the news division have saved the Czechoslovak federation? Ivo Mathé, the general director of Czech Television, believes that "even if we had had a Slovak in this position, he could not have salvaged the situation. As is well known, when a Slovak became a manager in the Czech lands, for Slovaks at home, he had ceased to be a Slovak. One person could not have changed the situation."[2]

THE MASS MEDIA IN CZECHOSLOVAKIA:
PATTERNS OF DEVELOPMENT

What was the media situation in 1989–92 Czechoslovakia? Our focus here is on the federal television—the main means of mass communication, which dominated the information market in both republics. What is especially significant is its potentially integrative role in the absence of federal daily newspapers. Newspapers and periodicals from one republic were hardly distributed on the territory of the other.[3] This was not caused solely by limited interest on the part of the readership. It was also due to the collapse of the former distribution monopolies of the postal newspaper services. Moreover, large Czech dailies were undergoing wild privatization by their own managements, who often transferred assets into their own hands with the participation of foreign investors, but without any transparency, contributing further to the chaotic situation in the print media.

Since 1953, Czechoslovak Television (ČST) had exercised a monopoly broadcasting role in communist Czechoslovakia. It was at first subordinated to the Czechoslovak Committee for Radio and Television. In 1959 it became a centralized organization under the auspices of the communist government. In 1964, the parliament approved law no. 18/64 on Czechoslovak television, which fortified the role of the television as an instrument of the ruling Communist Party even further. During 1968, the reformist wing of the Communist Party influenced Czechoslovak television for only a short period of time, as was the case with its influence in the society at large.

Television was finally liberated from party control in 1989. Until that time, ČST had been a massive ideological instrument of monopoly with more than 5,600 employees. After November 1989, a majority of the communist-era management personnel stayed on despite the changing circumstances. Moreover, some of the leading positions of the post-November 1989 ČST were assumed by people under the influence of the former state security apparatus. In addition, many employees who had been purged after 1968 were allowed to return after 1989, even though most of them had previously been active members of the communist *nomenklatura*. In other words, none of the managerial or the program posts in ČST were filled by people with experience in a similar line of work in the democratic part of the world. As a result, many of the so-called experts from the communist era were simply able to hold on to their positions, even though they had no real understanding of the proper role of the media in a democracy. All in all, this personnel situation had a negative impact on the ability of television to report adequately on events and developments in a democratizing society.

One of my immediate challenges in early 1992 was to cope with the repercussions of the lustration laws. The lustration laws of October 1991 banned the top officers and activists of the old regime from senior-level governmental posts for a period of five years. On 6 November 1991, the directive of the general director of Czechoslovak Television to implement lustration law no. 451/91 went into effect. The directive defined the positions that were subject to screening under this law, but its implementation was a protracted process. Since the party had controlled the media under communism, professional journalists, in the Western sense of the word, were hard to come by. It was difficult enough to find competent staff in the postcommunist context, and lustration often meant getting rid of individuals with experience who had been politically discredited. Their replacements, by contrast, often lacked any news experience whatsoever.

Western assistance did not always help the situation either. After 1989, the democratic world offered Czechs and Slovaks who had the requisite language skills a range of opportunities for study in the West. During my tenure at ČST in 1992, some of the first people who had won fellowships were returning from their study abroad with enviable qualifications. As it turned out, however, during 1989–91 such fellowships had been a field of opportunity for young communists and reliable cadres of the old regime, who were chosen on that basis. These "new experts" tended to come home and then leave the jobs that had been held for them during their absence because they could not meet the conditions of the lustration law. Such was the story of one of our young returnees: he spent 1991–92 as a Nieman Fellow at Harvard University, where no one had any clue they had hosted a high-level agent of the old regime. This experience underlines the long-term challenge of the personnel issue in ČST.

By the end of June 1992, the personnel situation in the news division reflected both the substantial effect of the lustration law and our considerable effort to recruit new employees. On 30 June 1992, the general director of Czechoslovak Television declared publicly that "not a single former agent of the security police (StB) is engaged any longer in the creation of the news programs of Czechoslovak Television."[4] Significantly, the leadership of neither the Czech nor the Slovak television and radio ever issued such a declaration. On the contrary, they offered ever greater advancement opportunities to those personnel who under the previous regime had compromised themselves significantly and who were forced to leave Czechoslovak Television after November 1989, owing to the lustration law.

Television employees culpable for their service to the old regime were especially eager to assist the new regime in the spirit of servility, out of fear that this new power could expose their carefully hidden past in service of the Communist Party, secret police, or unethical journalism that had bowed to the old regime. Surprisingly, the new regime quickly accepted this game, which in turn facilitated an unusually conflict-free coexistence with state television and radio and their monopoly position. This tradition of servility accounts, in some measure, for the very superficial and inadequate way in which radio and television covered political events and developments during 1990–1991; this coverage almost always failed to serve the public interest.

During the major public debate over the principles of economic reform at the turn of 1990–91, President Václav Havel expressed his own dissatisfaction with the work of these so-called professional journalists. He went as far as to offer to moderate television programs dealing with the economy himself, so as to prove that one could present the issues clearly enough for viewers to grasp the essence of the matters at hand as well as the opinions of various actors. Needless to say, Havel's offer was an unusual one for a sitting president, but it did convey the gravity of the personnel situation in ČST.

CREATING AN INDEPENDENT PROGRAM

While I was given a free hand to hire my news division staff, this proved much more difficult than I had originally anticipated. Even as I prepared myself in February and March 1992 to assume the post of editor in chief, I regarded (in agreement with the general director) ensuring quality programming from Slovakia for F1 as a top priority. For that reason, I made several working visits to Slovakia, where I held many meetings with this goal in mind. I searched for a well-qualified deputy editor, who would be able to develop a network of reporters from different Slovak regions, along the lines of what already existed in the Czech Republic. While they all acknowledged the importance of quality coverage from Slovakia, the most promising candidates for this position declined to serve.[5] For a while, it appeared that I would have to inform the general director that I had been unable to assemble the Slovak team I desired and therefore would have to postpone my start date. Just then, a colleague at the film academy, Fero Fenic, redirected my attention to the talents of a Slovak classmate of ours, Jozef Horal, who had directed Czech and Slovak documentary films. Horal, in the end, agreed to take on this difficult challenge.

I found my second deputy editor in Jan Dobrovský, who was recommended to me by Vladimír Mlynář. I also asked Dr. Petr Feldstein, who had headed the office, to stay on as one of my deputies. For the position of special advisor to the editor in chief, I managed to secure Michael Kraus, professor of political science at Middlebury College. His role as "the man from elsewhere," was at first difficult for the editorial staff to accept, but I felt it was essential to have an outside perspective, and here I was right. This was the team that took over the news division two months before the parliamentary elections of June 1992.

Since we were a state-funded television, we wanted to fulfill the spirit and the letter of the law, which stipulated the need to create an independent program, i.e., independent from the political majority of the moment. In a situation where many of us supported the new democratic government and were personal friends of high-level officials, it was not always easy to insist on the full application of democratic principles. That is why, for example, we adopted the practice of recording telephone conversations, so that our reporters had the opportunity as well as the duty to alert those who might attempt to pressure members of our staff to broadcast or not to broadcast something. We made it clear that attempts to apply such pressure would be recorded and possibly reported as news.

Another demand that I made at the outset was to put an end to the presence of the employees of the ministries of the Interior and Defense, clearly a legacy of the communist era, on our staff. The minister of defense, Luboš Dobrovský, replied that only the State Council of Defense, which had appointed them in the first place, could recall them. Negotiations concerning their presence, which had no legal basis, took months, but in the end, I was successful in removing them.

We also attempted to improve the personnel situation. Dr. Ladislav Špaček took over as the head of the domestic news section. Špaček had first proven himself as an excellent parliamentary reporter and correspondent and then further as an anchor and a commentator. The fundamental problem was the need to bring to the television new and qualified reporters who were not tainted by past experience with television under communism. On the very first day I arrived, I announced a recruiting campaign to fill vacancies that had been created by departing staff. These demanding recruiting efforts eventually bore fruit in the form of several outstanding television personalities who are well known today, but the training of those individuals was a long-term process. Given the then-still-persisting monopoly role of state television, there were no other training grounds where prospects could acquire the necessary skills before joining our staff. Therefore, while assuming significant responsibilities, our reporters had to learn on the job and inevitably committed mistakes.

TENDENCIES TOWARD DISSOLUTION

Inside television, negotiations dealing with reorganization and legislative changes concerning both radio and television broadcasting were also taking place. As a result, on 1 January 1991, ČST was reorganized on a new basis, with the creation of the so-called production centers and creative working groups. To any outsider, however, this reorganization seemed like some kind of a musical chairs game. It did not fundamentally open up programming jobs but on the contrary ensured that the existing personnel would retain key programming positions. With the exception of national searches that were conducted for the posts of editors in chief of the news and sports divisions and the directors of Czech Television and of Czech Radio, positions were filled without any outside search.

For illustrative purposes, I would like to mention the role of the Federal Council for Radio and Television Broadcasting of the ČSFR. It was headed by Ivan Medek, a Vienna-based veteran correspondent of the Voice of America. The council could have had some influence on the work of Czechoslovak Television, which had been given a federal mandate, because there still was no new law that dealt with the future of federal television programming. Both national televisions, however, took great initiative in the drafting of the new law. From the beginning, they wanted the federal television (F1) channel's programming to be comprised of only two national segments, furnished exclusively by Czech and Slovak television.

In support of this goal, they often used the most convoluted arguments. As Vladimír Just pointed out at the time, "The parceling out of F1 between Czech Television (ČTV) and Slovak Television (STV) would involve the liquidation of uncomfortable competition" from the federal television. But Ivo Mathé, the director of Czech Television, denied this, arguing: "The fears of monopoly are absurd. Should we create a second parliament because only one parliament does not guarantee democracy?" Just responded: "Every non-schizoid democratic state has only one parliament, but as Mr. Mathé surely knows, each state of this sort has still another essential guarantor of its democracy: pluralism of information, rather than an information monopoly."[6]

In Slovakia, the supporters of Vladimír Mečiar, giddy from their electoral success, expressed themselves quite openly from the summer of 1992 on. Jozef Darmo, director of the Institute of Journalism, was asked in August 1992 what the future would bring. As he put it: "We need to realize the full sovereignty and statehood of the Slovak Republic in its international dimensions. The sovereignty of the Slovak Republic, however, cannot be imagined without informational sovereignty."[7] Darmo's vision of informational sovereignty is today being fully realized, thanks to his censorious interventions in programming as director of Slovak Television.

The Federal Council for Radio and Television Broadcasting was the main supervisory body of electronic mass media in the parliament. Vladimír Just, then a council member, had argued that "the main task for the council was, or should have been, conceptual work: the preparation of the legal framework for the dual system of broadcasting in the Czechoslovak federation, including the conditions for licensing, the division of frequencies, the issuance of temporary licenses and so on." Instead, the council was preoccupied with its own internal divisions and the conflicting agendas of its individual members.[8] Dušan Slobodník, who would later become the minister of Culture in the first independent Slovak government, frequently criticized his council colleagues, while defending the words and actions of Vladimír Mečiar. According to Just, in the discussion inside the Council for Radio and Television,

> our Slovak colleagues constantly argued that this or that criticism would be counterproductive, but I have always been convinced that the ethics of reporting dictate that certain steps must be taken without regard for their likely impact. In the long run, it is unacceptable to hide from problems. There may well be some limits, such as state secrets, for example, but this was not the case here."[9]

In this sense, the council's infighting mirrored the deeper political divisions in society at large.

According to Ivo Mathé, head of Czech Television from 1991 to 1998—the main reason why all three television networks—Czech, Slovak, and federal—were so readily prepared for institutional division had historical roots:

> Ever since 1968, under the umbrella of Czechoslovak television, Slovak television was being built separately, with the tacit agreement of all power-holders. Indeed, the

federal television was well-equipped to accommodate the country's division, technologically, organizationally, and in terms of production. Even the separation of the television signal was not difficult to accomplish. The tendencies toward the division of Czechoslovak television were long in evidence, especially in Slovakia. All directors of Slovak television, of whom there were quite a few after November 1989, propounded the autonomy of Slovak television from the federal television under the flag of the right to "self-determination." Since 1968, the common denominator of the Slovak political arena was the motive to acquire as much independence as possible.[10]

On 24 May 1991, the Slovak National Council passed law no. 254/91, which created Slovak Television as of 1 July 1991. However, the federal parliament only approved law no. 468/91 concerning radio and television broadcasting on 30 October 1991, which legalized ex post facto the unilateral action of the Slovak National Council. Still later, on 7 November 1991, the Czech National Council passed law no. 483/91 concerning Czech Television, effective as of 1 January 1992. These legal changes launched the process of property and personnel division within the previously centralized Czechoslovak Television. It is important to note that the emerging institutional asymmetry—whereby federal Czechoslovak television had existed, for a time, alongside Slovak television without a Czech counterpart—produced a series of problems.

In the case of Slovakia, what was accepted was the so-called territorial principle, which meant that Slovak Television received all television assets located on Slovak territory, at an estimated value of 2.6 billion crowns. At the beginning of 1992, Czech Television received assets valued at 3.6 billion crowns, while Czechoslovak Television retained assets in the amount of 450 million crowns. The largest component of the latter was comprised of buildings where the federal news division, along with the newly created Czech news division, were each to produce their own daily news programming.* For fiscal year 1992, Czechoslovak Television could rely only on 398 million crowns from the federal budget.

The property division on the basis of the territorial principle significantly impeded the daily operations of Czechoslovak Television. There were several reasons for this. For starters, the division of assets meant, among other things, that federal television was suddenly deprived of all its employees who had been delivering the news from Slovakia; they had overnight become employees of Slovak Television. Similarly, on the Czech side, many employees were leaving federal television for posts in the new Czech Television, a trend that only accelerated with the growing prospect of the country's dissolution.

As a result of these organizational changes, when in early 1992 I assumed the position of editor in chief of the news division of Czechoslovak Television, our new team in Slovakia was yet to be created. Yet the news, including news from Slovakia, still had to be reported daily on federal television. Until the 1992 elections, therefore, we had to improvise in obtaining news coverage from Slo-

---

* Their offices resided across the hallway from one another.

vakia for the main evening news program of Czechoslovak Television (on the F1 channel). We relied on informal agreements and habits from the past, which were mutually unsatisfactory. Bratislava, understandably, did not want to be directed or perhaps even censored by Prague. The news division of Slovak Television, however, was under a great deal of political pressure. Its contributions to the most popular federal news program, *Deník ČST* (Diary of Czechoslovak Television), whose audience ranged from five to nine million viewers, were closely monitored by Slovak political elites for the "image of Slovakia" they conveyed. Slovak Television, which by early 1992 was an independent entity free of federal supervision, could beam live reports directly into all evening news programs, including *Deník ČST*. By law, I was responsible for the content of all ČST news programs, but in reality, I was in no position either directly or indirectly to influence the quality of journalistic work of the employees of the Slovak Television news division.

As a result, the news programs of ČST were increasingly under critical scrutiny by the print media, especially the Czech newspapers. For example, Vladimír Mlynář, a reporter for the weekly *Respekt,* noted the strange composition of the news, when during the seventh or eighth minute, the program would switch to Bratislava and the whole country would watch—without realizing that this was the case—what the employees of an entirely different organization had prepared for the broadcast.[11] The reason why the order and the content of the news was often not up to desirable standards had a lot to do with the fact that those of us who edited the program in Prague typically had no idea what sort of contribution we might receive from Slovakia as a live broadcast.

Our resources and equipment still reflected—as late as 1992—an era when the news coverage was governed by the directives of the Central Committee of the Communist Party. Although I was the editor in chief of the news division, the technical staff did not report to me. We had no archive to speak of, no news room, outdated computer hardware and software, and employees who were not trained to deal with state-of-the-art technology.

To compound the problem, the new Czech Television, as well as the federal television, both utilized the same equipment and technical staff, which was often a source of friction. This was especially the case when the staffs of both stations were preparing news programs; they had to fight for time with the requisite production equipment. Czechoslovak Television, for example, could not produce a live television broadcast of parliamentary proceedings without the support of Czech Television, which controlled the use of the transmission equipment. Czechoslovak Television, in turn, supplied Czech Television with editorial, archival, and production assistance. The regional television bureaus and staff belonged to Czechoslovak Television, but the editorial staff were employees of Czech Television.

At the same time, since Czechoslovak Television was state run, we were also at a disadvantage when it came to financial remuneration. The financial terms we could offer were dated and failed to motivate our staff under the prevailing circumstances of rising incomes in the journalistic profession. The newly born Czech Television attracted many of our experienced employees because they could offer a better financial package and—in a country that was falling apart— a more secure future. The uncertain fate of federal television precluded us from adopting policies that had a long-term perspective. Even if we had wished to do so, the budget at our disposal rendered this impossible.

The whole of Czechoslovak Television in 1989 had over 5,600 employees. By the beginning of 1992, over 3,700 employees had left to join the newly formed Czech Television. After all the reorganizations, the staff of the federal television had shrunk to 540 employees at the close of 1991, of which the news division had about 240 poorly paid employees, who prepared approximately three hours of daily programming. At the beginning of the year, we did not have a single employee in the Slovak Republic. As alluded to earlier, we had an understanding about cooperation with Slovak Television, which ensured the beaming of their news live into our main news programs. According to an agreed-upon timetable, Slovak Television also provided Slovak anchors for our federal news programs to maintain the bilingual character of the broadcast.

AFTER THE JUNE 1992 ELECTIONS

Czechoslovak Television's F1 was the only channel capable of broadcasting to the entire territory of Czechoslovakia. In 1992, F1's programs were supplied by all three televisions: Czechoslovak, Czech, and Slovak. More specifically, 51 percent of F1's programming was prepared by Czech Television, 24 percent was produced by federal television employees, and 25 percent was prepared by Slovak Television. At the same time, Czech and Slovak television collaborated in the liquidation of federal television, inasmuch as they both declared their readiness to divide its assets and to replace federal broadcasts with their own programming.

The aversion toward federal television on the part of some viewers, television employees, and politicians in Slovakia had several objective reasons. The most serious of these was the seeming monopoly of news broadcasting to Slovakia during prime time. *Deník ČST* was broadcast in Slovakia on both channels (federal and Slovak) simultaneously. Therefore, the Slovak viewer had no option of switching to another news program at 7 P.M. Slovak Television began to broadcast its own news in this time slot only as of 29 June 1992.

After the June 1992 elections, both national televisions and radios intensified their cooperation in dismantling the federal apparatus. On 5 August 1992, the representatives of Czech and Slovak television and radio held a joint session at the initiative of then–deputy minister of Slovak culture, Ivan Mjartan. The goal was to coordinate legal and legislative strategies for the liquidation of Czechoslovak Television and Czechoslovak Radio, including their assets and funding from the federal budget. Federal politicians and representatives of the federal media were not invited to this gathering.

Survey research conducted during the week of 2 July 1992 by the Prague-based Institute for the Survey of Public Opinion assessed the popularity and influence of the F1 channel. According to the results, 90 percent of the country's population tuned in to F1 at least once a week. More than half the population in both republics watched it daily.[12] The restructured news division contributed to the channel's popularity, especially in the period immediately preceding the June 1992 elections, when it became the focus of great interest. In contrast, the national televisions steered clear of election coverage. At that time, tensions between the news division of Czechoslovak Television and the news division of Slovak Television grew more intense. In the run up to the elections, the Slovak editors and reporters were afraid to provide coverage of political, economic, and ecological issues in Slovakia for F1. Our previous understandings unraveled. Instead of newsworthy items, we would receive reports about folk dancing, the cleanup of obscure ponds in Slovakia, and similar stories. Slovak reporters either studiously avoided the critical issues of the day or propounded their personal perspectives without consulting the editor of the broadcast. They would often send—without any previous consultation—their contributions directly into a live broadcast as a surprise from Bratislava.

Perhaps most damning were the threats emanating from Bratislava in May and June 1992 that any further unfavorable coverage of Slovak political developments by our channel would lead them to "pull the plug" on our broadcasts in Slovakia. Though such a measure would have been a clear violation of federal broadcasting law, intimidation and threats of this type raised the level of nervousness in our newsrooms, especially among our Slovak staff.

Soon after the elections, Slovak Television found itself under a great deal of pressure from the victorious political parties. Mečiar had all along insisted on putting an end to the federal television and endorsed the takeover of its programs by national televisions. On 24 June 1992, after the HZDS–ODS negotiations, he allowed for the possibility that Czechoslovak Television would not have to go out of business immediately. "I do not rule out the possibility that the post of interim general director of Czechoslovak Television before it expires could be filled by a representative of HZDS, so the staff of Czechoslovak Television can look forward to his appointment," Mečiar declared in an interview. Regrettably, such threats did have an impact on the work of our staff. So it happened that an otherwise easygoing, matter-of-fact, and disciplined anchor of *Deník ČST*, Mirka Všetečková, reported Mečiar's remarks during our evening broadcast, and added her own comment, with a smile: "We are looking forward to it."

Slovak Television had, until this point, broadcast *Deník ČST* at 7 P.M. on both F1 and the Slovak channel. It supplemented this federal programming with only one late evening news program of its own, *Aktuality*. After the elections, it finally launched its own prime time news program, which preceded the federal *Deník*

ČST on F1. While the ratings for the new Slovak program were initially very good, over time, Slovak viewers returned to watching the federal program.

After his victory in the June 1992 elections, Mečiar insisted on regular ten-minute weekly time slots for himself on Slovak Television. Jan Fulle, the Slovak editor in chief, at first resisted Mečiar's demands, but his position was complicated by pressure from other members of the Slovak media "to build a positive image of Slovakia."[13] Then, on 29 June 1992, without even a day's notice, Jan Fulle decided that his staff would no longer provide news for the federal broadcast and suddenly terminated the contracts of those Slovak employees who had been willing to remain as anchors in Prague. As a result, we faced the challenge of creating, from one day to the next, our own news coverage or being forced to report no news from Slovakia at all. Under the admirable leadership of our deputy editor in chief, Jozef Horal, as well as other accomplished Slovak reporters and anchors, such as Eugene Korda, Zuzana Bubílková, Lubica Lesná, Martina Balážová, and others, and with generous federal funding, we were able to create—almost immediately—new, autonomous studios in Slovakia with which to provide our own coverage. Consequently, up-to-date news reporting from Slovakia reached a new level of quality. For the first time, viewers in Slovakia were presented with a genuine choice of news programming. Despite this positive turn of events, the HZDS-orchestrated campaign to put Czechoslovak Television out of business only intensified.

In the anxious postelection atmosphere, the deadlocked negotiations of the election winners raised the question of whether a referendum was necessary to decide the division of the country. Regarding the referendum issue, the news division of Czechoslovak Television presented the full spectrum of views, without staking out a position of its own. Personally, I was already then a proponent of some aspects of direct democracy, such as referenda. However, I was rather apprehensive about the nature and consequences of any referendum campaign in the politically charged postelection climate. I feared it could only promote the rise of mutual acrimony, which would—in the context of "who is to blame for the country's demise" arguments—increase the likelihood of the conflict escalating into a civil war of the Balkan type. That is why in our 1992 broadcasts, ČST never advocated a referendum on the future of Czechoslovakia.

THE MASS MEDIA AND POWER

Our friends from abroad had a hard time grappling with some of our practices. The regularly established *Ten Minutes with the Premier* program, whereby the premier would sit in front of the camera and talk, answering a few questions, was one example. It was also one of the first things that I demanded had to go. In fact, I made this a condition of accepting my post as editor in chief. When General Director Jiří Kantůrek passed on the results of his conversations with the prime minister, he appeared to be surprised that Premier Marián Čalfa had accepted my demand.

Speaking generally, the relationship that the mass media had with newly emergent democratic power in the post-November 1989 federation was immature in character. The personal biases of comfortable and servile reporters or their bosses determined whose voices were heard. Reporters from the state-controlled mass media often preferred to forget their own questions and treated politicians and state employees with excessive reverence. This was a problem not easily solved, because the quality of news coverage reflected a deeper problem shared by all fledgling democracies. We had no experience with a functioning independent media in a democratic society. Hardly any of us had ever attended schools of journalism, and those of us who did under the communist regime were worse off for it. We had to learn on the job.

In 1992, some politicians chose to cease granting interviews and to stop defending their positions publicly, calling instead for "direct access to television whenever desired." This was the case with Vladimír Mečiar, who demanded that "the government ought to have access to mass media delineated by law so that it could inform the public of its deliberations whenever it deems appropriate and not when the media decides to give us air time." But in reality, Mečiar and his spokesmen consistently refused our invitations to participate in our preelection coverage.

There was, however, a legal justification for public officials to have the direct access to television that so many Slovak politicians dramatically demanded. Federal law no. 468/91 stipulated the obligation to "provide state organs with the necessary broadcasting time for important and essential announcements when the vital interests of the public are at stake." Yet when Michal Kováč, then chair of the Federal Assembly, wanted to broadcast his speech on the occasion of Havel's resignation from the presidency in July 1992, he did not invoke this law. Under the circumstances, I thought that fulfilling his request would have established an unfortunate precedent. Therefore, I rejected it. I had to turn down another of Kováč's proposals when he subsequently demanded an immediate and live broadcast of a session of the Federal Assembly. Our experience with broadcasts of this sort had not been good. What typically happened was that some deputies, upon realizing that we were broadcasting live, abandoned the topic under discussion and used television as a platform for self-promotion. As a result, parliamentary sessions grew unacceptably long, as did our live broadcasts. In such instances, we were vulnerable to criticism from both Czech and Slovak television, because our program spilled over into theirs, cutting into their regularly scheduled broadcasts. Such practices, in turn, were not conducive to cooperation among broadcasters from different stations.

Insufficient care to ensure a balanced representation of political parties in our broadcasts was a serious issue that we inherited from our predecessors. Consequently, already in the news-planning stage, representatives of some parties, such as the Civic Movement (OH) in the Czech lands, and the Christian Democratic Movement (KDH) and the Public Against Violence (VPN) in Slovakia, were being privileged over others. A certain degree of aversion toward Václav Klaus and his party, the Civic Democratic Party (ODS), was clearly discernible, even though in surveys of public opinion, ODS was the most popular party. Klaus was right to complain at public meetings that he received more attention from foreign television than from domestic. When a new hospital opened in the district of Kladno, the foreign minister and leader of OH, Jiří Dienstbier, made a television appearance, even though his hospital visit clearly had nothing to do with foreign policy. After the June 1992 elections and complaints from HZDS, we attempted to follow statistically our relative coverage record, only to discover that if we used our best judgment of the newsworthiness of any given event, our results were quite balanced. The outcome of the 1992 elections, as well as those of 1996, also demonstrates that appearances on television do not directly affect the electoral results of a given party.

In the 1992 circumstances of news monopoly, when our *Deník ČST* was watched by anywhere from 60 to 85 percent of the entire population, I insisted on ensuring a plurality of views inside our staff. That is why in April and May 1992, we created a system of shifts for our reporters, whereby leadership responsibilities for domestic and foreign coverage, for the deployment of reporters and supporting staff, and other management duties would rotate daily. In my view, this significantly limited bias in our broadcasts.

The assessment of broadcasts was a new and important corrective for the work of our team. It took place both immediately after the program was broadcast as well as during our staff meeting the following day. Members of different professions within the news division shared evaluation responsibilities, with varying degrees of success. By also relying on the views of outside experts and consultants, I tried to create an external, independent evaluation process, a practice later adopted by the councils for radio and television. The results of such evaluation, however, were mixed, for the inevitable criticism of shortcomings hardly inspired our staff, which was concurrently subjected to great psychological, physical, and time pressure.

To do our best to ensure balanced coverage, the main evening news programs were presented by Czech and Slovak anchors, who alternated on a weekly basis. Unfortunately, many of our Slovak colleagues were subject to great pressure back home, especially if they did not conform to the expectations of Slovak nationalists. As Mlynář notes, some Slovak anchors would call in sick rather than be seen interviewing someone such as Minister Bakšay, whom the Slovak nationalists dubbed a traitor of the Slovak people.[14] Along the same lines, I learned that a Slovak anchor quit his job on the very day that he was supposed to moderate a program.

In Mathé's view, "Slovak national television was perceived in Slovakia from the beginning as something intrinsically more trustworthy as a national and therefore reliable source of news information. In contrast, most Slovak viewers regarded the programs of Czechoslovak Television as 'something foreign from Prague.' The existence of Czechoslovak Television alongside Czech Television was perceived in Slovakia as giving the Czechs two television stations."[15]

CONCLUSION

The mass media, especially the broadcast media, played an important, if sub-sidiary, role in the unraveling of the federation. Legacies of the past in terms of both personnel and organizational issues heavily influenced the broadcast media during 1990–92. In my view, those responsible for the future of the state-funded mass media, the government and the parliament, were slow to act. They were also unsure of the optimal policy direction in rapidly changing circumstances. As a re-sult, at the turn of 1991–92, when I assumed my responsibilities, Czechoslovak Television was in its death throes, even as the country prepared for the most im-portant elections in its short history.

According to Vladimír Just, the federal broadcasting media did not contribute to the dissolution of the federation but instead advanced the public's understand-ing of its causes. As he puts it, they

> neither caused nor prevented the division of the state, but instead enhanced the civi-lized nature of the separation. The media were successful in giving representatives of both sides the opportunity to express their views. In that sense, they contributed to the uncovering of fundamentally different perspectives in the Czech lands and in Slovakia. Federal mass media quite clearly contributed to sustained reflection on the key issues, which the national mass media alone could not do with the same depth. The federal mass media produced better quality programs, and most importantly, were more objective. They were more realistic in their assessment of the situation in Czech–Slovak relations, especially when compared to their national counterparts. In the discussion inside the Council for Radio and Television, our Slovak colleagues constantly argued that this or that criticism would be counterproductive, but I have always been convinced that the ethics of reporting dictate that certain steps must be taken without regard for their likely impact. In the long run, it is unacceptable to hide from problems.[16]

In Ivo Mathé's view,

> the broadcast media certainly played a positive role and contributed to the peaceful nature of the federation's dissolution. In the course of 1992, the state television mo-nopoly ended, and competition between national and federal television quickly raised the standards of all television journalism, which in turn improved the quality of information available to the public.[17]

To answer the question whether the mass media caused the dissolution of the federation, I tend to agree with Just's and Mathé's perspectives. In my view, the end of the Czechoslovak federation was rooted in the undemocratic nature of the 1968 constitution, which allowed for the minority veto. When communist totali-tarianism had come to an end, the mass media could not save the federation, for they did not exist apart from society; on the contrary, they were very much part of it. By the time Czechoslovakia was coming to an end, both republics had at least three sources of television news: Czechoslovak Television, Czech Television, and Slovak Television. Each alternative source of information, even if providing news from a different perspective, had its own significance. Most important, in contrast to the situation in the former Yugoslavia, where much of the federal television apparatus was transformed into an instrument of Serbian chauvinism, exacerbating ethnic tension, federal television in Czechoslovakia instead contributed to a peaceful parting of ways.

NOTES

1. My own notes have been supplemented by interviews with the general director of Czech Television, Ivo Mathé, and with the writer and theater critic Dr. Vladimír Just, who was a member of the Federal Council for Radio and Television Broadcasting attached to the Federal Assembly of the Czechoslovak Federal Republic during 1992.
   2. Interview with Ivo Mathé, 15 May 1996.
   3. See the chapter by Owen Johnson in this volume.
   4. *Lidové noviny,* 1 July 1992.
   5. The top candidates included Martin Šimečka, Ivan Hoffman, and Sergej Michalic.
   6. See the exchange in *Literární Noviny,* 12 August 1992.
   7. *Koridor,* 17 August 1992.
   8. Interview with Vladimír Just, 20 May 1996.
   9. Interview with Just.
   10. Interview with Ivo Mathé, 15 May 1996.
   11. Vladimír Mlynář, "Na Kavčích Horach strach" (Fear on Kavky Hill), *Respekt,* 29 October–3 November 1991.
   12. *Prostor,* 5 August 1992.
   13. See, for example, Pavel Rusko, "Televizne spravodajstvo v pražskom objatí" (Television News in Prague's Embrace), *Nový čas,* 27 May 1992, and "Kroky k objektivite na obrazovke" (Steps toward Objectivity on the TV Screen), *Národná obroda,* 22 June 1992.
   14. Mlynář, "Na Kavčich Horach Strach." Ladislav Bakšay, a Slovak, was minister of foreign trade for the federal government.
   15. Interview with Mathé.
   16. Interview with Just.
   17. Interview with Mathé.

Part V

Czechoslovakia's Dissolution in Comparative Perspective

18

On Ethnic Conflicts and Their Resolution

Stanley Hoffmann

A WORLD OF ETHNIC CONFLICTS?

Let us compare, schematically, the world of the Cold War and the present international system. In the former, as had been the case for several centuries, the state was viewed as a coherent entity—Carl von Clausewitz assumed that it could be compared to a person endowed with reason and intelligence. The floor of the system was made of states. Another metaphor, used by realists, was that of states as billiard balls. Between the fundamental norm of state sovereignty (from which was derived the imperative of nonintervention in other states' domestic affairs) and the ideal of national self-determination, endorsed by liberals, there were, obviously, conflicts. Self-determination led to the secession of Belgium from the Netherlands, to that of Greece from the Ottoman Empire, to the reunification of Germany and Italy at the expense of the many states into which these nationalities had been split, to the recurrent fragmentation of the Ottoman Empire, to rebellions in partitioned Poland and in Hungary. But successful national self-determination led to the formation of new states, as in Central and Eastern Europe after World War I; and in the process of decolonization after World War II, emancipation from colonial rule often had little to do with *national* self-determination: in much of Africa, unlike in India or Palestine, the new states' borders were simply those that the colonizers had artificially carved up. The "floor" of the international system was periodically rearranged; it was not dismantled.

In the Cold War system, the main question was ideological. The central conflict was over the legitimacy of the government in the sovereign state; the "free world" and the communists had radically different conceptions of legitimacy, although both claimed to stand for democracy. And the central risk was that of a violent conflict between the rival blocs, now armed with nuclear weapons. This fundamental danger led to lesser conflicts among states belonging to the two camps: e.g., the two Koreas, the two Vietnams. It also led to many interventions by the superpowers in the domestic affairs of weaker states in order to change the character of the governments there (the United States in Iran, in Guatemala, in Santo Domingo, in Nicaragua; the Soviet Union in Hungary in 1956 and in Dubček's Czechoslovakia in 1968) or to prevent a "friendly" government from falling (the United States in El Salvador, the USSR in Afghanistan). To be sure, there were many other interstate conflicts that had little to do with the Cold War: on the Indian subcontinent, in the Middle East, in Cyprus, among others; but even these tended to become, so to speak, hitched to the central conflict.

The present international system, by contrast, is one in which many billiard balls disintegrate, torn by internal conflict or flawed in their construction. The damaged floor of international politics is a heterogeneous collection of sturdy states, of new and often still untested ones produced by the collapse of the Soviet Union, and of failed or corrupt states. The principle of self-determination appears mainly as a factor of fragmentation and turbulence more than as a lever of human liberation; it is a threat to the territorial integrity of states, an engine of secessions and splits, actual (Ukraine, Central Asia, Georgia, Azerbaijan, Eritrea) or potential (Sri Lanka, Québec). Moreover, it often collides with another norm of contemporary international law: the respect for and protection of human rights, individual or (in the case of minorities) collective. The Yugoslav tragedy provides many examples.

In this system, the central question is one that had already troubled nineteenth-century thinkers: what constitutes a nation? Insofar as nationalism is the one universal ideology that, after the collapse of communism, is left to coexist (most uneasily) with liberalism (celebrated a bit too hastily by Fukuyama as having established a kind of intellectual "end of history"), Joseph Renan's old question—*qu'est-ce qu'une nation?*—is more pressing than ever. But there is a second central question, in ironical counterpoint to the first: Is the sovereign state (national or not) still an effective shelter and provider for its members in an age of pervasive insecurity where the state cannot defend its subjects either from nuclear attack at the cosmic level, so to speak, or from terrorism at the microscopic one; in an age of economic interdependence in which practically no state is self-sufficient, and, furthermore, where the global capitalist market, a network of individuals and private corporations, severely constrains and shapes the "operational" sovereignty of the states?

The main risks in this system are both violence and anomie: the violence of often genocidal conflicts within or over the ruins of states, and the anomie of chaos, due to the deficiencies of international governance; for whenever state sovereignty has become atrophied or meaningless, the international public and private institutions that have developed remain too weak to provide adequate substitutes or to regulate a global economy whose sudden somersaults shake and shock the states that are at its mercy.

Let us now focus on a few facts. First, many of the inter- or intrastate conflicts in the present system are not ethnic at all. In the Somalia of 1991–94, in Liberia, in Afghanistan, in Nicaragua, in Albania, in Cambodia, in Zaire, in Angola and Mozambique, in Korea, violence has been fueled by political gangs, by ideological parties and armies, by tribal rivalries, by personal ambitions, and similar causes. Prolonged political repression is a powerful breeder of such violence, as in Albania and Algeria. Religious forces and fanaticisms are another major source of bloodshed—in the Sudan, in Algeria, in Afghanistan, between Sunnis and Shiites in Iraq, between Sikhs and Hindus in India, to name only a few.

Second, what constitutes an *ethnie* is far from clear. The Yugoslavs were all South Slavs, the Czechs and Slovaks are Slavs (and the Serb- and Croat-based notion that the Yugoslav conflict was a war among Catholics, Orthodox, and Moslems—a notion rashly endorsed by Samuel Huntington in his muddled thesis about the clash of civilizations—is pretty hard to swallow, if one remembers that much of the population was secular and that the leaders were communists reconverted into nationalists). The line between tribalism and ethnicity is thin, or artificial (Rwanda and Burundi, Nigeria). We need to resort to the concept of subethnies. Each one of them is based on a combination of religious, historical, and cultural factors, and the dubious concept of race is not of much help. What matters most is the self-perception of the group—but even in this respect we must remember that it is often fabricated by the leaders.

Third, the phenomenon of nationalism is difficult to account for in purely rational terms. What one can show is that the choice of a nationalist strategy may be perfectly rational for an ambitious leader or elite. But the heart of the phenomenon is a human need for social identity in a world in which the traditional and rather static hierarchies have collapsed, in which what Karl Deutsch called social mobilization and others call modernization occurs. This identity, first in Britain, in France, and in the rebellious British colonies of America, focused on the nation, and on the right of the nation to have a state of its own, both for domestic reasons (the provision of security, education, services) and for external ones (protection from foreign domination and intrusion). The idea of the nation and the nationalist ideologies that it bred thus filled the needs of human emotion and imagination in an otherwise "disenchanted" society of bureaucratic regulations and capitalist calculations. In a world of functional hierarchies, this idea (or ideal) and these ideologies provided human beings with a sense of equality as citizens, of common membership despite and across social divisions. Social scientists, including Marx and Ernst Gellner, have tended to underestimate the powerful nonrational elements that provide the glue of the nation-state or confused the (modernizing) function of nationalism with its source and essence.

If we turn to the dimensions of ethnic and subethnic conflict in the present international system, three points stand out. First, we find an extraordinaryly *widespread* occurrence of such explosions: when empires break up, as in the case of the Soviet Union and within some of the units that resulted from its disintegration (in Russia—the war in Chechnya, in Georgia and Azerbaijan); when the state structure was weak (Yugoslavia after Tito; Sudan, Rwanda) or weakened by war (Iraq 1991, Afghanistan); when repression was ruthless enough to provoke collective resistance but not enough to wipe it out (Kurds in Turkey and Iraq); when an incipient process of democratization fulfilled John Stuart Mill's expectation that democratic self-government would be fatal to multiethnic states (Yugoslavia 1990–91, Czechoslovakia after the fall of communism); when a minority receives support from an outside power dominated by the same ethnie (Turks in Cyprus, Albanians in Kosovo, Armenians in Nagorno–Karabakh, Russians in Moldavia, transnational "Pan-Tutsiism" in Central and Eastern Africa).

Second, ethnic and subethnic conflict has become a major *disruptive* factor both in international relations and in domestic affairs. In world politics, it destroys the status quo and produces a kind of universal security dilemma: it puts into jeopardy existing borders (cf. the Ibo rebellion in Nigeria); it creates headaches for other states concerning the recognition of new units (cf. the Organization of American States' reluctance to recognize Eritrea, the intra-European squabbles over the recognition of Slovenia and Croatia); it raises questions about the devolution of treaty obligations to successor states. It produces huge masses of refugees, thus provoking frequently hostile and inhumane reactions of closure in "invaded" countries (cf. the restrictions on asylum in Germany after the Yugoslav war, and the Schengen provisions) and putting an almost unbearable strain both on the international regime for refugees and on the resources of the United Nations High Commission for Refugees. It fuels lasting conflicts among states: between India and Pakistan, Greece and Turkey, Israel and Syria, Israel and the potential Palestinian state. It fosters unilateral external interventions—from within the region (Turkey in Cyprus) or from a faraway power (France in Rwanda). It creates major problems for international law and a UN Charter still founded on the norms of sovereignty and nonintervention (which includes a ban on humanitarian intervention without the consent of the targeted state).

From the viewpoint of a state prey to ethnic or subethnic conflict, difficult choices have to be made. Should a secession be allowed, and if so, how? (Cf. the pending Canadian crisis.) Should it be averted by a reshaping of domestic institutions in a federal, confederal, or consociational direction, or by a granting of extensive rights of autonomy to an ethnic minority—but wouldn't this actually encourage it to escalate its claims? Can it be averted by a policy of assimilation that treats all members as equal citizens—but in the process either erases or relegates to the purely private domain the ethnic or subethnic characteristics of minorities (the French and, to a large extent, the U.S. approaches)?

Third, there is something *intractable and often murderous* about ethnic conflict. War lords come and go, gang members melt into jungles and mountains, ideological armies fade or compromise, but ethnic feelings (and often religious ones as well: e.g., Northern Ireland) have a way of surviving even if they go underground for a while. As I have argued elsewhere, nationalism is ubiquitous, polymorphous, parasitic on other ideologies. It can be openly ethnic, singling out "its" ethnie as radically unique; it can be civic and voluntaristic—and develop around the sense of superiority of such a democratic formula over ascriptive ones. It can be a means to, or a companion of, liberal, representative institutions; it can also be authoritarian and aggressive. It can graft itself even on a cosmopolitan creed such as communism, or on as transnational a force as Islamic fundamentalism, or Pan-Arabism.

It does not only have multiple faces. It also has multiple parents. It often depends on the determination of elites to triumph over foreign domination or over nonnational rulers (cf. the role of the Congress Party in the Raj). It certainly depends on intellectuals, who construct a national idea if not ex nihilo, at least often on the flimsy basis of an imagined past or even an almost vanished language (such as Hebrew), and whose all-important role is to provide the myths and the *lieux de mémoire* for national unity. It requires masses willing to fight and suffer for it.

Precisely because so much can be invested into nationalism by so many, it risks degenerating into warfare, in two ways. One is the kind of total war humanity has experienced twice in this century. The horizontal complicity of monarchs and diplomats before 1914 was destroyed by the European nationalisms that grew harder after 1871, and by the fear they inspired in a multinational state such as Austria–Hungary. The Second World War was initiated by the hideous racist nationalism of Hitler and revived Russian nationalism after June 1941—also, I would add, the American nationalism that inspired "unconditional surrender" and the dropping of the atomic bombs on Japan. The other form is genocide: the Holocaust was the product of Nazi nationalism (and we have to remember that its victims were not only the Jews but other "inferior" peoples as well: Slavs, Gypsies, homosexuals). Genocide has reappeared, despite all the pious post-Holocaust promises of never again, both in Yugoslavia and in Rwanda (and, on a somewhat smaller scale, in East Timor). The Cambodian killing fields resulted not from ethnic but from ideological fury. But in all cases of genocide, we find the manipulation of the many (killers) by the few (leaders, political or military—sometimes, as in the Serbian case, with the help of the media).

ETHNIC CONFLICT RESOLUTION

Given the importance and the consequences of the problem, what is to be done? This is not the only conundrum of world politics, since we must also worry about the proliferation of weapons of mass destruction and of acts of terrorism (two kinds of tools nationalism can use) as well as about the effects of global capitalism (a form of cosmopolitanism that is both open to national manipulations and a breeder of nationalist reactions and resistance). But it is assuredly the central *casse-tête* of modern diplomacy. I would like to distinguish between the present scene and the long term.

Much has been written recently about the prevention of ethnic violence. It can take two forms. One, already alluded to, is from the inside of a threatened country. It can decide to give a special status to a minority, by law or by agreement with the country that sees itself as the natural protector of the minority (cf. Hungary's recent agreement with Romania—an agreement in which outside powers were actually involved: France with Balladur's idea of a stability pact, the EU that Hungary and Romania wanted to please so as to make future membership easier). This was also the case in South Tyrol. But the willingness of a state to concede extensive autonomy to minorities depends not only on the nature of the regime (it is hard to envisage Saddam Hussein granting genuine power to the Kurds, or the Turkish military allowing for Kurdish autonomy) but also on its philosophy (French Jacobin assimilationism leaves little room for Corsican or Alsatian assertions of distinctiveness) and on the danger of contagion (these last two factors have made successive Indian governments hostile to a recognition of minority rights). It also depends on the degree to which a state could fear that such a recognition would ignite rather than extinguish foreign meddling of the kind that Hitler practiced in the Sudetenland and in Poland. As for the creation of an institutionalized form of multiethnicity, it has sometimes worked: in the Swiss confederation, in Spain in relation to Catalonia. But sometimes, as in Canada and Belgium, it is shaky, even when (as in India and Canada) there are multiethnic parties cutting across the dividing lines. Here again, we have to look at the state's philosophy: Zionist Israel does not envisage becoming a binational state, and Milosevic's Serbia much preferred a greater Serbia to a revamping of the Yugoslav Federation that would have increased the autonomy of Slovenia, Croatia, and Bosnia–Herzegovina, hence their power over Serb minorities in the last two cases. We must, of course, look also at the mind-set of the ethnic or subethnic groups fighting against the existing states. The Basques are not willing to settle for what the Catalans obtained. The Québécois nationalists want the principle and symbols of independence.

This means that there are cases in which permanent warfare (as in Sri Lanka) and secession (or partition) are the only alternatives. As in the case of Eritrea, or in that of Chechnya, or in the earlier one of Bangladesh, secession can be bloody—especially when fostered with outside help (Bangladesh, Cyprus partition). The only contemporary example of voluntary secession is the Velvet Divorce between the Czech Republic and Slovakia, a fascinating case in which the relative indifference of one key negotiator (Klaus) to the whole issue of nationalism versus the multiethnic state, because of his preferred emphasis on economic issues, led to an agreement between leaders without popular consultation (a condition most political philosophers writing about secession insist on).

The other kind of prevention, through outside good offices, has known some successes. If many ethnic dogs growled but didn't bark in Eastern Europe or in Macedonia, the efforts of the Organization for Security and Cooperation in Europe (OSCE) and the magnetic pull of the EU are largely to be credited. The

OSCE and the Council of Europe have pressed the Baltic states to treat Russian minorities fairly. These successes suggest that regional organizations may be best equipped to provide the diplomatic good offices and, if necessary, the peace-keepers prevention requires. And yet, the Organization of African Unity (OAU)—often paralyzed by the fear that any questioning of existing borders could lead to destabilization all over the continent—has had a poor record. As for the UN, it has not done much better. Many research institutes have proposed set-ting up indicators of impending troubles, but the problem lies much more in the willingness of the secretary general to ring the alarm bell and of the member states to act. International law and the charter being what they are, this should be easier when the possible conflict is interstate, but in the Arab–Israeli conflict the UN has been increasingly pushed aside by the United States, and in the conflict over Cyprus, NATO plays a more important role. When, as in the majority of cases, the conflict is an internal one, the UN is handicapped by the need to es-tablish that there is a threat to peace and security—something that is easier to de-termine when the conflict has already broken out—by the need to get the consent of the troubled state's government (which may well see UN good offices as le-gitimizing the minority that agitates against it), and by the reluctance of govern-ments to start on a slippery slope that could lead to military intervention and ca-sualties. Although, in 1994 in Rwanda, and in 1996 in the case of the Tutsi revolt in Zaire, small outside forces might have prevented the massacres that ravaged the area (in the opinion of many high officials of the UN), neither the OAU nor the Security Council decided to raise them. Indeed, in the Zairian case, African states such as Uganda intervened to help the Zairian Tutsis and later the anti-Mobutu forces. In the Yugoslav drama, even though political developments in Slovenia and Croatia in 1989–91 made a breakup predictable, the UN did practi-cally nothing (the secretary general's interest was focused on Africa) and the EU did too little too late. Only in Macedonia—but not in Bosnia—was a preventive force sent in time. The fact is that preventive intervention by the UN or a regional organization *is* a highly intrusive affair. It may involve interference in and the re-drafting of internal constitutional arrangements, a very delicate operation indeed. And it may necessitate the sending of forces, which can run either into the reluc-tance of states (many of whom have ethnic skeletons in their closets) to set a precedent that may boomerang on them or into a state's preference for a decisive victory by one side in the conflict, rather than for the shaky standstill that a mil-itary intervention could ensure (as in Cyprus, where the international force keeps the country divided and the conflict unresolved).

If prevention fails (or isn't even attempted), what about the methods of settle-ment of a conflict that has turned violent? In ethnic conflicts between states we find a somewhat greater ratio of success when the risks of escalation—in inten-sity or in geographical scope—are very high. The UN has (with the active help of the major powers) stopped several conflicts between India and Pakistan; it has obtained cease-fires in the 1967, 1973, and 1982 Arab–Israeli wars, but the cost, frequently, has been (as in Cyprus and in Southern Lebanon) a freezing of a miserable status quo; and when one of the parties is a major power—China in its wars against India and Vietnam, the Soviets in Afghanistan, the British–Argentinean war over the Falklands—the UN has remained on the sidelines.

In intrastate ethnic conflicts, we find few cases comparable to the settlements (tenuous as many may be) achieved in instances of ideological or gang conflicts (as in Liberia, with the help of Nigeria and other West African states; in Angola and Mozambique under U.S. and UN auspices; or in Cambodia or El Salvador). To be ultimately effective, they require either a disarmament of the factions or a willingness to share power; when neither occurs, the settlement comes from the victory of the stronger side, as in Kabila's case in Zaire. What we find instead in ethnic international conflicts is a mixed record of external unilateral and collective interventions. In the first category, we can place India's intervention in East Bengal, which ensured the partition of Pakistan, i.e., the victory of the weaker side, and India's intervention against the weaker side, the Tamils, in Sri Lanka—which ended in a fiasco. We can also place there the misguided intervention of the Greek colonels against Makarios in Cyprus, which helped mobilize the Turks, as well as a variety of post-1991 Russian interventions in the "near abroad," which helped Shevardnadze against his foes in Georgia and one faction against others in Tajikistan. In none of these cases did the outside intervener facilitate or make possible a negotiated settlement. (The same can be said about French support for the Hutus in Rwanda.)

Collective intervention in internal ethnic conflicts by the UN also presents us with a blurry picture. The criteria legitimizing intervention have remained narrow: the existence of a threat to international or regional peace and security, and (only in the case of the Kurds in Iraq) a record of brutal oppression—but only as a kind of appendix to collective security. Those criteria have not been applied consistently (contrast action in Yugoslavia with inaction in the Sudan); and of course great powers, such as China in Tibet or Russia in Chechnya, have not been sanctioned. When the UN Security Council chose to intervene, the burdens created by these operations often seemed doubly disproportionate—too flimsy to be effective tools of settlement, too complex and costly for the meager financial and operational resources of the UN. Humanitarian assistance, both in Yugoslavia and in Rwanda, has run into formidable obstacles: obstruction by some of the parties (the Serbs in Bosnia, both the Tutsis and the Hutu armed gangs in refugee camps in Rwanda and Zaire), the Sisyphean nature of the humanitarian effort as long as war keeps raising the number of the wounded, the hungry, and the exiled, the lack of means at the disposal of relief and refugee agencies to prevent the diversion of their aid for war purposes, and so on. The definition of the political mission, beyond humanitarian assistance, has often been fuzzy (as in Somalia) or contradictory (as in the Bosnian conflict, where the Security Council planted one of its feet, firmly, in the soil of a political settlement among parties deemed equally good—or bad—and the other foot gingerly in the soil of collective support to the Moslem

Bosnians against ethnic cleansing and massacres). Or else, as in the Dayton agreements, after the cease-fire and separation of forces finally were achieved through the belated use of NATO force against the Serbs, the missions given to the successors—NATO's Implementation Force (IFOR) and NATO's Stabilization Force (SFOR)—of that hapless hostage, the UN Protection Force (UNPROFOR), were both too limited and too handicapped by lack of political will to enforce the peace and to deal with war criminals.

The problem of political support for such collective interventions remains crucial. Contrast the Gulf War (up to and including the protection of the Kurds after the coalition's victory) and the Yugoslav tragedy. We can be reasonably sure that a new Iraqi invasion of Kuwait would provoke a new demonstration of collective security. We do not know today what the UN or NATO will do if Dayton fails, war resumes, and the Bosnian Serbs are responsible for that resumption. The reluctance of national armed forces, geared to fighting enemies of their nation, to intervene in police operations among foreign factions fuels the reluctance of states to get engaged too deeply in such adventures. Settlements still elude international society—both in the interstate ethnic conflicts of the Middle East (despite Oslo) and in internal ones in Yugoslavia and Rwanda. And of course, civil violence not deemed to threaten peace and security goes on: in Sri Lanka, East Timor, Algeria, and the Sudan, to name a few.

When we turn to the long term, we are reduced to the normative (in the sense that Hegel gave to international law, a law that tells us how we ought to act but says little about how we actually act). Rather than producing a long laundry list of oughts, I will limit myself to three sets of exhortations.

The first, which I have developed elsewhere, concerns international governance. If one is convinced that ethnic conflict is both a threat to peace and security (in part because of the role of contagion in this epidemic phenomenon, nationalism) and a threat to fundamental liberal values of respect for life and diversity, then one must provide mechanisms capable of accomplishing the tasks of prevention and settlement that are so badly carried out at present and that cannot be left to often questionable, fragile, and selfish states. What this requires is, on the one hand, the scrapping of the sacrosanct distinction between interstate and intrastate conflicts, once the latter begin to threaten peace or to violate fundamental human rights. On the other hand, since in human affairs—domestic as well as global—the triumph of reason so often rests on the threat or the use of force, international and regional agencies need to be provided with standby forces specially trained and earmarked by their members, or with the kind of volunteer army Sir Brian Urquhart has suggested, for war preventing, peacekeeping, and peace-enforcing purposes. They would still require the consent of a number of states in order to be legitimately used. But this would amount to a major revolution in world affairs.

The second imperative deals with the tension between the norm of state sovereignty and the principle of national self-determination. Each one, if pushed too far, has unacceptable effects both on international order and on the lives and rights of individuals. Solutions will have to be found through strict limitations on both. Concerning sovereignty, liberal representative government is largely an effort to curb it inside the borders of the polity: it splits the powers of government among many branches and levels and creates a zone of inviolable human rights. External sovereignty is already being eroded by the facts of interdependence as well as by international norms for the protection of human rights. We need to move to a situation in which it is clearly understood and enshrined in international law that sovereignty is justified by and limited to the protection of the polity from outside threats and interference and to the provision of order, justice, welfare, and self-government. Sovereignty should be subject not only to the self-imposed restrictions that result from treaties but also to the authority of international and regional organizations with the right and power to enforce these restrictions, to ensure collective security, and to protect human rights both through collective interventions and through a system of international criminal justice.

As for self-determination, a debate is proceeding among political philosophers, between those who consider it a fundamental human right—the right to a nation and nationality of one's own—and those who reject this view either because they consider it disruptive of world order and dangerous for the vital good of peace or because they are appalled by the injustices self-determination often breeds, through the mistreatment of minorities and the excesses of nationalism—or for both reasons. There is, in my opinion, no way anymore of removing national self-determination from the list of rights granted by international law to individuals and peoples. To revoke it would also be disruptive of world order and peace, and license to new imperialisms. But there is a need for serious conditions and curbs to be imposed on it. They would concern secession and the recognition of new states. Secession should be a last resort, after all other attempts at reaching a solution that reconciles autonomy for the group that claims it with the territorial integrity of the state have failed; and these attempts, if they do not succeed through bilateral negotiations, should continue through the good offices of a regional organization or of the UN. Also, it should occur only if the grievances of the claimants are serious (economic exploitation, legal discrimination, danger of cultural extinction, political oppression) and recognized as such by a regional organization or the UN. It should be accompanied by statutory measures protecting the rights of minorities within the seceding entity. And it should be (despite the Czechoslovak precedent) endorsed by a qualified majority of the people who claim independence.

Recognition of a new state should be denied if such conditions are not met. (If this condition had been observed, the recognition of Croatia would have been refused or delayed.) Beyond recognition, membership in regional organizations should meet an additional condition already required by the EU, the Council of Europe, and, increasingly, the Organization of American States: democratic institutions (including free media).

A third imperative, which gets us close to the shores of Utopia, is a gradual decline in the significance of ethnicity in international relations, the prevalence of multiple, overlapping identities over a hierarchy in which ethnic identity and loyalty to one's nation are valued as supreme. This means no less than a decline of nationalism. Patriotism, attachment to one's nation (whether it is defined in ethnic terms or in "civic," "melting pot," or multicultural ones) should be compatible with loyalty to a state composed of several nations and to suprastate institutions whose aim is to provide those services (including peace and security) that states can no longer deliver. This is, in essence, what the European Union tries to accomplish. Its example shows both that it is not an entirely utopian dream and that it is a very difficult task. The creation of "international regimes" in which both ethnicity and state borders are devalued is a worthy goal. What makes it so hard to reach is, of course, the resistance of nations and states and the danger of backlash among citizens who resent the transfer of powers to often technocratic suprastate institutions and continue to see the national cocoon as the condition of their independence, as the shelter of their distinctiveness, and as the framework of their political and democratic autonomy. The conditions that made the launching of European integration possible are hard to replicate and even to reproduce in the larger Europe that emerged from the fall of the iron curtain. But in international affairs we always need to remember the old dictum: it is not necessary to hope in order to undertake, or to succeed in order to persevere.

BIBLIOGRAPHICAL NOTE

The literature on this subject is enormous. I have found the following works especially helpful:

Ernst B. Haas, *Nationalism, Liberalism and Progress* (Ithaca: Cornell University Press, 1997), vol. 1.
Yael Tamir, *Liberal Nationalism* (Princeton: Princeton University Press, 1993).
Daniel Philpott, "In defense of self-determination," *Ethics*, vol. 105, no. 2 (January 1995), pp. 325–385.
A paper by Nancy Kokaz on secession, still unpublished.

This chapter draws on related essays I have written in recent years:

"The politics and ethics of military intervention," *Survival*, vol. 37, no. 4 (Winter 1995–1996), pp. 29–51.
The Ethics and Politics of Humanitarian Intervention (South Bend: Notre Dame University Press, 1996).
"Yugoslavia: Implications for Europe and for European Institutions," in *The World and Yugoslavia's Wars,* ed. Richard Ullman (New York: Council on Foreign Relations, 1996), pp. 97–121.
"Nationalism and world order," for the Nobel Symposium, Stockholm, September 1997; still unpublished.
"The delusion of world order," *New York Review of Books*, 9 April 1992.

19

Lessons from the Breakup of Czechoslovakia

Michael Kraus and Allison Stanger

Surveying the universe of now extinct communist federations, the case of the former Czechoslovakia presents a curious anomaly: it is the only one of these entities that disintegrated in entirely peaceful fashion. At the most basic level, the Communist parties of Czechoslovakia, Yugoslavia, and the Soviet Union pursued quite similar tactics in their efforts to contain ethnic conflict. All three countries had federal constitutions that subscribed to the dualistic Stalinist notion of simultaneous republic and union sovereignty without institutionalizing any sort of legal mechanism—such as the supremacy clause of the U.S. constitution—to arbitrate disputes between the center and its constituent parts. Instead, the Communist Party, rather than the constitution itself, was the ultimate authority on rights and obligations. Václav Havel has aptly referred to this institutional arrangement as "federalized totalitarianism."[1]

The constitutions of the communist federations, therefore, became an invitation to power struggle absent the party's status as unchallenged arbiter. Yet each of these three countries attempted to govern in the transition with federal constitutions they had inherited from the one-party state. The obvious problem was that once the party's monolithic power had been challenged and undermined, it was possible for both center and periphery to find ostensibly legal support for mutually exclusive claims to sovereignty. Perpetual constitutional crisis was the inevitable result, yet since these states did not yet have credibly independent constitutional courts to mediate competing claims, peaceful resolution remained beyond the grasp of existing institutions. Confronted with this common problem, however, Czechoslovakia disbanded without the contending parties to the constitutional dispute taking up arms. How was this possible? There are at least four factors that merit careful consideration.

The first and most compelling explanation of the relatively tranquil nature of divorce Czecho–Slovak style is the absence of past violent conflict between the two member nations. While plenty of Czechs saw Slovakia's secession from Czechoslovakia under Hitler's shadow as a betrayal, and many Slovaks viewed the unitary state that ultimately emerged from the Pittsburgh Agreement in similar terms, neither Czechs nor Slovaks sought organized revenge through armed struggle. To be sure, Czechoslovakia's history is characterized by Czech domination of the political landscape—to a degree disproportionate to the two-to-one ratio of Czech to Slovak citizens in the common state—as well as by Slovak indignation at this state of affairs. Whether this tendency to resolve disputes by peaceful means is a trait embedded in the Czech and Slovak national characters by years of domination from without, or whether it is instead a hallmark of an already democratic political culture is a matter beyond the scope of this paper.[2] Suffice it to say, the history of Czech–Slovak relations, when compared to that of the Serbs and the Croats, or to cite another example, the Armenians and Azerbaijanis, is distinguished by a noteworthy degree of moderation. Significantly, during 1990 to 1992, no organized political grouping and no influential voice was heard advocating the use of violent means. A 1991 proposal to create a Slovak militia was quickly defeated.

The second factor that sets the case of Czechoslovakia apart from other former communist federations is the very low degree of ethnic territorial interpenetration. To be sure, numerous Slovaks were educated in Prague and continued to live in the Czech Republic after their education years had ended, and some Czechs settled in Slovakia for a variety of reasons, yet the overarching pattern is that the vast majority of Czechs remained in the Czech lands and only a minority of Slovaks settled in Bohemia and Moravia. At the time of the country's dissolution, only 1 percent of Slovakia's residents were Czechs, and no more than 4 percent of the Czech Republic's residents were Slovaks. In sharp contrast to the former Yugoslavia or Soviet Union, significant enclaves of ethnic minorities within territory controlled by ethnic majorities were not a prominent feature in the former Czechoslovakia. As Carol Skalnik Leff has so aptly put it, the demographic map of Czechoslovakia was a blanket rather than a quilt. Czechoslovakia's distinctive demographic geography made it easier to divide the country and allow the small minority of Czecho–Slovak citizens whose daily lives were profoundly disrupted by the split to choose whether they wished to be citizens of the Czech Republic or Slovakia. Most important, competing territorial claims were not a feature of the Czech–Slovak political landscape as they were for postcommunist elites in the former Yugoslavia and Soviet Union.

The third explanation for the Czecho–Slovak exception points to the timing and sequence of postcommunist elections.[3] Unlike the first two factors, this difference involves elite decisions where alternative courses of action were possible. The makers of the Velvet Revolution endorsed a plan for the first free and contested elections in postcommunist Czechoslovakia that called for simultaneous elections to federal and republic-level institutions in June 1990. In so doing, democratic legitimacy was conferred on the representative institutions of both the federation and its two member republics. In contrast, while the Soviet Union held partially free elections to the first Congress of People's Deputies in March 1989, the first elections that were not rigged in favor of the Communist Party took place at the republic level, not the union level. This created an unfortunate situation where the republican representatives had been endorsed by the voice of the people in a way that union representatives, the guarantors of state unity, had not.

Under these circumstances, it is not surprising that the coup attempt of August 1991 succeeded in bestowing democratic legitimacy upon Russia's newly elected president, Boris Yeltsin. In the former Yugoslavia as well, democratic elections first took place at the republic level, not the federal level. In either country, those responsible for making these electoral choices may well have thought that democratizing the center simultaneously would only destabilize the situation still further, but the opposite was actually true: in circumstances where significant liberalization has already taken place, when republics have representatives who have been elected by the people in fair elections and those of the center do not, popular support will naturally gravitate to those who have been elected and away from those who have not. In this sense, ethnic separatism can be fueled or tamed by the early decisions that political elites take.

Finally, and related to the third point, a comparative exploration of now extinct communist federations reveals the distinctive contribution that political leadership can make to keeping man's vices at bay. While some might fault Václav Havel for failing to keep the country together, and indeed he himself would probably cite this as his greatest regret, to focus on what he did not succeed in accomplishing is to run the risk of missing what he did. In the negotiations over the future of the common state, as the gap between Czech and Slovak perceptions of the principal tasks at hand widened, rather than throwing the weight of his authority behind the status quo, President Havel instead assumed a highly constructive mediating role between the often self-interested representatives of Czech and Slovak interests. His painstaking and patient efforts to facilitate compromise rather than confrontation stand in direct contrast to the actions of Slobodan Milosevic, who instructed the dominant nation—of which he, like Havel, also happened to be a member—to keep the state intact by any means possible. While Soviet and Yugoslav leaders used force to deal with ethnic conflict, Havel openly declared that there was no role for the military in resolving the Czech–Slovak dispute.[4] Relatedly, the consensus that developed among Czech and Slovak political elites that Czechoslovakia could not be salvaged also made an important contribution to the peaceful character of the common state's dissolution.

Weighing the competing explanations of Czechoslovakia's demise, what patterns have emerged from our investigation? What are the lessons, if any, for other states torn by ethnic conflict? Two lessons, we believe, are especially worthy of sustained attention.

The first lesson that an examination of the Czechoslovak case illuminates is the critical role of political elites in determining whether the state will hold. As already noted, early decisions by the political elites comprising interim governments can have a major impact on ethnic conflict. During December 1989 to January 1990, Civic Forum had the power to decide the timing of elections, choose the electoral system, and set the duration of the first democratic parliament's term. Among those decisions that may have adversely affected the country's ability to contend with the Czech–Slovak dispute, Petr Pithart, the former Czech prime minister, has singled out the initial two-year term for the parliament as "apparently a gross error," since it unnecessarily limited the time available to reach a constitutional compromise.[5]

If Czechoslovakia's fate demonstrates anything, it is that elite opinion matters more than mass opinion, especially when both the political and economic systems are simultaneously in transition. While there was plenty of talk about deploying a referendum to consult the people themselves on the common state's desired future—indeed, over two and a half million Czechs and Slovaks signed a petition demanding such—no referendum was ever held, either in the Czech lands or in Slovakia. This outcome is hardly surprising, given that polling data consistently indicated that while Czechs and Slovaks might disagree on the desired path of political and economic transformation, the majority of both Czechs and Slovaks favored preserving Czechoslovakia right through the June 1992 elections. To be sure, voters delivered a referendum of sorts in those elections, where the Czech lands threw their support behind Václav Klaus's Civic Democratic Party (ODS), which had minimal support in Slovakia, and Slovak voters endorsed Vladimír Mečiar's Movement for a Democratic Slovakia (HZDS), a party that had no organizational structure whatsoever in Bohemia and Moravia. That is to say, Czechs and Slovaks voted for the political leaders who engineered the split. Yet the stubborn fact remains that sentiment for separation in mass political opinion was always a minority position; clearly, voters thought they were supporting values in the ODS and HZDS platforms other than a declaration of irreconcilable differences. In this sense, political elites must ultimately bear the lion's share of responsibility for the country's fate, since it is difficult to construct an argument supported by hard evidence that either the Czech or Slovak governing party was pressured by its constituents to pursue a divorce, while there is ample polling data to indicate the opposite.

So why did Klaus and Mečiar pursue the course that they did? While the record of their negotiations on the future of the country remains closed, the available evidence suggests that the leaders of ODS and HZDS grew weary of seeking to overcome the impasse that had been reached after some two years of fruitless Czech–Slovak negotiations. On the Czech side, the search for a speedy solution was motivated by a widespread apprehension that with Mečiar at the Slovak helm, Czechoslovakia would have a deadlocked government at best, and slide into chaos at worst. On the Slovak side, even though Mečiar's party never publicly called for Slovakia's independence, its election campaign platform demanded international recognition and a seat in the United Nations for Slovakia. When Mečiar introduced this stipulation as a nonnegotiable demand, Klaus found no way to accommodate it in the context of a common state.

The impatience of the HZDS and ODS leadership can be further explained by examining the personal interests of both parties to the negotiations. Both HZDS and ODS in general, and Mečiar and Klaus in particular, stood to enhance their relative power after the country had been partitioned. To generalize this point, we might say that states disintegrate when political leaders construct a calculus of power where the prospects of anarchy and violence are outweighed by the potential for individual self-advancement. To use Lijphart's language, Czechoslovakia was partitioned because political elites did not sufficiently fear the alternatives to working out their differences.[6] As 1992 drew to a close, ODS leaders claimed to have simply accepted the historical strivings of the Slovak nation for self-determination. According to leading Slovak sociologists Martin Bútora and Zora Bútorová, however, "the creation of an independent Slovak republic was more an unintended outcome of postcommunist panic and confusion exploited by ambitious politicians than the culmination of Slovak national emancipation."[7]

Even though Czechs and Slovaks managed to part ways peacefully, for reasons outlined above, it is this calculus of elite interest and power that needs to be directly addressed to preserve the peace in other instances where ethnic animosity threatens existing state structures. This is where external pressure or action that serves to shape elite perceptions of their interests can potentially play a critical role, especially in small states, which are usually unable to pay the price of unilateral action in the face of powerful external opposition. Turning to the Balkans, it seems fair to say that it was only too late in the game that the West affected the calculus of elite power in the former Yugoslavia in a positive way. The United States may have had the right rhetoric, but that rhetoric was unlikely to encourage individual leaders to transcend self-interest, since it was clear that the Americans were reluctant to back up words with deeds and if forced to act were determined not to shed American blood for the cause.

The case of the former Czechoslovakia, therefore, illustrates how the demands of transition politics only serve to magnify the importance of political leadership. What all states in the postcommunist context shared was a situation in which public opinion had been successfully mobilized against the ancien régime. This mobilization dealt a fatal blow to the illusionary legitimacy that communist regimes had enjoyed prior to Gorbachev's rejection of the Brezhnev doctrine. Yet preserving unity in opposition to some regime or principle is always infinitely less difficult than preserving unity in support of something. Maintaining popular support for acts of construction rather than mere destruction is notoriously difficult. It only seems possible in instances where extraordinary leadership of the ostensibly selfless variety holds sway. Czechoslovakia was fortunate to have such a leader in the form of Václav Havel, but he was also a man, like his dissident counterparts in other lands, who had to learn on the job. Having devoted his life to opposing totalitarian power, he was suddenly thrust into a situation where he bore the lion's share of the responsibility for shaping a positive vision of the country's future. Under these circumstances, it is not surprising that Havel took decisions early on in his tenure as Czechoslovakia's president that he might not have resolved in the same fashion were the identical choices presented to him after the world of practical politics had grown familiar to him. We might find fault with some of those early decisions, but at the same time, one can only wonder where the successor states of Czechoslovakia would be today without the moral force of Havel's leadership in the immediate aftermath of totalitarianism's demise. Along similar lines, few would disagree that Nelson Mandela made all the difference in postapartheid South Africa.

The second lesson that the Czech–Slovak parting of ways highlights is the important role of political institutions, which can either exacerbate or ameliorate ethnic conflict. In societies divided by ethnic cleavages, it is democratic institutions that have proven most successful in containing group animosity while preserving liberty.[8] Democratization of necessity entails the construction and legitimation of new institutions, yet as the recent history of Central Europe shows, since the postcommunist agenda was full, institutional reform tended to be relegated initially to a lesser priority by the opponents of communist power. In Poland, Hungary, and the former Czechoslovakia, opposition leaders embraced the constitutions of the outgoing order as a stopgap measure until new charters could be drafted and ratified. By amending communist constitutions beyond recognition, democratic life was to be breathed into institutions that had not been designed to function outside the shadow of the one-party state.

In the former Czechoslovakia, the decision to abide by the old regime's rules for the time being placed an insurmountable obstacle in the path of those seeking to forge new institutions to improve upon the old. Czechoslovakia's born-again parliament was bound by the *zákaz majorizace,* which gave blocking power on all legislation pertaining to institutional renovation to nationalist Slovak deputies in the lower chamber—more blocking power than any other minority of legislative bodies in the world. Regimes do not typically begin and end in legal fashion, yet would-be democratizers in the former Czechoslovakia and elsewhere initially endeavored to abide by the letter of communist law in remaking the institutions of the communist regime. What this meant, in practice, was that every step forward required a consensus between Czechs and Slovaks before it could be taken. Not surprisingly, the machinery of federal government under these terms ultimately ground to a halt.

What went wrong with power sharing in Czechoslovakia? After all, at least on its face, any minority veto is designed to forge ethnic cooperation, not confrontation. Here a distinction needs to be made between politics as usual in an established democratic regime and the extraordinary politics that by definition exist in any democratic transition. Since power in the communist era resided in the party apparatus rather than in state institutions, rules governing constitutional amendments had little practical significance; political life was elsewhere. Under democratic conditions, those same rules, however, became absolutely critical. What the case of Czechoslovakia seems to suggest is that norms and procedures that foster harmony in mature democracies may have precisely the opposite effect when democracy is in its infancy. Building democracy requires a focus on what unites a country's citizens as opposed to what divides them. Czechoslovakia's inherited institutions, the legacy of communist divide-and-rule tactics, directed the attention of Czechs and Slovaks to what divided them. The minority veto encouraged citizens to think of themselves as members of a group first and as citizens second. While this logic might preserve the peace and pluralism when democratic institutions are already in place, it proved enormously damaging for those seeking to build those institutions in the first place.

To make the same point in slightly different fashion, consociational or power-sharing decision-making rules are meant to reinforce an existing pattern of tentative elite accommodation; elites originally commit to the rules themselves because they fear the alternatives. Although it is highly unlikely to be remembered in such stark terms, the critical founding moment is very much compelled by the fear that the state itself will not survive under any other circumstances and that the death of the common state would fatally compromise the identities of its constituent parts. The supposition here is that external forces stand poised to swallow up the fragments resulting from elite failure to find common ground. Once consociational decision-making rules are institutionalized, they facilitate further cooperation, even though the mutual apprehension that prompted their adoption in the first place may have dissipated on all sides. The problem in Czechoslovakia was that Czechs and Slovaks had never really worked together in the fashion that the communist regime's voting rules seemed to presuppose, especially from the Slovak perspective. In the minds of many Slovaks, Slovak consent to the common enterprise had never been fully given, even though the very existence of Czechoslovakia would have seemed to indicate otherwise. As a result, the Slovaks demanded that consent first be forged where Czechs saw it as already existing. Yet opening up the question of what values were at the very foundation of the common state in an international environment that had overnight grown benign was surely to tempt fate. What both sides discovered was that the forces that had originally cemented their partnership—the threat of German and Russian hegemony—were no longer compelling. The Cold War and the subsequent collapse of the Soviet Union, that is, had dramatically lowered the price of agreeing to disagree.

The transformation of the external environment was a necessary condition for the dangerous game of roulette between the elected representatives of Czech and Slovak interests that transpired after communism's collapse. The stake in this face-off became the survival of the common state. The task of fostering cooperation was rendered all the more difficult by an ever-widening gap between Czech and Slovak perceptions of the challenges at hand. From the typical Czech perspective, the Czechs were attempting to move forward and put the past behind them, while the Slovaks were bent on derailing the process of change. From the Slovak perspective, the Czechs were once again ignoring their concerns, unaware that Slovak consent was a prerequisite for building a new order in which Czechs and Slovaks could coexist in mutual respect and dignity. Over time, this perception gap only widened, fueling the dialogue of the deaf between the two parties. Their differing points of departure in thinking about their common problems led the Czechs to be increasingly preoccupied with pragmatic concerns and the Slovaks to focus on symbols with seemingly little practical significance. Bridging this gap would have required symbolic concessions from the Czech side, ones that Klaus and his coalition partners saw as pathetically beside the point.

The contemporary world has a number of examples of multiethnic states—Belgium, Canada, India, South Africa, Switzerland—that have thus far survived the powerful external shock to domestic structures dealt by the collapse of the bipolar international system. Is there some sort of lesson in their success that might be applicable here? In all of these states, with the exception of Belgium and Switzerland, who were never colonized, decolonization and democratization did not occur simultaneously. As for Belgium and Switzerland, each had longstanding democratic traditions that predated the collapse of the Cold War order, muting the destabilizing effects of change from without. Czechoslovakia, unlike any of the aforementioned multinational survivors, had to face the twin challenges of democratization and decolonization simultaneously. That it weathered this storm without bloodshed is perhaps its greatest achievement.

NOTES

1. *Jana Klusáková a Jiří Dienstbier rozmlouvají nadoraz* (Prague: Primus 1993), p. 25.

2. Here one would also need to consider the degree to which social cleavages in the former Czechoslovakia were cross cutting rather than reinforcing when compared with patterns of social stratification in the former Yugoslavia and Soviet Union. For example, Czech and Slovak religious divisions, while they existed, did not compound ethnic tensions as they did in the Serb–Croat conflict.

3. Juan Linz and Alfred Stepan have singled out the importance of this factor. See "Political Identities and Electoral Sequences: Spain, the Soviet Union, and Yugoslavia," *Daedalus*, vol. 121, no. 2 (spring 1992).

4. Bratislava Domestic Service, 14 March 1991, as reported in "Havel Addresses Slovak Military: Stresses Unity," *FBIS-EEU*, 15 March 1991, pp. 15–16.

5. Petr Pithart, *Po devětaosmdesátém: kdo jsme?* (Bratislava: Kalligram, 1998), pp. 26, 36–37.

6. For an exploration of Lijphart's consociational theory, see chapter four by Petr Kopecký in this volume.

7. Martin Bútora and Zora Bútorová, "Slovakia: The Identity Challenges of the Newly Born State," *Social Research*, vol. 60, no. 4 (winter 1993), p. 720.

8. Rita Jalali and Seymour Martin Lipset, "Racial and Ethnic Conflicts: A Global Perspective," *Political Science Quarterly*, vol. 107, no. 4 (winter 1992/93., p. 605.

Appendix

Narrative Chronology of the Czech–Slovak Conflict, 1990–1992

11 January 1990
Vladimír Mečiar becomes Slovak minister of the interior.

25 January 1990
In an interview with the *New York Times,* Czechoslovakia's new foreign minister, Jiří Dienstbier, announces that Prague plans to ban weapons sales. Historically, Czechoslovakia was a leading arms producer, ranking seventh in the world as an arms exporter in 1984–1988.

27 February 1990
Federal premier Marián Čalfa, in a speech to the parliament, announces that the Central Directorate of Czechoslovak film will be abolished at the end of the year. Film enterprises that act on Czech territory are to taken over by the Czech Republic, those that operate on Slovak territory by the Slovak Republic.

7 March 1990
In an interview, federal deputy prime minister Ján Čarnogurský states that the Slovaks would rather meet the challenge of Pan-European or central European integration as an autonomous entity than through Czechoslovakia's mediation.

28 March 1990
"Hyphen war" erupts. In a letter read to the Federal Assembly on 28 March, President Václav Havel attempts to break the impasse surrounding the country's post-communist name, requesting that the assembly approve either the name Czecho-Slovak Republic or, alternatively, Czechoslovak Federal Republic.

29 March 1990
After weeks of intense debate during which three proposals were rejected, including those made by Havel and a Slovak proposal to call the country the Czecho-Slovak Federal Republic, the Federal National Assembly reaches a compromise on a new name for the republic. The compromise allows the Slovaks to incorporate the hyphen in the country's written title as the Czecho-slovak Federative Republic, with the s in Slovak uncapitalized. The Czechs may write the name without the hyphen as the Czechoslovak Federative Republic.

30 March 1990
The Movement for an Independent Slovakia leads an unauthorized demonstration in Bratislava calling for a separate Slovak state. The demonstrators, who number 5,000, gather in front of the Slovak parliament in Bratislava to protest the country's new dual name.

11 April 1990
Representatives of the governments of the Czech and Slovak republics meet for the first time in twenty years. They issue a joint statement maintaining that conflicts between both nations are the consequence and remnant of the centralized command system.

20 April 1990
The Federal Assembly approves another new name for the country: the Czech and Slovak Federal Republic. There are to be separate versions of the name in both the Czech and Slovak languages.

8–9 June 1990
Czechoslovakia's first postcommunist elections take place.

27 June 1990
Vladimír Mečiar becomes Slovak prime minister

5 July 1990
The Federal Assembly reelects Václav Havel as president.

11 July 1990
With the endorsement of the Christian Democratic Movement (KDH), a memorial plaque is unveiled in Slovakia to commemorate Jozef Tiso, president of the wartime fascist Slovak state. Tiso was tried for war crimes and executed by the postwar democratic government of Edvard Beneš.

20 July 1990
Tensions mount after the Czechoslovak Socialist Party daily *Svobodné Slovo* publishes an article falsely accusing one of the of the most prominent prewar Slovak nationalist leaders, Andrej Hlinka, of being a "fascist murderer."

21 July 1990
Slovak nationalists demand the removal of all plaques, statues, and names associated with former Czechoslovak president (a Czech) Edvard Beneš.

29 July 1990
The KDH declares: "We support a confederal framework for the Slovak and Czech Republics and for Slovakia to enter Europe as a sovereign and equal entity."

8–9 August 1990
Federal, Czech, and Slovak government leaders meet behind closed doors in Trenčianské Teplice. Guidelines are drawn up for the experts who will draft the governments' new constitutions. Decision-making power will be shifted from the federal to the Czech and Slovak governments as of 1 January 1991. The federal government is to become a coordinating agency that will help the two independent states to work harmoniously together. It will retain control over defense and border security, establish legal standards, maintain a standard currency, fight crime, and assume responsibility for taxation, price controls, and foreign policy. Slovak representatives propose (unsuccessfully) that three reserve banks be created, two at the republican level and one at the federal level.

14 August 1990
Representatives of the Slovak National Party and eight smaller parties reject the Trenčianské Teplice agreements and call for an immediate passage of a new constitution, establishing an independent Slovak state.

18 August 1990
Czech premier Pithart announces that the agreement reached in Trenčianské Teplice was and is the only alternative to the disintegration of the state.

25–26 August 1990
A memorial celebration of Andrej Hlinka in Slovakia is attended by 15,000 participants. Speakers proclaim, "Down with the Czechoslovak federation," "Long live the Slovak state," and call on the Slovak National Council to declare Slovak sovereignty. Slovak prime minister Mečiar criticizes the nationalist tone and substance of the Hlinka celebrations.

3 September 1990
Foreign Minister Jiří Dienstbier meets with Slovak prime minister Vladimír Mečiar and Slovak minister of international relations Milan Kňažko to discuss how the federal and Slovak governments should divide responsibility for foreign policy. Dienstbier and Mečiar agreed that "a unit for international relations" headed by a Slovak government member with ministerial rank should be attached to the Slovak government. Some Czech politicians see these moves as the first steps toward Slovak independence.

7 September 1990
Ten Slovak political parties, meeting at the initiative of the Public Against Violence (VPN), issue a statement supporting the Slovak government's call for a united Czechoslovak state. The Slovak National Party also signs but says its long-term goal is a confederal agreement.

7 October 1990
After a call by the Slovak Heritage Foundation (Matica Slovenská), thousands demonstrate in Bratislava to demand that the Slovak National Council make Slovak the official language in Slovakia.

14 October 1990
Václav Klaus is elected chairman of Civic Forum (OF).

25 October 1990
The Slovak parliament adopts a law making Slovak the official language in Slovakia but allowing ethnic minorities to use their native languages in an official capacity in areas where they make up at least 20 percent of the population.

28 October 1990
In a television speech marking the seventy-second anniversary of Czechoslovakia's founding, President Havel urges Czechs to disavow all remnants of superiority in their relations with the Slovaks and Slovaks not to succumb to nationalist demagoguery.

5 November 1990
Federal prime minister Marián Čalfa, Czech prime minister Pithart, and Slovak prime minister Vladimír Mečiar meet in Prague. After their meeting, they announce that they have resolved most of the problems related to the division of powers. With a few exceptions, the agreement is identical to the one reached at Trenčianské Teplice. The prime ministers agree to maintain the federal government's right to make decisions on economic strategy, defense, foreign policy, banking, and federal taxes; in all other areas, the republics are to be free to set their own policies.

6–7 November 1990
The Slovak and Czech governments approve the division-of-powers document (born in Trenčianské Teplice) on 6 and 7 November, respectively, but the federal government agrees only in principle; it views some of the provisions as adversely affecting the ability of federal agencies to function properly.

13 November 1990
Prime ministers Čalfa, Pithart, and Mečiar, as well as the heads of the Slovak and Czech parliaments, Dagmar Burešová and František Mikloško, reach a revised agreement in Prague on sharing power among the federal and republican governments. The accord (a draft constitutional amendment) must be approved by all three governments before being submitted to the republican parliaments and then to the Federal Assembly to become law.

15 November 1990
The federal government unanimously approves the draft on sharing power among the federal and republican branches.

16 November 1990
The Czech government approves the power-sharing agreement.

19 November 1990
The Slovak government unanimously approves the power-sharing agreement.

21 November 1990
The Slovak National Council approves the power-sharing agreement.

29 November 1990
The Czech National Council approves the power-sharing agreement.

6 December 1990
Mečiar and the Slovak cabinet arrive unannounced to Prague to inform Prime Minister Pithart's cabinet that Czechoslovakia's days may be numbered. According to Mečiar, the Slovak National Council is preparing an imminent declaration of the supremacy of Slovak laws over those of the federation. The only way to prevent the dissolution of Czechoslovakia is for the Czechs to make concessions on power sharing. Also, Mečiar demands the replacement of four federal cabinet ministers because they are not "federal" enough. Fearing a chaotic dissolution of the state, Czech political representatives begin immediately to prepare a "catastrophic script," i.e., a plan of action in the event of Slovak secession.

10 December 1990
Following the intensification of discussion surrounding the power-sharing agreement, including a threat by Slovak leaders to declare the supremacy of Slovak

laws over those of the federation, Havel asks the Assembly to adopt immediately laws providing for the establishment of a constitutional court and for holding referendums in times of political crises. He also requests that his powers be broadened until new federal and republican constitutions have been passed.

11 December 1990
A poll conducted by Slovak Television in early December shows that 53 percent of Slovaks favor a federal system, 26 percent a confederation, and 5 percent an independent state.

12 December 1990
The Federal Assembly passes the constitutional amendment on power sharing between federal and republican institutions (basically the draft agreed on in November with only a few amendments). The new system gives broad economic powers to both republics, while the federation retains control of defense, foreign policy, economic and financial strategy, and ethnic minority affairs. The Federal Assembly retains the right to control energy distribution in emergencies.

9 January 1991
Mečiar announces that Slovakia will defy Prague's ban on arms exports.

18 January 1991
Slovak prime minister Mečiar tells journalists that Slovakia will try to expand its role and profile on the international scene, accusing two Prague papers of spreading misinformation about Slovakia. By presenting Slovakia as unstable, they might discourage investment from abroad.

21 January 1991
The federal government approves an emergency bill stipulating that a state of emergency can be declared by the president with the consent of the federal government or one of the two national governments. It includes provisions for limiting the freedom of assembly and the right to strike. A state of emergency could be proclaimed for a maximum period of ninety days if the constitutional system were endangered, in case of war, or other extraordinary circumstances.

22 January 1991
The Slovak National Council rejects the state of emergency bill for leaving too much power in the hands of the federal government.

3–4 February 1991
President Havel gathers top officials in Prague to discuss the preparation of new constitutions for Czechoslovakia, Slovakia, and the Czech Republic. On behalf of the KDH, Ján Čarnogurský demands that national parliaments first approve the

constitutions of their respective republics, then agree to enter into a state treaty, and only then create a federal constitution.

17 February 1991

During the second round of constitutional talks, the Christian Democratic Movement (KDH) of Slovakia continues to insist that a state treaty be concluded. Moreover, the idea has gained the support of other Slovak political parties, including the Public Against Violence (VPN), presently the leading political force in Slovakia, and the Slovak Democratic Party, the coalition partner in the Slovak government of both the KDH and the VPN. After the talks, Havel maintains that neither the Czech Republic nor Slovakia could sign a state treaty, since neither has the status of a sovereign state, which is required by international law for the signing of such a document.

27 February 1991

The Federal Assembly approves the establishment of a constitutional court by a vote of 215 to 7. The court will settle disputes over the division of powers between the federal government and the Czech and Slovak republics.

2 March 1991

Tens of thousands of people rally in Brno, Ostrava, and Olomouc to demand that the government and other legislative bodies promptly settle Moravia's status within the federation. They call for autonomy and better treatment.

5 March 1991

Slovak prime minister Mečiar and fourteen other members walk out of the Public Against Violence council meeting in Bratislava, saying they intend to draw up a new platform of their own.

6 March 1991

The Public Against Violence splits into two groups: one advocating the movement's original program, which emphasizes Slovak national concerns within the existing federal framework, and the other intent on putting Slovak issues before all others.

7 March 1991

Five radical nationalist groups issue a Declaration of the Sovereignty of Slovakia. The declaration proposes steps leading to the full independence of Slovakia.

8 March 1991

Federal prime minister Čalfa points out that the supporters of the declaration of Slovak sovereignty are primarily political forces that had opposed the current government.

Havel and Mečiar meet. The Slovak prime minister assures the president that he is an advocate of the federation. Both politicians agree that a referendum on Slovak independence should be held soon, and Mečiar tells Havel that he believes the voters will choose to remain in Czechoslovakia.

10 March 1991
Responding to the possibility of demonstrations, Mečiar says that the declaration's demands will not be approved by the Slovak parliament, since the Slovak people do not support Slovak independence.

11 March 1991
Thousands fill a large square in Bratislava, chanting slogans supporting Slovak independence and criticizing the federal government.

Presidential press secretary Michael Žantovský proposes that both the Czechs and the Slovaks be given the right to say in a referendum whether they want to remain in one state.

Federal prime minister Čalfa declares that the Slovak National Council is not constitutionally entitled to adopt a declaration of sovereignty.

Dagmar Burešová, the chair of the Czech National Council, announces that she does not believe that the majority of Slovaks want to break up Czechoslovakia. Arguing that such an important question should not be addressed in the streets but through constitutional means, she calls for a referendum. The leadership of the Public Against Violence repeats its call for a referendum. The presidium of the Czech government issues a statement that the future of the federation is being decided in Slovakia.

12 March 1991
The call for a referendum receives support from the Slovak Heritage Foundation. Chairman Jozef Markuš says that his group favors a referendum on the sovereignty issue. The group, however, also urges the Slovak National Council to make an immediate declaration of sovereignty.

13 March 1991
Slovak nationalists honor the leader of the Slovak fascist state of World War II. Between 5,000 and 10,000 people attend a ceremony in a Bratislava cemetery to consecrate a cross on the grave of Jozef Tiso.

14 March 1991
5,000 people gather in the center of Bratislava to celebrate the fifty-second anniversary of the founding of the Slovak state, which also signified the end of democratic Czechoslovakia. On a one-day visit to Slovakia, Havel unexpectedly ap-

pears at the rally, accompanied by his supporters and bodyguards. Angry demonstrators scream abuse at the president, and some attack him and his entourage. Havel escapes unscathed, but several scuffles break out between nationalists and supporters of Havel. In a television address to the Slovak nation that same day, Havel warns against attempts to attain independence by unconstitutional means but also declares that he would respect the decision of the Slovaks to live in an independent state if that decision were made in a referendum.

16 March 1991
Federal government issues a statement warning against the country's disintegration.

17 March 1991
The VPN passes a vote of no confidence in Vladimír Mečiar.

18 March 1991
Despite losing the support of VPN, Mečiar says he will not step down. The charges against him include sympathizing with separatists and using the files of the former communist secret police to blackmail opponents.

19 March 1991
Under increasing pressure from the government coalition, Mečiar does not attend a Slovak cabinet meeting, allegedly because of illness.

22 March 1991
At a press conference during his visit to the Netherlands, President Havel promises to hold a referendum on Slovak independence.

23 April 1991
The Slovak parliament votes to dismiss Prime Minister Mečiar and replace him with Ján Čarnogurský.

28 April 1991
In his weekly radio address, President Havel describes the Slovak parliament's ouster of Mečiar as a triumph for parliamentary democracy.

1 May 1991
The Public Against Violence formally splits in two. The new faction, led by former prime minister Vladimír Mečiar, is to call itself the Movement for Democratic Slovakia (HZDS).

21 May 1991
In a closed session, the Czech National Council discusses various scenarios drawn up by the Czech government in the event of the disintegration of the federation.

24 May 1991
HZDS, the new political group led by former prime minister Mečiar, asks the Slovak National Council to take steps similar to those taken by the Czech National Council on 21 May.

5 June 1991
Slovak prime minister Ján Čarnogurský says Slovakia will seek separate membership in the European Community if Czechoslovakia becomes a member and "if the time is ripe." Since EC members are required to yield part of their sovereignty, it would be just as easy for Slovakia to do so as for all of Czechoslovakia.

17 June 1991
At a meeting in the Moravian town of Kroměříž, leading federal, Czech, and Slovak politicians agree on the principles for adopting the state treaty and, subsequently, the federal constitution.

3 July 1991
In a statement on the Yugoslav conflict, Slovak opposition leader and former prime minister Vladimír Mečiar says that the struggle of Slovenes for their identity is a model for the struggle of Slovaks.

7 July 1991
Václav Havel says that the Czechs would not hinder the Slovaks if they want to secede from the federation, but if a referendum were held, it looked as if the majority of Slovaks would opt to remain in Czechoslovakia.

19 July 1991
The Federal Assembly approves the so-called Law on Referendums that enables referendums to be held on the constitutional setup of the country. It also provides for a referendum aimed at determining whether either or both republics wish to secede from the federation, in effect ending the existence of Czechoslovakia.

22 July 1991
Slovak prime minister Ján Čarnogurský says that he expects to see an independent Slovakia by 2000.

Federal Assembly chairman Alexander Dubček leaves the VPN, which he had helped found in 1989, because it has abandoned its "centrist policy."

5 September 1991
Havel meets with Slovak prime minister Ján Čarnogurský to discuss the future structure of the federal government and Slovak economic troubles. Havel promises to step up the process of working out a new government structure.

Čarnogurský wants to guarantee the Slovak Republic's sovereignty through a state treaty with the Czech Republic.

5–6 September 1991
The presidiums of the Czech and the Slovak national councils meet in Bratislava to discuss problems surrounding the preparation of the federal and republican constitutions. The meeting takes place amid growing tension between the Czech and federal authorities on the one hand and the Slovak representatives on the other. A communiqué is issued listing all of the issues on which the two sides have been able to agree, stating that by the end of 1991 all "basic documents" on the constitutional setup of Czechoslovakia should be completed.

12 September 1991
Mečiar and thirty-four other leading Slovak politicians and intellectuals sign a document entitled the Initiative for a Sovereign Slovakia. The document states that no progress has been made since the talks in Kroměříž and that the Slovak National Council should adopt the declaration of Slovak sovereignty issued in March and approve a "full" Slovak constitution, meaning one whose content and form are distinct from that of the federal constitution.

16 September 1991
No fewer than 1,000 prominent Slovaks issue a statement condemning all efforts aimed at presenting the division of the country to Slovaks as a fait accompli. The signatories also called for a referendum on the future of Czechoslovakia.

Another petition ("A Call to Citizens," calling for a referendum on whether Czechs and Slovaks should continue to live in a unified state), originating from the Bratislava headquarters of the magazine *Kulturný život* and initiated by Havel's adviser Pavel Tigrid, gathers 1,300 signatures in a few hours, including those of a number of prominent Slovaks. The petition asserts that dividing Czechoslovakia would cause irreparable economic and moral damage. By the end of October, more than half a million Czechs and Slovaks have signed it.

Slovak prime minister Ján Čarnogurský criticizes the Initiative for a Sovereign Slovakia, saying that the sovereignty of Slovakia is already anchored in the current Czechoslovak constitution. He also points out that the text of the declaration of Slovak sovereignty violates the current Czechoslovak constitution.

19 September 1991
Some 30,000 Slovaks demonstrate in Bratislava for Slovak independence. Federal president Václav Havel supports the call for a referendum but appeals for unity, saying a declaration of sovereignty would create enormous problems.

20 September 1991
The Czech National Council adopts a resolution stating that the declaration of full sovereignty by one of the two republics would be an unconstitutional act. In such a case, the other republic would start taking immediate steps to "secure its own independent existence." Such steps would be coordinated with the federal bodies. What remained of Czechoslovakia after one of the republics has seceded would be entitled to become Czechoslovakia's successor in international affairs. This means that the republic that unilaterally takes steps ultimately leading to full independence will have to seek international recognition, including membership in international organizations.

23 September 1991
The Slovak National Council rejects a bid by a group of deputies to force a vote on a declaration of Slovak sovereignty. The motion for an immediate vote on sovereignty is supported by 61 of the 132 deputies present.

24 September 1991
After opening the fall session of the federal parliament, Václav Havel says he wants a national referendum on the future relationship between Slovakia and the Czech Republic before the end of the year.

25 September 1991
The Slovak National Council rejects yet another bid to force a vote on the declaration of Slovak sovereignty.

The former Slovak prime minister Vladimír Mečiar declares that a referendum is not the way to decide whether Czechoslovakia will remain a unified state.

29 September 1991
President Havel repeats his call for an early referendum on the country's future setup.

16 October 1991
Slovak parliamentary chairman František Mikloško complains publicly that not a single step forward has been made during the eighteen-month discussions on the future setup of Czechoslovakia.

28 October 1991
At a rally in Bratislava commemorating the seventy-third anniversary of the united Czech and Slovak state, President Havel is booed off stage by Slovak pro-independence demonstrators when he calls for a moment of silence to commemorate the anniversary of a united Czechoslovakia.

30 October 1991
926,000 Czechoslovak citizens have signed a petition urging the Federal Assembly to call an early referendum on the country's future.

1 November 1991
At the founding meeting of the Moravian–Silesian Council, representatives of thirteen political parties and movements call for equal and independent status for Moravia and Silesia in the Czechoslovak federation. In the event of the breakup of the Czechoslovak federation, the Moravian and Silesian factions say they will support a federative arrangement within the Czech Republic, which comprises Moravia, Silesia, and Bohemia.

3 November 1991
Havel invites leading Czech, Slovak, and federal politicians to join him at his summer retreat in Hrádeček, northern Bohemia, to discuss outstanding constitutional issues. It is the twelfth such meeting called by Havel since the beginning of 1991.

5 November 1991
Alarmed by the lack of real progress in the talks between the presidiums of the republican legislatures, and after an emergency session, the federal government issues a statement asserting that both the federal government and the Federal Assembly will have to start playing a more active role in the constitutional talks.

6 November 1991
The Federal Assembly passes a bill setting down procedures and guidelines for all referendums. The law requires referendum questions to be answerable by a clear yes or no; a campaigning period of twelve days; and a span of at least twenty days between the calling of a referendum and the actual vote.

7 November 1991
The Federal Assembly passes a bill finalizing procedures for laws to be reviewed by the country's constitutional court. The law establishes procedures the court will follow when considering the constitutionality of referendums, power-sharing disputes, and international agreements.

13 November 1991
The Federal Assembly fails to agree on the wording of a referendum question on the fate of the country, despite the fact that President Havel and the major political parties presented no less than six alternative questions for consideration. The majority of Slovak and virtually all communist deputies band together to defeat all six drafts.

In Bratislava, the Slovak parliament rejects (by just six votes) a proposal to put a declaration of Slovak sovereignty on the agenda.

17 November 1991
In response to the stalemate, President Havel proposes a number of constitutional and other changes on the second anniversary of the Velvet Revolution. The changes would empower Havel to call a referendum without the parliament's approval and to dissolve the Federal Assembly if necessary; they would also give him special powers before new elections are called. Havel also proposes that the Federal Assembly have only one chamber instead of the current two.

Gustav Husák, former Communist Party leader and president, dies. Ján Čarnogurský, Slovak prime minister (and former prisoner of Husák's secret police), attends the funeral.

3 December 1991
The president urges the federal parliament to grant him extra powers in an effort to forestall a constitutional crisis that could split Czechoslovakia.

31 December 1991
"A Call to Citizens" petition in support of a referendum on the future of Czechoslovakia gathers 2,259,000 signatures.

21 January 1992
The federal parliament rejects two of five amendments proposed by President Havel: that a new constitution be adopted only after it has been approved by the Czech and Slovak parliaments and that a referendum be held on whether Slovakia should remain in the federal state.

22 January 1992
Havel withdraws a third proposed amendment whereby the bicameral federal parliament would have been reorganized into one chamber.

28 January 1992
The Federal Assembly rejects President Havel's proposal that the president be given the power to dissolve the parliament.

29 January 1992
Slovak prime minister Ján Čarnogurský states at a political rally in Košice that Slovakia wants, step-by-step, to achieve the same sovereignty enjoyed by other European nations.

9 February 1992

After months of negotiations, an agreement is reached at Milovy on an accord defining the relationship between the two republics in the future federation. The treaty was drafted by a commission of experts formed by the Czech and Slovak parliaments. The draft will now be submitted to the republican and federal parliaments for discussion. President Havel hails the agreement as a great step forward.

12 February 1992

The Slovak parliament's presidium rejects by only one vote the Milovy accord aimed at keeping the country together.

15 February 1992

Federal prime minister Čalfa calls the Slovak parliament's rejection of the Milovy accord the beginning of the separation of the Czech and Slovak republics.

18 February 1992

The Czechoslovak Federal Assembly fails to approve amendments to three sections of the country's constitution aimed at establishing new relations between the president, the parliament, and the government. The amendments failed to gain the necessary total of forty-five votes among the Slovak deputies in the Chamber of the Nations.

19 February 1992

Prime Minister Ján Čarnogurský warns that the rejection of the draft treaty between the Czech and Slovak republics (the Milovy accord) by the presidium of the Slovak parliament has increased the danger of Czechoslovakia disintegrating.

20 February 1992

In a television address, Čarnogurský calls on Slovakia's parliament to avoid illegal moves toward independence.

28 February 1992

In an interview with *Le Figaro,* Slovak prime minister Čarnogurský says he wants Slovakia to enjoy the same international status as the former Soviet republics and to have its own representation in the EC. He adds, however, that he would be willing to share a foreign affairs and defense ministry and a national bank with the Czech lands. In Čarnogurský's view, there are two possible paths for Slovakia: (1) to immediately seize the opportunity for international recognition while it exists, or (2) to work for the same goal through gradual steps. He is in support of the latter.

3 March 1992
The presidium of the Czechoslovak parliament announces that general elections will be held on 5 and 6 June.

4 March 1992
In an interview with the *Frankfurter Allgemeine Zeitung,* Václav Havel criticizes those who advocate an independent Slovakia but oppose a referendum; they know that a clear vote for unity would undercut separatism for a long time.

7 March 1992
The Christian Democratic Movement in Slovakia splits into two factions because of differences over Slovakia's position within the federal Czechoslovak state. Both parties announce they will remain in the Slovak ruling coalition to avert a government crisis.

11 March 1992
After more than a year of failed efforts to agree on Czechoslovakia's future state structure, the leaders of the Czech and Slovak parliaments, Dagmar Burešová and František Mikloško, say that further Czech–Slovak talks should be suspended until new parliaments are elected in June.

15 March 1992
Alexander Dubček joins the Social Democratic Party in Slovakia.

20 March 1992
The Czech parliament announces its decision to establish a Foreign Ministry for the Czech Republic on 1 June. The Czech prime minister denies, however, that the move is being made in reaction to the creation of the Slovak Ministry of International Relations some two years earlier.

22 March 1992
The HZDS draft election program is adopted. It outlines the following sequential postelection imperatives: (1) The sovereignty of the Slovak Republic will be declared unconditionally and without consultation with anyone at all; (2) a new Slovak constitution will be promulgated, with a president as the head of state; and (3) a referendum will be held on which form coexistence with the Czech Republic should take—if the latter is really interested in coexistence.

23 March 1992
Slovakia's parliament rejects another attempt to proclaim the republic's sovereignty.

1 April 1992
Vladimír Mečiar predicts that Slovakia will declare its sovereignty after the June parliamentary elections and will achieve it by the end of 1992.

13 May 1992
The twenty-three-day general election campaign officially begins in Czechoslovakia amid concern that the results could lead to a breakup of the federation.

5–6 June 1992
In general elections in Czechoslovakia, Václav Klaus's Civic Democratic Party (ODS) wins in the Czech Republic, while Vladimír Mečiar's Movement for Democratic Slovakia (HZDS) triumphs in Slovakia.

7 June 1992
Václav Havel asks Václav Klaus to form a new government, a move promptly criticized by Mečiar, who argues that talks between the political parties should precede negotiations on forming the government.

9 June 1992
After the first round of postelection talks between Klaus and Mečiar in Brno, Klaus maintains that the Slovak side perceives the future federal government as one of liquidation and that he is unwilling to become federal prime minister under such circumstances.

11 June 1992
The second round of talks between the winner of the Czech elections, Václav Klaus, and his Slovak counterpart, Vladimír Mečiar, takes place.

16 June 1992
Mečiar tells reporters in Vienna that if Czech leaders continue to reject his call for a confederation of two sovereign states, Slovakia will have to go it alone. The Slovak premier also states that public opinion polls show that 78 percent of Slovaks want Slovakia to be a subject of international law, but at the same time they also want to maintain the common state.

17 June 1992
Vladimír Mečiar and Václav Klaus hold another round of talks on the future of the Czechoslovak state. As in the two previous rounds, the two leaders fail to agree on the fundamental principles of a new federation. They do, however, decide to form a caretaker federal government. Klaus tells the press that he would rather be Czech prime minister than head a federal goverment programmed to self-destruct. Mečiar says he plans to become Slovak premier.

18 June 1992
President Havel shrugs off Klaus's decision to turn down the post of federal prime minister and dismisses the claim that the incoming government will serve only long enough to dissolve the federation.

21 June 1992
In his regular radio address, Havel insists that the future setup of the country should be decided by a referendum, but he welcomes the fact that both parties have agreed to form a temporary federal government. He also reaffirms his intention to stand for another term as federal president. In response, the former Slovak communists, now the democratic left, announce that they will act with Mečiar's party to block Havel's reelection.

23 June 1992
At its opening session, the new Slovak parliament instructs Mečiar to form a new Slovak government. Mečiar tells reporters that he expects the new parliament to declare Slovak sovereignty in July and adopt a new constitution in August.

24 June 1992
The new Slovak government is sworn in, with Vladimír Mečiar as prime minister.

1 July 1992
Speaking in Bratislava, Václav Havel announces the composition of the caretaker federal government, which he acknowledges might have a limited term but should still be seen as legitimate.

Four right-of-center parties represented in the new Czech National Council sign a coalition agreement that Václav Klaus should become Czech prime minister.

2 July 1992
The new federal and Czech governments are sworn in. The growing significance of the republican bodies is reflected in both the composition and the structure of the republican governments. Not only do they have more ministries than the federal government, but they are also composed of the most prominent representatives of the parties that emerged victorious from the elections of 5–6 June.

3 July 1992
Havel fails in his bid to be reelected Czechoslovak president in two consecutive rounds of voting in the Federal Assembly.

7 July 1992
Mečiar announces that his party wants Slovakia to elect its own president at the end of August, adding that the Czech Republic should do the same. The Slovak

and Czech presidents, he argues, could then serve as Czechoslovak president and vice president.

8 July 1992

Czech prime minister Václav Klaus announces that the Czech parliament will soon start to discuss a draft constitution, including plans to introduce the post of Czech president.

13 July 1992

Klaus presents his government's program to the Czech National Council. It involves all necessary measures to enable the republic to exist as an independent state, including the adoption of a republican constitution and the creation of the post of Czech president. Klaus also vows to pursue radical economic reforms based on rapid privatization and to build a state based on the rule of law.

14 July 1992

Klaus's program is approved by a vote of 105 to 60.

Mečiar presents his new government's policy statement to the Slovak National Council, outlining the sequence of constitutional steps that Slovakia will take: (1) declaration of sovereignty, (2) adoption of a new constitution, and (3) a referendum on these measures.

15 July 1992

The Slovak National Council approves the program presented by the Slovak government.

16 July 1992

The federal government program, presented by Prime Minister Jan Stráský, is approved by the Federal Assembly. The document calls for the Czech and Slovak parliaments to reach an agreement on the future of Czechoslovakia by 30 September; it is criticized by some deputies as being too provisional. Until the country's fate is decided, the federal government will maintain control of foreign affairs, finance, defense, transport and communications, economic policy, and environmental affairs.

17 July 1992

The Slovak National Council overwhelmingly approves the Slovak Republic's declaration of sovereignty. Opposition to the declaration comes only from former Slovak prime minister Ján Čarnogurský's Christian Democratic Movement and from members of the Hungarian coalition.

Within minutes of the close of the ceremony in the Slovak National Council, one of President Havel's advisers delivers a letter to the Federal Assembly in

Prague in which the president announces that he will resign on Monday, 20 July, at 6:00 P.M.

19 July 1992
In his last regular weekly radio address, Havel says that his decision to resign was not an "impulsive act of protest" against the Slovak declaration of sovereignty; he simply did not want to stand in the way.

20 July 1992
At 6:00 P.M. the presidential flag is lowered over Prague castle, as Václav Havel officially steps down from the presidency.

22–23 July 1992
Klaus and Mečiar meet in Bratislava and agree to submit a law entitled "On the End of the Federation" to the Federal Assembly by 30 September. They also agree to split up the Czechoslovak Security and Information Agency and propose to privatize state radio and television and the official news agency ČSTK.

24 July 1992
Alexander Dubček, the former chairman of the Federal Assembly, says that a referendum is the only legitimate way to decide whether Czechoslovakia should be split into two states. Speaking to reporters in Prague, Czech prime minister Klaus responds that a referendum is an option but simultaneously notes that referendums have never been held at critical points in Czechoslovak history.

30 July 1992
In the third round of federal presidential elections, none of the three candidates is elected. The Federal Assembly cancels the fourth round of elections, which had been scheduled for 6 August, as no candidates have been proposed.

5 August 1992
Vladimír Mečiar tells the Slovak parliament that a referendum on the future of Czechoslovakia is now contrary to Slovak interests. At this point in time, a referendum will only complicate the question of the "successor rights" of the two new states.

20 August 1992
Speaking on television, Czechoslovak prime minister Jan Stráský says that there are indications that HZDS is retreating from its original separatist positions. Stráský points out that it is still possible to save the federation but suggests that splitting Czechoslovakia would be the better solution to the country's problems.

The ministers of internal affairs of Czechoslovakia, Slovakia, and the Czech Republic meet in Bratislava to discuss the transfer of the federal ministry's powers to the republican ministries in the event of a breakup. The ministers agree to set up seven commissions to solve legal issues associated with the transfer of powers. The commissions will also deal with cataloging the federal ministry's property, dividing its archives, and establishing the border between the Czech Republic and Slovakia.

24 August 1992

Czech prime minister Klaus announces that the Slovak prime minister has refused to participate in the HZDS/ODS talks on Czechoslovakia's future scheduled to take place on 27 August in Prague. In a letter to Klaus dated 21 August, Mečiar outlined his reasons, which include the ODS failure to apologize for recent statements suggesting that HZDS was orchestrating a left-wing putsch.

25 August 1992

The talks between Mečiar and Klaus on the breakup of Czechoslovakia will take place after all. The two leaders will meet in Brno on 26 August, and the meeting's agenda will remain the same. No reason for Mečiar's about-face is given.

26 August 1992

Meeting in Brno, Klaus and Mečiar agree that the Czechoslovak federation should split into two separate states by 1 January 1993. Their timetable calls for the Federal Assembly to adopt a law on the dissolution of the federation, division of property, and delineation of successor rights by the end of September. It also envisages that by the end of November each republic will have passed legislation on areas of future coexistence, including economic and political ties. The two sides agree to set up a customs union and a transitional monetary union; the long-term goal, however, is to create two separate currencies.

27 August 1992

At a press conference in Prague, Klaus says that he hopes that the federal parliament will approve a constitutional amendment abolishing the Czechoslovak federation.

31 August 1992

A session of the Slovak National Council devoted to drafting the Slovak constitution opens in Bratislava.

1 September 1992

The Slovak National Council adopts a new Slovak constitution.

2 September 1992

Radio Budapest reports that Magyar deputies in the Slovak parliament believe that the new Slovak constitution does not guarantee the protection of Slovakia's national minorities.

3 September 1992
In a ceremony at the Bratislava castle, Vladimír Mečiar and parliamentary chairman Ivan Gašparovič sign Slovakia's new constitution. The constitution goes into effect immediately after the signing ceremony, but some of its provisions are frozen until 1 January 1993 to avoid clashing with federal law.

8 September 1992
Speaking to reporters in Prague, the Czech Republic's new foreign minister, Josef Zieleniec, says that the Czech Republic and Slovakia will exchange ambassadors early in 1993. He also explains that the priorities of Czech foreign policy will remain the same as those of Czechoslovak foreign policy, but that the Czech Republic will wield less international influence and will consequently scale down some of the foreign policy projects initiated by former Czechoslovak foreign minister Jiří Dienstbier. Attaining membership in the EC, NATO, and the West European Union will be priorities.

18 September 1992
In an interview on Slovak radio, Mečiar reveals that the territorial principle has been adopted for the division of Czechoslovakia's assets; assets will be kept on the territory where they presently reside.

22 September 1992
The Federal Assembly asks the government to submit to it by 15 October a program of steps to prevent an unconstitutional breakup of the federation, and by 15 November contingency plans for Czech–Slovak cooperation in the event of a constitutional split.

1 October 1992
The Czechoslovak Federal Assembly fails to pass a law on permissible ways of splitting the country. Currently, secession by one republic based on the results of a referendum held in that republic is the only "constitutional" means of dissolving the country.

3 October 1992
After an emergency session of the Czech government, Klaus makes it clear that he has no intention of postponing scheduled meetings with the Slovak government to discuss further steps toward dividing the country, although Mečiar has urged him to do so. Klaus also says that Czechoslovakia will cease to exist on 1 January 1993.

Making his first public appearance since his resignation on 20 July, Havel urges acceptance of the breakup of Czechoslovakia (at a news conference held at Divadlo Na Zábradlí). He makes recommendations to the Federal Assembly for doing such in a civilized manner, reminding them that "states do not begin and end constitutionally."

4 October 1992

At a press conference, Mečiar pronounces the federal government's proposals on the division of state property to be "unacceptable" to Slovakia. The federal government had proposed that all fixed property located on the territory of either republic should be awarded to that republic and that the rest should be divided on a two-to-one basis in favor of the Czech Republic (whose population is twice the size of Slovakia's).

6 October 1992

After an eight-hour meeting of the leadership of ODS and HZDS in the Moravian town of Jihlava, Klaus and Mečiar sign an agreement, which confirms earlier agreements between the two parties stipulating that Czechoslovakia will cease to exist on 1 January 1993; a series of treaties specifying the relationship between the two new states will go into effect that same day. The agreement does not define specific terms for Czechoslovakia's split.

8 October 1992

The Federal Assembly passes two constitutional amendments aimed at transferring federal powers to the Czech and Slovak republics. The first amendment reduces the number of federal ministries from fifteen to five (foreign affairs, defense, internal affairs, economics, and finance). The second bill gives the republics the power to investigate crimes against the state and jurisdiction over state media institutions; it also ends the federal monopoly on film.

10 October 1992

At a meeting near Prague, Klaus and Mečiar agree to introduce a customs union and to maintain temporarily a common currency following the breakup of the federation.

19 October 1992

HZDS announces that a referendum will be held in December 1992 to confirm the creation of an independent state (the referendum never takes place).

26 October 1992

Czech and Slovak leaders, meeting in Javorina, Slovakia, conclude a total of sixteen agreements designed to govern Czech–Slovak relations after the dissolution of Czechoslovakia on 1 January 1993.

27 October 1992

The draft law on the abolition of the Czechoslovak federation is approved by the federal government and submitted to the Federal Assembly.

29 October 1992

Klaus and Mečiar sign the sixteen agreements defining relations between the Czech and Slovak republics after the breakup of Czechoslovakia on 1 January 1993. The agreements include provisions for creating a customs union and retaining a common currency after 1 January 1993. The accords will be sent to the Czech and Slovak republican parliaments for ratification.

7 November 1992

Alexander Dubček dies.

10 November 1992

The Czech government submits a draft constitution to the parliament for approval.

13 November 1992

Federal Assembly deputies pass a bill on the division of federal property, laying the foundation for the "civilized" separation of Czechoslovakia. Movable assets will be divided according to a two-to-two ratio, while fixed federal property will remain the property of the republic on which it is located. The division of some property, including the assets of federal television and radio, will be covered in separate legislation. The Czechoslovak parliament also adopts a law on the dissolution of the Federal Security and Information Agency.

16 November 1992

Former Czechoslovak President Václav Havel announces that he will run in the Czech Republic's presidential elections.

17 November 1992

On the third anniversary of the Velvet Revolution, both the Czech and Slovak republican parliaments pass resolutions recommending that the Federal Assembly pass a bill on the dissolution of the federation.

18 November 1992

The Federal Assembly fails to approve legislation on the dissolution of the Czechoslovak federation. The bill had to be approved by a three-fifths majority in all three parts of the Federal Assembly. It gains the necessary majority in the Chamber of the People and in the Czech section of the Chamber of the Nations, but fails by three votes in the Slovak section. Passage is blocked by opposition deputies demanding that a retroactive "ratification referendum" on the split be held in December.

19 November 1992

The Czech National Council approves a resolution declaring that it is assuming "full responsibility" for the republic, falling just short of a declaration of sovereignty. Most opposition deputies walk out before the vote. Klaus tells Czech Television that the declaration was needed to give the Czech government a stronger mandate.

23 November 1992

Czech and Slovak government leaders meet in Bratislava to discuss Czech–Slovak relations after the dissolution of Czechoslovakia, including an agreement on army archives and one on cooperation in defense matters. The leaders sign nine agreements but fail to agree on how to divide immovable property belonging to federal institutions. The Czech side insists that such property remain in the possession of the republic on whose territory it is located—as stipulated by the 13 November constitutional law on the division of the federation's assets. But since there is more than twice as much such fixed property in the Czech Republic, the Slovaks want financial compensation for the Czech share that exceeds the stipulated two-to-one ratio.

24 November 1992

The Czech parliament approves fifteen and the Slovak parliament sixteen treaties governing relations between the Czech Republic and Slovakia after 1 January 1993.

25 November 1992

After two unsuccessful attempts, the Czechoslovak Federal Assembly finally approves legislation providing the legal basis for the federation's dissolution; the measure is passed by a very narrow (three-vote) majority.

2 December 1992

The Federal Assembly approves the dissolution of Czechoslovak Television, Czechoslovak Radio, and the Czechoslovak Press Agency (ČSTK) on 1 January 1993. While Czechoslovak Television and Radio will continue to operate until 31 December 1992, ČSTK was abolished de facto in November, when its assets were divided between two newly established republican press agencies—the Czech Press Agency (ČTK) and the Press Agency of the Slovak Republic (TASR). The Federal Assembly also votes to dissolve the Czechoslovak Academy of Sciences as of 1 January 1993 and to transfer its assets to the Czech Academy of Sciences and the Slovak Academy of Sciences. The Czechoslovak Red Cross organization will be divided into the Czech Red Cross and the Slovak Red Cross following the split of the federation on 1 January 1993.

4 December 1992

The presidium of the Czech National Council releases a statement saying that the governing coalition and the opposition are unable to agree on a draft Czech constitution.

16 December 1992

Lawmakers from the Czech Republic finally endorse a new constitution, which provides for a two-chamber parliament and a weak presidency once the Czechoslovak federation dissolves 1 January 1993. The final vote is 172-16 with 10 abstentions. The constitution will go into effect 1 January 1993. Deputies vote on nearly ninety amendments to the constitution in one session, adopting about twelve changes on the floor. Not surprisingly, the final text is not immediately available to journalists. Among the key compromises are the addition of a bill of rights as an amendment to the constitution. Deputies will still have to resolve how the new upper house or senate will be created.

17 December 1992

The federal parliament holds its final session.

In the first unanimous vote in recent memory, 151 deputies in the Czech National Council approve a law making the Czech flag identical to the flag of the Czechoslovak Federation. This violates the law on splitting the federation, which forbids either side from using any Czechoslovak state symbols. Slovakia has no official reaction to the Czech move.

1 January 1993

The Czech and Slovak Federal Republic ceases to exist.

Index

Adamec, Ladislav, 139, 142
Africa, conflicts in, 288–290, 292–296. *See also* ethnic conflicts
Agrarians, Slovak, 31, 33, 46n11. *See also* First Republic
Antal, Jozsef, 210. *See also* Hungary
Arab-Israeli conflict, 293. *See also* intra- and interstate conflicts
arms industry. *See* Czechoslovakia, Czech Republic, Dienstbier, economic conditions, foreign policy, Mečiar, Slovakia
Austria, 70, 91, 194. *See also* Austro-Hungarian Empire, economic conditions
Austro-Hungarian Empire, 80, 91, 184, 195, 291; compromise of 1867, 61. *See also* First Republic

Baltic republics, struggle for independence, 89, 248, 253
Beneš, Edvard, 2, 41, 46n6, 201, 263; nationalist philosophy, 3; relations with Soviet Union, 201, 203. *See also* Czechoslovakia, First Republic
Bil'ak, Vasil, 50–51. *See also* Communist Party in Czechoslovakia
Bohemia, 1–2, 5, 210, 229, 241, 300, 302. *See also* Czech-Slovak relations, World War II

Bratislava, 2, 9, 171, 174, 210. *See also* constitution and state treaty, 1989–1992; Slovakia
Brezhnev, 201, 216n6
Brno, constitutional and state treaty negotiations at, 244–246
Burešová Dagmar, 53, 55, 57, 251; common state, view of, 255

Čalfa, Marián, 52–53, 169, 244, 250, 280; arms sales, 208; "federal Slovak", 251; Government of National Understanding, interim federal prime minister, 139. *See also* constitution and state treaty, 1989–1992; dissolution
Čarnogursky, Ján, 18–20, 56, 59, 77; constitution and state treaty negotiations, role in, 140, 146, 148–149, 223–224, 243, 252–254; dissolution, analysis of, 18–19, 221–225; European Community, membership in, 213–214, 224–225; fall of communism, impact on Czech-Slovak relations, 221; Maastricht, as model for Czechoslovakia, 211; nationalism, role of, 236; Slovakia, views on independence of, 212–214; Soviet coup of 1991, views of, 211. *See also* Christian Democratic

Czechoslovakia, foreign policy, Hitler, Munich Agreement of 1938, Sudetenland, World War II
Gorbachev, Mikhail, 6, 95, 139, 303. *See also* Soviet Union
Gottwald, Klement, 204. *See also* Communist Party in Czechoslovakia, Stalin
Government of National Understanding. *See* Čalfa
Great Moravian Empire, 1

Habsburg Empire, 3, 46n2. *See also* First Republic
Havel, Václav, 18, 20, 40, 53, 59, 62, 75, 99, 150, 209, 214; arms sales and disarmament, 208; Charter 77, 6; constitution and state treaty negotiations, 20, 75, 137, 141–142, 146–152, 223, 232–233, 262, 264, 301, 304; dissolution of Czechoslovakia, reasons for and attitudes toward, ix, 6–8; "federalized totalitarianism," 18, 203, 206, 299; foreign policy views, 202; hyphen war, 52, 249; leadership, compared to Milosevic, 301; leadership, moral force of, 304; media, professionalism of, 271–272; Public Against Violence, support of, 222; reaction to Soviet coup of 1991, 211–212. *See also* Civic Forum, constitution and state treaty, dissolution, elites, foreign policy, political and institutional parties, referendum, Velvet Divorce, Velvet Revolution
Hitler, Adolph, 4, 5, 18, 201, 291–292. *See also* ethnic conflicts, Munich Agreement of 1938, World War II
Hlinka Populists, 31–33, 92–93, 169. *See also* First Republic, Slovakia, Tiso
Hungary, 82, 91, 188, 192, 201, 210–211, 267, 287; minority in Czechoslovakia, 210, 267; rule of Slovak lands, 2, 5; Slovakia, relationship with, 210–211; Slovakia and Ruthenia, former

provinces of, 3. *See also* Austro-Hungarian Empire, Czechoslovakia, Eastern Europe, economic conditions
Huntington, Samuel, 287
Hus, Jan, 2
Husák, Gustav, 50–51, 140, 204, 250. *See also* Communist Party in Czechoslovakia
hyphen war. *See* Czech-Slovak relations

intelligentsia, 4–5
interstate system: collapse of Soviet Union, changes following, 202, 216; dissolution of Czechoslovakia, impact on, 200; what constitutes a nation, 288; World War II, changes following, 200–202. *See also* Cold War, ethnic conflicts, foreign policy, self-determination, sovereignty
intra- and interstate conflicts: examples of, 289–290, 292–297; resolution of, 23, 292–297; use of force in, 295. *See also* Cold War, ethnic conflicts, self-determination, sovereignty

Jewish community, 3
Jičínsky, Zdeněk, 141, 241. *See also* constitution and state treaty

Kalvoda, Jan, 56, 148–149, 264
Klaus, Václav, 9–10, 10, 25n16, 59, 154, 176; constitution and state treaty negotiations, 24n3, 43, 48n42, 57, 100, 154, 244–246, 292, 302–303; media coverage of, 281; meetings with Mečiar, 48n42, 57–63, 81, 89, 96, 99, 175, 244–246, 256; mission to Košice, 242–243; *See also* constitution and state treaty, Civic Democratic Party, Civic Forum, dissolution, elites, Havel, Mečiar, political institutions and parties
Klepáč, Ján, 56, 58
Košice Program of 1945. *See* Czech-Slovak relations
Kováč, Michal, 21, 25n18, 60, 244–245

About the Editors and Contributors

Jan Čarnoguský is chair of the Christian Democratic Party and was prime minister of the Slovak government from 1991 to 1992.

Václav Havel is the current president of the Czech Republic and was the president of Czechoslovakia from 1989 to 1992.

Stanley Hoffmann is Buttenwieser University Professor at Harvard University.

Owen V. Johnson is professor of journalism at Indiana University.

Petr Kopecký is lecturer in the department of politics at the University of Sheffield.

Michael Kraus is Federick C. Dirks Professor of Economics and Political Science and chair of political science at Middlebury College.

Daniel Kroupa has been a Czech senator since 1998 and was a member of Czech parliament from 1992 to 1996.

Carol Skalnik Leff is associate professor of political science at the University of Illinois, Urbana-Champaign.

Miroslav Macek is deputy chair of the Civic Democratic Party and was formerly deputy premier of the federal government of Czechoslovakia.

Petr Pithart is deputy chair of the Czech Senate and was formerly prime minister of the Czech government from 1990 to 1992.

Jan Rychlik is senior research historian at the T. G. Masaryk Institute in Prague and was advisor to Petr Pithart from 1991 to 1992.

Allison Stanger is associate professor of political science and director of international politics and economics at Middlebury College.

Jan Svejnar is Everett E. Berg Professor of Business Administration and executive director of the William Davidson Institute at the University of Michigan Business School. She is also director of the Economics Institute at the Academy of Sciences of the Czech Republic.

František Turnovec is professor of economics at Charles University and director of the Center for Economic Research and Graduate Education (CERGE) at Charles University in Prague.

Martin Vadas is associate professor at the Academy of Creative Arts and was director of the news division at Czechoslovak Fedearl Television in 1992.

Sharon Wolchik is professor of political science at George Washington University.

Peter Sajac is director of the Institute of Slovak Literature at the Slovak Academy of Sciences and was formerly the leader of the Public Against Violence.

Milan Zemko is director of the department of internal politics in the office of the president of Slovakia and was formerly a historian at Comenius University.